EXPLORATION FAWCETT

Colonel Percy Harrison Fawcett was born in 1867 in Devon, England. At the age of nineteen he was given a commission in the Royal Artillery. He served in Ceylon for several years where he met and married his wife. Later he performed secret service work in North Africa. Fawcett found himself bored with Army life and learned the art of surveying, hoping to land a more interesting job. Then in 1906 came the offer to join the Royal Geographical Society: his ticket to adventure.

It was summer 1925 when Colonel Percy Fawcett passed a final message to his wife. "You need have no fear of any failure," he wrote before setting off deeper into the Mato Grosso region of the Amazon jungle on his quest to discover a fabled lost city of gold. He never found it. Instead, he vanished in baffling circumstances, leaving a mystery that has become one of the most enduring of the 20th century.

EXPLORATION FAWCETT

JOURNEY TO THE LOST CITY OF Z

Lt. Col P. H. Fawcett

Arranged from his manuscripts,
letters, log-books, and records by
BRIAN FAWCETT

With line drawings by
BRIAN FAWCETT

WEIDENFELD & NICOLSON

A W&N PAPERBACK

First published in Great Britain in 1953
by Hutchinson & Co
This paperback edition published in 2001
by Weidenfeld & Nicolson,
an imprint of Orion Books Ltd,
Carmelite House, 50 Victoria Embankment,
London EC4Y 0DZ

An Hachette UK company

1 3 5 7 9 10 8 6 4 2

A CIP catalogue record for this book
is available from the British Library.

ISBN 978-0-7538-2790-1

Printed and bound in the UK
by Clays Ltd, Elcograf S.p.A.

www.orionbooks.co.uk

The lot of the one left behind is ever the
harder. Because of that—because she
as my partner in everything shared
with me the burden of the work
recorded in these pages—this
book is dedicated to my wife

"CHEEKY"

PERCY HARRISON FAWCETT.

Stoke Canon,
Devon.
1924.

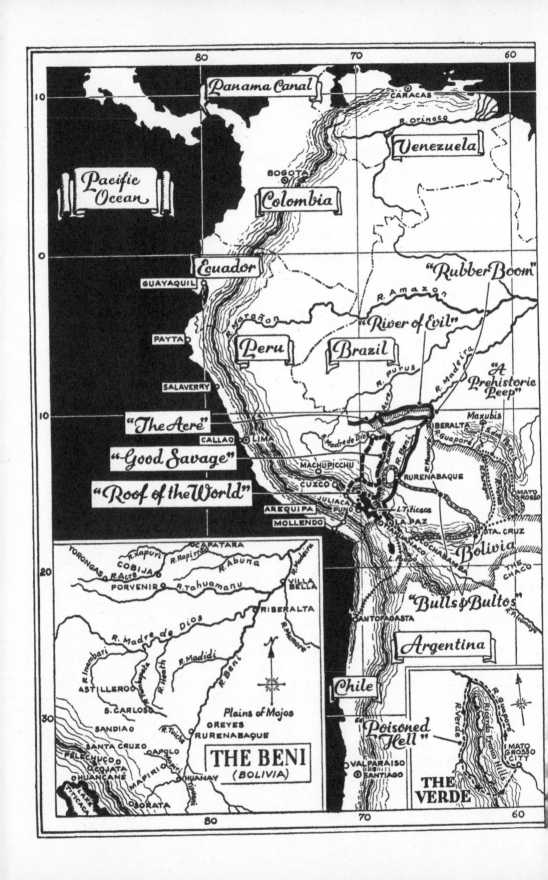

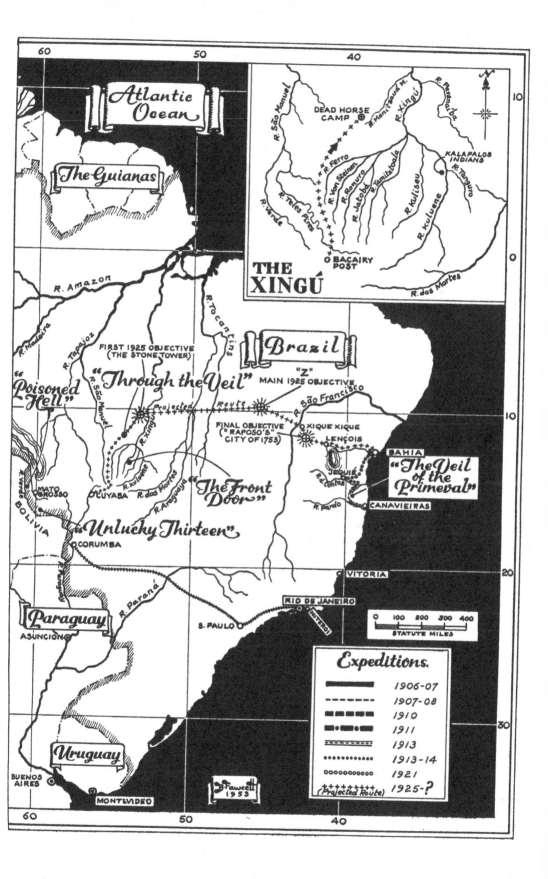

ACKNOWLEDGEMENTS

The author wishes to thank Mrs. George Bambridge, daughter of the late Rudyard Kipling, for permission to quote two verses from her father's poem, "The Explorer". Thanks are due also to Messrs. Methuen and Co., Ltd., publishers of *The Five Nations*, in which this poem appears.

CONTENTS

ILLUSTRATIONS

Between pages 174 and 175

Except where otherwise acknowledged, all photographs are by Col. P. H. Fawcett.

xiii

PROLOGUE

"WHAT a story!"

I put down the last sheet of the manuscript with regret. It was like saying good-bye to a close friend. For several days I had spent my lunch hours in the office reading entranced this tale which had recently come into my possession. Even the difficulty of deciphering the tiny, close handwriting could not turn me from the sense of personal adventure as in thought I accompanied my father on his expeditions, sharing with him the hardships, seeing through his eyes the great objective, feeling with him something of the loneliness, the disillusionments and the triumphs.

Looking from my office windows into the leaden greyness of the Peruvian coastal winter I felt the vastness of South America. Beyond the barrier of the Andes, towering up there to the east above the low, dripping ceiling of cloud, lay the enormous expanse of the wilderness, hostile and threatening, holding inviolable its secrets from all but the most daring. Rivers twisting crazily through the silent curtains of jungle—sluggish, muddy rivers full of death. Forests in which animal life could be heard but not seen—snake-infested swamps—hungry, fever-haunted wilds—savages ready to resist with poisoned arrows any invasion of their privacy. I knew something of it—enough to enable me to follow my father vividly in the pages of that manuscript as he took me with him back into the barbarism of the Rubber Boom's last years, with all its debauchery and cruelty; to the silence of unexplored frontier rivers; and, finally, in search of the lost remnants of a once mighty civilization.

The manuscript was not entirely new to me. I could recall his writing it before I came to Peru in 1924, and on occasions hearing him read out extracts from it. But it was never finished. There remained a finale to be added later—the great climax which his last expedition should have supplied. But the forest, in allowing him a peep at its soul, claimed his life in payment. The pages he had written in the confidence of sure achievement became part of the pathetic relics of a disaster whose nature we had no means of knowing.

When evidence of death is entirely lacking it is not easy to believe that never again will a member of one's family be seen. My mother, who had in her possession the manuscript, was convinced that some day her husband and eldest son would return. It is in no way strange that she should think so. Reports of the fate of my father's party came in one after another, some credible, some fantastic, but not one conclusive. But a belief that my father would write the climax of his own story was not the only reason for withholding the manuscript from publication. There was also the desirability of maintaining some measure of secrecy as to the supposed whereabouts of his objective, not from motives of jealousy, but because he himself, fearful of other lives being lost on his account, urged us to do everything possible to discourage rescue expeditions should his party fail to come back.

More than fifteen years had gone by since he left on that fatal expedition in Matto Grosso, and here at last was the story of all that led up to it. Previously I had not seen his work in South America in true perspective. I knew the main events, but had lacked the material necessary to enable me to assemble them in my mind into a complete whole.

"You, as his only surviving son, should have all his papers," my mother had told me, when she dug out of a trunk his log books, letters and manuscript, and handed them to me. Item by item I took them to the office with me, to peruse during the long South American lunch period, for I valued those two quiet hours more for getting my own business done than for eating. It was my accustomed time for writing and study.

I finished reading the manuscript with a growing determination to publish it—to carry out as far as possible my father's object in writing it. That object was to stimulate an interest in the mystery of the sub-continent, which, if solved, might alter our whole conception of the ancient world. It was time, I felt, that the full story should be told.

But a war was on. The railroad on which I was engaged as a mechanical engineer was a war project, and shortly after I had enthusiastically begun to type the manuscript circumstances took from me much of my spare time. Perhaps it was just as well, for when a semblance of normality eventually returned I could see that the task was too involved to be merely an avocation. To prepare it required my undivided attention; so the work was not done until I quit railroading altogether.

Art would have woven the structure of a tale with the material of but a single one of the episodes related. I hesitated to release a story so top-heavy with episodes, and lacking a climax—the great climax it should have had. But it was not an attempt to win beauty of literary expression, I reflected—it was a man's own narrative of his life's work and adventures; artlessly written, no doubt, but a sincere record of actual happenings.

'Fawcett the Dreamer', they called him. Perhaps they were right. So is any man a dreamer whose active imagination pictures the possibilities of discovery beyond the bounds of accepted scientific knowledge. It is the dreamer who is the investigator, and the investigator who becomes the pioneer. But he was also a practical man—a man who in his time excelled in soldiering, in engineering and in sport. His pen drawings were accepted by the Royal Academy. He played cricket for his county. It is not to be wondered at that the young artillery officer who in his twenties built singlehanded two successful racing yachts, patented the 'Icthoid Curve' —which added knots to a cutter's speed—and was offered a position as design consultant with an eminent firm of yacht builders, should later achieve outstanding success in the difficult and venturesome delimitation of frontiers which in the great Rubber madness were bloodily contested by three countries. True, he dreamed; but his dreams were built upon reason, and he was not the man to shirk the effort to turn theory into fact.

'Fawcett the Mystic!'

An accusation, perhaps, or a subtle suggestion of eccentricity to explain the tenacity with which he followed what many considered to be nothing but a fantasy. But any man risks being termed 'mystic' who seeks knowledge beyond the material. He made no secret of his interest in the occult, and it has been quoted in his disfavour, the insinuation being that anyone so credulous as to believe in 'psychic hocus-pocus' must not be taken seriously. There are respected people in the worlds of science and letters who might be similarly condemned! After all, he was an explorer— a man of inquiring turn of mind whose desire for knowledge led him to explore more channels than one. Mystic or not, his work as geographer received scientific recognition, and has been incorporated into official maps.

But both dreamer and mystic dissolved into the essence of the explorer, archæologist and ethnologist when he was on the trail, and it is essentially of the expeditions that his manuscript deals. A certain amount of editing was unavoidable. From time to time he wrote detailed letters to my mother from remote settlements—letters that took months to emerge from the wilds into civilization. I have salted the text with quotations culled from these letters; and also from the log books which cover every expedition up to his last one.

Would that the record of his final ill-fated trip had come to light! It may yet be found—who knows?

BRIAN FAWCETT

PERCY HARRISON FAWCETT
Pelechuco, 1911

CHAPTER I

THE LOST MINES OF MURIBECA

WHEN Diego Alvarez struggled landwards through the Atlantic swell in a welter of wreckage from the disintegrating caravel, it was to land, exhausted, on a shore absolutely unknown to this sixteenth-century Portuguese. Only twenty-four years previously Columbus had discovered the New World and fired the imaginations of Iberian adventurers. The dawn of knowledge was only just breaking after the dark night of the Middle Ages; the world in its entirety was yet a mystery, and each venture to probe it disclosed new wonders. The border between myth and reality was not fixed, and the adventurer saw strange sights with an eye distorted by superstition.

Here, on the coast of Brazil where Bahía now stands, anything might exist. Behind the forest's edge on top of those cliffs were surely to be found wonderful things, and he—Diego Alvarez—would be the first of his race to set eyes on them. There might be dangers from the natives of the country—perhaps even those weird people, half human, half monster, who, tradition had it, lived in this land—but they had to be faced if he was to find food and water. The spirit of the pioneer had driven him to join the ill-fated voyage; it spurred him on, and nothing short of death could stop him.

I

The place where he came ashore, sole survivor from the wreck, was in the territory of the cannibal Tupinambas. Perhaps he escaped being eaten by reason of his strangeness; perhaps his captors considered it a triumph over neighbouring tribes to display their captive alive. For his salvation the Portuguese had principally to thank an Indian girl named Paraguassu, the Pocahontas of South America, who took a fancy to him and became his wife—ultimately the favourite among several.

For many years the Portuguese mariner lived with the Indians. A number of his countrymen came to Brazil, and he was able to establish friendly relations between them and the savages. Finally he managed to bring Paraguassu into the fold of the Church, and a sister of hers married another Portuguese adventurer. The child of her sister's marriage, Melchior Dias Moreyra, spent most of his life with the Indians, and was known by them as Muribeca. He discovered many mines, and accumulated vast quantities of silver, gold and precious stones, which were worked by the skilful Tapuya tribes into so wonderful a treasure that the early European colonists were filled with envy.

Muribeca had a son called Roberio Dias, who as a lad was familiar with the mines where his father's vast wealth originated. About 1610 Roberio Dias approached the Portuguese King, Dom Pedro II, with an offer to hand over the mines in exchange for the title of Marquis das Minas. He showed a rich specimen of silver-bearing ore and temptingly promised more silver than there was iron at Bilbao. He was only partly believed, but the royal greed for treasure was strong enough to cause a patent to be drawn up for the marquisate.

If Roberio Dias thought he would leave the court a marquis he was mistaken. Old Dom Pedro II was too cunning for that. The patent was sealed and delivered to a commission entrusted to hand it over only after the mines had been disclosed. But Dias in his turn had suspicions. He was not one to trust blindly to the King's faith. While the expedition was some distance from Bahía he managed to persuade the officer in command of the Commission to open the envelope and allow him to see the patent. He found that he was down for a military commission as captain, and no more—not a word about the marquisate! That settled it. Dias refused to hand over the mines, so the enraged officer took him back by force to Bahía, where he was flung into prison. Here he remained for two years, and then he was allowed to buy his freedom for 9,000 crowns. In 1622 he died, and the secret of the mines was never disclosed. Diego Alvarez had been dead for a long time; Muribeca himself had gone, no Indian would talk even under the most frightful tortures, so Dom Pedro was left to curse his ill-judged deceit and read over again and again the official reports of the assays made of Roberio Dias's specimens.

The secret of the mines was lost, but for years expeditions scoured the country in an effort to locate them. As failure succeeded failure, belief in their existence died away to survive only as myth, yet there were always some hardy souls ready to brave hostile savages and slow starvation for the chance of discovering a New Potosi.

The region beyond the São Francisco River was as unknown to the Portuguese colonists of those times as the forests of the Gongugy are to the Brazilians of today. Exploration was too difficult. Not only was it too much to contend with hordes of wild Indians shooting poisoned arrows from impenetrable cover, but food was not available to provide for an expedition large enough to protect itself from attack. Yet one after another ventured it, and more often than not was never heard of again. They called these expeditions *Bandeiras*, or Flags, for they were officially sponsored, accompanied by Government troops, and usually by a contingent of missionaries. Occasionally civilians banded together for the purpose, armed a number of negro slaves, enlisted tame Indians as guides, and disappeared into the *Sertão* (bush) for years at a time, if not for ever.

If you are romantically minded—and most of us are, I think—you have in the foregoing the background for a story so fascinating that I know none to compare. I myself came upon it in an old document still preserved at Rio de Janeiro, and, in the light of evidence gleaned from many quarters, believe it implicitly. I am not going to offer a literal translation of the strange account given in the document—the crabbed Portuguese script is broken in several places—but the story begins in 1743, when a native of Minas Gerais, whose name has not been preserved, decided to make a search for the Lost Mines of Muribeca.

Francisco Raposo—I must identify him by some name—was not to be deterred by wild beasts, venomous snakes, savages and insects from attempting to enrich himself and his followers as the Spaniards in Peru and Mexico had done only two centuries before. They were a hardy lot, those old pioneers—superstitious, perhaps, but when gold called all obstacles were forgotten.

It was always difficult to take cargo animals through the trackless hinterland. There were numerous rivers and bogs everywhere; pasture was coarse, and the continuous attacks of vampire bats soon finished the animals off. Climate ranged from very cold to extreme heat, and total drought would be followed by days of sheer deluge, so that a fair amount of equipment had to be carried. Yet Raposo and his band gave little consideration to such drawbacks, and set out hopefully into the wilds.

Exactly where they went I have only lately discovered. It was roughly northwards. There were no maps of the country in those days, and no member of the party knew anything about land navigation, so the clues in the record they left are entirely unreliable. Indians accompanied them from point to point and suggested the routes taken, otherwise they merely wandered into the unknown and left it to fortune to bring them to the coveted objective. In the manner of all pioneers, they lived on what fish and game they could secure, and on fruit and vegetables pilfered from Indian plantations or begged from friendly tribes. It was thin living, for game is timid in the South American wilderness, but men lived more simply in those days and consequently their endurance was greater. Raposo, his compatriots, and their black slaves survived to continue their wanderings for ten years. Not counting the Indians who joined them from time to time and who would vanish when it suited them, the party was about eighteen strong. Perhaps that was the secret of their survival, for the usual *Bandeiras* numbered at least five hundred, and there is a record of one 1,400 strong, not a single member of which ever returned! Few might live where many would starve.

The time came when the party was travelling eastward again, towards the coast settlements, tired of this seemingly endless wandering, and disheartened by their failure to locate the lost mines. Raposo was almost ready to believe them a myth, and his companions had long ago decided that no such mines existed. They had come through swamps and bush country when jagged mountains showed up ahead, beyond a grassy plain broken by thin belts of green forest. Raposo in his narrative describes them poetically, "They seemed to reach the ethereal regions and to serve as a throne for the wind and the stars themselves." Anyone who has passed months on end in the monotonous flatness of the plains will appreciate his rhapsody.

These were no ordinary mountains. As the party came nearer, the sides lit up in flame, for it had been raining and the setting sun was reflected from wet rocks rich in crystals and that slightly opaque quartz which is so common in this part of Brazil. To the eager explorers they seemed to be studded with gems. Streams leaped from rock to rock, and over the crest of the ridge a rainbow formed, as though to hint that treasure was to be found at its feet.

"An omen!" cried Raposo. "See! We have found the treasure house of the great Muribeca!"

Night came down and forced them to camp before reaching the foot of those wonderful mountains; and next morning, when the sun came up from behind them, the crags appeared black and menacing. Enthusiasm waned; but there is always something fascinating about mountains for the explorer. Who knows what may be seen from the topmost ridge?

To the eyes of Raposo and his comrades their height was vast, and when they reached them it was to find sheer, unscalable precipices. All day they struggled over boulders and crevices, seeking a way up those glassy sides. Rattlesnakes abounded—and there is no remedy for the bite of the Brazilian species. Wearied by the hard going and constant vigilance to avoid these snakes, Raposo called a halt.

"Three leagues we have come and still no way up," he said. "It would be better to return to our old trail and find a way northwards. What do you say?"

"Camp!" was the reply. "Let's camp. We've had enough for one day. Tomorrow we can return."

"Very well," answered the leader; and then to two of the men, "You, José and Manoel—off you go to find wood for the fire!"

Camp was pitched and the party was resting when confused shouting and a crashing in the bush brought them to their feet, guns in hand. José and Manoel burst into view.

"*Patrão, Patrão!*" they cried. "We've found it—the way up!"

Searching for firewood in the low scrub they had seen a dead tree at the edge of a small wooded creek. This was the best fuel to be had, and they were making their way towards it when a deer sprang up on the other side of the creek and disappeared beyond a corner of the cliff. Unslinging their guns the two men followed as quickly as they could, for here was meat enough to last them several days.

The animal had vanished, but beyond the outcropping of rock they came on a deep cleft in the face of the precipice, and saw that it was possible to climb up through it to the summit. Deer and firewood were forgotten in the excitement.

They broke camp at once, shouldered their packs, and set off with Manoel leading. With ejaculations of wonder they entered the crevice in single file, to find that it widened somewhat inside. It was rough going, but here and there were traces of what looked like old paving, and in places the sheer walls of the cleft seemed to bear the almost obliterated marks of tools. Clusters of rock crystals and frothy masses of quartz gave them the feeling of having entered a fairyland, and in the dim light filtering down through the tangled mass of creepers overhead all the magic of their first impressions returned.

The climb was so difficult that three hours passed before they emerged torn and breathless on a ledge high above the surrounding plain. From here to the ridge was clear ground, and soon they were standing shoulder to shoulder at the top, gazing, dumb with amazement, at the view spread out below them.

There at their feet, about four miles away, was a huge city.

Immediately they flung themselves down and edged back behind the cover of the rocks, hoping that the inhabitants had not seen their distant figures against the sky, for this might be a colony of the hated Spaniards. Then again, it might be such a city as Cuzco, the ancient capital of the Incas in Peru, inhabited by a race of highly civilized people still holding out against the encroachments of the European invaders. Was it perhaps a Portuguese colony? It might be a stronghold of the Orizes Procazes, remnant of the mysterious Tapuyas, who showed unmistakable signs of having once been a highly civilized people.

Raposo wriggled up to the crest once more and, still lying flat, looked around him. The ridge stretched as far as he could see from south-east to north-west, and away over to the north, hazy with distance, was unbroken forest. In the immediate foreground was an extensive plain patched with green and brown, broken in places by shining pools of water. He could see where a continuation of the rocky trail they had ascended dropped down the side of the mountain to vanish below the range of vision, appearing again and winding over the plain to lose itself in the vegetation surrounding the city walls. No sign of life could he see. No smoke arose in the still air; no sound broke the utter silence.

He gave a quick sign to his followers, and one by one they crawled over the ridge and dropped down beyond the skyline to the shelter of scrub and rock. Then they made their way cautiously down the mountain-side to the valley floor, and left the trail for a camp site near a small stream of clear water.

No fires were lit that night, and the men talked in whispers. They were awed by the sight of civilization after those long years in the wilds, and by no means confident of their safety. Two hours before nightfall Raposo had sent off two Portuguese and four negroes to reconnoitre and find out what sort of people lived in this mysterious place. Nervously the rest of the party awaited their return, and every forest noise—every insect song and whisper of the foliage—was sinister. But the scouts had nothing to tell when they came back. Lack of cover had kept them from venturing too near the city, but no sign of occupation had they seen. The Indians of the party were as mystified as Raposo and his followers. By nature superstitious, certain parts of the country to them were 'taboo', and they were filled with alarm.

Raposo, however, was able to prevail on one of the Indians to scout forward singlehanded after sunrise next morning. No one had slept much during the night, and their curiosity about the Indian's fate kept them from resting in the more comfortable light of day. At midday he crept back into camp, obviously terrified, and insisting that the city was uninhabited. It was too late to push forward that day, so they spent another restless night listening to the strange forest sounds around them, ready to face some unknown danger at any moment.

Early next morning Raposo sent ahead an advance guard of four Indians and followed towards the city with the rest of the party. As they came near the overgrown walls the Indians met them with the same story—the place was deserted—and so with less caution they followed the trail to an entrance under three arches formed of huge stone slabs. So impressive was this cyclopean structure—similar, probably, to much that can yet be seen at Sacsahuaman in Peru—that no man dared speak, but slipped by the blackened stones as stealthily as a cat.

High above the central arch characters of some sort were graven deeply into the weatherworn stone. Raposo, uneducated though he was, could see that this was no modern writing. A feeling of vast age brooded over everything, and it took a distinct effort for him to issue in a hoarse, unnatural voice the orders to advance.

The arches were still in a fair state of preservation, but one or two of the colossal uprights had twisted slightly on their bases. The men passed through and entered what had once been a wide street, but littered now with broken pillars and blocks of masonry rank with the parasitic vegetation of the tropics. On either side were two-storeyed houses built of great blocks fitting together with mortarless joins of almost incredible accuracy, the pòrticos, narrow above and wide below, decorated with elaborate carvings of what they took to be demons.

The description, coming from men who had never seen Cuzco and Sacsahuaman, or the other wonder cities of old Peru—which were incredibly ancient when the Incas first came upon them—cannot be lightly dismissed. What they saw and related tallies closely with much that we can still see today. Uneducated adventurers could hardly invent an account so closely corroborated by the cyclopean remains now familiar to so many.

There was ruin everywhere, but many buildings were roofed with great stone slabs still in position. Those of the party who dared to enter the dark interiors and raise their voices ran out at the echoes flung back at them from walls and vaulted ceilings. It was impossible to say if any remnants of furnishings remained, for in most cases inner walls had collapsed, covering the floors with debris, and the bat droppings of centuries formed a thick carpet underfoot. So old was this place that perishables such as furniture and textiles must have disintegrated long ago.

Huddled together like a flock of frightened sheep, the men proceeded down the street and came to a vast square. Here in the centre was a huge column of black stone, and upon it the effigy, in perfect preservation, of a man with one hand on his hip and the other pointing towards the north. The majesty of this statue struck deep into the hearts of the Portuguese and they crossed themselves reverently. Carved obelisks of the same black stone, partially ruined, stood at each corner of the square, while running the length of one side was a building so magnificent in design and decoration that it must have been a palace. The walls and roof had collapsed in many places, but its great square columns were still intact. A broad flight of ruined stone steps led up and into a wide hall, where traces of colour still clung to the frescoes and carvings. Bats in countless thousands winged in circles through the dim chambers and the acrid reek of their droppings was suffocating.

The explorers were glad to get out into the clean air. The figure of a youth was carved over what seemed to be the principal doorway. It portrayed a beardless figure, naked from the waist up, with shield in hand and a band across one shoulder. The head was crowned with what looked to them like a wreath of laurel, judging by Grecian statuary they had seen in Portugal. Below were inscribed characters remarkably like those of ancient Greece. Raposo copied them on a tablet and reproduced them in his narrative.

Opposite the palace was the ruin of another huge building, evidently a temple. Eroded carvings of figures, animals and birds covered the walls that remained, and over the portal were more characters which again were copied as faithfully as Raposo or one of his followers was capable of doing.

Beyond the square and the main street the city lay in complete ruin, in some places actually buried under mounds of earth on which not a blade of grass or other vegetation grew. Here and there were gaping chasms, and when the explorers dropped rocks into these not a sound came up to indicate bottom. There was little doubt now what had devastated the place. The Portuguese knew what earthquakes were and what destruction they could do. Here whole buildings had been swallowed, leaving perhaps only a few carved blocks to show where they had stood. It was not difficult to imagine something of the awful cataclysm that had laid waste this glorious place, tumbled columns and blocks weighing perhaps fifty tons and more, and that had destroyed in a matter of minutes the painstaking labour of a thousand years!

The far side of the square terminated in a river about thirty yards wide, flowing straight and easily from the north-west and vanishing in distant forest. At one time a fine promenade had bordered on the river, but the masonry was now broken up and much had subsided into the water. On the other side of the river were fields that once were cultivated, still covered with abundant coarse grass and a carpet of flowers. Rice had propagated and thrived in the shallow swamps all about, and here the waters were alive with duck.

Raposo and his party forded the river and crossed the swamps towards an isolated building about a quarter of a mile away, and the ducks scarcely troubled to move from their path. The building was approached by a flight of steps in stone of many colours, for it stood on a rise and its frontage extended for 250 paces. The imposing entrance, behind a square monolith with deeply engraved characters, opened into a vast hall where carvings and decorations had resisted the depredations of time in an amazing manner. They found fifteen chambers opening off the great hall, and in each was a carved serpent's head with a thin stream of water still flowing from it into the open mouth of another stone serpent beneath. The place could have been the college of a priesthood.

Deserted and ruined the city was, but its environs of rich fields provided far more food for the explorers than they could find in the virgin forest. It is therefore not surprising that in spite of their awe of the place none of the men was anxious to leave it. Their fear gave way to a lust for treasure, and this increased when João Antonio—the only member of the party to be mentioned by name in the document—found a small gold coin in the rubble. On one face it bore the effigy of a youth on his knees, and on the other a bow, a crown and a musical instrument of some sort. The place must be full of gold, they told themselves; when the inhabitants fled they would have taken only the things most necessary for their survival.

The document hints at the finding of treasure, but no details are given. It may well be that the heavy aura of calamity hanging over the place was in the long run too much for the nerves of these superstitious pioneers. Perhaps the millions of bats deterred them. At any rate, it is unlikely that they brought any quantity of it out with them, for they still had a formidable journey ahead if they were ever to see civilization again, and none of them would have been anxious to burden himself with more equipment than he already had.

Gathering rice from the swamps and hunting duck—if hunting it could be called—were perilous. Anacondas big enough to kill a man were common; and poisonous snakes, attracted by the game, swarmed every-where, feeding not only on the birds but also on jerboas—'rats jumping like fleas', as the narrator describes them. Wild dogs, large grey brutes as big as wolves, haunted the plains, yet not a man would sleep within the city. Camp was pitched just beyond the gate where they first entered, and from here they watched at sunset the legions of bats emerging from the great buildings to disperse in the gloaming with a dry rustling of wings like the first breath of an approaching storm. By day the sky was black with swallows, greedy for the prolific insect life.

Francisco Raposo had no idea where they were, but at last decided to follow the river through the forest, hoping that his Indians would remember the landmarks when he returned with a properly equipped expedition to comb the wealth out of these ruins. Fifty miles down they came to a mighty waterfall, and in an adjoining cliff face were found distinct signs of mine workings. Here they tarried longer. Game was plentiful, several of the men were down with fever and the Indians were nervous about the possibility of hostile tribes in the vicinity. Below the fall the river broadened out into a series of swampy lagoons, as these South American rivers have a way of doing.

Investigation proved the suspected mineshafts to be holes they had no means of exploring, but at their mouths lay scattered about a quantity of rich silver ore. Here and there were caves hewn out of the cliff by hand, some of them sealed off by great stone slabs engraved with strange glyphs. The caves might have been the tombs of the city's monarchs and high priests. The men tried in vain to move the stone slabs.

The adventurers pictured themselves as rich men and agreed to say nothing to anybody except the Viceroy, to whom Raposo owed a debt of gratitude. They would return here as soon as possible, take possession of the mines, and remove all treasure from the city.

In the meantime a scouting party had been sent out to explore farther down river. After traversing the lagoons and backwaters for nine days they caught a glimpse of a canoe paddled by two 'white people' with long black hair and dressed in some sort of clothing. They fired a shot to attract attention, but the canoe made off and vanished from view. Weary of the fatiguing business of making wide detours around the swamps, and afraid to continue farther down with so small a party, they returned to the fall.

Raposo felt the need of caution now that he and his followers had fortunes within their grasp. He had no wish to risk an encounter with hostile Indians and so he struck off eastwards. After some months of hard travel they reached the bank of the São Francisco River, crossed from there to the Paraguassu, and at length came to Bahía. From here he sent to the Viceroy, Don Luiz Peregrino de Carvalho Menezes de Athayde, the document from which this story is taken.

Nothing was done by the Viceroy, and one cannot say if Raposo returned to his discovery or not. At all events, he was never heard of again. For nearly a century the document was pigeonholed at Rio de Janeiro, till the then State Government turned it up and commissioned a young priest to investigate. This exploration was entirely unsuccessful, apparently carried out with little intelligence.

It was difficult for an administration steeped in the narrow bigotry of an all-powerful Church to give much credence to such a thing as an old civilization. Egypt in those days was still a mystery, and the ecclesiastical spirit which wilfully destroyed the priceless records of Peru and Mexico was rife as ever.

I know that Raposo's lost city is not the only one of its kind. The late British Consul at Rio was taken to such a place in 1913 by a half-caste Indian; but it was a city far more easily reached, in non-mountainous country, and completely buried in forest. It too was distinguished by the remains of a statue on a great black pedestal in the middle of a square. Unfortunately a cloudburst carried away their cargo animal and they had to return immediately to avoid starvation.

There are other lost cities besides these two; and there exists another remnant of an old civilization, its people degenerate now, but still preserving records of a forgotten past in mummies, parchments and engraved metal plates. It is just such a place as described in the story, but far less ruined by earthquakes—and very difficult to reach. The Jesuits knew of it, and so did a Frenchman who in the present century made several unsuccessful attempts to reach it. So too did a certain Englishman, much travelled in the interior, who had learned of it from an old document in Jesuit keeping. He was a victim of advanced cancer, and either died of it or was lost.

I am probably the only other who knows the secret, and I obtained it in the hard school of forest experience backed by careful examination of all available records in the archives of the Republic as well as certain other sources of information by no means easy to tap.

Outside of South America the details I have given here are not familiar, in fact even the countries most concerned with the mystery know little about it. Nevertheless, both native and foreign scholars of considerable erudition in Brazil agree that an old and forgotten civilization can be the only key to the riddle of the remarkable pottery and inscriptions that have been discovered. They know the legends current at the time of the Conquest, and they realize the vast extent of the unexplored forests.

One eminent Brazilian man of letters writes that his studies have convinced him that

"The autochthons of America lived in the remotest ages in a state of civilization vastly different from the present. For a number of reasons this civilization degenerated and tended to vanish, but Brazil is the country where its vestiges may still be sought."

He adds:

"It is not unlikely that in our still little-known forests there may be ruins of ancient cities."

General Cunha Mattos, founder of the Historical Institute of Rio, strongly endorsed this opinion.

It is my belief that they are perfectly right, and I only hope that public enterprise will sponsor responsible exploration before the vandals get there!

Intelligent Brazilians support exploration and ethnological survey, as was evidenced in the address to the Congress of National History at Rio de Janeiro in 1914, when the Roosevelt Expedition, royally escorted along the Matto Grosso telegraph line to the Rio Duvida, was hailed as "the inauguration of a new era opening to us a knowledge of our unknown lands and the people who inhabit them".

It is more than that: it is research of world-wide interest, for what can be more enthralling than penetration into the secrets of the past, and throwing light upon the history of civilization itself?

CHAPTER II

THE STONE IDOL

I HAVE in my possession an image[1] about ten inches high, carved from a piece of black basalt. It represents a figure with a plaque on its chest inscribed with a number of characters, and about its ankles a band similarly inscribed. It was given to me by Sir H. Rider Haggard, who obtained it from Brazil, and I firmly believe that it came from one of the lost cities.

There is a peculiar property in this stone image to be felt by all who hold it in their hands. It is as though an electric current were flowing up one's arm, and so strong is it that some people have been forced to lay it down. Why this should be I don't know.

Experts at the British Museum were unable to tell me anything about the idol's origin.

"If not a fake," I was told, "it's quite beyond our experience!"

Fakes are not made except to sell as antiquities, and what would be the use of making such an article if no one was in a position to form even a false opinion of it? I am quite sure it is not a fake, for fourteen of the twenty-four characters inscribed on it occur separately on various pieces of ancient Brazilian pottery.

I could think of only one way of learning the secret of the stone image, and that was by means of psychometry—a method that may evoke scorn from many people, but is widely accepted by others who have managed to keep their minds free from prejudice. Admittedly, the science of psychometry is yet in its infancy in our western countries, though highly developed in the Orient; and great care must be taken to

[1] See the illustration facing page 33.

sift out from the results the crumbs of telepathic communication liable to mix with it. It is based on the theory that every material object preserves in itself the record of its physical vicissitudes, and that this record is available to a person sensitive enough to tune in to the particular vibrations involved. The analogy of a radio receiver is by no means out of place, for the science of radio communication is delving deep into what a hundred years ago would have been regarded as rank superstition. Anyway, I am going to give the facts and leave it to you to accept or reject them, as you please.

I was quite unknown to the psychometrist, who held the figure in one hand and in complete darkness wrote the following:

"I see a large irregularly shaped continent stretching from the north coast of Africa across to South America. Numerous mountains are spread over its surface, and here and there a volcano looks as though about to erupt. The vegetation is prolific, and of a tropical or sub-tropical nature.

On the African side of the continent the population is sparse. The people are well-formed, but of a varied nondescript class, very dark complexioned though not negroid. Their most striking features are high cheek-bones and eyes of piercing brilliance. I should say their morals leave much to be desired, and their worship borders on demonology. I see villages and towns revealing signs of fairly advanced civilization, and there are certain ornate buildings which I take to be temples.

I seem to be transported across the country to the western side. Here the vegetation is dense, the flora most gorgeous, and the inhabitants far superior to the others. The country is hilly, and elaborate temples are partly hewn from the faces of the cliffs, their projecting façades supported by beautifully carved columns. Processions of what look like priests pass in and out of these temples, and a high priest or leader is wearing a breastplate similar to the one on the figure I am holding. Within the temples it is dark, but over the altars is the representation of a large eye. The priests are making invocations to this eye, and the whole ritual seems to be of an occult nature, coupled with a sacrificial system, though whether human or animal I cannot see.

Placed at various parts of the temple are a few effigies like the one in my hand—and this very one was evidently the portrait of a priest of high rank. I see the high priest take it and hand it to another priest, with instructions to retain it carefully, and in due course deliver it to an appointed one, who in turn must pass it on until at length it comes into the possession of a reincarnation of the personage it portrays, when numerous forgotten things will through its influence be elucidated.

The teeming population of the western cities seems to consist of three classes; the hierarchy and the ruling party under an hereditary monarch, a middle class, and the poor or slaves. These people are the absolute masters of the world, and by a great many of them the black arts are practised to an alarming extent.

I hear a voice saying: 'See the fate of the presumptuous! They count the Creator as under their influence and subject to their powers, but the day of retribution has come. Wait and watch!' Then I see volcanoes in violent eruption, flaming lava pouring down their sides, and the whole land shakes with a mighty rumbling sound. The sea rises as in a hurricane, and a huge portion of land on both east and west sides disappears under the water, leaving the central part flooded but visible. The majority of the inhabitants are either drowned or destroyed by the earthquakes. The priest to whom the effigy was given rushes from the sinking city towards the hills, where he places the sacred charge in hiding and then continues his flight eastwards.

Some of the people accustomed to the sea take to the boats and sail off; others escape to the central mountains, where they are joined by refugees from north and south.

The voice says: 'The judgment of Atladta will be the fate of all who presume to deific power!'

I can get no definite date of the catastrophe, but it was long prior to the rise of Egypt, and has been forgotten—except, perhaps, in myth.

As to the image; it is a maleficent possession to those not in affinity with it, and I should say it is dangerous to laugh at it. . . ."

Other psychometrists held the stone figure, and gave impressions tallying closely with the above. At all events, whatever its story may be, I look on it as a possible key to the secret of the Lost City of my quest, and when the search is continued it will accompany me. The connection of Atlantis with parts of what is now Brazil is not to be dismissed contemptuously, and belief in it—with or without scientific corroboration—affords explanations for many problems which otherwise are unsolved mysteries. Later on I shall have much more to say about this subject.

At the time of writing these words[1] I am awaiting with what patience I can muster the culmination of plans for the next expedition to search for the city discovered by Raposo and his party. I now have what I believe to be the correct bearings, and given normal luck we'll reach it. Bearing in mind the very hard conditions of the journey, no risk will be taken in selecting the rest of the party. I have been prevented from reaching my objective before by lack of stamina in my companions, and I have often regretted that it is not within my power to do it alone. It will be no pampered exploration party, with an army of bearers, guides and cargo

[1] 1923.—ED.

animals. Such top-heavy expeditions get nowhere; they linger on the fringe of civilization and bask in publicity. Where the real wilds start, bearers are not to be had anyway, for fear of the savages. Animals cannot be taken because of lack of pasture and the attacks of insects and bats. There are no guides, for no one knows the country. It is a matter of cutting equipment to the absolute minimum, carrying it all oneself, and trusting that one will be able to exist by making friends with the various tribes one meets. Game may or may not be obtainable; the chance that it will makes a ·22-calibre rifle desirable, but even this is a burden one grudges. Certainly, the weight of express rifles, revolvers and the ammunition for them is out of the question. It is far more dangerous to shoot a large beast than to leave it alone, and as for savages—well, the savage who is intent on killing you is invisible; and a rifle cannot compete with poisoned darts or arrows in a forest ambush!

My eldest son Jack will accompany me on the next trip, and the third member of the party will be his school friend, Raleigh Rimell, who at present is in Los Angeles, California. Raleigh I have not seen for a long time and therefore know little about his physical condition today, but Jack has the makings of the right sort. He is big, very powerful physically, and absolutely virgin in mind and body. He neither smokes nor drinks. Nor do I. One loses the habit when supplies of liquor and tobacco are cut off, and I gave them up a long time ago. The addict is under a handicap almost insurmountable when unable to obtain these things in the forest, and more than one of my companions has cracked up for lack of them.

So far I have had with me only two men able to withstand the prolonged hardships. One of them is now dead, and the other has married and settled down, so it would be unfair to ask him to come again. I am sure of Jack, however. He is young enough to adapt himself to anything, and a few months on the trail will toughen him sufficiently. If he takes after me, he will not contract the various ills and diseases rife in the South American wilds, and in an emergency I think his courage will stand. Raleigh will follow him anywhere.

Jack and Raleigh will have to learn to swim, as it were, by being flung into deep water. With no former experience they will be taken into a supreme endurance test. I myself worked up to it more gradually, and in any case had behind me many years of army life in the tropics. Being by nature a lone wolf and rather abstemious, I was not softened by gin and whisky when the first South American adventure came along; and as each succeeding expedition was harder than the last, the toughening process was continuous.

Much as I loathed army life, it had the merit of leading up to the work most attractive to me, and it served as an apprenticeship for that which seemed so much more worth while. Perhaps it was all for the best that my childhood in Torquay was so devoid of parental affection that it turned me in upon myself, although with my elder brother and sisters I had some grand times. There were school years at Newton Abbot, with canings that did nothing to alter my outlook. Then came cadet years at Woolwich; and in 1886, at the age of nineteen, my commission in the Royal Artillery, and early manhood in the garrison at Trincomalee, Ceylon. It was here I met my future wife, whose father was at the time a District Judge at Galle.

Life in Ceylon was as pleasant as army life can be. There was interesting work to do, plenty of sport—especially yachting in the incomparable harbour—and not too much restriction. Actually I could have enjoyed a longer period of service in that most beautiful of all islands, but the early '90s saw me back in England, taking the Long Course of gunnery instruction at Shoeburyness. Then came a turn at Falmouth; and, in January of 1901, marriage.

My wife caused much of the old reserve to lift from me; but the 'lone wolf' habit was not to be shaken off, and I continued to seek paths of my own rather than take the well-trodden ways. There was an interesting secret-service job to do in North Africa in 1901, and this was followed by a spell in Malta, when with my wife's capable help I learned the art of surveying. To our great relief we went East again in late 1902, and after a brief spell in Hong Kong found ourselves back in our beloved Ceylon, where our eldest son was born at Colombo in 1903.

It was with aching hearts that we left Ceylon in 1904 and came back to be stationed at Spike Island, Co. Cork, Ireland. But we were close now to the gateway of a new life. In 1906 the offer of boundary delimitation work in Bolivia was made to me.

The South America in which my story opens was very different from that of today. In 1906 Peru and Bolivia had not yet recovered from the devastating war against Chile—the Pacific War of 1879–82. The West Coast republics had scarcely felt the influence of growing industrial development; they were principally agrarian and imbued with the traditions of Colonial Spain, though their potential mineral wealth was being exploited by foreign concerns. Chile, thriving on its nitrate, was perhaps more awake to the existence of modernity than the others, but in all of them was much that to the foreigner appeared ridiculous, and the European was inclined to forget that but a scant century before he also was passing through the same stage.

Lack of restrictions made it the happy hunting-ground of the ne'er-do-well, the remittance-man and the fortune-hunter; the seaports were roaring hotbeds of vice in which hordes of sailormen from the many windjammers, tramps and coasters carried on with complete abandon. There was of course the serious foreigner too, and doubtless his beneficent influence played a big part in bringing about the changed aspect of today. Many of these worthy people felt the desire to give to the country of their adoption as well as to take from it, and the hospitable, long-suffering national observed this and extended the hand of sincere friendship.

The same countries today are in the vigour of their youth and beginning to take their true place in the world; the toys of childhood and the crudities of adolescence have been put aside for ever; and their limbs, which are their peoples—one in race, though segregated by political boundaries—will inevitably become conscious of unity. The grandeur that is to come may be only just beyond the horizon, if not already in view.

All who have lived in these lands, and learned to know them, fall captive to their irresistible charm. It would be the greatest mistake were the reader to judge their present condition from my impressions in the first decade of the century, for society then was no more like today's than that of the Napoleonic era was like ours.

What have not changed are the silent rivers rolling on through the forests of the interior, for to them the passage of a millennium is but a day, and they still shroud behind their impenetrable veil the mysteries of which I write, and the curtain rolls back on scenes utterly removed from the everyday world. Come with me now, and see for yourself!

CHAPTER III

PATH TO ADVENTURE

"DO you know anything about Bolivia?" asked the President of the Royal Geographical Society.

Its history, like that of Peru, had always fascinated me, but beyond that I knew nothing of the country, and said so.

"I've never been there myself," he said, "but its potential wealth is enormous. What has been exploited up to now is not much more than a scratch on the surface. One usually thinks of Bolivia as a country on the roof of the world. A great deal of it is in the mountains; but beyond the mountains, to the east, lies an enormous area of tropical forest and plains not yet by any means completely explored."

He took a large atlas from the side of his desk and fingered over the pages.

"Here you are, Major—here's about as good a map of the country as I have!" He pushed it over to me and came round to my side of the desk to point out its features. "Look at this area! It's full of blank spaces because so little is known of it. Many of the rivers shown here are guesswork; and the places named along them mostly no more than rubber centres. You know it's rubber country?

"The eastern frontier of Bolivia follows the River Guaporé up from Corumba to Villa Bella, at the confluence of the Mamoré River, where the Beni becomes the Madeira, and eventually flows into the Amazon. North it runs along the Abuna, to the Rapirran, and then overland to the River Acre. All this northern frontier is doubtful, as accurate surveys have not yet been made of it. The western frontier comes down to the

18

Madre de Dios and along the Heath—a river that has not been explored to its source—then continues south and crosses the Andes to Lake Titicaca. On the southern frontier there is the Chaco, which is the border with Paraguay, and, further westwards, the frontier with Argentina—the only border which has been definitely fixed.

"Now, up here in the rubber country along the Abuna and the Acre, where Peru, Brazil and Bolivia meet, there is considerable argument about the frontier, and so fantastically high is the price of rubber now that a major conflagration could arise out of this question of what territory belongs to whom!"

"Just a minute!" I interrupted. "All this is most interesting—but what has it got to do with me?"

The President laughed. "I'm coming to that. First of all I want you to get the picture. . . .

"The countries concerned in the dispute about the frontiers are not prepared to accept a demarcation made by interested parties. It has become necessary to call in the services of another country which can be relied on to act without bias. For that reason the Government of Bolivia through its diplomatic representative here in London has requested the Royal Geographical Society to act as referee, and to recommend an experienced army officer for the work on Bolivia's behalf. As you completed our course in boundary-delimitation work with outstanding success, I thought of you at once. Would you be interested in taking it on?"

Would I! Here was the chance I had been waiting for—the chance to escape from the monotonous life of an artillery officer in home stations.

The War Office had frequently promised that boundary-survey work might come my way if I acquired the training, and so I had gone to great trouble and expense to make myself competent. Time passed without my hopes being fulfilled, and I began to doubt those promises. Now, from an unexpected quarter, there came the offer I most desired! My heart was pounding as I faced the President, but with an effort I assumed an air of caution.

"It sounds interesting, certainly," I remarked, "but I'd like to know a little more about it first. It must be more than just survey work."

"It is. What it really amounts to is exploration. It may be difficult and even dangerous. Not much is known about that part of Bolivia, except that the savages there have a pretty bad reputation. One hears the most appalling tales of this rubber country. Then there's the risk of disease—it's rife everywhere. It's no use trying to paint an attractive picture for you, and I hardly think it's necessary, for if I'm not mistaken there's a gleam in your eye already!"

I laughed. "The idea appeals to me—but it depends on whether the War Office will agree to second me."

"I realize that," he replied. "You may have some difficulty, but with the backing of the R.G.S. I have no doubt they will release you in the end. After all, it's a wonderful chance to enhance the prestige of the British Army in South America."

Naturally I accepted the offer. The romantic history of the Spanish and Portuguese conquests, and the mystery of its vast unexplored wilds, made the lure of South America irresistible to me. There were my wife and son to consider, and another child was on the way; but Destiny intended me to go, so there could be no other answer!

"It would have surprised me had you refused," said the President. "I shall recommend you at once, then."

One difficulty after another cropped up, and I became anxious about the chances of being released. However, it was finally arranged, and I left Spike Island with the hope that before long my wife and the children would be able to join me in La Paz. With a young assistant named Chalmers, we embarked on the North German Lloyd flagship *Kaiser Wilhelm der Grosse* in May 1906, and sailed for New York.

This ship was at that time the last word in luxury liners, but as travel of this sort had little appeal for me I was bored, and quite indifferent to the overfed passengers who sprawled about the decks. There were gales and fog; we nearly collided with a roving iceberg, invisible till it was almost too late to avoid it. A high-pressure cylinder burst and left us rolling for hours in the troughs of a terrific sea; but it all happened in the brief space of a week, and soon we were in New York.

The energy and bustle were things I had never known before. Accustomed to the calm deliberation of the English and the solemn dignity of the East, America at first shocked me. We were not allowed beyond the area of the docks, and so my impressions were mainly of noise, advertisements, and reporters by the score. The speed of street traffic, the fussiness of the tugs in the harbour as they pushed and shouldered the innumerable railroad car-floats and lighters, the incessant shouting, all jarred on my nerves; but to soothe them again there was the truly wonderful sight of that unique skyline, the green of Governor's Island, and the elegant tracery of the Brooklyn Bridge.

We had a brief glimpse of New York and no more. The same afternoon we boarded the S.S. *Panama*, and the Statue of Liberty sank out of sight astern. This ship was the antithesis of the floating palace we had left, for it was a dirty Government ship full of "Diggers" bound for the Isthmus of Panama. White-collar workers, adventurers, toughs, would-be toughs, and leather-faced old scoundrels crowded every foot of available space, and when walking up and down the deck we had to dodge foul squirts of tobacco-juice. Their chief occupations were drinking and playing ruinous crap games, and the noise that went on all the time made my study of Spanish grammar a difficult matter. There were sourdoughs from the Klondike, Texas Rangers, and gunmen from south of the border, boomer railroad men with stacks of forged service letters, a few prostitutes, and fresh young college boys on their first adventure. They were all good fellows in their way, and each played his part, however small, in making that masterpiece of engineering, the Panama Canal. To Chalmers and myself it served as a useful introduction to an aspect of life we had not hitherto known, and much of our English reserve was knocked off in the process.

The port of Cristóbal was known as Aspinwall in those days, and ships tied up to a long jetty stretching far out into Limón Bay. Beyond the docks lay Colon, more restricted than it is now but otherwise much the same. Liberally sprinkled with Hindu curio shops and saloons, it was composed largely of alleys where drunken laughter and the tinkling of pianos seemed to uphold its reputation for having more brothels than any town of its size in the world. Notices shouted at you to come in and have a drink! Sailors were everywhere, in all stages of intoxication, reeling from saloon to saloon, and from brothel to brothel. Quarrels flared up on street corners and died down again; here and there a scuffle attracted an interested group of spectators; down some side street a screaming prostitute would fling curses at a *perro muerto*, or patron who left without paying the score. There was no attempt at keeping the peace—the Panamanian police knew better than to try!

Alongside the front street ran the tracks of the Panama Railroad, and the fussing yard engines moved up and down with scarcely a pause, their bells clanging monotonously. Every now and then there came from beyond the town the long-drawn wail of a chime whistle, and a freight or passenger train would come romping in from across the Isthmus and draw up in the station with thumping air compressor and the soft sigh of releasing brakes.

We left the jetty in a buggy driven by a somnolent Jamaican, bumped over the railroad tracks, and clip-clopped along the edge of Colon to the station. The town was comparatively quiet at this time of day, except for the activity in the railroad yards and a subdued tinkle of glasses from the saloons, with perhaps an occasional oath or a shout of laughter. By day it is too hot to do anything but laze and sleep, and it is after sundown that the town wakes up. It rests all day and dances all night, like the fireflies in the pandemonium of the Chagres woods.

The rail journey across to Panama City gave us our first sight of the forest of tropical America—the buttressed, ghostly pale tree boles; the hanging tangle of lianas and moss; the almost impenetrable scrub and bush. Fever was rampant, and in one of the way stations through which we clattered I noticed the platform piled to the roof for its whole length with black coffins!

For us, Latin America began in Panama City. There was little attempt at sanitation, the smells were almost overpowering, yet the narrow streets and overhanging balconies were not without their charm. In the *Plaza* was the 'Grán Hotel'—it is always 'Grand', 'Royal', or 'Imperial', however humble, and what it lacks in status it makes up in grandiose title! This one turned out to be an insect paradise; and the proprietor was greatly annoyed when I pointed out that the bed-linen in my room was overdue for the laundry.

"Impossible!" he roared with a flurry of gesticulation. "All the linen goes to the laundry at least once a month. If you don't like it, there are plenty of others who would be glad to have the room. Every bed in my hotel is occupied, some by two—even three—and every bathtub as well! Yours is a big room, and I am losing money by letting you have it to yourself."

There was nothing I could say. After all, every hotel was over-crowded.

Everywhere the lottery vendors hawked their ticket strips, cafés and saloons abounded, and from the balconies we were ogled by scantily clad ladies. Down by the shore was a sea wall forming the outer defence of a crowded jail, and here you could stroll in the evening, toss coins to the scrambling prisoners beneath, and sometimes see an execution by firing squad. With so much entertainment it was impossible to be bored.

We were glad to leave Panama, all the same, when at length the time came to embark on a Chilean ship—a narrow-gutted, rakish vessel with side-loading holds, and superstructure running from the extreme stern to within a few feet of the clipper bow—designed for coast service in little dog-hole ports where no dock facilities existed. The best ships on the Coast were those of the Pacific Steam Navigation Company of Liverpool, and had time permitted we should have preferred to wait for one of these, for their officers were a cheerful lot, with a genius for deck golf, and the knack of making the trip pleasant for the passengers. But we were on the trail of Pizarro, and nothing else mattered.

As a boy I was held spellbound by the romantic histories of the Conquests of Peru and Mexico, and the long-dormant yearning to visit these countries was now about to be satisfied. Like many other readers of Prescott's masterpieces, my sympathies were not with the daring and rapacious Spaniards risking all for gold, but with the Incas for the loss of their ancient civilization which might have told the world so much.

Guayaquil was at this time a veritable pest-house! One evening we steamed up the Guayas River through dense clouds of mosquitoes, which invaded cabins and saloon alike, penetrated to every corner of the ship, and stung us mercilessly. I had never known anything like it before. The agonies of Pizarro and his followers must have been beyond description when these pests crept out of scratching range and bit under their shelter-ing armour! Guayaquil's appalling lack of sanitation had much to do with the yellow-fever endemic. As the anchor roared down into the black mud of the filthy river, evil-smelling bubbles burst upwards—and I was reminded of Malta. But Yellow Jack hardly seemed to worry the people, for the streets were crowded, trade was brisk, and well-kept launches lined the wharves. A new Minister to London was due to leave in a north-bound steamer of the same line as ours, so numerous Ecuadorian flags waved over the city's public buildings, and we watched him with his gorgeously uniformed staff played aboard by brass bands.

The clean freshness of the Pacific welcomed us when the fever-haunted Guayas River vomited us out on its muddy tide. Rounding Cape Blanco, where the giant blanket fish leap and drum and where every wave is split by the twin triangles of sharks' fins, we came to the Northern Peruvian port of Paita. This was a nondescript village of wooden houses, standing at the foot of unbroken sandhills, and here we were fumigated with formaldehyde for our indiscretion in visiting Guayaquil.

Salaverry was the next port of call—one of those places where you should if possible go ashore, but generally can't. It is not far from Trujillo, itself one of the oldest Spanish settlements on the Coast and site of an ancient Chimu city and burial grounds, dug up over and over again in search of treasure. The tradition is that somewhere in this vicinity lies hidden the treasure of the 'Big Fish'. The 'Little Fish' was discovered about two hundred years ago and is said to have realized twenty million dollars for its lucky finder! 'Big Fish' is worth considerably more, and is believed to contain the emerald god of the Chimus, cut from a single stone eighteen inches high.

Callao is the port of Lima, capital of Peru, and here we lay off-shore, the ship rolling her rusty bottom out in the huge swell some distance from the *embarcadero*, or landing-stage. Soon we were invaded by shouting, struggling boatmen who fought their way to the ladders, and from their rocking launches bargained with shore-going passengers, breaking off every now and then to hurl streams of invective at one another. To jump from ladder to launch in this bedlam was anything but easy. One moment the lowest step of the ladder would be at a giddy height above the crowding boats, then there was a scramble to avoid a ducking as the sea came foaming up almost to deck level. It was a matter of biding your time, and then jumping, in the hope that the chosen launch would be there when you landed! Huge jellyfish—medusae—drifted about on the surface and as far down in the clear water as the eye could see.

Once ashore we found a choice of three railways for the nine-mile trip to Lima. There was the famous Central of Peru, masterpiece of that indefatigable engineer, Henry Meiggs; the 'English Railway', opened to traffic in 1851 and claimed as the first in South America; and an electric line whose inter-urban cars even at that time could do a mile a minute.

Lima turned out to be a fine city, with admirable shops and wide avenues to bear witness to the progressive policy of the late President Pierola, whose object it was to beautify the place. Motor-cars were yet few, and the principal conveyance was the victoria, though in every one of the main streets horse-cars crawled along tracks set in the cobbles. Almost anything could be bought—at a price—but that price was generally four times as much as in London! Don Francisco Pizarro, resurrected from a niche in the crypt of the Cathedral and placed in a glass coffin to preserve him from the memento-hunting fingers of travelling Americans, was one of the chief sights for the visitor, and I paid my doit for the privilege of gazing on his emaciated remains.

The Maury Hotel was a welcome change from the ship. I was told it was the best in Lima, and could readily believe it, for we found it clean, comfortable and efficient, and the food excellent. For a week it was our home, and during that time I saw what I could of Lima and its environs. A duty call on the British Minister led to introductions to other English residents, all of whom were most hospitable and kind. The Minister himself was an amusing man of rather eccentric habits, and he generally met callers clad in a dressing-gown at the top of a long flight of stairs connecting his apartments with the street. He was always ready to defend himself, for a constant stream of alcoholic seamen sought him for the purpose of asserting what they were pleased to call their 'rights', and it was said that he was not above resorting to violence to get rid of them!

The manager of the Central Railway of Peru, Mr. Morkill, was kind enough to offer me a run to Rio Blanco, 11,000 feet up in the Andes, with an excursion train put on for the sake of sailors from two visiting British warships. He had a private car hooked on the rear of the train for my exclusive use—a courtesy that was quite new in my experience. Never had I seen anything like this railway, which is the highest of any standard-gauge system in the world, and is only beaten as the highest of any gauge by the Antofogasta-Bolivia Railway, which wins by a scant ten feet! The Central runs from sea level to almost 16,000 feet in little over a hundred miles, climbing steady grades of one in twenty-five, backing up many zig-zags or reversing switches, and passing through innumerable tunnels. The run up to Rio Blanco left me speechless, not only at the grandeur of the scenery, but also at the engineering enterprise that built this extraordinary railway.[1]

We rejoined the ship in Callao for the remainder of the voyage, and steamed out of the port, round San Lorenzo Island, and down the coast. The setting sun lit the towering *Cordilleras* thirty miles back from the

[1] When my father received a cable advising him of my birth on the day he arrived in Lima, little did he know that in less than eighteen years' time the new arrival would be a resident in Lima, and working under Mr. Morkill's son on the Central Railway of Peru. Indeed, by some odd concatenation of circumstances, the same private car my father used on his trip to Rio Blanco—the old 'Chalaca'—stood for some years, retired from service and transformed into a watchman's shelter, just outside my office in the locomotive works.—ED.

shore in a magnificent panorama, topped by snowy summits. There were calls at Cerro Azul and Pisco, where we were able to go ashore and stroll up-town to the *plaza* beneath a high canopy of *ficus* trees. The ship held a course remarkably close to the land, so close that here and there we could see Inca ruins and an intensive cultivation of cotton in green strips irrigated by mountain rills. But what interested us more was the teeming bird and fish life of the ocean around us.

On the third morning after leaving Callao we woke to find the engines stopped and the ship rolling over almost to her beam ends in an enormous swell. We lay off Mollendo, chief port of Southern Peru, and from the scuttle I could see a cliff, almost obliterated in a welter of foam from the mighty breakers, with a huddle of miserable-looking wooden houses on top. All about us were lighters, pitching and bobbing, now on the crest of the waves, now lost to view in the troughs.

Disembarking was not so bad as we had feared. The ship rolled so badly that to pass from ladder to launch was too dangerous, and passengers were unloaded into the boats in baskets swung from the ship's derricks. Once in the launch you fully appreciated the size of the swell, and the women screamed every time one of those twenty-five-foot combers towered astern of us. But the boatmen were used to this work, and without shipping a drop of water we rounded into the small harbour, open to the fierce rush and retreat of the waves. The final hazard was in being lifted from the crazily pitching launch by a dock crane, one passenger at a time, seated in a kitchen chair to which no less than four or five yelling stevedores were clinging.

Mollendo was even more miserable a place than it looked from the ship. Much of it had been ruined by disastrous fires, and what was left was shabby. It also suffered from outbreaks of bubonic plague. The best part of it was undoubtedly the station and busy yards of the Southern Railway of Peru.

We reserved seats on the first train for Arequipa and enjoyed a most interesting journey inland. At Ensenada the train turned away from the shore and began the tortuous ascent of a long 4-per-cent grade to the plateau at Cachendo; and as the Tambo Valley opened out to us we caught a glimpse of green fields and extensive areas under sugarcane. We stopped for breakfast at Cachendo, and then the train rolled on over the sandy *pampa* of La Joya, and the snows of *Misti* and *Chachani*, guardian mountains of Arequipa, came into view. For miles and miles hundreds of white sand dunes littered the plain, changing their position constantly under the force of the wind. In the gullies were large quantities of kaolin, once used by sailing vessels as ballast until the authorities woke up to its value.

"Oranges! Bananas! Buy my fruit, *señores*! Limes—*chirimoyas— grenadillas*!" At Vitor the train was invaded by hordes of market-women

who thrust their baskets of fruit in our faces. The idea was to sell the
entire lot, basket and all, and then clear off before we found that under
the attractive top layer the fruit was hardly fit to eat. Prices, high when the
train arrived, plummeted down as the departure-bell tolled in the station,
and the noisy bargaining was still going on as the train began to move.

At Quishuarani we came on one of those exquisite scenes alluded to
by Prescott—snow-capped *Misti* in the background and the serrated crest
of *Chachani* towering up into an impeccably blue sky. In the midst of a
billowing ocean of many-coloured sandhills was a deep canyon, its sides,
streaked with pink and yellow sandstone, sloping down to a vividly green
valley. Through this valley ran the tiny River Chili, bursting into miniature
cascades of silver spume among the *adobe* huts and rich fields.

Misti is a volcano reputed to be inactive, but from its crater a whiff
of smoke rises every now and then, as though to tell the citizens of
Arequipa that it only sleeps. Occasionally it erupts with disastrous
results. The houses are for the most part of only one storey, built of
gleaming white lava blocks called *sillares*. The climate is delightful, for
Arequipa lies at nearly 8,000 feet above the sea and well beyond the fog
pall of the littoral. With its many sources of medicinal waters in the
neighbourhood it might be a health resort, but at night, when the setting
sun has ceased to guild the Cathedral spires and *Misti's* cone, evil smells
pollute the air from the open sewers running through every street.

We spent only one night in Arequipa, city of pretty women, fine shops,
and green fields, and on the following day took train for Puno. Almost at
once the heavy climb began, and at 13,000 feet llamas made their appearance—those proud and dignified relatives of the sheep that are so unsheep-
like in character. Then we reached Vincocaya, at 14,000 feet, and caught
sight of the shy vicuña, smallest of the llama family, whose exquisite fleece
was valued highly by the Incas.

The summit of the line is at Crucero Alto, 14,666 feet above sea level,
and after that the train descends past a series of picturesque lakes to
Juliaca, junction of the Puno and Cuzco divisions. Then it runs on
beside reedy flats and gleaming fingers of water to the port of Puno,
12,500 feet up on the shores of Titicaca, highest navigable lake in the
world.

How strange it is to see steamers in operation up here on the roof of
the world! Yet here they are, and sizable vessels too. There is an interesting story behind them. The first was brought up from the coast piecemeal
on the backs of mules, and assembled at the lakeside. The other ships
were also delivered in sections, but came up by rail for assembly on the
Peruvian Corporation's slip. Lake Titicaca can become surprisingly rough
sometimes, and perhaps nowhere else is it possible for a traveller to suffer
from sea-sickness and mountain-sickness at the same time!

Docked at Puno Mole, the *Coya* gave a weird impression of ocean travel as we embarked that night, for here was no flat-bottomed river craft or shallow-draught stern-wheeler. This was a regular ocean-going steamer, with accommodation comparable to any. There were the formalities of the Customs, the shouting of stevedores, the white-coated stewards waiting at the gangway to take passengers' hand-luggage down to the cabins, all the familiar to-do at the start of an ocean voyage. The rattle of winches and the shudder of the deck greeted us as we went aboard, and in the warm paint-filled atmosphere of the stateroom we could feel the vibration of the auxiliaries down below and hear the occasional clang of a shovel in the stokehold. It was unbelievable that all this could be at 12,500 feet above sea level! Then came the shattering blare of the hooter, the jangle of engine-room bells, and we slid away from the mole into the darkness.

Next morning we were up at dawn to see the magnificent view of the main *Cordillera* of the Andes sharply defined in the crackling frosty atmosphere, a chain of jagged snow-covered peaks dominated by the white masses of *Sorata, Huaynapotosi, Murarata* and *Illimani*—seventy miles of unbroken snow. As we passed the Island of the Sun, legendary birthplace of the Incas whose palaces now lie in ruins, I wondered what the lake was like in its palmy days before the Conquest. Passing the Straits of Tiquina, with the Island of the Moon astern, we saw on either side lofty hills terraced and cultivated to their summits, and ahead numerous small islets of red earth with golden crops glowing in the light of the rising sun. Beyond were still more islands dancing in the mirage, misty and blue with distance, losing themselves in the soft white haze hanging over the southern margin of the lake. At the foot of the hills were *adobe* houses with red-tiled roofs, brightly garbed Indians grouped about their doorways. Sailing or paddling over the silvery surface of the lake were reed *balsas*, rafts whose design has not changed in centuries. Thousands of ducks fled from the vicinity of the ship, half running, half flying over the water in their efforts to get out of the way. The colouring baffles description—but the chill air nipped us to the bone.

The *Coya* glided into Guaqui port, and we disembarked in Bolivia. Then we boarded the narrow-gauge train of the Guaqui-La Paz Railway, and we had our last glimpse of the ship as she lay alongside the mole mirrored by a perfect reflection in the glassy surface of the canal. Soon we were passing Tiahuanaco, whose ancient ruins are perhaps the oldest in existence anywhere—older even than the Sphinx.

Tiahuanaco was built, as Sacsahuaman and much of Cuzco were built, by a race who handled cyclopean boulders and carved them to fit so perfectly that it is impossible to insert a knife-blade between the mortarless joins. Looking at these remains it is not difficult to believe the tradition that they were erected by giants—indeed, skeletons of giants are said to have been discovered in rock tombs in the vicinity of Cuzco. In my opinion, Tiahuanaco, which covers an area of about a square league, was built on an island in a lake. Much of it is still buried below the present level of Titicaca, and the remains scattered and tumbled over the surface of the ground are not necessarily the ruins of the original city. Excavations may disclose several cities, built one upon another—as in Cuzco. It was destroyed by the frightful seismic upheavals which are so evident all over the continent. The lake was bodily lifted thousands of feet with the Andes, and then burst its barriers and rushed through a cleft south of *Illimani*. After that, a new lake may have formed, for Tiahuanaco was undoubtedly submerged for a long time. The level of the present lake was once considerably higher, for on the surrounding hills can be plainly distinguished the old high-water mark. Today, people scrape in the sand covering the ruins and unearth bits of pottery and arrow-heads of obsidian —now and then little golden relics—of which the museum in La Paz has an interesting collection. But I believe that these belong to the degenerate days following the great catastrophe, when the gathering refugees from the Pacific spread over the uplands of the Province of Charcas. Intermittent and quite inadequate efforts have been made to disclose Tiahuanaco's secrets.

An eminent German archæologist, who spent a lifetime excavating at Tiahuanaco, invited me some years ago to offer the British Museum twenty-four packing-cases full of pottery, stone and golden figures, weapons, and other relics from the unique collection he had made there, expressing his willingness to accept the Museum's valuation. This I did; but it was refused.

"To tell you the truth, the things are of no particular interest to us," was the answer I was given. Britain lost incalculable treasure that day!

Speaking of treasure, you cannot be in Peru or Bolivia a day without hearing talk of treasures, and not by any means Inca treasures only. It was the custom of the Spanish invaders and natives alike to bury all their possessions in the ground or conceal them within recesses in the walls of their houses during the revolutionary epoch following the Conquest; and until recent times the same thing has been done at the first hint of trouble.

On one occasion, while engaged in repairing an old house in Arequipa, some workmen came upon a hole in one wall and were wild with excitement at finding a cavity extending beyond it. With palpitating eagerness they enlarged it and were rewarded by the discovery of a number of silver dishes. They broke their way in farther and disclosed crockery; farther still, and they came to warm food on a plate—and beyond it, the infuriated visage of the lady next door, whose larder was being ransacked!

Seriously, though, real treasure is found not infrequently. Farmers turn up hoards with their ploughshares, and, if unwise enough to declare the find to the authorities, are promptly jailed, and held *incomunicados* until it is established that they have kept back none of it! In Colombia, a few years ago, a man fell into a hole while hunting, and on recovering found himself in a cave. When his companions finally located him the cave was explored, and they discovered a million dollars' worth of plate and valuables, secreted there since the days of the Conquest.[1]

The level of the great Andean plateau, or *Altiplano*, is between twelve and thirteen thousand feet above sea level, and the view from the *Alto*—fifteen hundred feet above La Paz—is superb. La Paz nestles at the bottom of a deep canyon beside a rushing mountain stream, and when approaching by rail you look down on red-tiled roofs and a chequerboard of gardens. On all sides as far as the eye can reach are the gashed and rain-eroded hills. The towers of many churches rise from among the roofs and gardens, and white houses gleam like jewels in the pattern of green and yellow farm lands on the hillsides. *Illimani's* 21,000-foot summit dazzles the eye to the south-east, seeming only five miles away, but in reality fifty; and the glory of snowy peaks lends infinite grandeur and beauty to the scene. Everywhere are Indians, whose bright garments display every conceivable colour.

Foreigners may feel the altitude of La Paz at first. On closer acquaintance the city has its drawbacks, but I can easily imagine a worse fate than being obliged to live there permanently. The market on a Sunday morning must be one of the sights of the world, when the Indians from the *Yungas*—the warm valleys—come in to buy and sell.

They come in their thousands, with *ponchos*, skirts and shawls of dazzling colours; but the dress of the *Cholita*, or half-caste Indian woman —who considers herself superior to the full-blooded Indian—is perhaps the most striking. Many of these women are very pretty, and know it! They wear short, full skirts of silk, allowing a peep of lace petticoats; their stockings are of silk, and their high-laced boots of Spanish style; over their blouses they wear plush or velvet jackets and brilliantly coloured shawls; and to top it off they wear at a coquettish angle round white straw hats with narrow brims. Their free gait and swinging skirts give them an attractive swagger; and when to all this are added lively dark eyes, the rosy cheeks of the hill folk, and an abundance of jewelry, you have a fascinating picture indeed.

The *Cholos*—male counterparts of the pretty *Cholitas*—are vicious and

---

[1] A similar case happened in the Republic of Panama in 1937. However, the cases you hear of are few and far between, and it can only be supposed that the unreported finds are more common. Treasure hunters waste much time and money in seeking for hoards that are either non-existent or have already been lifted. They seem to forget that people who find treasures are usually anxious to keep the fact secret!

Cocos Island, in the Pacific, is reputed to have several buried treasures, but the principal one is that of Lima Cathedral, which is said to have been buried there in 1820 during the War of Independence. Hopeful seekers have dug the island up from end to end, much to the annoyance of the South American Republic whose property it happens to be, yet the treasure they seek never left Lima! I know the place where it is supposed to be hidden, and the site is romantic and risky enough to satisfy any adventurer.—ED.

invertebrate specimens of humanity, by no means physically or mentally up to the standard of their womenkind. The real Indians offer a striking contrast to both. Ugly and short, but sturdy and virile, picturesquely garbed in *ponchos*, slashed trousers and felt hats, and full of good humour, they appeal to you at once. They look honest, and suggest strength. They may be called lazy rascals, but my own belief is that they by no means deserve the universal condemnation they receive. Those who know the Tibetans find a distinct resemblance.

To the foreigner the drawbacks of La Paz are its steep streets and the rarefied air of the high altitude. Any physical exertion results in a racing heart and panting breath, and many suffer for a time from *soroche*, or mountain-sickness. The dry air causes lips to crack and noses to bleed; the mind is less active, and nerves become jumpy. Newcomers generally overtax themselves before becoming acclimatized, and ignore the fact that if alcohol and excessive exertion be avoided the unpleasant sensations are greatly reduced.

Yet La Paz with its street cars, its *plazas*, *alamedas* and cafés, is essentially a modern city. Foreigners of all kinds throng the streets. True, the proximity of the wild places can be sensed plainly. In the midst of the frock coats and top hats of the townsmen you see the frayed Stetsons and 'thousand-milers' of the prospectors; but somehow the wired soles of shoe packs don't look incongruous among the high-heeled pumps of the fashionable ladies. The miner and prospector are everyday types, for mining is the be-all and end-all of the Bolivian *Sierra*, and now and then you will see the emaciated yellow face of one who has lately come from beyond the mountains—from the steaming hell of the vast wilderness into which we were about to plunge.

CHAPTER IV

FRINGE OF THE WILDERNESS

TROUBLE began when I complained of the delay in settling matters for the expedition. I was new to the country, ignorant of the customs, and impatient to get started. As usual, money was the chief obstacle. How could one hire the mules or purchase the supplies without it? I had my first taste of '*mañanas*', and was put off from one day to another. Then, as I continued to pester them, the delays were extended from one week to the next! 'Passing the buck' between departments wore my patience thin, and I asked the British Consul to see what he could do to hurry things along.

"But of course you must have the money," said the Bolivian official with whom I was most concerned. "There will be four thousand pounds for your expedition expenses."

I was surprised. That was far more than I had expected.

"I will make out the order for that sum to be paid you at once," he concluded.

Next day the Minister for Foreign Affairs sent for me.

"That is a grave mistake, about the four thousand pounds," he informed me, with a cold asperity. "There is no need for such a large sum. The arrangement was to pay you four thousand *Bolivianos*—not pounds."

I made a quick exchange calculation, and objected. It was not enough.

"Nonsense!" retorted the Minister. "Stores are unnecessary. You can obtain all you require on the Beni; and you will find instruments for the work awaiting you at Rurenabaque."

"Without stores or enough money to buy them it's quite impossible to carry out the work," I replied, "and if I don't get them here, I must have an official guarantee of getting them there, before I leave for the Beni."

The Minister lost his temper at that, and smote his temples with the flat of his hand. I bowed respectfully and withdrew.

The British Consul tried to smooth things over with the Government. In doing so, a network of difficulties came to light. The first official was hurt because we hustled him, and his order for payment of £4,000 was intended to show us in the light of making excessive demands. There was a very natural desire on the part of the Government for the boundary line to be run by a Bolivian engineer, because of rubber interests—in fact, the Government might not be anxious to run the line at all until tension with Peru had diminished.

"They may even back out of the contract," the British Consul told me. "They resent your presence, and will discredit you in any way they can. However, another interview is arranged for you, and it will be interesting to see what comes of it."

Something did come of it. The interview was tense and explosive, but arrangements were fixed for 4,000 *Bolivianos* for travelling expenses and 6,000 for stores. An agreement was drawn up, and I was docked then and there ten *Bolivianos* for official stamps! Some time passed before all the necessary ministerial signatures had been appended to the order for payment of the cash.

This distasteful business once concluded, I tried to make peace with the ruffled authorities. La Paz rang with the tale of how scurvily Ministers of the Government had been treated by the British Commission, and in diplomatic circles there were chuckles about it. Nevertheless, when it was all over my advances were greeted generously, and, superficially at any rate, peace was established.

There were no baths in La Paz at that time, and the alternative of a tin basin was an ordeal in this cold climate. You were seriously told that a cold plunge would stop the heart altogether at this altitude, and the stranger was in no position to deny it. Besides being bitterly cold, the city was frequently covered with snow, for it was the wet season. The Minister of the Colonies—as the interior of the country is called—made anxious enquiries about my comfort, and I told him a bath would transport me to the very heavens. He said that my services were too valuable to permit it —a bath at that altitude where evaporation is so rapid would be certain to result in pneumonia.

Ventilation was another problem. At my hotel there was no window in the first room I occupied, and the door opened on to a gallery encircling a small *patio*. Whenever I left it open to admit a little fresh air, some well-intentioned passer-by would close it for me. In one wall was another door, a glass affair covered by a frayed curtain, and one night I decided to give this a trial, so, after unfastening a number of bolts and screws, I opened it. Beyond was a dark space of some sort. I investigated with a candle, and to my horror found that it was another bedroom, with a woman sitting up in bed and staring at me speechless. Fully expecting screams of outraged modesty, I apologized as well as my text-book Spanish allowed, and retreated. She made no sound.

The delays were considerable, but at last I received £1,000 in gold from the Government—and considered the transaction a quick one compared with the time it takes to extract even the meanest sum from the British Treasury! So much gold made me feel enormously important, though the cost of mules, stores, and hotel bills soon reduced it to £800. With this treasure jingling in the saddle-bags, Chalmers and I set out over the *Altiplano* on the fourth day of July, 1906, bound for Sorata and the Beni.

We crossed a rolling plain, where an unbroken stream of cargo animals—mules, donkeys, llamas and Indians—carried grain, rubber and llama-dung fuel to the markets of La Paz. Llama dung was at the time the only fuel in general use there, and strangers had to get used to the acrid taste it imparted to food.

It was snowing hard when we left, and I put on my *poncho*—the first time I had worn this new acquisition. The llama- or alpaca-wool *poncho* is a garment in general use amongst the Mountain Indians. It serves as a waterproof, an overcoat, and a bed-blanket; but it is really part of the men's clothing—the Indian women never wear them. As a protection against driving snow nothing can be better. Yet my mule objected to it. The trailing corners of the *poncho* flapped in the wind, and before I realized the danger I was thrown by a sudden buck. I tied up the corners of the *poncho* to keep them from flapping, and remounted.

The snow fell thicker and thicker, till visibility was reduced to no more than twenty yards, and the stiffening wind whipped it under our *ponchos*. I decided to remove the *poncho* and put on a long slicker instead. Just as I was drawing my head and arms through the stiff folds the confounded mule bucked again, and once more I was flat on the ground. Then it took to its heels, and with sinking heart I listened to its receding hoof beats and the fainter and fainter jingling of my gold in the saddle-bags.

The *arriero*, or drover, was in the rear, and when he came up it took me some time to explain in my bad Spanish what had happened. Taking in the situation at last, he dived into the white pall in pursuit. He told off passing Indians to help, and in the hue and cry I waited, hardly expecting to see my money again.

To my amazement the mule was brought in from the opposite direction by two Indians who had found it making for home. They sensibly assumed that the owner was somewhere ahead. The saddle-bags were untouched, and I marvelled at the honesty of those Indians, who might easily have taken the gold, without the slightest risk of being caught. I rewarded them handsomely, and they were amazed at the folly of a *Gringo*[1] in even recognizing their service!

The snow stopped when we came to Lake Titicaca, and we had a wonderful view of the lake. No wind was blowing and its still surface reflected perfectly every cloud. The sun was brilliant. Little puffs of white cumulus lay along the skyline, as though some huge locomotive had idled across below the horizon. Birds were everywhere, so tame that they scarcely troubled to keep out of our way. Every hillside was terraced and cultivated to its summit, just as in the remotest times of the Incas.

We found *posadas*—inns—along the fairly good road, and stopped for beer or coffee. We passed through villages, where the dogs turned out to greet us with a frenzy of barking. It was a long day's journey, and before we reached the end of it the snow was falling again, heavier than ever.

At night we put up in the *posadas*. They were dreadful places, incredibly dirty, cruelly cold, and devoid of any vestige of sanitation. Pigs wandered in and out at will, for as in Lima the real scavengers are the carefully protected vultures, so here on the *Altiplano*—and elsewhere for that matter—the pigs fulfil that office.

There are some horrifying stories about these *posadas*—especially the ones farther down the Mapiri trail, where the outermost fringes of the forest reach up into the mountains. In one of them was a room where, one after another, travellers were found dead, their bodies black from the action of some horrible poison. Suspicious of foul play, the authorities investigated, and after some time discovered in the thatched roof of the room a huge *apazauca* spider—a sort of black tarantula so large that a plate would scarcely cover it. This monster lowered itself down at night on the sleeper beneath, and its bite meant death.

Gruesome stories about inns are familiar enough in fiction, but in Bolivia you have them in fact. There was one about a *posada* on the trail east of Santa Cruz de la Sierra, where the landlord, a villainous-looking half-caste, did to death no less than forty travellers, probably by knifing them in their sleep. He was summarily executed.

Our aching muscles and joints prevented us from sleeping that first night on the trail. Both of us were soft from easy living on board ship and in hotels, and it would be several days before we began to harden up. From the inn next morning we looked out on a world completely covered in fresh snow, but the sky was clear and gave promise of a better day.

---

[1] The word *Gringo* belongs to the slang of Latin America, and denotes broadly any foreigner of the fair-complexioned races. The origin of the word is not certain, but it is believed that in the old days visiting sailormen sang 'Green Grows the Grass . . .' with such fervour that the first two words were borrowed as a nickname for them.—ED.

We breakfasted in a hut at 14,000 feet, and then crossed the Divide, catching a last wonderful view of Titicaca spread out in a great sweep of shimmering silver, and reflecting the surrounding snow-covered mountains with absolute clarity. Then to the north we saw another unforgettable picture—the thin ribbon of the Mapiri River in a misty gorge thousands of feet below, half hidden by drifting clouds that were beginning to disperse in the warmth of the mounting sun. We could see the carpet of forest where sub-tropical vegetation began, and the flanks of the mighty hills rising up to break through the blanket of cloud and tower skywards with gleaming white snow crests. Away off on the other side of the gorge, tucked out of sight under the slopes of *Illampu*, was Sorata, our destination for that night.

We zig-zagged down a precipitous trail for seven thousand feet. At every turn we came upon some breathtaking view. Never had I seen mountains like these, and I was crushed by the grandeur—speechless with the overpowering wonder of it! As we dropped lower the vegetation increased. The bunch grass of the summits gave way to fields of vetch and a cactus-like moss; a few stunted trees made their appearance, short and twisted, like witches suddenly transformed by some magician's art while engaged in an unholy sabbath; then we were in the midst of organ cactus, its dismal grey candles springing up from the slightest crevices in the rocks. We stopped and drank from a mountain stream whose water was melted ice. Eucalyptus and algarroba trees appeared. We filed down and down, twisting and turning, until at last the valley floor was reached, and weary from the muscular tension of holding back in the saddle we crossed the river on a swaying suspension bridge of wire and laths. There followed the short climb to Sorata, where our cavalcade was greeted by a party excitedly awaiting us.

"Please accept a *copa* of *chicha*, *señores*," said the leader of the party, and several men advanced filling earthenware bowls from large jugs of the native maize beer. We accepted it gratefully, and when they had filled bowls for themselves the leader offered a toast to us.

"*A su salud, señores!*" The *chicha* was delicious, thick but refreshing, food and drink in one.

Within the village we were carried off by a hospitable German named Schultz, in whose house we lodged for two nights. There was an excellent dinner—cocktails—wine—and then an hour or two of yarning with our host before turning in for a deep sleep.

I awoke stiff the next morning, but standing at the bedroom window forgot it in the joy of filling my lungs with the delicious mountain air. After a real breakfast—and not the mere roll and coffee of the customary *desayuno*—we arranged about our baggage and the care of our animals, and then we were taken by Schultz to a picnic on his land beside the river, a thousand feet below. We bathed in the river, and were surprised to find the water not unbearably cold, though it came from the snows only eight miles away. Then the party, including some ladies and a few local bigwigs, sat in the flower-filled grass and consumed a picnic lunch that would have astonished even Mr. Pickwick for its abundance and variety.

Sorata is an important centre for the preparation of *chalona*, which is mutton, skinned, spatchcocked and dried under a hot sun in the rarefied atmosphere of 15,000 feet. It keeps in good condition for a long time, even when sent down to the hot forest regions. We were rash enough to cook a half-prepared piece to try it, and were seriously inconvenienced. Here too, as indeed all over the *Altiplano*, a species of small hard potato is dried and frozen to form what is known as *chuñu*, an indispensable part of the diet throughout the mountains.

On the morning after the picnic we said good-bye to Schultz, took our leave of the good townspeople, and started off up a precipitous trail towards the pass at 17,300 feet above sea level. It took us two hours to cover four miles, and in that time we had climbed 6,000 feet. The mules struggled up ten yards at a time, and then halted with pumping lungs. When heavily laden they sometimes bleed at the nose and die. At Ticunamayo we reached a *tambo*, or rest-house, and here we spent the night. There was no accommodation inside, so we slept outdoors in bitter cold and damp fog.

Next morning we could see Sorata, showing crystal-clear away beneath us, its houses glimmering in the light of the rising sun. We had our last view of it when we were close under the pass, and then a turn of the trail hid it from sight and a freezing wind from the snow-fields howled down on us. With the mules slipping and stumbling on the ice, we struggled up the last slope and over the top.

The next halt for the night was the Government rest-house at Yani, once the centre of a rich gold placer which was worked in a very primitive manner. There is a story about this place that may appeal to lovers of the uncanny.

About the turn of the century, two Bolivian army officers arrived here late one night on a return trip from the Beni, and, seeing a handsome girl in the doorway of a house adjoining the *tambo*, tossed up to decide who should try his luck at courting her. The loser stayed with the village headman—the *Corregidor*—and next morning to his horror discovered his brother officer dead on the broken stone floor of a ruined house, which he could have sworn was not only whole but occupied on the previous night.

"The house has been a ruin for years," declared the *Corregidor*. "There was no maiden or doorway, *mi capitan*. It was a *duende* [ghost] you saw!"

"But why is it haunted, then?" asked the officer. "Why should we both have seen the ghost? Was some crime once committed here?"

"I cannot say, *mi capitan*. We know of nothing—no explanation for the *duende*. We only know that from time to time she is seen by strangers —never by us who live here!"

People familiar only with Europe and the East can scarcely imagine what these Andean trails are like. The Indians and mules—and, of course, the ubiquitous llama—are about the only creatures able to negotiate them successfully. The narrow tracks are strewn with loose boulders and shifting gravel, they climb thousands of feet up what I can only describe as like the side of the Great Pyramid, and then drop down a precipice on the other side in a twisting series of tight zig-zags. Over huge boulders resembling a giant's stairway the mules jump cat-like from one to another. On either side of razor-backed ridges the path drops down to an abyss filled with mud. Bones of dead animals line the trail, and here and there a quarrelling tangle of vultures fight over the decomposing carcass of a horse or mule. In places the tortuous way becomes nothing but a narrow ledge cut in the sheer rock hundreds of feet above the valley floor, and here the mules elect to make their way at the extreme outer edge. The rider looks down into space and carries his heart in his mouth, knowing that accidents frequently take place. It is then that you recall the tales of false steps on loose rubble, and the screaming fall of animal and rider never to be seen again.

Many Indians come up the trail from the rubber estates, carrying on their backs heavy loads suspended by a thong about their brows. They carry no food with them, but sustain themselves on the ten-day journey without appreciable loss of strength by chewing a cud of *coca* leaves and lime. Europeans cannot chew *coca* with impunity, for it requires genera-tions of the habit to become immune to the ill effects, the essence being, of course, cocaine. Even the Indians give the impression of being partially drugged, and perhaps this is the reason why their brains act sluggishly.

A foreign doctor joined us on the Mapiri trail, and waxed so eloquent about diseases that I began to suspect his qualifications. One day he stopped a passing Indian and dismounted to examine a large swelling on the man's cheek.

"Apparently a cancerous growth or tumour," he observed. "These people are full of disease."

As he spoke, the 'growth' was shifted from one cheek to the other. It was a wad of *coca*! The doctor eyed the Indian with distaste, remounted without a word, and spoke no more for several miles.

Descending the eastern side of the mountains we spent a whole day, now panting up steep slopes, now slipping and sliding down rubble that rolled from under the mules' hoofs. We could see nothing beneath us but a sea of cloud pierced by the mountain tops. At 13,000 feet the timber line was reached—a thin scattering of tortured, stunted trees not more than the height of a man. Then, as we dropped lower through the reeking pall of cloud, ferns and flowers began to show, and the biting air of the altitude gave way to the warm breath of the *Yungas*. Next day we emerged into clear air again and into thick, sub-tropical vegetation. We worried our way down a hair-raising descent and came to cabbage palms and magnolias. The heat was noticeable now, so we were glad to throw off some of our clothing. Another 3,000-foot drop brought us to the tropics —into hot gorges where the tangle of forest caught and held the lazy wisps of moist cloud that hung from the heavy banks above, and through which no hint of the sun could penetrate.

We were to take to the river, but tertiana fever was so bad at Mapiri that we decided to stop at the rubber *barraca* of San Antonio, managed by an Austrian named Moll. The only remarkable thing about this place —which was nothing but a huddle of huts in a small forest clearing— was a child of seven, half Chinese and half Indian, who not only marketed at Mapiri but cooked for the whole personnel of the station—and first-class cooking at that! These children are invariably very precocious, but they do not develop much after childhood and seldom live to an advanced age.

Thatched palm leaves over rough frames formed the miserable mud-floored huts, of which Mapiri boasted fifteen. These were set around a weedy space representing the *Plaza*; and the church was nothing but a half-ruined hut with a tottering cross above it.

When we rode into town, the Governor sat on one of the doorsteps watching a *fiesta*. The rest of the population, numbering fifty or sixty, were drunk. Some lay flat on the ground, unconscious; others shuffled in a rude dance to appalling music coming from an absolutely unfurnished hut called the 'Grán Hotel'; an Indian woman was struggling to undress herself; and the decomposing body of a man, grotesquely holding a bottle in his hand, lay in a gutter. Yet this place was of some importance, for a good deal of rubber passed through here, and though the Mapiri River is not altogether good rubber country it paid to gather it at a price reaching nearly ten shillings a pound.

At Mapiri I obtained the services of a Jamaican negro named Willis, who when sober was an excellent cook. He and another coloured man had been making a living by washing gold, but his friend was now sick and in a bad way. As Willis informed me, "He wanted to dead, but couldn't dead nohow." Willis, tired of waiting, was glad to join our party.

From Mapiri the journey down river is by *callapo*, which is a raft consisting of three floats, joined by cross-pieces. A float, or *balsa*, consists of seven layers of a peculiarly light wood, plentiful in some parts of the Upper Amazon tributaries but scarce where there is much navigation. The logs are fastened together at several points by strong, fibrous palmwood pins, and on the log next the outer one pegs are driven in to support on cross-ties light platforms of split bamboo for passengers and cargo. The length of these craft is about twenty-six feet, and the beam four. The crew consists of three *balseros*, or raftsmen, in front, and three astern. The load carried is about three tons of cargo and two passengers.

To take a *balsa* down these Andean streams with only one companion, as I did on many occasions later on, is a highly exhilarating sport, and one which demands a great deal of skill. There are rapids every hundred yards, sharp turns to negotiate, rocks to avoid, and always whirlpools at the bends, often big enough to wreck a *balsa* or *callapo*. At times the speed is terrific, at others barely a crawl, but the scenery is fascinating—a never-ending delight.

We pushed off from the river bank at Mapiri with a crew of Lejo Indians, drunk with that maddeningly intoxicating beverage *kachasa*. All the inhabitants sober enough to stagger down to see us off stood by and cheered. Our first experience of river travel put our nerves on edge, for our merry *balseros* were in no condition for the team work required for such tricky navigation, and until the mouth of the Tipuani River was reached it was one narrow escape after another.

The Tipuani is one of the best gold rivers in Bolivia, and it could produce vast quantities of the metal were it not for the frequent and sudden risings of the stream. Bedrock is exposed one minute, and the next a wall of water is hissing over it, caused by a cloudburst or sudden storm in the mountains above. To be caught in one of these floods is fatal—and there is no telling when they will come.

At the mouth of the Tipuani River is Huanay, a village consisting of a few huts and nothing else, but a *callapo* station of some importance. We stayed here for the night, being hospitably received at a trading establishment belonging to our friend Schultz in Sorata. Our Lejo Indians came from a nearby village belonging to their tribe, and celebrated their arrival with more drinking. Huanay was full of unusual excitement when, in addition to our visit, a number of Indians from the independent village of Challana came in with a large amount of goods to trade.

Challana is independent because it has resolutely defied the Bolivian Government. There are many quite incorrect stories about this place, but the real facts are that some years ago a family called Montes discovered valuable rubber lands farther south and laid claim to them, evicting the Indians from the *Yungas* who had settled there and starting small plantations. These Indians migrated northwards to the waters of the upper Challana, and, finding there both rubber and gold, built a village; but so as to avoid a repetition of their ill-treatment, they declined to allow any stranger to enter the community. However, they were joined by various outlaws and renegades, and elected as chief an ex-captain of the Bolivian army. At Huanay they exchanged their rubber and gold for such goods as they required, and steadfastly refused to pay taxes to the State. The Government sent an expedition to enforce taxation. The place was attacked from three directions—but thanks to the merchants of Sorata, the people of Challana were well armed, and beat off the soldiers with ease. Since then no further attempt has been made to subjugate them. They have their own cattle and produce, and thumb their naughty noses at the world!

After a good rise in the Tipuani River, one pound's worth of gold a day can be panned easily upstream, and at Huanay about an ounce from twenty pans of gravel. White miners don't consider this worth working for, as owing to the lack of transport there the cost of living is exorbitant.

Between Huanay and the Beni are three dangerous rapids, 'Malagua', 'Retama' and 'Nube'. At the first of these the drop is a good twenty feet in three hundred yards. Rounding a sharp bend into the rapid, our *callapo* struck a rock, which smashed a baulk and brought down all the cargo piled in the centre of the platform. The craft tilted, and the Doctor was pinned down by boxes. Men sprawled and shouted. They were still rather drunk and scarcely knew what was happening. I grabbed the camera and rifles, fearing that these would be lost overboard or get a drenching, and the *callapo*, though half submerged, was carried down that wild shute of water in some miraculous way without capsizing. Once in smooth, deep water, we poled ashore and made good the damage. Chalmers, in the next *callapo*, came through in fine style.

At Isapuri rubber station, between the rapids, we put up for the night. Here Schultz had an agent, who made us comfortable and fed us well, and we spent the evening drying our gear and cleaning the guns.

The scenery was magnificent throughout the trip. We passed under huge cliffs of conglomerate and red sandstone, through narrow gorges, and under overhanging forest where the flamboyant trees were a glory of colour, and full of parrots and macaws. We camped on beaches in the rain, and were pestered by sand-flies. Out in midstream we were free from insects, but the moment we neared the shore mosquitoes and tiny biting flies attacked us in clouds. We sweated in temperatures like the inside of a hot-house, when not a breath of wind stirred; and we shivered in cold so penetrating that it felt like an English winter!

Chalmers, who followed with Willis on the other *callapo*, found a rifle in a wrecked boat and took it. His raftsmen had intended to have this rifle themselves, and were so annoyed at Chalmers for getting there first that they deliberately let the *callapo* run on a snag, where it was wrecked. Twenty-eight cases of freight were lost, including five of ours and the stands belonging to the plane tables. This was serious, for it put these useful instruments out of action.

On the seventh day after leaving Mapiri we floated gently into the port of Rurenabaque. The 'port' was a beach of mud, covered with upturned *balsas* and refuse, where vultures croaked and quarrelled. Behind lay a collection of roughly framed huts, thatched with palm leaves and walled with split bamboos, and clustering about a grass *plaza* at the foot of a lofty ridge. In the maps I had seen the name of this place marked in capitals, and I had hopefully expected at least a show of permanent architecture. This miserable settlement seemed scarcely fit for habitation by whites. My heart sank, and I began to realize how truly primitive this river country was. I was to learn later that after months in the wilds Rurenabaque could look like a metropolis!

My spirits rose at the very tasty breakfast dished up for us in the unfurnished hut serving as an hotel, and after meeting some of the inhabitants I was inclined to look on the place with less disgust. There was a company of Bolivian infantry in town, with two or three officers who turned out to be excellent fellows. Their commander, a thoroughly good man called Colonel Ramalles, was Governor of the Beni Province. We also found two English traders—for rubber was booming—and three Americans, two of them rather impoverished prospectors, and the third a Texan gunman of renown, who had come here to take refuge from the outer world, where he was 'hot'. Various Customs officials and a few Indians made up the rest of the population. Most of the inhabitants appeared to be suffering from one or other of the many diseases common in the interior, such as *beriberi, espundia* and malaria, the degree of severity depending on how far alcohol and vice had undermined their health.

Colonel Ramalles welcomed us with a banquet; I responded with another. Champagne, at fabulous cost, flowed like water! Food was plentiful. There was no lack of meat, for the great cattle plains of Mojos lay just beyond; and, moreover, on the previous day a large sounder of peccary had come across the river, chased by a stealth of hungry jaguars. The whole town turned out with guns and knives to slaughter about eighty of the weird pig-like creatures.

Jaguars are very common on the cattle plains, and the great sport is not to shoot them, but to lasso them on horseback. Two men take part, keeping the roped beast between them. It requires good mounts and considerable dexterity with the lasso, but given these it is not nearly so dangerous a sport as it sounds.

Jaguars can sometimes be tamed, and do not make dangerous pets if caught as cubs. There was a practical joker at Reyes, a few leagues from Rurenabaque, who had quite a large one which he allowed to wander like a dog about the house. His great delight was to take his pet along the trail towards Rurenabaque and wait for travellers on muleback. At a signal the jaguar would leap out from the bushes and the mule would bolt, usually unseating its rider, whose terror at finding himself face to face with the beast can be imagined.

Mules are more afraid of jaguars than of any other living thing, and it is said that the paw of a freshly killed one carried in a saddle-bag is better than any spur to accelerate the pace of a stubborn mount.

CHAPTER V

RUBBER BOOM

I WAS in the dumps and feeling very homesick. What kind of an ass was I to exchange the comfort of Spike Island for conditions which I was beginning to realize might make even Rurenabaque seem a paradise? My salary had seemed good, but this was an illusion. In Bolivia I was no better off than I was as an artillery major—less so, in fact, for in the garrison our lodgings were free. On accepting the post I had not realized what the difficulties would be of even getting my salary paid into my bank in London. Those who claimed to have experience told me that very likely nothing would be paid until a substantial sum stood to my credit, when promises of an early payment of the whole lot would be given together with an offer of a small part of it on account.

More than once I was tempted to resign and return home. The hope of bringing my wife and family out to La Paz had gone. It was out of the question. Not only was a house almost impossible to obtain, but rents were more than I could afford. At that time it was no place for an English-woman on her own, while for children the food would be unsuitable and the altitude a drawback.

Even under favourable conditions Rurenabaque was over a fortnight's travel from La Paz; and Riberalta—where much of my time was bound to be spent—was another three weeks' journey down river. But there were no regular passenger services between these places. The traveller had to wait his chance, often for weeks in some out-of-the-way place, until a *callapo* or raft turned up bound for where he wanted to go. To get from Mapiri to the *Altiplano* depended on whether mules could be obtained. The rivers of the Bolivian *Montaña*—as the forest region is called—were in fact more remote from La Paz than was England. Here we were, cut off from everything, before us the prospect of three years' most difficult and dangerous work—years that commenced on arrival at the Beni—with letters from home reaching us only at rare intervals, and with no escape to a more favourable climate for rest and recuperation. And I had willingly allowed myself to be condemned to this!

We were now on the fringe of the real rubber country, and about to find out for ourselves what truth there was in the stories told about it. Many people had doubted the Putumayo disclosures, but it is a fact that from the start the exploitation of rubber in both Bolivia and Peru led to shocking barbarities. Not that the Governments of these countries were indifferent to the abuses that went on—they were very deeply concerned—but the great distance of the rubber regions from any effective State control encouraged unscrupulous foreigners and, for that matter, Bolivians and Peruvians of the same ilk. In fact, most of those rubber exploiters were degenerates tempted by the chance of making big money the easy way. Believe it or not, but the huge scattered labour force of the rubber industry had little understanding of the real causes underlying their sufferings, and were even quite willing to fight to keep things as they were if to do so was the wish of the *patrón*. So long as the individual did not suffer he cared little what happened to the others—in fact their misfortunes rather amused him.

No Government inspector who valued his skin would venture into the rubber country and send back an honest report. The arm of vengeance was long, and in the *Montaña* life was held very cheap. For instance, a judge was sent to the Acre to get evidence of the particularly brutal murder of an Austrian, and found that powerful people on the rivers were involved. Had he told what he knew, he would never have left there alive. It was prudent to say nothing, to return safely to the *Altiplano* with a nice gift of 'hush money', and to close the case by paying a small compensation to the relatives. Who can blame him?

No instruments awaited us in Rurenabaque. "You need not worry about them," said Colonel Ramalles. "They will be ready for you in Riberalta. General Pando is there, and he has them."

"The sooner we get on, the better," I remarked. "There's no object in our staying here."

"I will, of course, do what I can for you, but it may take time. Meanwhile, there is Independence Day, and the way they celebrate it here I doubt if anything can be done till the effects of it are over!"

The celebrations passed in an orgy of drinking, and were followed by a period of '*mañanas*' lasting a full week. Then there arrived in town two Customs officials from La Paz in a hurry to reach Riberalta, gentlemen of such impressive dignity that at last a *batelón* was found to take them and us.

Now, a *batelón* is the clumsiest and worst-designed of all boats. It originated in the mind of some foreigner who knew nothing about building or designing, and it keeps the same form in spite of its obvious defects. The keel is the trunk of a tree, adzed roughly into shape and opened up over a fire; and there are a rude stem and sternpost, to which a number of thick hardwood planks are fastened carvel fashion with large iron nails bent over on the inside. The midship section forms a blunt 'V', and aft there is a platform carrying a palm-leaf shelter and some rough seats for the crew. It invariably leaks like a sieve, for the gaping seams are practically impossible to caulk effectively, so one or two members of the crew must be continually employed in bailing. It is forty feet long, twelve feet broad, and draws about three feet. The freeboard is not more than four inches, and the load carried is usually about twelve tons of cargo. Anything from ten to twenty-four Indians make up the crew.

Not very many of Rurenabaque's population had recovered from the celebrations, and those who were sober enough to walk saw us off with salvos of Winchester 'forty-four-forty'.[1] Fortunately, no one was hit. When we reached the Altamarani rapids we made the passage by what can only be described as miraculous intervention. But the two bailers were unable to cope with the alarming leakage of the *batelón's* hull, and ten miles below the town we were forced to beach. Then we had to unload all the cargo and set about the job of forcing great masses of *estopa*—beaten palm fibre—into the seams of the boat with the pommel of a *machete* from inside or outside, whichever way it would go in better.

We camped ashore at a *chacra* (smallholding) belonging to the English engineer of a small Government steam-launch. This ingenious man, Pearson by name, managed to keep in service a decrepit vessel whose working parts were held together for the most part with wire or string. It was on the stocks when we arrived, and Pearson pointed out his running repairs proudly. The boiler shell must have been nearly paper-thin in places, and, however low the pressure carried, a danger to life or limb.

During the night, quite suddenly, there was thunder and a deluge of rain—rain so heavy that it fell as solid water. The river rose by nine feet; the launch was swept off its stocks, turned over on its side and hurled against the trees; and we made an excited rush to save the baggage from being carried away. It was the height of the dry season, but in the Amazon forests heavy rain must always be anticipated at full and new moon—

---

[1] 'Forty-four-forty' ammunition, being common to Winchester carbine and Colt six-shooter alike, was at one time available even in the most out-of-the-way places in South America. For this reason, the Winchester .44 carbine became the favourite 'revolution gun', and its tremendous hitting power, handiness and reliability made it the prized possession of every would-be *politico*. The sale of 'forty-four-forty' weapons and ammunition was banned in some republics because of this, I believe.—ED.

usually at new moon. It is frequently followed by a *surusu*, a south or south-west wind bringing cold so intense that thin ice is occasionally found in the early morning!

The river went down to its normal level almost as rapidly as it had risen, leaving on the banks a tangle of flotsam full of moribund *migales*—the great bird-catching spiders—and half-drowned snakes. As we were breakfasting in Pearson's dwelling, in came José, an employee of the launch, looking very scared.

"A jaguar was in my hut last night," he said. "I woke up to see it standing in the middle of the floor watching my lighted candle-lantern. I could have stretched out of my hammock and touched it, *señores*!"

"Why didn't you shoot it?" Pearson enquired. No one slept in those parts without a gun handy, and José's Winchester was always within reach.

"He was too close to me, Señor Pearson. If I had tried to grab my gun he might have attacked. And if I had failed to kill him at once he'd have got me. I lay as still as the dead, and by and by he left so quietly and swiftly that I could scarcely believe he'd ever been there."

The Beni on both sides is the haunt of venomous snakes—worse in this respect than many other places, for here is the junction of forest, plains and hills, abounding in the dry scrub they love. Commonest is the rattlesnake. There are five different kinds, but in length they seldom exceed a yard. Largest of the snakes is the *Surucucu*, that double-fanged abomination known elsewhere as the *Pocaraya* or Bushmaster, which sometimes reaches the prodigious length of fifteen feet, with a diameter of a foot at the thickest part, so I was told. Then there is the *Taya*, a greyish, light-brown snake, fierce and very agile, which, like the Hamadryad of India, attacks human beings at sight during the breeding season. Anacondas are common—not the giant kind, but up to twenty-five feet long, and quite big enough. Those snakes were so constant a danger that we soon learned to take precautions against them.

Not far from where we now were lived the *Barbaros*, wild and hostile savages much feared by the rubber people of the Beni. I was told hair-raising stories about them, but I met them later, and found that there was a great deal of exaggeration in these. At some distance in the forest near Altamarani lived an old half-caste woman with her daughter. This old lady was a natural clairvoyante. She possessed a crystal globe, and was consulted by people the whole length of the river between Rurenabaque and Riberalta. She looked just like the traditional witch, and was a herbalist, fortune-teller and distiller of love-potions. Though believed to have amassed a considerable fortune, no one dared molest her, and the *Barbaros* treated her with the greatest respect. She, for her part, despised them.

MIGHTY SACSAHUAMAN. "Piled by the hands of giants for godlike kings of old",
the key to the mystery of who built these immense Pre-Incan ramparts may one day be
found in Brazil

MACHUPICCHU. Probably the fabled Vilcabamba, unsuccessfully sought by the *Conquistadores*, this wonder city of the Incas was discovered in 1911 by Hiram Bingham and
the Yale-Peruvian Expedition

THE TUMBLED RUINS OF TIAHU-ANACO. These may be the remains of the most ancient buildings in existence, pre-dating the rising of the Andes

TWO ANCIENT STONE IDOLS. They stand beside the entrance of Tiahu-anaco Church

Carved from black basalt, this ten-inch statuette is believed to have come from one of the ancient Brazilian lost cities

THE "SUNDIAL" AT MACHUPICCHU. To the Incas of old this and other monuments of remotest antiquity were just as much a mystery as they are today

Photo by Brian Fawcett

A CUZCO STREET. In the wall on the right can be seen the Incan stonework upon which the Spanish conquerors built their city.

"FROM SORATA WE MUST CLIMB TO THE PASS UNDER THE SNOWS OF ILLAMPU"

CALLAPOS ON THE MAPIRI RIVER

Every year the natives here celebrate a kind of sabbath in the forest. They gather round an altar of stones and brew the native beer, *chicha*, which they drink in huge quantities over mouthfuls of strong tobacco. The mixture maddens them, and men and women then give themselves up to a wild orgy. This often continues for a fortnight.

The *Barbaros* use palmwood bows from five to ten feet long, and arrows of the same length. The bowstrings are made from bark cord. Boys are taught to use the bow by shooting over a hut at a papaw fruit on the other side. Sometimes they use the bow vertically in the customary way; sometimes by lying on the ground, bearing against it with both feet and drawing back with both hands. They become expert in firing up in the air to land on the mark with deadly accuracy. The feathers are put on the arrows with a twist, so as to rotate the shaft rifle-fashion and give it a straighter flight. Is it possible that the idea of rifling firearms originated from this? Women and children are armed with double-pointed jabbing-spears of bamboo, whose barbs are of monkey-bone bound with native cotton and fixed with gum wax. In warfare, spears and arrows are usually tipped with poison.

The *batelón*, plugged with masses of *estopa*, was reloaded and continued its journey down river. Threading our way through forests of snags, we had one miraculous escape after another. These snags are the trunks and branches of dead trees which fall into the river or are washed away in floods. In the struggle for existence in the primeval forest, trees are crowded out, strangled by parasitic growths, or blown down in storms. Often they cannot even fall, but are upheld to rot in position by the other trees around them. The eroding current of the rivers eats away the muddy banks, and a number of trees topple into the water to become snags. Sometimes they show just their tops above the surface; the more dangerous ones are those which are submerged a few inches out of sight. Their twisted boughs are eaten away into wicked spikes, and, as the timber is often nearly as hard as iron, these spikes can rip through a swiftly moving boat as though it were paper.

We drifted along with the current at about three miles an hour, day after day of deadly monotony, for the scene on the shores never changed. Little events became mightily important, and we searched hungrily for signs of life in the vast wilderness. Duck and wild geese were plentiful, and, of course, monkeys, the black *Marimono* and *Manechi* predominating. The latter is the South American Howler, the *Bugio* of the Brazilians, and in the early morning its roaring challenge wakes the forest.

Game of any kind is usually hard to find, so monkeys are looked on as good eating in these forests. Their meat tastes rather pleasant; but at first the idea revolted me because when stretched over a fire to burn off the hair they looked so horribly human. The newcomer has to become hardened to these things and leave his fastidiousness behind him—or else starve.

At one spot in the river bank I saw a complete burial-urn. I am sorry now that we did not take it, for very interesting pottery has been unearthed at Rurenabaque, and it might have turned out to be a find of ethnological value.

On the second day out from Altamarani we ran full tilt on a snag. Four of the crew were hurled into the river, and the Doctor panicked and leapt in after them, while the pompous Customs officials looked green with terror. The moment we struck, the rest of the crew jumped out instantly and kept the boat from filling. To them it was a huge joke. I thought the *batelón* was finished for certain, and was surprised to find that beyond a few extra leaks no harm was done. Quickly we stopped the leaks with a few pounds of *estopa* and carried on. When the wood of a *batelón's* hull is new, it probably requires a rock and a twenty-miles-an-hour impetus to split one of the planks and tear out those great bent nails.

No sooner were we on our way again than the crew began yelling with excitement, and paddled frantically for a large sandbank where we could see a sounder of pigs. The boat was run ashore, and every member of the crew made after them with his Winchester. Shortly after we heard the thump of shots, as though miles away in the forest. These Tumupasa Indians are fine trackers, and in less than an hour they were back with two pigs. In the thick jungle a European could scarcely hope to avoid losing himself, with no sun or compass to guide him, but those Indians seem to be able to feel their way through the bare soles of their feet.

Moving with the current was easy, but our daily mileage was not great, as this was the season for turtles' eggs and we made frequent stops to search for nests. The *Tartaruga*, or large tortoise, is common in the Purus and most Amazonian affluents, and lays over fifty eggs at a time. Strangely enough, it is not found in the Beni. Instead, there is the *Tracaya*, or small tortoise, which is plentiful and lays about twenty eggs to the clutch. These eggs are considered a great delicacy, but man shares this liking with the storks, and the birds are expert in discovering the nests. The tortoise lays her eggs at night and hides them by smoothing over the sand on top. Nature, on teaching the creature that much, left off without providing her with the means of erasing her tracks, so unless it is raining it is easy to trace the spot where eggs are hidden. It takes some time to get used to the eggs, for they have an oily taste. They are soft-shelled and about the size of a golf ball.

We camped one night at the *chacra* of an Englishman, a renegade from civilization, who lived in the forest with an old Indian woman. His past was lurid—the case with most of these hermits. He was an educated man who at one time held a position of importance. In this isolated spot he found a contentment denied him in the outside world, and the bouts of insanity that ailed him worried no one but himself and his companion.

We were plagued by sand-flies, particularly those known as the *Tabana* and the *Marigui*, called in Brazil the *Pium*. Clouds of *Marigui* attacked us by day and left small blood-blisters where they bit. The *Tabana* came singly, but advertised their presence by a probe like the thrust of a needle. The bites of both insects itch abominably, and are liable to turn septic if scratched.

Below Rurenabaque is a stretch of the Beni known as 'The Desert', too low-lying for any settlements, and in the dry season the haunt of savages in search of turtle eggs and fish. Our crew said that savages kept to the west bank, so camp was made always on the other side. A number of tragedies had taken place hereabouts, vengeance exacted by the savages for the cruelties practised on them by unscrupulous employees of the rubber concerns.

A Swiss and a German from a *barraca* below the confluence of the Madidi had recently raided the savages here with a sizable force. A village was destroyed, men and women butchered, and children killed by dashing their brains out against trees. The raiders returned proudly with a prize of eighty canoes, and boasted of the exploit! The only reason for it was that a few timid Indians had come into camp and an attack on the *barraca* was feared. I was told that these warriors from the *barraca* considered it grand sport to throw Indian babies up in the air and catch them on the points of *machetes*.[1] Decent people on the river were disgusted at the whole affair; and the Government were also indignant when they heard about it, but could do nothing.

Slaving raids on the savages were a common practice. The prevailing idea that the *Barbaro* was nothing better than a wild animal accounted for many of the atrocities perpetrated on them by the degenerates who were the straw bosses of the *barracas*. I met the Guarayo Indians later, and found them intelligent, clean, and infinitely superior to the drink-sodden 'civilized' Indian of the rivers. True, they were hostile and vengeful; but look at the provocation! My experience is that few of these savages are naturally 'bad', unless contact with 'savages' from the outside world has made them so.

Their custom was to attack at dawn, by riddling the *toldetas* with arrows. These *toldetas* were mosquito-nets of cheap cotton cloth, and beneath them slept every member of the boats' crews, Bolivian and Indian alike. Any who survived the shower of poisoned arrows had little reason for self-congratulation when the savages laid hands on them. General Pando, who ascended the Heath a little way from the Madre de

---

[1] The *machete* is the broad-bladed hacking-knife essential for travel in the forests, and an indispensable possession of every rubber gatherer.—ED.

Dios and crossed the swamps to the upper waters of the Madidi, told me that he and his men planted their *toldetas* as a decoy, and slept well away from them.

"In the morning we often found them riddled with arrows," he said. "We never experienced a direct attack, probably because my party was a large one, but all the time they harried us from the bush, and remained invisible."

In 1896 an important Bolivian Government official was travelling on the Beni with his wife and step-daughter when Guarayos attacked one morning at dawn. There was a stampede for the *batelón*, and in the panic the wife was left behind on the sandbank where the camp was pitched; her absence was discovered only when the craft was some distance down river. The lady was kept by the savages in their village for several years, and was eventually found by a slave-raiding expedition. The leader of the raiders restored her, and four semi-savage children, to the husband, charging him £300 for the service. Meanwhile, the husband had married his step-daughter, and the shock of seeing his wife again killed him. The lady, with her children, took up residence with the daughter in Santa Cruz de la Sierra, and delighted to tell of her unique experiences.

In Riberalta I met an Austrian lady—vivacious and handsome—who from time to time went off alone into the forest to live with the Pacaguaras Indians. Her collection of tooth necklaces and other savage curios was unequalled.

In the strength-sapping heat of the forests you were sorely tempted to bathe from the *batelón*. It was unwise to do it, but if the desire proved too strong it had to be done with caution because of the prevalence of the *Puraque*, or electric eel. Two varieties of this creature are found in these rivers; one is about six feet long and brown in colour, and the other— the more dangerous of the two—is yellowish, and half the length. One shock is sufficient to paralyse and drown a man—but the way of the *Puraque* is to repeat the shocks to make sure of its victim. It seems that to deliver the shock the eel must move its tail, for when quite still it can be touched without harm. Nevertheless the Indians will not handle even a dead one.

Another loathsome fish to be found throughout the Amazonian rivers—and particularly common in the tributaries of the Madeira—is the *Candiru*. Its body is about two inches long and a quarter of an inch thick, ending in a narrow swallow-tail. It has a long bony snout and sharp teeth and its skin is covered with fine back-swept barbs. It seeks to enter the natural orifices of the body, whether human or animal, and once inside cannot be extracted because of the barbs. Many deaths result from this fish, and the agony it can cause is excruciating. While I was in Riberalta an Austrian doctor cut two out of a woman; and a Japanese doctor at Astillero, on the Tambopata River, showed me one of a different species taken from a man's penis. This species sometimes reaches a length of five inches, and looks like a newly hatched eel.

Poisonous stingrays lurk on the sandy river bottoms. They are not large, but the gash of the mucous-covered barbed lance is extremely painful and sometimes dangerous. The people of the rivers say that the best remedy is to urinate on the wound. Whether this is so I cannot say, but I know that the sting of the sea urchin is so treated by the natives in the West Indies. The stingray makes good eating, and the lance is used by the Indians for tipping arrows.

The monotony of drifting down river day after day, with nothing to do but watch the unchanging shore, proved too much for our companions, the two Customs officials. In their charge were mailbags for delivery in Riberalta, and it was not long before they had broken the seals of these and helped themselves to any newspapers and periodicals they found inside.

"It doesn't matter," was the excuse. "In any case the papers become public property when they get there!"

By the time we reached Riberalta most of them had been lost, and many people who counted the days from one mail to the next were forced to make the best of it, and wait with what patience they had for the next mail, which might come in a month's time—or in three!

At the mouth of the River Madidi, at the edge of the Plains of Mojos, stands the Mission of Cavinas, where remnants of an Indian tribe, once part of a large and powerful nation known as the Toromonas, had a settlement of a few well-kept huts. The Indians always managed to keep their plantations free from weeds, whereas those of the white people were rank with them; and Cavinas was a pleasant contrast to the ill-kept, unproductive lands of the white settlements.

From here on there were rubber *barracas* on both sides of the river, but only one of them made us welcome. The drunken, degenerate-looking proprietors must have had bad consciences. The only one that received us hospitably was at Concepción. The owner was well educated and widely travelled, his wife and children altogether charming, and his business a happy one. He was optimistic about the future of rubber on the Beni, but I couldn't agree with him. It seemed to me that its decay and eventual abandonment was inevitable unless the whole region could be developed by organized immigration.

After a journey of twenty days from Rurenabaque we reached Riberalta on August 28. Here I met General Pando, ex-President of the Republic and Delegate of the Beni Province, a man of striking appearance and marked ability. He had carried out extensive explorations in Bolivia and probably knew more about the country than any of his compatriots. What was so encouraging to me was the fact that he was the first official I had met who really knew what work was required of the Commission.

No instruments awaited me here—I would find them at Bahía, or as it was called later, Cobija! I knew enough by this time to believe in them only when I saw them!

"A boat will be provided to take you up the Rio Orton," he told me. "Then, from Porvenir, there is an overland trail to the River Acre."

"How long do you reckon the work on the Acre will take me?" I asked.

"I fear you are not going to find it easy, Major. I should say it will take you all of two years to complete."

I certainly had no intention of spending two years on the Acre—nor was I going to allow the grass to grow under my feet as far as the work was concerned. I didn't tell him that, though.

Where the Beni and Madre de Dios Rivers join there is a width of 500 yards from shore to shore. Riberalta, standing at the confluence, was almost a town, for the palm-leaf huts were arranged in blocks, a few roofs were covered with rusty *calamina*,[1] and there was even one building of *adobe*,[2] headquarters of Suarez Hermanos, the principal rubber firm. Although the Suarez building was a simple, one-storeyed affair encircling a central *patio*, its cost, I was told, amounted to more than £12,000! The price of everything here was ten times more than in the outside world. In spite of extortionate prices, there appeared to be plenty to eat, and in some inexplicable manner everyone contrived to live on credit. Bread sold at fourpence an ounce. But beef, the staple diet, was plentiful, and half-wild cattle from the Plains of Mojos could be bought at under four shillings each, the only snag being that the buyer must catch his purchase after the transaction—if he dared.

Situated almost in the heart of the continent, Riberalta is only 500 feet above sea level. It is built on the site of an old entrenched Indian village, and the ground is not more than six feet above the highest summer water level. The heat here can be almost intolerable, yet there are frequent *surusus*, when the temperature drops suddenly from 110 degrees in the shade to 40—and sometimes even to freezing-point. On such occasions, the people retire to their open, draughty huts, and bury themselves under all the blankets they possess until the *surusu* passes.

When we arrived in town a mutiny had just taken place in the Madre de Dios, at the mouth of the River Heath, where the soldiers of a small detachment murdered their officers and fled into Peru. One soldier—an Indian—returned to Riberalta, and said that he had refused to take part

---

[1] Corrugated iron. It is the curse of South America—from the standpoint of the picturesque — and destroys the looks of what might otherwise be attractive. The *Tejas*, or Spanish tiles, are more durable and a distinct embellishment, but they cost more and require more effort to fit, so the cheap and hideous *calamina* has won a firm foothold!—ED.

[2] *Adobe* is a mud-like clay used for building throughout Latin America. It is the poor man's brick, and is often dug beside the building site.—ED.

in the affair. He was tried by court martial, found guilty, and sentenced to 2,000 lashes with the cat.

The cat, as employed on the Beni, was a short stick with four well-knotted rawhide lashes. It was expected that the sentence would finish off the Indian and so bring about a result that for lack of sufficient authority could not be resorted to directly. The foreign residents protested, but to no purpose. The man took his flogging; and the Doctor, who witnessed it, gave me full details afterwards.

The victim was spreadeagled flat on the ground, and a soldier on each side of him gave one lash per second for the duration of a minute, when the cat was passed to the next soldier in a queue of waiting men, who one after another carried on, without any break in the tempo. Any beater who failed to lay on hard enough received fifty lashes himself. The victim fainted seven times without any halt in the proceedings, and when it was over he was left lying where he was. Later on he was salted. His flesh was literally stripped from the bones, leaving these in places exposed—yet he survived!

There were three Englishmen in Riberalta at that time. One was the best of men, untouched by the vices of a community in which he had spent a quarter of a century. The second died shortly after we arrived there, and was notable for nothing except a mania for litigation. The third was one of the most vicious and degenerate men I have ever come across. He held a lucrative position in one of the rubber firms, but lost it, I believe, and blew his brains out in London a few years afterwards.

Drink reigned supreme, as it did in most of these places. There was every excuse for it. Surrounded by brutality and bestial passions, living in unbelievable squalor, isolated by vast distances, lack of communications and impassable jungle, it is not surprising that people sought escape in the only way they knew—by means of the bottle.

I saw General Pando frequently, and missed no opportunity of urging arrangements for our departure. I wanted to get to work as soon as possible.

"I don't think you'll get away to Bahía for three or four weeks yet," he observed; "and when you reach there I expect there will be a delay until the river rises. Why not put in the time running a preliminary survey for a railway between Porvenir and Bahía? It would be a great service to the Government if you would."

Discussing details of the boundary work with him, I decided to do the Acre section first, and then return to Riberalta to plot the frontier. After that I would do the middle section, and again return to plot. Finally, the Abuna section would be done. Calculating on a month of plotting, time taken in travelling to and fro, and six months spent on each section, two years and a half would be required, or nearly the total duration of the contract.

A Customs official, down with *beriberi*, came in from the Acre, and I asked him what to expect when we reached that river.

"I have seen it for over a hundred miles in a large steamer," he said. "It has all been explored before—in fact there are rubber *barracas* all the way up."

CHAPTER VI

BORN TO SORROW

IT is no exaggeration that nine out of every ten of Riberalta's inhabitants suffered from diseases of one kind or another. There were the partially paralysed victims of *beriberi* who hobbled along on crutches and crowded round whenever there was the prospect of an *aperitivo*, or free drink. Some people had Tertiana fever, some consumption, and many had ailments that the doctors could not diagnose. Every mercantile establishment in town did a roaring trade in quack remedies, sold at extortionate prices. The healthy person was regarded as a freak, an exception, extraordinary. *Beriberi*—a kind of dropsy—was the normal ailment on the rivers, probably caused by the poor quality of the food and its lack of vitamins. You could get fresh meat, but the staple foods were *charque* (strips of salted, sun-dried meat) and rice. The rice was brought from Santa Ana, Santa Cruz, or Manaos in Brazil, and was generally mouldy when sold after at least two years in storage. (I can remember a time in the Acre when you could not even get this.) The *charque* was usually crawling with maggots. It smelled so bad that it could only be swallowed after boiling three times, yet in Riberalta it sold at one shilling and eightpence a pound. People washed this diet down with large draughts of *kachasa*—the wicked cane alcohol. No wonder they died like flies!

In town there were many forest Indian slaves. They had been brought in as children, and became members of the Church. Some managed to adapt themselves to the new life, but for the most part they were untamable. If caught as boys they sooner or later felt the call of the wild and escaped back to the forest. Yet those young savages never forgot what they had been taught. They absorbed education readily, and on returning to the tribe they initiated their people into the ways of civilized man. Exceptional Indians were sent as far afield as Europe to study.

The owner of a thriving business in Riberalta, a German named Winkelmann, purchased a young savage girl, had her educated in Germany, and married her. I had tea with them several times, and found her not only nice-looking but very well-mannered, speaking four languages, perfectly adapted to her position, and the mother of a charming family. As a rule, however, those forest people were either shot at sight like dangerous animals or ruthlessly hunted down to be sent as slaves to distant rubber estates where escape was impossible and every sign of independence beaten out of them with the whip.

The most tragic cases on the Beni occurred in the town and province of Santa Cruz de la Sierra. Here the labourers were brought down in chain gangs of fifty at a time and sold. It was against the law, of course, but temporary syndicates found in the peonage system a way of circumventing it. So long as all transport on the rivers was in the hands of the big firms there was no hope for those people. Any attempt to escape was almost certain to end in disaster.

Once four men did manage to escape from a French firm, and made their way down river in a canoe. The labour foreman, better known as the *Mayordomo*, gave chase, caught up with them, and, instead of taking them back, dashed their brains out with the butt of a Winchester as they knelt before him begging for mercy. Legal redress was unlikely in such cases. The local judges drew salaries of only about £16 a month and depended on bribes for a living. With all money and power in the hands of the rubber firms there was little chance of justice being done.

I visited a Frenchman in the Riberalta jail who had murdered his employer in a fit of jealousy. While imprisoned he was fed by his woman, whom one day he seized and strangled, and he was condemned to death. He escaped and fled into Brazil, thanks to the judge who sold him a file!

Usually a bribe directly offered would be considered an insult. The common method was to buy at a huge price some timber or other goods belonging to the judge. In legal cases both sides would bid for the goods, and of course the highest bidder won. Before condemning such barefaced corruption, remember that these places were incredibly remote and extremely primitive—and, for that matter, the same thing regularly took place in England before the Industrial Age.

Once in the hands of the big firms it was difficult for any man, black or white, to leave against the will of his employers. An Englishman in Riberalta told me a story to illustrate this.

"I travelled on the Orton with a man who had quit his job with a well-known firm and was clearing out with all his savings—about £350. He was a useful man, you understand, and they didn't want to lose him, so what did they do but decoy him ashore at one of the firm's *barracas*, where they soon made him drunk.

"They kept him like that for three days—so drunk he didn't know what he was doing. At the end of that time they let him sober up, and then pushed a bill under his nose for £75 more than the whole of his savings. What could he do? No court would have upheld his case if he had made a claim against the swindlers. Probably no court would even have listened to him. He was forced to sell his wife and daughter to cancel the debt, and then get back up river to work, where he was before. It was on the way up river that I met him, and what made him mad when he told me the story was not so much the trick they played on him, but that his womenfolk had gone for too low a price!"

I remarked that it was largely his own fault. At least he was no slave.

"It amounts to the same thing, though," replied the Englishman. "Don't think that white men are never sold into slavery! There's the well-known case of two brothers who came down the Beni on a trading project. They stopped at a *barraca* where play was high, got mixed up in a poker game, and the elder of the two lost heavily. Next morning, when the younger one tried to get into the boat, the *Mayordomo* caught him, threw him back on the shore, and started to lace into him with a whip. His elder brother had sold him to cancel the debt! When he heard that, the younger one became violent and was given 600 lashes to calm him down. I believe he escaped eventually, but what happened after that I don't know—shouldn't think he felt much brotherly love, anyway!"

Two of the big firms in Riberalta kept forces of armed toughs for hunting Indians, and wholesale butchery went on. The wretched captives were taken to work so far away from their tribes that they lost all sense of direction, and so escape was all the more difficult. They were given a shirt, the necessary tools, and a portion of rice, and ordered to produce an annual total of about seven hundred pounds of rubber under threat of the whip. This may not seem a great deal, but rubber trees were scattered sparsely over a huge area, and unceasing toil was necessary to locate and work them. With rubber at the boom prices of those days the system brought immense profits to the firms.

The more capable a man, the harder it was for him to escape from the clutch of the rubber concerns. White, black, or Indian, once enmeshed in the toils of debt, had little hope of ever winning free again. Credit was generously given with the object of ensnaring men. It was easy for a firm, which besides paying a man's wages supplied him with all his needs and deducted the cost from his pay, to 'cook' the accounts in such a way that he remained always in debt—and therefore always a servant. But this was not true slavery—after all, the man was paid. He was virtually a prisoner, but not a slave. Outright slaving was another matter, yet no man was beyond the danger of it.

George Morgan, a negro, was bought by one of the Riberalta Englishmen—the bestial one—for £30. Miserably treated, he had no prospect of any other fate but slavery, and possibly being sold up river to a *barraca* where his treatment would be worse than at the hands of the human devil who owned him. The other English and German residents signed a petition to the Government to order his release and sent copies to Lima and to England, but nothing was done—probably the letters never got out.

Besides spending twenty-four hours in the stocks at the police station, debtors had to work off what they owed to their creditors. A Peruvian employed at one *barraca* died, and his wife and six children in Riberalta were seized and sent into slavery at another *barraca* of the same firm. This is a fact.

A German, in debt to a large firm, was sent off to one of the most isolated *barracas*, where all the other workers had died. There was no hope of his ever being able to escape from this place. An Englishman named Pae started a business in Riberalta and aroused the jealousy of the bigger houses. They undersold him, ruined him, ran him into debt, and he was taken for service at a nominal wage—not quite a slave, but hopelessly bound.

I could cite case after case—not from hearsay, but personal knowledge. The sickening tale has no end, for Riberalta was only one place in that hell where such things were going on. If an escaped man survived long enough to be caught and brought back, the punishment was at least a thousand lashes—or as much as it was considered he could stand without dying. The atrocities on the Putumayo in Peru, disclosed by Sir Roger Casement, were only a fraction of the terrible story. Slavery, bloodshed and vice reigned supreme on the rivers, and there was no halt to it until the bottom fell out of the rubber market. The labourers on the Madeira River had an average working life of five years. On the other rivers it was little more. East of Sorata an old person of either sex was a rarity! South America is not a country of mediocre proportions. Everything is on a grand scale, and the atrocities of the rubber-boom days were no exception.

At Santa Cruz, a small village only ten miles from Riberalta, there were many deaths from a peculiar kind of fever, never classified. In the true spirit of local enterprise, the *curé* of the village exploited the epidemic to make his fortune. He divided the graveyard into three sections—Heaven, Purgatory and Hell—and charged accordingly for burial!

On September 25 we left Riberalta in a small *batelón* with ten Ixiamas and eight Tumupasa Indians, a steersman, and a young army officer to act as interpreter, his father a Scotsman who had lived all his life in La Paz and his mother a Bolivian. This young officer turned out to be a good companion—when sober.

The day after sailing we entered the Orton, a river notorious for its snags, *pirañas*,[1] *candirus*, crocodiles, anacondas, stingrays and flies, as

[1] The *Piraña*, or *Piranba*, is a small flesh-eating fish which attacks in shoals capable of stripping an animal to the bones in a matter of seconds. It haunts the vicinity of riverside slaughter-houses, and is attracted from great distances by the smell of blood or an open wound.—ED.

well as for the absence of any game. It proved to be a sluggish stream running between fairly high banks at the edge of extensive swamps, and besides combining all the worst features of Amazonian rivers, was navigable by launch only in the wet season. The *piums* settled on us in clouds. We were forced to close both ends of the *batelón's* palm-leaf shelter with mosquito-nets, and to use head-veils as well, yet in spite of that our hands and faces were soon a mass of tiny, itching blood-blisters.

It was here we first heard the *seringero* bird—three low notes in *crescendo* followed by a 'Wheet-wee-o', and a shrill cry. It is an active, gay bird about the size of a thrush, and its presence indicates that rubber trees are near, for it feeds, presumably, on the parasites found on these. The rubber gatherers—*seringeros*, as they are called—listen for the bird's cry when searching for trees.

At a *barraca* called Palestina we found traces of the trouble with Brazil in 1903, which led to the rearrangement of the frontier. The place was much entrenched and fortified, and from it a trail led through the forest to the Rio Abuna, and to the Acre at Capatara, below the Brazilian town of Xapury. I must say that the entrenchments didn't impress me and I doubted the knowledge and experience of the officers responsible for them. They were laid out according to those ancient plans you find in the textbooks, and could have been enfiladed easily.

So far there were no signs of barbarities on the Orton; apparently the whip was used only when everything else had failed. Nothing could be seen of the underlying slave system, yet we knew it was there. Not far away, on the Madre de Dios, there was a *barraca* which concerned itself not with rubber but with breeding children for the slave market, and was said to have about six hundred women! Most of the local managers and overseers were dishonest, cowardly and brutal—quite unfit for the control of labour—yet some spark of decency kept them from practising their brutalities openly. They were never tired of telling me that the half-caste and Indian understood only the whip. As often as not they themselves were half-castes—and as to the Indian, my own experience proved again and again how readily the indigene responded to decent treatment.

It was at Palestina that the man who pioneered rubber on the Orton —and, indeed, in Bolivia—is said to have flogged men to death, or by way of change to have tied their legs together and their hands behind their backs and flung them into the river. Those who suffered the latter fate were the lucky ones! I met an Englishman once employed by him who told me of these mad crimes. He was himself inclined to be tarred with the same brush!

The flies nearly drove us crazy. There was no respite from them, for the night shift of biting insects was nearly as bad as the day shift. When taking observations my torments were almost unbearable—there was no protecting my bare hands and face from them.

The *batelón* leaked, and crashed repeatedly into snags. Caulking with masses of *estopa* was a routine that could not be relaxed for even an hour. So wide did some of the seams gape that the *estopa* quickly worked out. Dan, the Anglo-Bolivian, was for the first day or two quiet and contemplative—recovering from a last drinking bout in Riberalta. Then, when his head cleared, he became rather a nuisance, and I had to reprimand him severely. For all that, he was a cheerful youth.

We passed one *barraca* after another, and usually stopped for a meal, or, if they were worked out and abandoned, gathered papaws and other fruit from the rank plantations. Sometimes we camped on a strip of sandy beach, sometimes we slept in the insect-haunted interior of a hut. Once or twice our camp was invaded by a vast army of driver ants, which swarmed over everything and destroyed all living creatures in their path. The heat was stifling, and we could seldom bathe in the river because of the deadly *pirañas* and the stingrays. The awful monotony of the forest, crowding down to the water's edge on both banks, was unbroken day after day, except where a rough clearing was cut for a *barraca* that looked, with its thatch and cane, almost a part of the jungle itself. At times we felt as though our sanity could stand the plague of insects no longer!

We found the wife of General Pando's nephew living with her family at the *barraca* of Trinidad in far more luxury than would have been procurable at Riberalta. They had their own plantations and poultry and cattle which had been brought overland during the dry season when trails were passable. Here we were entertained royally, and for a day or two were able to forget the miseries of the journey.

A lady at the *barraca* was a victim of advanced *espundia* in the ear, a disease common in these regions. At that time and for long after it was not recognized as due to the Leishmann Donovan microbe, and the same disease as the *Bouton de Biskra* of Tripoli, and the Delhi boil of India. By drastic and painful treatment it can be cured in ten days, or in advanced cases in under six months, for it responds to methylene and strong antiseptics. In the forests, where it is usually allowed to run its course, it develops into ghastly facial growths, or a mass of leprous corruption on legs and arms.

There was a strange case here of a *mozo* (as the labourer is usually called in Bolivia) who was bitten by a poisonous snake. The venom was not strong enough to kill him, but it caused two of his fingers to shrivel and drop off. Deaths from snakebite were frequent here, for everyone went barefooted. Unprotected, even the most careful walker runs great risks, for some of these snakes are tiny but deadly. Snakes were so common and of so many varieties that it is practically certain they were not all known and classified.

At Trinidad we were provided with English magazines and a copy of *Martin Chuzzlewit*. Starved of reading matter, we read and re-read every page of these—every advertisement—even the proprietors' imprints. They were riddled with termite holes and stained by the damp, but to us were more valuable than gold!

The River Tahuamanu was swollen with recent rains when we commenced the ascent, yet the going was hard. Fallen trees blocked the way, and snags bristled ahead of us. It needed continuous axe-work to cut a way through, and by the time we reached comparatively clear water we were exhausted. Our eight Indians proved to be good workers, but we nearly lost them, for one night they filled Willis's pipe with mud for a lark and next morning he retaliated by letting them have it with a stick. Had they been able to leave and go home, I have no doubt they would have done so; but it blew over, and when their sore backs were better they settled down again. As a matter of fact, these Tumupasa Indians had been growing rather insolent, and the thrashing from Willis did them good.

In the forest they believe that every *Gringo* knows something of medicine, and at Bellavista *barraca* I was asked to treat a case of blackwater fever, an uncommon malady here. This case was due, I think, to drinking water from a filthy, stagnant pool. I had a small medical book with me, and studied methods of treatment from this—and they worked! Possibly it was something of a faith cure, but the important thing is the man recovered.

Forty-three days of hard going, unrelieved torture from flies and tiny bees, and deadly monotony, brought us to Porvenir. The village—if you could call it a village—was composed of two huts only; but one of these had two storeys, and so was no ordinary hut. The *batelón* returned down river to Riberalta, but the eight Tumupasa Indians stayed with us to freight a quantity of stores overland to Cobija, twenty miles away. I sent Dan to Cobija to procure mules for the transport of our equipment.

The Tahuamanu was extensively worked by the rubber firms, and at any of the *chacras* there were bananas and papaws to be had. As Willis was not only a good cook but a clever fisherman too, we were well off for food. We lived so well, in fact, that the news spread to Cobija, and there was a stampede of half-starved soldiers, together with the inhabitants of that place, to beg food and drink from us. We were able to feast them when they arrived, thanks to our Indians, who had just captured a twelve-foot anaconda, a handsome snake in red, green and yellow—and good eating.

Cobija is on the border between Bolivia and Brazil, where the frontier is the River Acre itself. On the way there from Porvenir, as we passed the grave of Colonel Aramallo, killed in the fighting of 1903, one of the soldiers escorting our cargo mules broke away from the party and flung himself down on the grave with almost hysterical grief. This interested me because Bolivians were fond of asserting that the Indian is incapable of affection. I was told that this Indian soldier showed his grief every time he passed the grave—and we felt inclined to show ours when we reached our destination, for of all dismal places Cobija must be the worst!

It was now a river port of some importance, as its elevation of less than eight hundred feet above sea level permitted uninterrupted navigation all the way to the Atlantic. It had been a *barraca*, but was abandoned and became overgrown. In 1903 the Brazilians captured it, and then were wiped out by the Bolivians, who attacked with Indians. They fired the huts with burning arrows bound in petroleum-soaked cotton, and then picked off the defenders as they were forced into the open. Not a single Brazilian escaped. Even when we arrived there—three years afterwards—skeletons still littered the ground. Brazilians occupied the place once more, but as workers, and here and in the Purus region they numbered about sixty thousand.

My anxiety over the instruments was relieved at last. There were no chronometers, as one had been stolen and the other was in Manaos for repair; and the only theodolite was so badly damaged that it could not be used. The frontier survey—an important if not vital matter for Bolivia —would therefore be run with my own sextant and chronometer watch. The work would be done, I determined, in spite of the lack of interest and the inefficiency of the authorities responsible—but I admit that for a while I was so annoyed that I almost decided to throw my hand in.

The big launches working up river beyond Cobija earned fabulous freights—often as much as 100 per cent a voyage—but in the dry season from April to November communication was cut off except for canoes and small boats known as *igarités*. Syrians and Armenians swarmed on the river in the traffic season. Their *batelónes* were piled with cheap merchandise to barter for rubber, and they made fortunes far more rapidly than their brothers, the indefatigable *Mercachifleros*, or pedlars, of the highlands. When the river traffic was at its height, Cobija was not quite so dismal.

As a rubber-collecting station for two big firms it had a garrison of twenty soldiers and thirty civilians, governed by a drunken *Intendente* who was an army major. One or two were foreigners, good chaps, but fond of the bottle. At least twenty of the fifty inhabitants suffered from *beriberi*, which in a few cases was *beriberi galopante*, a particularly rapid kind that carried off its victim in twenty minutes to twenty hours. Each soldier of the garrison drew weekly rations of two pounds of rice, two small cans of sardines and half a can of potted prawns—and on this he lived. That men leading a strenuous life should be expected to keep in condition on such rations simply staggered me. No wonder there was a run on stores we brought with us, and we let the men draw on them freely.

The doctor of the house of Suarez's station here, who claimed to have studied all the local diseases, told me that *beriberi* was caused by poor food, drink and debility, and is a bacillus passed contagiously, no one knows how. *Espundia*, he said, was the same.

"Wait till you get to the Abuna," was his cheerful warning. "There is a form of tetanus very prevalent up there, which is almost immediately fatal!"

Beriberi and other diseases caused a death rate of something like half Cobija's population every year—a staggering figure! It was no wonder, for beyond a few ducks and chickens, the uneatable *charque* and rice were about all they had. The forests had plenty of game, but the people of Cobija were far too languid and diseased to go hunting.

The *Intendente*, an uneducated rascal who could hardly sign his name, was fond of cards. We were lodged only a biscuit-toss away from the hut that served as army headquarters, and one night we heard him order his subaltern to join him in a card game. The subaltern refused. There were roars of drunken rage at that, and the young officer left the hut in disgust. The *Intendente* drew his rusty sword and staggered out after the subaltern, who was standing by the barrack-room door. He kicked him in the groin and then slashed at the youngster with his sword, hurting him badly. Hearing the noise, the *Intendente's* secretary ran out to see what was going on, and was unwise enough to remonstrate with his superior. The *Intendente* then turned on him and chased him round the hut, taking wild double-handed slashes at the poor fellow which would have cut him in half had they landed. The only refuge the secretary could think of was our room, and he rushed in, white-faced, to beg our help.

Hard on the secretary's heels the *Intendente* thundered in.

"Where is that dirty so-and-so?" he roared. "Where have you *Gringos* hidden him?"

"Steady!" I said. "You ought to be ashamed of yourself, attacking unarmed men with your sword!"

He caught sight of his trembling secretary in a dark corner and was about to push past me, but I held him off.

The *Intendente* spat an obscene oath at me and flung back to fumble at the holster on his hip. "I'll teach you, you damned interfering *Gringo!*" he yelled.

As he drew his revolver I grabbed his wrist and twisted the weapon out of his grasp.

At the same moment the injured subaltern came in with some soldiers, gripped the struggling, cursing *Intendente*, and dragged him away to the headquarters hut, where they tied him to a bed and left him to sober up.

An official investigation followed, and it came to light that the *Intendente*, having exhausted all his credit, had put in a requisition to the house of Suarez for several cases of drink, ostensibly for the 'English engineers'. He had sold all the stores he could lay hands on, and embezzled public money, so he took the chance of obtaining drink against our expense account. I at once wrote to General Pando objecting strongly to having the expedition charged with drink bills; and not long afterwards a new *Intendente* arrived from Rurenabaque—a fine man who was a firm friend of mine.

The official exchange rate stood at 12.50 *Bolivianos* to the pound sterling, but here on the Acre I found that our golden sovereigns were worth only four and it cut down our purchasing power alarmingly. For the first time in my experience gold was at a discount. The reason for this I never discovered.

I had no wish to waste time in Cobija, and soon completed what investigation and topographical work had to be carried out in the vicinity. Rains were already heavy, the river rose and fell spasmodically, and so we had hopes of procuring launches. By the time I had dispatched to General Pando a plan and estimate for a metre-gauge railway between Porvenir and Cobija, arrangements were under way for our departure up river with the object of mapping it to its source.

The premature death of a large duck from some obscure complaint provided an opportunity of giving a banquet to the chief members of the community. The dead bird cost me £1; a fowl in addition another thirty shillings. We bought eggs at two shillings each, and canned lobster and fruit were added from our own stores. There were fifteen bottles of champagne, six of gin, one of brandy, and three of rum to go with the coffee. Willis was entitled to the credit for procuring all these things—he could smell out food and drink as a hound smells out a rabbit. The guests had no difficulty in disposing of the lot, and I, having a distaste for liquor, had no need to help them. They even ordered more supplies to keep the party going—on credit, of course!

A launch came into port a day or two afterwards, towing a lighter freighted with stores, and the crew told us that the travelling priest of the Acre was on his way up river. He had been collecting funds for the cathedral of Manaos for as long as anyone could remember, and was said to make about £1,000 per voyage. He solemnized marriages at £30 each, masses were said for £6, baptisms and burials cost £10; and in addition to these he gave harmonium or phonograph concerts for seven shillings and sixpence per head, the listeners providing their own seats.

Rubber was extraordinarily profitable on the Acre. The Brazilian *seringeros* who worked it were free of any form of constraint beyond a contract, and every one of them was making between £500 and £1,500 a year. They were well fed, clothed and armed, and lived in *centros*, huts erected on the river bank close to their *estradas*, or circuits of 150 trees each. Some were educated men, and most possessed phonographs. Here the whip was unknown and there was no regular slave trade, but savages were occasionally hunted and fetched about £60 each. The trade was not extensively practised, mainly because the tribes had wisely moved out of the region.

Christmas Day, 1906, was welcomed with another banquet, this time at the house of a trader. I was voted into the chair and obliged to make a speech, which a growing fluency in Spanish enabled me to do without a breakdown. All the guests in turn managed during the evening to 'make use of the word', as they say in Spanish, and every speech was practically identical. There was much smiting of chests, much use of the words 'heart' and 'noble sentiments'. All the speeches were applauded with thunderous volleys from the guests' rifles—and where the bullets might lodge was nobody's concern! There was music, and dancing and unlimited liquor. At four o'clock in the morning those guests who were still conscious went to another house for a refresher of beer, and from there only three emerged—myself, Dan, and a Peruvian named Donayre.

In a fusillade of farewell rifle-shots we left Cobija next day, accompanying Señor Donayre up river in his boat.

Yorongas

CHAPTER VII

THE ACRE

SEÑOR DONAYRE was the manager of a *barraca* several days' journey up river. He was an interesting man. At one time the German firm for which he worked on the Purus sent him to the Putumayo to contact Indians on that river, learn their language, and report on the chances of rubber and trade. In one large tribe he was given a wife, and stayed with them for two years.

"These people were cannibals," he said, "and many a time I have seen bits of men—white men—cooked. They didn't care so much for eating whites—men of other Indian tribes were preferred. The taste is rather like monkey meat."

"Did you ever sample the flesh yourself?" I asked.

"I lived with them, remember, and it was necessary for me to adopt their habits. If I had refused to do what they did I wouldn't have lived to tell the tale!"

"How developed were they—I mean mentally, socially . . .?"

"Oh, they were intelligent all right! They had an organized government; and while each separate community had its own chief, there was a supreme chief who acted as king over the whole tribe. They sometimes cremated their dead, but usually ate them. Women were plentiful, and though polygamy was practised, their morals were of a high order.

"It's easy to condemn cannibalism as disgusting, Major, but when you come to think of it, is it any worse to eat a dead man than a dead beast or bird? It at least provides a reasonable motive for killing a man, which is more than you can say for civilized warfare; and it's a convenient way of getting rid of the dead, without occupying valuable ground and polluting clean air by burying the corpse! Of course, it's a matter of viewpoint. One's first thought is that cannibalism is revolting, but when you are familiar with it there seems little to object to."

"What caused you to leave them?"

"My wife told me of a plot to kill all white men. They thought the brutalities which the whites practised on the Indians were an attempt to wipe them out, and they were eager to retaliate. I don't suppose they wanted to kill me, but I was a white, so I must be eliminated with the others of my race. Anyway, I escaped without any trouble, and I was sorry to leave them. Savage life has its compensations, and the more civilized a man is the more ready he is to slough off the old life and relapse into an existence of extreme simplicity. Most of the whites I have met who 'went savage' were people of good education. It is they who seem to be the most adaptable.

"You meet whites who have gone Indian, and sometimes you see Indians who are white. I've seen them myself—people with red hair and blue eyes, like a *Gringo*. Ask any of the men in the Brazilian *barracas* up this way, and they'll tell you the same."

This was the first time I heard of the 'White Indians'. I, also, have seen them, and later on shall have more to say on the subject.

Between the Purus and the Acre was a large triangular area that Bolivia had sold to Brazil for two million pounds. In less than three years Brazil took considerably more than this value of rubber out of it. I myself saw masses of rubber worth up to £70,000 waiting in the *barracas* for launches to freight it out to Manaos. As I have said, the owners calculated on earning one hundred per cent the value of the rubber each voyage, with luck, that is; but it sometimes happened between May and December that the launches were caught and stranded by a falling river. The snags in the Acre often broke propeller blades, so a number of spares had to be carried—in fact there was the case of one big launch that lost no less than thirty-two propellers in a single voyage! The river's width was not over fifty yards, and deep-draught launches could navigate it only when the shallow, snag-filled stream rose at least twenty-five feet with the rains, and even then its many small rapids were difficult to negotiate.

On the other side of the frontier, in Brazilian territory, all the houses were well-built, roomy and well-furnished. At Porto Carlos, a large Brazilian *barraca* where launch navigation ended, the owner and his family lived in luxury, with a fine home, and plenty of everything, including many cattle brought up from Manaos.

River etiquette frowned on the traveller who failed to stop at these *barracas* and *centros* to take at least a cup of coffee with the residents. People so isolated were hungry for news of the outside world, and this was their only hope of getting it. To see a new face, to enjoy fresh conversation, was to feel once more the touch of remote civilization. On our way up river we stopped at a few places, but not a soul was about, everyone being apparently busy in the *estradas*. Valuable rubber, guns, clothing, gramophones and property of all kinds lay around for the taking, yet nothing was ever touched. Sometimes there was a notice saying 'Everything here has an owner', but it was hardly necessary, for theft was considered by all so heinous a crime that no one dreamt of it. Murder and rape were tolerated, but not robbery! At one *centro* far up the owner may have been killed, for creepers covered the hut, and grass had grown over the *bolachas* of rubber, yet nothing had been disturbed. An average *bolacha* of rubber was at that time worth £30, and to take it out was easy, as it would float behind a canoe.

Savages were not numerous on this part of the river, though I heard complaints of isolated bands descending on the *centros* and purloining any metal articles they could lay hands on, sometimes even attacking and killing the rubber pickers. The once large native population had been much reduced in warfare with the whites, and many of the survivors had cleared off to remoter regions upstream.

We passed the night at a *centro* where a score of rubber pickers got together to celebrate the New Year. The hut was a single room set on piles six feet above the ground, for Brazilians wisely avoid sleeping at ground level. We all passed a reasonably good night with the exception of Willis, who elected to swing his hammock underneath the hut's floor because he feared rain. The floor was made of widely spaced slats of fibrous palmwood, so that we inside were by no means shut off from the outer world—nor Willis from us. After turning into my hammock I listened for some time to the noisy hawking and spitting of the Brazilians, and Willis, who was right in the line of fire beneath, sent up bitter curses.

Near this place lived the most beautiful woman I have ever seen. She was a Brazilian half-caste, with long silky black hair, perfect features, and the most glorious figure. Her large black eyes alone would have roused a saint, let alone an inflammable Latin of the tropic wilderness. I was told that no less than eight men had been killed fighting for her, and that she had knifed one or two herself. She was a she-devil, the living prototype of the 'jungle girl' of novel and screen, and dangerous to look at in more ways than one. Twelve men had possessed her up to then, and probably many more followed.

One night we camped in the forest near the mouth of the Yalu River, and as I climbed into my sleeping-bag something scuttled up my arm and over my neck—something hairy and revolting. I brushed it off, and there fell on the back of my other hand a gigantic *apazauca* spider. It clung to me tenaciously as I attempted to shake it off, and finally dropped to the ground. It was a bit of luck that the brute didn't bite me, for this species is very poisonous and can sometimes kill a man.

At Rosario, while we waited a few days for arrangements to be made to continue up river, a Bolivian arrived who was one of an expedition to ascend the Tahuamanu six weeks before. He told me that thirty-six days up from Porvenir they struck a wide Indian trail, followed it northwards to the Yacu River—a tributary of the Purus—and captured a large number of savages. The expedition was of course a slaving raid. They killed many Indians, but the party lost a number of their own men. The 'proceeds' of the journey were profitably disposed of, and the survivors considered themselves lucky in coming out alive, for not all such expeditions were so fortunate.

"There was one expedition of no fewer than eighty men," the Bolivian told me. "It crossed from the Tahuamanu to the Rio de Piedras, or Tabatinga, which has its source not far from that of the Acre and the Purus, and runs into the Madre de Dios near Maldonado. In spite of the party's numbers, so many of them were killed with poisoned arrows that the rest abandoned the trip and retired. There's a tribe there called the Inaparis—light-complexioned people, who don't like to be molested —and probably they were the ones who did it."

Donayre was looking seedy, and I suspected worms. I treated him, and my reputation as a doctor was established when he was relieved of an ailment that had worried him for months. He tried very hard to persuade me to accept a fee in rubber to the value of six *contos*, or £360, and burst into tears when I refused it!

Again and again I was asked—even begged—to map private rubber concessions for staggering fees, and had I nothing else to do I might have done it. I was once offered the equivalent of £5,400 for a survey that would have taken about three weeks to complete. A map of a concession was always required before it became legally valid. The regular surveyors were far too scared of diseases and savages to risk their lives in these regions, even though they could have made their fortunes in very little time. As for savages, I don't suppose we met half a dozen in all the territory between Rosario and the source of the Acre. The sight of rifles frightened them, and they vanished as soon as we saw them. To shoot at them was the last thing I would have done.

There was plenty of evidence that the rubber industry on the Acre was past its heyday, in fact on its last legs—as indeed it was throughout Bolivia. Demand was still good, and prices were high, but insect pests and pigs did untold damage to the grown trees, and the young trees reached a height of five or six feet only to shrivel up and die. I often wondered why hevea was not planted, but was told that the attempt had been a failure. Possibly the difficulty could have been overcome had it not been for the general desire to get rich quick. One rubber picker could collect over two tons a year under existing conditions—as was the case in the Acre—and everyone profited so much that no serious consideration was given to the idea of waiting fifteen years for planted trees to mature.

In a large *batelón* obtained from Donayre we left Rosario on January 9, and were at once in difficulties. The snag-filled river shoaled. The boat was really too big for this section, but there was nothing better to be had. To make matters worse the rain came on in torrents, until the roar of it was like an express train making up time on a tight schedule. Mosquitoes and *mariguis* pestered us; and when we camped that night it was in wet hammocks. However, next day the going improved, for the rain brought up the level of the river.

We were able to exchange our large boat for two canoes at the *barraca* of Tacna, at the confluence of the Acre and Yaverija, and so the problem of navigating the upper reaches of the Acre was solved. A double-handed duel had just been fought here between two brothers and their two partners for possession of a seventeen-year-old Peruvian Indian girl, who was delighted at the compliment. She was no beauty —to my eye—but possibly she had other charms that inflamed the passions of these four idiots. At all events, one of the brothers was shot in the arm and bled to death through neglect, one partner fled, and the remaining two embraced and swore eternal friendship. The house was riddled with bullet holes, so the duel must have been quite exciting while it lasted.

The Indians in this region were troublesome, and they took care to hide their villages at some distance from the river. They also marked out good escape paths from slavers. In making these paths the practice was to end them suddenly, leave a strip of untouched jungle, and continue again well to one side, always avoiding proximity to a river.

A little distance above Tacna we came to Yorongas, last *barraca* on the river. Beyond was unknown country, for there had been no incentive to explore it owing to the growing scarcity of rubber trees and the hostile Cateana Indians. The forests in the neighbourhood were full of game. There were *capibaras*, and *antas* or tapirs, very good eating, though believed to be poisonous in certain regions on account of something they fed on. Peccary were also numerous and in large sounders, which suggested that the Indians, who are keen hunters, lived a fair distance away.

By Brazilian law, one man is limited to working an area of land with a river frontage of twelve miles and six miles deep. This limit can hardly be exceeded anyway, both on account of the savages and because of difficulties in transporting the heavy *bolachas* of rubber at a distance of more than two leagues from the river. The *centros* were frequently attacked here, and the wild Indian was therefore shot at sight, for no punitive expedition against the tribes was allowed by the Brazilian Government, whose policy it was to protect the indigene. That doesn't mean to say that the shooting was sanctioned—far from it—but there was no way of preventing it in the more inaccessible places. The Indians found on the Acre are the Cachitis, Cateanas, Maritinaris, and Guarayos, these last probably being the remains of a once large nation, for they are dispersed widely between the Purus and the Beni.

In the Purus and Acre is found a large catfish called the *Pirurucu*, whose rough tongue, tough as the sole of a shoe and like it in form, is used as a rasp for grating food and polishing wood. Stingrays are common here because of the sandy river bed; and I shot an eleven-foot crocodile, a rarity so far up river. The manager at Yorongas told me he killed an anaconda fifty-eight feet long in the Lower Amazon. I was inclined to look on this as an exaggeration at the time, but later, as I shall tell, we shot one even larger than that.

Everyone here took *Guaraná* tea, a beverage originated by the Guaraná Indians of the Lower Amazon, who prepared it from a plant to be found only near a village called Manes. It is made in the form of a short, hard cylinder, from which powder is rasped with a catfish tongue, and added to cold water. It is an excellent tonic, and appears to have no serious effects. No Brazilian in the wilds will be without it. It is in great demand, and genuine *Guaraná* tea always fetches a high price, but there are imitations which are not only inferior but may even be harmful. The taste is rather like *Maté*.

The administrator at Yorongas was a cheerful man and harboured no grudge against the Indians, in spite of their having driven him out of one *barraca*, burnt his house, and destroyed fifteen tons of his rubber. He was tolerant enough to say that perhaps the attacks were well deserved, for he himself had seen expeditions treat the Indians with incredible barbarity. It was out of the ordinary to hear a rubber baron speak like this, and my respect for him increased greatly in consequence.

We had miscalculated the condition of the river above Yorongas; the largest of our two canoes was too big to get up, so we were forced to exchange it for two smaller ones. Fallen trees blocked the river everywhere, and the labour of cutting through them, or lifting the canoes and supplies over them, was endless and back-breaking. We were amazed at the tameness of all wild life, and even the tapir—usually the most timid of animals—stood his ground and watched us with mild curiosity. Little *capibaras* sat on their haunches while we passed, and made no attempt to escape. Monkeys were everywhere, of course, including a kind almost white and smaller than the common brown monkey. I saw these nowhere else but on the upper Acre, and the little creatures are so delicate that in captivity they die at once.

Bird life was so prolific and tame that it was hard to restrain our Indian crew from slaughtering the birds with sticks. There was a peculiar carrion bird, something like a pheasant in appearance, which hopped about on the river banks and hissed loudly at us. A species of otter, known as a *lobo*, popped head and shoulders out of the river and barked in Willis's face while he was fishing from the stern of a canoe, and he was so surprised that he fell backwards into the water. We pulled him out, and he muttered something about devils, for never before had he seen such an animal. The otter's presence told the rest of us that there were no crocodiles, for the croc is afraid of otters and carefully avoids the same stretch of river.

As we poled our way along, the bones of large animals showed in the high, red sandstone bluffs bordering the river, where the banks had caved in and fallen. Fossil remains were common here; and lower down we saw petrified tortoises in perfect state. Had we stopped to investigate we might have found signs of extinct monsters, or animals now no longer seen in these forests.

Four days up from Yorongas we struck a sounder of peccary, and at once there was wild excitement. The crew were out like a flash—everyone scrambled ashore—rifles barked and bullets whizzed in all directions—whining ricochets crashed through the foliage and slapped viciously into solid timber. Not even a pitched battle could have been more dangerous, for every man fired into the struggling mass with an utter disregard of consequences. Men shouted and yelled; pigs screamed and fled in panic; Willis was bowled over by a peccary boar running between his legs, and sought refuge in a tree. So terrified were the peccary that they never tried to attack, and when it was all over we found five of them lying dead on the ground. Heaven only knows how many were wounded! It was a miracle that no men were hit—not even Willis, who on coming down from his tree proclaimed that he was a dead man. We took a piece of one pig and found it excellent eating, in fact it is regarded as the best meat the forest provides. There was no doubt about the crew's opinion of it, for they consumed the whole lot in one glorious feast lasting from dusk to dawn.

Animal life abounded. In the great trees there squeaked and chattered legions of little grey monkeys known as *Leoncitos*, slightly larger than marmosets; at night we were pelted with buds and other missiles by those saucer-eyed members of the lemur family, the *Nocturnos*, or night monkeys; and in camp stores had to be guarded from the depredations of the mischievous brown monkeys.

There were signs of Indians now—tracks on the sandbanks and trails in the forest—but we caught no more than a glimpse of them, for they were careful to keep out of sight as much as possible. Here and there a tree trunk had been hacked laboriously into the shape of a cone a foot high, probably with a religious motive. Had there been no Indians in our party the savages might have shown themselves. It was trying to the nerves, knowing all the time that our every movement was watched, yet seeing almost nothing of those who were watching. It meant keeping a guard out at night, the sentries working in three-hour shifts.

We passed the *Cascada de Avispas*, a small fall of only a foot or two in height, where one could bathe safely, the only discomfort being the yellow stinging *tabana* flies. It was hard work going up stream, for we negotiated no less than a hundred and twenty rapids and cataracts, some three or four feet high, and the heavy dug-out canoes had to be dragged and lifted over them. Red sandstone gave way to black rock, and at length we came to a fairly high waterfall, beyond which the river's width dwindled to no more than a yard. Canoes could go no farther. I should have liked to continue on foot to the source, which could not have been more than a few miles distant, but the Indian crew refused to go on, and I was afraid to leave them behind with the canoes in case they made off with them and left us stranded. We therefore carved a record of the expedition on a large tree and turned back. We reached Yorongas on February 7, and stayed there for several days, while Willis went down to Tacna to purchase flour for bread-making.

Yorongas had fine plantations of bananas and mandioca, the latter superior to the potato and a staple food throughout the interior of Brazil. In the Acre planting was always done four days before or after the full or new moon, according to the crop; in fact, it was then quite common throughout South America to plant in accordance with the moon's phases, and any neglect to observe these was said to render crops more liable to attack from pests. The same precautions were taken when thatching with palm leaves, in the belief that fronds cut during a waning moon or too near a new moon were liable to be rapidly devoured by insects. It is unwise to condemn these as primitive superstitions until they are proved unfounded. Personally, I believe we have yet much to learn about the moon's influence.

During the stay at the *barraca* I developed the photographs taken up river. This was a job that had to be done as soon as possible after exposure, for in the humidity of the forest damp attacked all film not sealed in watertight containers. The difficulty was to find water cool enough. Many otherwise good results were spoilt by development in too high a temperature. At this time I was using a camera made by the Stereoscopic Company, taking roll film four inches by six and a half—a big picture compared with present-day ideas. Later I favoured smaller sizes, as more exposures were obtainable for a given weight of film—and weight meant everything when all we took had to be packed on the back. The number of important exposures lost through mishaps was heartbreaking, but we finished the expeditions with enough to form a comprehensive record.

Dan left us here and returned to Tacna, probably hoping for an orgy of drink. This young man had been left behind dead drunk at Tacna on the way up, and caught up with us after we had left Yorongas, coming into camp full of apologies and swearing never to touch a drop again. He had very little respect for Chalmers, and I quite expected a blow-up between the two, but fortunately it never came to that.

The manager of Yorongas and several of his men were annoyed because a young Cateana girl whom they had captured, and kept chained up like a dog, had managed to break loose and escape. Later on she turned up at Tacna, lured back to the dangerous proximity of whites by a passion for one of the *seringeros*. There she remained, and no chains were required to keep her.

Dan had drunk himself into a stupor when we reached Tacna. I left him there, took Willis and Chalmers, and set off up the Yaverija, a small tributary of the Acre which required mapping. It was a difficult stream to negotiate owing to the snags and fallen trees, and the work was made harder by the amount of shirking that went on whenever my back was turned. Protruding from the surface of a hardened clay deposit in the river bank well upstream we found the skull and some bones of a petrified saurian. The skull was over five feet long, but too damaged by the action of water and pebbles to warrant its removal, though I did manage to collect a few black teeth which happened to be intact. Not far away was the skeleton of an even larger monster, plainly to be seen at the bottom of a deep, quiet pool, but there was no way of getting at it.

We were wrecked three times on snags in this river, but luckily lost nothing of value, in spite of the fact that Chalmers fell overboard each time with the compass in his hand. The instruments and the precious chronometer were saved by the waterproof metal case we kept them in. When we returned to Tacna it was to find that Dan had gone on to San Miguel with the crew, and when after hours of stiff paddling we caught up with him he was drunk again and the *batelón* had continued without him. We carried on, and came to Rosario, where Donayre's wife welcomed us, for her husband was away from camp.

Letters reached us in all sorts of places, and it was an agreeable surprise to find a mail waiting for us at Rosario. All travellers were ready to carry mail with them if asked to do so; and I, for one, never heard of any letters being lost or stolen.

We were four days at Rosario, waiting the return of the *batelón*, and during this time I was engaged in doctoring Donayre's infant son, treating Willis for fever, and developing films. So far, the rainy season had been slight, and I came to the conclusion that accounts of its effects were exaggerated. There is reason to believe that the intensity of the rains is decreasing with the gradual changes in the South American climate, though regularly every seven years there is a bad wet season. Many a time I have seen high-water marks on the river banks far above any recorded level, showing clearly that in the past flooding was more serious than now. The spate of water is caused by snows melting in the Andes, but the snows are also diminishing with the decrease in precipitation and the receding forest line.[1]

About three miles below Rosario was the *barraca* of a man who was a great devotee of the phonograph, and the music travelled along the surface of the river with perfect clarity after sunset. Its stridency softened by distance, there was something extraordinarily glamorous about the sound coming up to us in the gloaming of the tropical evening at that precise moment when for the second time in twenty-four hours the insect orchestra ceased and all was still. *Estudiantina* was a favourite tune of his, and to this day whenever I hear it there comes to me a vision of the Acre, reflecting a golden sky against which the top of the jungle wall on the bank stands out in sharp silhouette. It is said that the savages can communicate with one another up to twenty-five miles by means of their wooden gongs, and the peculiar note these produce. Having listened to that distant phonograph, clear as though it were in an adjoining room, I can quite believe it. In the forest the human voice is lost at a distance of two hundred yards; a rifle-shot can be heard only half a mile away, or less. Yet the notes of some birds seem to travel much farther—even certain insects can be heard at surprising distances.

Bird song in the forest is strangely beautiful, and has a hollow echoing sound rather like the sounds you hear outside the bird house at the Zoo. No single bird has the variety of song that our English thrush and blackbird have, but they repeat over and over again two or three bell-like notes. Some chatter, some croak, others whistle or hiss. Without seeing what creature is making the noise it is difficult to decide whether it is made by bird or insect. Strangest of all the bird noises is the cry of the *Trompetero*, the big black Trumpeter bird. It begins with a series of staccato clucks, increasing in tempo like an accelerating motor-cycle till it becomes a loud and sustained trumpet-call, then slows to staccato notes once more, growing more and more hesitant till it dies away altogether.

Talking of birds, all through the Peruvian and Bolivian *Montaña* is to be found a small bird like a kingfisher, which makes its nest in neat

---

[1] At the time of which my father wrote, the Central Railway of Peru had to operate a snow-plough frequently during the wet season in the vicinity of the summit (15,806 feet above sea level). I remember the old wedge plough stored at Ticlio Station, but never saw it in use; and in 1926 it was removed and sent down to the coast for scrap. I was in charge of motive power in the Mountain Section for many years, and noted the steadily decreasing annual snows. In 1924 I remember depths of about two feet, but by 1946 no more than a few inches would fall, even in the fiercest blizzard.—ED.

round holes in the rocky escarpments above the river. These holes can plainly be seen, but are not usually accessible, and strangely enough they are found only where the birds are present. I once expressed surprise that they were lucky enough to find nesting-holes conveniently placed for them, and so neatly hollowed out—as though with a drill.

"They make the holes themselves." The words were spoken by a man who had spent a quarter of a century in the forests. "I've seen how they do it, many a time. I've watched, I have, and seen the birds come to the cliff with leaves of some sort in their beaks, and cling to the rock like woodpeckers to a tree while they rubbed the leaves in a circular motion over the surface. Then they would fly off, and come back with more leaves, and carry on with the rubbing process. After three or four repetitions they dropped the leaves and started pecking at the place with their sharp beaks, and—here's the marvellous part—they would soon open out a round hole in the stone. Then off they'd go again, and go through the rubbing process with leaves several times before continuing to peck. It took several days, but finally they had opened out holes deep enough to contain their nests. I've climbed up and taken a look at them, and, believe me, a man couldn't drill a neater hole!"

"Do you mean to say that the bird's beak can penetrate solid rock?"

"A woodpecker's beak penetrates solid wood, doesn't it? . . . No, I don't think the bird *can* get through solid rock. I believe, as everyone who has watched them believes, that those birds know of a leaf with juice that can soften up rock till it's like wet clay."

I put this down as a tall tale—and then, after I had heard similar accounts from others all over the country, as a popular tradition. Some time later an Englishman, whose reliability I cannot doubt, told me a story that may throw some light on it.

"My nephew was down in the Chuncho country on the Pyrene River in Peru, and his horse going lame one day he left it at a neighbouring *chacra*, about five miles away from his own, and walked home. Next day he walked over to get his horse, and took a short cut through a strip of forest he had never before penetrated. He was wearing riding breeches, top boots, and big spurs—not the little English kind, but the great Mexican spurs four inches long, with rowels bigger than a half-crown piece—and these spurs were almost new. When he got to the *chacra* after a hot and difficult walk through thick bush he was amazed to find that his beautiful spurs were gone—eaten away somehow, till they were no more than black spikes projecting an eighth of an inch! He couldn't understand it, till the owner of the *chacra* asked him if by any chance he had walked through a certain plant about a foot high, with dark reddish leaves. My nephew at once remembered that he came through a wide area where the ground was thickly covered with such a plant. 'That's it!' said the *chacarero*. 'That's what's eaten your spurs away! That's the stuff the Incas used for shaping stones. The juice will soften rock up till it's like paste. You must show me where you found the plants.' When they came to look for the place they couldn't find it. It's not easy to retrace your steps in jungle where no trails exist."

After an easy journey down stream on a rising river we reached Cobija on February 23, and found the seasonal rubber traffic in full swing. The population was no longer faced with starvation, launches had come and gone, others were expected, and the Customs were raking in money. But here in Bolivia the rubber industry was being ruined by the ruthless tapping of trees, giving them no rest. In Brazil, every picker ran three *estradas*, so that the trees were tapped only once in three days, and after ten years of cutting were allowed to rest for eight years. It was calculated that between its collection by the *seringero* and delivery at Manaos or Pará the product lost fifty per cent of its gross weight value as pure rubber, a loss borne by the gatherer, who nevertheless found it a profitable business so long as prices remained at their high level. All the same, the *seringero's* life was a terribly hard one, and few were free from ailments of one sort or another. His day commenced at 4 a.m. with the round of his *estrada* of 150 trees, placing his cups on the trunks over a distance often considerable in poor forest. He then had to cut wood for his fire, and collect the nuts used for obtaining the white smoke necessary for curing the rubber. Rounds had to be made a second time to collect the milk, and on returning there was the laborious process of smoking it into *bolachas*, during which one drop of rain to dilute the milk would ruin the day's work. Besides this, he must keep his plantation going, hunt game, build his own house and maintain it, make his own canoe, and transport his rubber to headquarters.

The day is bound to come when all forest country free from inundation will be inhabited by civilized folk, and the whistle of the locomotive and the drone of the aeroplane will be heard where previously the myriad voices of insects were the only sound. The forest is not in itself unhealthy; disease is spread from the villages of civilized settlers, where gross self-indulgence is responsible for the greater part of it. When uncontaminated by the settlers the indigenous tribes enjoy good health —and they would certainly not elect to live where they do were life disagreeable and land unproductive.

On the north bank of the river above Cobija, near Porto Carlos, are seepages of petroleum, black and thick, but inflammable. Somewhere in the area between the Purus River and the Chaco vast supplies of oil may later be found.[1]

We were longing for news of the world we knew, and expected to find at Cobija all our newspapers from home, sent up in bundles from

[1] Oil wells are now being worked at several places in the forest country, but the chief obstacle to intensive exploitation is the lack of transport.—ED.

Riberalta. Yes, the bundles had arrived all right, but every paper had been eaten by official mules in lieu of fodder! Maltese goats live mostly on scraps of paper, but I had never suspected that mules would sink so low. We were forced to accept this explanation for the loss. The word of the postal authorities was not to be doubted, and the mules were incapable of denying the charge.

A period of enforced idleness and dreadful monotony was enlivened by a German named Keller, master of a big launch that came in from Manaos. He was a keen chess-player, and we spent most of our time together crouched over a chessboard. Keller told me that freights between Manaos and the upper Acre reached £24 a ton, and exports of rubber £30 a ton. No wonder launches were prepared to take risks—and that Manaos in the height of the rubber boom was paved with gold!

RURENABAQUE.
A dismal heap on the way in—a metropolis on the way out!

SAN ANTONIO *BARRACA*.
Outpost of the great Bolivian rubber empire

GROUP AT PORVENIR, 1906. Fawcett is the seated figure

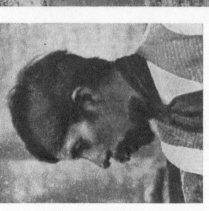

ESPUNDIA VICTIM. First his nose will rot away, then his mouth. He will live to have a horrifying, fleshless face

CASCADA DE AVISPAS, ON THE
UPPER ACRE

END OF THE TRAIL, ON THE
UPPER ACRE

PORTAGE OF THE *BATELON* AT THE *CACHUELA* OF RIBERON

COL. PLACIDO DE CASTRO AT CAPATARA.
This great Brazilian was murdered shortly after the picture was taken

CHAPTER VIII

RIVER OF EVIL

THE *batelón* slid round a wooded bend of the river, and there came
a sudden cry of surprise from the man in the bow. I looked up.
Lying beside the bank, not two hundred yards ahead, was an ocean-going
steamer.

"Come out, quick!" I shouted to Dan and Chalmers, who were
arguing together inside the shelter. "Here's something you don't often
see!"

They crawled on deck and stood up beside me, gasping with
amazement.

She was a small vessel as steamers go—displacing perhaps a thousand
tons—but in that minute of unexpected encounter she seemed mightier
than the *Mauretania*, grander than the *Olympic*. We could hardly believe
our eyes. It seemed incredible that we should find a real steamer from
the other side of the world—here, in the heart of the continent, walled
in by rank jungle, separated from the ocean on one side by the sky-
scraping *Cordilleras*, and on the other by sixteen hundred miles of
river! Her black hull and dingy yellow upperworks were streaked with
rust; her boot-topping showed a clear eight feet above the surface of the
water; the tall, thin black funnel was clear of smoke, but above it the
atmosphere shivered to the hot furnace gases; and she lay slightly canted
over shorewards, so that the trucks of her stumpy masts almost mingled
with the thick foliage of the marginal forest trees.

As we glided past we saw the name *Antonina* in faded letters on
her bow. A steward came out on the deck under the bridge, emptied

79

a bucket of slops overboard, and straightened his half-naked figure to watch us—a small man with a mop of tow-coloured hair and narrow pinched shoulders. No one else appeared, and there was no activity ashore, but it was the hour when Europeans would be lunching. Stained canvas wind-catchers were stretched over the high boiler-room ventilators and from open scuttles air scoops protruded. On her counter appeared the name again, '*Antonina*, Hamburg', and a blade of her single screw showed beneath.

"Hey!" ejaculated Dan. "What about going aboard her and having a beer? I bet they have real German beer fresh from the cask!"

It was too late. Already the current had carried us past, and to drive back alongside would be difficult. We should have thought of that before instead of standing like fools and looking at her!

"Wonder what she's doing here?" murmured Chalmers.

"Rubber," Dan said. "She's come to load rubber. Probably brought machinery and trade goods. Fancy bringing a ship right up this far!"

That was the thing that amazed me. Steamers were occasionally seen on the Madeira, but none of us expected to find one on the Acre. Its presence there proved that the river was navigable up to that point at least.

We were some miles down river from Xapury, most southerly Brazilian village on the Acre. After leaving Cobija we entered Brazilian territory, and at once a change was noticeable in the flourishing *barracas*, well-built houses and prosperous owners. After Cobija, Xapury seemed a luxurious place, for it boasted an hotel—of a kind—where there was an inclusive charge of fourteen shillings a day, which, as prices on the rivers went, was not expensive.

As in the Bolivian villages, liquor and disease were rife in Xapury. It was here that the 'toughs' of the Acre congregated to make merry, so the town was frequently 'hot' in more senses than one. Dan was the 'dude' of our party, and the pay he received in Cobija was spent on a new suit, a gilt watch-chain, and a pair of hideous yellow boots with high heels and elastic sides. How he escaped the attentions of the toughs I don't know, for they were an evil lot capable of anything, and a little horseplay at Dan's expense would have enlivened an hour or two for them. These river villages attract the worst characters in Brazil. The local rowdies were not above raiding *centros*, stealing the rubber, and clearing off with it before the *seringeros* realized their loss. To dispose of it down river was easy. They were experts with their guns and knives, and ready to use them without the slightest compunction. No ordinary man dared meddle with them.

The sight of a ship was a refreshing glimpse of civilization, but our soaring spirits soon dropped again when we landed at the *barracas* along the river. At one of these mortality was twenty-five per cent of the staff each year. At another, all the mules had died of some obscure complaint—oh, that it might be from a surfeit of newspapers! Alcohol was the origin of most of the human diseases.

Even worse than Xapury was Empreza, another Brazilian settlement, but there we stayed only long enough to pick up Colonel Placido de Castro, Governor of the Acre, who accompanied us as far as his *barraca*, Capatara. It was due to him that at Capatara we were able to obtain mules for the overland trip to the Abuna, his hospitality and entertaining conversation placing us still more in his debt. The upper affluents of the Abuna had to be explored and mapped, for they were extremely important in the frontier arrangements.

We stayed at a place called Campo Central in order to trace the sources of certain rivers and find their position. While doing this we came upon enormous circular grass clearings, a mile and more in diameter, the site a few years earlier of large villages of the Apurina Indians. A few of these Indians still lived at another place called Gavion, and some others, lucky enough to escape slaving expeditions, fled northwards some leagues into the forest, where they became friendly with rubber pickers and quickly deteriorated under the influence of alcohol. They were in any case miserable-looking people, very small, and apparently harmless. They buried their dead in a sitting posture and everywhere in the clearings were graves.

The little band at Gavion had submitted to civilization and seemed content enough, except for the malice of an evil spirit named Kurampura. Bad luck in hunting was looked on as the work of Kurampura, and appeasement of the god was often sought by tying a man to a *Palo Santo* tree as a sacrifice. The *Palo Santo*—Sacred Tree—is one of the commonest pests in the South American forests. It is a soft, light wood, usually found near the river banks, and is the favourite haunt of colonies of the Brazilian fire ant, a vicious insect with an extremely painful bite. Touch the tree, and armies of these ants rush out from holes in the trunk eager to attack, even dropping from branches above on to the trespasser. To be tied to the tree for a couple of hours must be indescribable agony— yet it is a custom of the Indians, and I have known depraved whites in these parts to use the same form of torture. Like so many poisonous insects, the fire ant attacks a man's neck if possible—only wasps seem to go for the eyes. The *Palo Santo* tree has no branches on the lower part of the trunk, and within a radius of several yards not a leaf or a blade of grass will grow.

I had a narrow escape near Gavion. Along the trail were a number of deep channels bridged by roughly hewn logs. In wet weather mules prefer the outer log to walk on, because it appears less slippery, and these logs are therefore the most worn and dangerous-looking ones. I was frankly nervous, but comforted myself with the thought that instinctively, or from familiarity, the mule must know what it was doing better than I. It was while crossing one of these sheer-sided streams that the log my mule was walking on broke with a rending crash, and we went down with a tremendous splash into the water. I sank underneath the animal, whose weight pushed me down into the muddy bed of the stream. Had the bottom been hard not a bone would have been left whole in my body, for the mule struggled and kicked frantically in its efforts to get right side up. It succeeded not a moment too soon, for every bit of air had been driven out of my aching lungs, and I managed to get my head above surface in the nick of time. A near thing, but apart from a ducking no harm was done.

Accidents always come in a run. One of our Indians partly hacked through a large tree out of sheer mischief, and that night it fell with an appalling crash on the sleeping camp. No one was hurt, but hammock awnings were torn to ribbons and guy-ropes broken. Legions of small, very aggressive black ants swarmed over us from the fallen branches, and the *katuki* flies rushed to attack our exposed persons with their needle-like stings. For the rest of the night there was no sleep for anyone —the insects saw to that.

Heavy rains and flooding of the trail to the Abuna forced us to stay some days at a *centro* called Esperança, where someone stole two of our saddles and fled with them into the forest. If the thief was ever caught I am sorry for him, for these saddles belonged to Placido de Castro.

Three rubber pickers died from snakebite the day we arrived at Santa Rosa, on the Abuna. Situated in the midst of swamps, this place was a paradise for snakes of all kinds, including anacondas—in fact, so feared were the latter that the *barraca* was regarded as a penal settlement, and rubber pickers worked in couples because so many lone men had disappeared mysteriously. It was one of the dependencies of Suarez Hermanos, and lay in Bolivian territory—quite the most depressing place I have ever been in, but very rich in rubber all the same. The only redeeming feature of the building was that it had two storeys, but being located only a few feet above normal river level it was often flooded, and in the dry season surrounded by an ocean of mud. The manager was a Frenchman of good family, who, in spite of being a sick man, relieved the utter boredom of life by keeping a harem of four rather pretty Indian women. Constant labour shortage was Santa Rosa's trouble. I hesitate to give the death-rate, for it is almost unbelievable.

One species of snake here had a head and one third of its body flat as a tape, while the rest of it was round. Another kind was completely red in colour, with a white cross on the head. Both were reputed to be venomous. At night the gleam of anacondas' eyes was quite common, reflecting luminously the smallest light in points of fire.

"There are white Indians on the Acre," this Frenchman told me. "My brother went up the Tahuamanu on a launch, and one day, well up river, was told that white Indians were near. He didn't believe it and scoffed at the men who told him, but nevertheless went out in a canoe and found unmistakable signs of Indians. The next thing he knew, he and his men were being attacked by big, well-built, handsome savages, pure white, with red hair and blue eyes. They fought like devils too, and when my brother shot one of them dead the others rallied to recover the body, and got away with it.

"People say these white Indians don't exist, and, when it's proved they do, that they are half-breed mixtures of Spanish and Indian. That's what people say who never saw them, but those who have seen them think differently!"

Fever and insects were too much for Chalmers. For some time I had observed his gradual break-up, and fearing that if he stayed with me he might not survive the hardships, I suggested his return to Riberalta. Half expecting him to refuse, I was surprised when he accepted with alacrity; and on April 10 he set off with five of the Tumupasa Indians, who were also suffering from fever. That left me with three Indians, Willis and Dan, with whom to ascend the Abuna and accurately determine its course. We had already mapped the source with our inadequate instruments, and to finish the job properly it was necessary to survey the rest of the river. Not that it was unexplored—it had been ascended in the 1840's, and had several *barracas* in the upper waters—but it was a river with an evil reputation, frequently overflowing its banks into vast lagoons and swamps, and infested in its middle reaches by the dreaded Pacaguaras Indians, who were always hostile. They had recently killed a Brazilian, and carried many prisoners into the forest. Here, too, were to be found the giant anacondas, mightiest of all constrictors, haunting the extensive fever-ridden swamps.

What a pity it is that the rivers lost their old Indian names, for these furnished an indication of their character! The Acre was really the Macarinarra, or 'River of Arrows', because on it were found the flowering bamboos from which arrows were cut. Rapirran, a frontier affluent of the Abuna, was the 'River of Sipos', a vine used extensively in house-building. Another little river, Caipera, was 'River of Cotton'—and so on. Some day the old nomenclature may be forgotten, a loss in areas where strategic minerals are sought.

Placido de Castro came over to say good-bye before we started off from Santa Rosa in an *igarité* that I managed to purchase. As usual, the Colonel was accompanied by a pack of dogs, of several breeds, which had the habit of sitting down every minute to scratch. In the forest, dogs scratched all the time—they spent their lives scratching; the wonder of it was that their hides wore out only in patches instead of

being scraped off their bodies altogether! It was the last time I saw the
Colonel, for shortly afterwards he was shot by unknown assassins while
on the trail. His death was a loss to the Brazilian rubber country, for
he was a good and enlightened man.

The Colonel, who took an important part on the side of Brazil
against the Bolivians in the 1903 trouble on the Acre, told me that at
the outset he clothed his men in khaki, but found casualties so great
that he changed the uniform to green. This proved less conspicuous in
the forest and at once reduced the losses to a negligible figure. His
opinion was that misgovernment had precipitated the trouble. Of his
own exploits he was modestly reticent, but his renown had spread far
beyond the Acre.

The position of rubber picker was a very humble one, yet a *seringero*
I met here, who had received six years' schooling in England, had dropped
all his European habits and clothing and returned here of his own
free will. A man, however well educated, who has once sampled extreme
simplicity of existence will seldom return to the artificial life of civilization. The burden of it is not realized until it has been laid aside. There
was a man I met on the Madeira River who was one of the crew of a
batelón, perhaps as hard a life as there is. He spoke English and French
perfectly, but preferred this body-breaking labour, with its alcohol, its
charque and mouldy rice, and its sandbanks for a bed, to anything a more
luxurious life could offer!

"You'd better look out for yourselves on the Abuna!" was the
warning everybody seemed to enjoy giving us. "The fever there will
kill you—and if you escape that, there are the Pacaguaras Indians. They
come out on the banks and make a boat run the gauntlet of poisoned
arrows!"

"A German engineer was attacked there the other day, and three of
his men killed," said someone. Another nodded confirmation ponderously
and shook a finger at us.

"Not so long ago forty-eight men went up the Rio Negro—that's
an affluent of the Abuna—in search of rubber. Only eighteen came out,
and one of them was stark, staring mad from the experience!"

Had we listened to all the grim warnings we should have got nowhere.
By this time I was beginning to form my own opinions, and was not
prepared to believe all the tales I heard about savages.

It was one of the gloomiest journeys I had made, for the river was
threatening in its quiet, and the easy current and deep water seemed to
promise evils ahead. The demons of the Amazonian rivers were abroad,
manifesting their presence in lowering skies, downpours of torrential
rain and sombre forest walls.

Before reaching the confluence of the Rapirran we stopped at the
barraca of a Tumupasa Indian called Medina, who had made a fortune

in rubber. In this filthy place Medina had a daughter who was one of the prettiest blonde Indians I have seen—tall, with delicate features, small hands, and a mass of silky golden hair. Beautiful enough to grace a royal court, an asset to any European ballroom, this superb girl was destined to join the harem of the manager at Santa Rosa and languish as the fifth member of that enterprising Frenchman's seraglio. I took several photographs of her, but together with all those of the Abuna, except a few developed at Santa Rosa, they were destroyed by the constant damp.

On this river is to be found a bird called the *hornero*, which builds itself a cunning clay-domed residence in branches just above high-water level. Another bird called the *tavachi* seeks, cuckoo-like, to usurp this dwelling whenever possible, and the *hornero*, finding its nest occupied, walls in the raider with clay, leaving it to perish miserably in a sealed tomb. Nature has its reasons for everything, but I could never fathom the sense in this wasteful disposition, nor can I understand why the instinct of the *tavachi* does not warn it of an almost certain death.

Here, too, you see the *bufeo*, a mammal of the manatee species, rather human in appearance, with prominent breasts. It follows boats and canoes as porpoises follow ships at sea, and is said to be very good eating, though I never succeeded in catching one to prove the truth of this. It is neither helpless nor inoffensive, and will attack and kill a crocodile.

"Have you anything to sell?" That was the question at every *centro* we passed. When Syrians came up this river with a trading boat, as they sometimes did, their voyages must have been exceedingly profitable.

We were drifting easily along on the sluggish current not far below the confluence of the Rio Negro when almost under the bow of the *igarité* there appeared a triangular head and several feet of undulating body. It was a giant anaconda. I sprang for my rifle as the creature began to make its way up the bank, and hardly waiting to aim smashed a .44 soft-nosed bullet into its spine, ten feet below the wicked head. At once there was a flurry of foam, and several heavy thumps against the boat's keel, shaking us as though we had run on a snag.

With great difficulty I persuaded the Indian crew to turn in shorewards. They were so frightened that the whites showed all round their popping eyes, and in the moment of firing I had heard their terrified voices begging me not to shoot lest the monster destroy the boat and kill everyone on board, for not only do these creatures attack boats when injured, but also there is great danger from their mates.

We stepped ashore and approached the reptile with caution. It was out of action, but shivers ran up and down the body like puffs of wind on a mountain tarn. As far as it was possible to measure, a length of forty-five feet lay out of the water, and seventeen feet in it, making a total length of sixty-two feet. Its body was not thick for such a colossal length—not more than twelve inches in diameter—but it had probably been long without food. I tried to cut a piece of the skin, but the beast was by no means dead and the sudden upheavals rather scared us. A penetrating, foetid odour emanated from the snake, probably its breath, which is believed to have a stupefying effect, first attracting and later paralysing its prey. Everything about this snake is repulsive.

Such large specimens as this may not be common, but the trails in the swamps reach a width of six feet and support the statements of Indians, and rubber pickers that the anaconda sometimes reaches an incredible size, altogether dwarfing that shot by me.[1] The Brazilian Boundary Commission told me of one they killed in the Rio Paraguay exceeding *eighty* feet in length! In the Araguaya and Tocantíns basins there is a black variety known as the *Dormidera*, or 'Sleeper', from the loud snoring noise it makes. It is reputed to reach a huge size, but I never saw one. These reptiles live principally in the swamps, for unlike the rivers, which often become mere ditches of mud in the dry season, the swamps always remain. To venture into the haunts of the anaconda is to flirt with death.

There was plenty of excitement for us on this river. We had shot several *marimonos*—black monkeys—for food, and to keep the store of carcasses safe while in camp we suspended them from the high branches above. In the middle of the night I was awakened by a bump under my hammock as though some heavy body had passed underneath, and peering out I saw in the light of the moon the form of a large jaguar. It was after the monkey-meat, and had little interest in me, but in any case it would have been foolhardy to shoot in the uncertain light, for a wounded jaguar at close quarters is a terrible thing. I saw the beast raise itself on its hind legs and claw at a carcass. In the moment of grasping what it sought the rustle of my hammock disturbed it; it turned with a snarl, bared its teeth, and next moment was gone as silently as a shadow.

Long stretches of the river bank seemed to have nothing but *Palo Santo* trees, from whose vicinity the forest had, so to speak, withdrawn the hem of its garments. There was no mistaking them, for they stood like lepers, the ground all round them absolutely bare of vegetation. Dan was so tired on pitching camp one evening that he slung his hammock from two of these trees, and turned in without realizing what he had done. In the middle of the night blood-curdling yells brought us out of our hammocks in alarm, reaching for rifles in the belief that savages were attacking. With the tatters of broken sleep still blinding us, we could almost feel the poisoned arrows ripping into our unprotected bodies—

----

[1] When this serpent was reported in London, my father was pronounced an utter liar!—ED.

almost see the dim shapes flitting through the bush at the camp's perimeter! Then our eyes opened to the sight of Dan running madly for the river, screaming as he went. There followed a loud splash, and the yells were smothered.

Satisfied that Indians were not attacking, we followed Dan to the river bank to learn what all the noise was about. Legions of ants from the two *Palo Santo* trees had made their way along the hammock ropes, covered him from head to foot, and sunk their venomous mandibles into every centimetre of his person! Dripping wet, he climbed into a canoe, and there spent the rest of the night picking the insects off himself. Next morning it took us a long time to release his hammock and beat it clear of ants.

"Savages!"

The cry came from Willis, who was on deck watching the approach to Tambaqui Rapid. Dan and I tumbled out of the shelter and looked in the direction the negro was pointing. Several Indians were standing on the bank, their bodies painted all over with the red juice of the *urucu*, a bean common in the forest. Their ears had pendulous lobes, and quills were thrust from side to side through their nostrils, but they wore no feather head-dresses. It was my first sight of these people, whom I took to be Karapunas.

"We'll stop and make friends with them," I said; but before the order to put into the bank could be given our Indian crew had spotted them. There were cries of alarm and the paddles moved at a frenzied rate.

Shouts came from the savages, and loosing their great bows they shot some arrows in our direction. We couldn't see them coming, but one ripped through the side of the boat with a vicious smack—through wood an inch and a half in thickness, and right through the other side as well! The force behind that arrow amazed me, and without seeing for myself I would never have credited such penetrating power. Why, a rifle could scarcely do more!

It was the custom of these savages to come out two or three hundred strong on the banks, and give any passing boat a hot reception. The middle of the river was within range from either side, so there was no escaping them. I knew an instance on another river of a steamer being attacked in the same way. An arrow transfixed an Englishman through both arms and chest, and pinned him to the deck with such force that it took some time to release him.

The *igarité* slid through the water at so lively a clip that we soon came up to the Tambaqui Rapid and rushed it without mishap, the crew still paddling furiously in their fear of more arrows. It was not a very formidable rapid—by no means as bad as the next one, Fortaleza, which had a ten-foot fall, and of which the noise alone was frightening. The water rushed with a flurry of foam over an outcrop of the same granite that is to be found in the Madeira and all rivers to the east of it between eight and ten degrees South Latitude—the significance of which I came to recognize later, when studying the geology of the ancient continent. The boat had to be portaged past this fall, hauled overland on rollers made from tree trunks—a labour that left us well-nigh exhausted, so short-handed were we.

On the bank lay the half-dried body of a dead anaconda, its hide nearly an inch thick. Possibly when quite dry it may have shrunk to less than that, but even so the fine tough leather would equal in quality that of the tapir.

Four hours below Fortaleza we reached the confluence with the Madeira River, so wide that it seemed like an ocean after the narrow Abuna. There we found a Bolivian Customs post, in conditions as unhealthy as it is possible to conceive. Everyone was either ill with fever or drunk—and if ever drink was justified it was there! Night had fallen, and as we drifted in to land we heard the clinking of guitars and the tuneless wail of drunken voices, as though to warn us of the degeneracy to be found there. Rubber exported from Bolivia paid lower duties than from Brazil, so it was customary for all the Abuna rubber, whether it came from the Bolivian or the Brazilian side, to pass out by way of this post. In any case, the river was not yet fixed definitely as the frontier. Stores were landed on the Brazilian side and carried across by night, a mild form of smuggling which the Customs people found better to favour than hinder. How much of the duties collected ever reached the Government is a question I cannot answer. Only one official handled money; the other nine had nothing to do but run up debts.

There were six soldiers under the command of an *Intendente*, who had been taken from Mapiri while looking for rubber and sent to this miserable post with all his possessions, which comprised a tin of salt, two swords, an alarm clock, and a dented chamber pot. The post had to be filled. His predecessor had the unfortunate habit of slashing at the soldiers with his sword, so at last they turned on him, shot him, and crossed over to Brazil. The drunk and wounded officer escaped into the forest and followed the river bank up to Villa Bella. Some idea of the state in these out-of-the-way places may be gathered from the fact that when the Bolivian Customs were handed over to Brazil there were 7,000 cases of freight at San Antonio, a shipping port below the rapids of the Madeira, awaiting transport to the Beni, and that 5,000 of them contained liquor!

At the mouth of the Abuna *charque* and rice were the only foodstuffs. No one bothered to fish or hunt, or even to dress, and sweating in their filthy rags they sang their drunken catches or groaned in the throes of sickness, as the case might be. No medicines were available, and even if any had been, there was no mind clear enough to administer them. The only healthy person was a young German who came in on his way up river, a cheerful and wholesome youth who made no bones about Anglo-German relations. The burning desire of Germany, he said, was for war, in order to damage the commercial prosperity of her rivals and secure colonies.

After eight days in this vile place we managed to obtain passage aboard *batelónes* with freight for Villa Bella, a port at the mouth of the Mamoré and half-way back to Riberalta. As we pushed out into the river there came to us like a dirge of farewell the tinkle of the guitars and drone of voices.

The Madeira-Mamoré Railway was not yet in being—that back-woods system running from 'nowhere' to 'nowhere', whose white officials received salaries so high that in ten years they could retire—if they lived so long! Instead, it took about twenty days of killing work to transport the heavily laden boats past the many rapids between San Antonio and Villa Bella. A *batelón* carrying twelve tons of freight had no more than three inches of freeboard, and it was necessary to hug the river bank closely. In the smooth stretches the crew of twenty Indians paddled; but where the water was swift and broken the boat had to be swung round rocks at the end of a long rope. Great skill was needed to avoid the ever-present dangers, and by nightfall the crew were utterly exhausted. The moment they threw themselves down on the hot rocks beside the river they were fast asleep, and in consequence pneumonia was rife amongst them—so much so that sometimes a whole crew would be carried off by it, and the boat forced to await the arrival of a fresh crew before it could go on.

Four of the men in our boat died during the first half of the voyage. Any man who fell ill became the butt of the rest, and when he died there was tremendous hilarity. The staring corpse was tied to a pole, and sparsely covered in a shallow trench scraped out with paddles on the river bank, his monument a couple of crossed twigs tied with grass. For funeral there was a drop of *kachasa* all round, and ho for the next victim!

The river here was over half a mile wide, but full of rocks, and the swift current made navigation difficult. The dangerous little rapids of Araras and Periquitos were passed without difficulty, but the more formidable one of Chocolatal took three days to negotiate. Life here was far from dull. The pilot went out to inspect the road where the *batelónes* would be portaged to by-pass the rapid, and was shot by Indians not half a mile from the boat. We found him with forty-two arrows in his body. At the time I had gone out in search of a turkey for the pot, but fortunately met no savages. My impression was that this tribe, although by no means amenable to civilized overtures, had no particular animosity towards white men.

In the Mamoré, near Villa Bella, the savages did at one time come in to the *pescanas*—recognized camping places—to engage in barter, but slaving expeditions had since estranged them. While trading up the Mamoré, a well-known Bolivian was visited by a group of the Araras Indians, who pretended to be greatly interested in his rifle and begged him to fire it again and again, clapping their hands with pleasure at the noise. When the magazine was empty the chief called attention to his bow and arrow, as though to show what he could do with it, and drawing it out to the full, suddenly turned and sent the arrow clean through the Bolivian. In the resulting confusion the Indians melted away.

A brother of the victim took revenge by leaving as though by accident some poisoned alcohol at the *pescana*. Subsequently eighty corpses were found there. These Indians are still numerous and troublesome, but the construction of the railway has cleared them out of the Madeira.

A half-caste told me that near the Chocolatal Rapid he and some other men captured a canoe with two Indians in it only a short time previously.

"One of them refused all food and died," he said. "The other started a hunger strike, too, but we strung him up to a tree by the heels and had a little rifle practice on him. He died at the eighth shot. It was great fun!"

Freighting in *batelónes* was good business here. They cost 1,800 *Bolivianos* (£144) to build, and were hired out at 400 *Bolivianos* per voyage for four voyages a year, the hirer taking all responsibility for loss.

The crew of the *batelón* almost collapsed with laughter when one of my Tumupasa Indians developed *beriberi* on this journey and became paralysed in the legs. He died in Villa Bella.

No more hair-raising experience could be imagined than the approach to Riberón Rapid. For a mile we clung to rocks or the bank where it afforded some sort of hold, and then let ourselves go, paddling wildly through a thirty-yard stretch of water rough enough to be capable of swamping the deep-laden boat. We must have shipped at least a ton of water during the ordeal. One of the four *batelónes* capsized and sank, its crew being too weak to paddle effectively. The cargo was lost, but there were no deaths, for all Indians swim like otters.

We camped at Riberón, where the boats had to be discharged for the heavy portage round the rapid. No sooner had we settled down, utterly exhausted, than we were invaded by an army of black ants, countless millions of them, which swarmed over everything in their path, setting up a shrill hissing noise, weird and fearful, at any living obstruction. They stop for nothing, and woe betide the sleeper who fails to wake at the soft rustle of their coming in time to make his escape! They did no damage in camp, but annihilated all insects, and marched on. They often visit huts in the forest and clean them of vermin.

At Misericordia, the next rapid, there was a big whirlpool, beside which dwelt an old man who had made a comfortable fortune by collecting wreckage, rubber, and anything else washed up on the shore. It was a very dangerous spot; and once in the clutch of the whirlpool no boat could escape disaster. The passage down river was most perilous, for the speed through the maze of rocks was greater, and skilful though the pilots and crews might be, they were usually drunk on leaving Villa Bella for the journey. Wrecks were frequent in the days before insurance was tightened up, for it often paid the consignors to lose a cargo deliberately.

Whoever was responsible for Bolivian place-names was guilty of gross irony when he named the port at the confluence of the Mamoré and Beni Rivers 'Villa Bella'. A foul black morass occupied the middle of the place, and the mortality was at times enormous. The death-rate among the crews of the *batelónes* working to San Antonio and back amounted to fifty per cent per year—a figure I was getting accustomed to by now. That was the toll taken by Bolivian rubber at this period, and I don't think it is an exaggeration to say that every ton shipped out cost a human life.

Reeking in undisguised filth, its inhabitants drink-sodden and degenerate, Villa Bella was nevertheless one of Bolivia's most important Customs posts. The fear of the Beni seemed to have kept away officials of a decent type; and I was treated as a Government stool pigeon. No official had the politeness or sense of duty to do anything to help us in our work, and one inhabitant even went to the extent of taking shots at me with his Winchester, fortunately with uncertain aim on account of drink. Being unable to get anything done I bluntly told the acting administrator of the Customs that if transportation was not provided immediately a formal complaint against him would be made to the Minister of the Colonies. That did the trick—I was indeed a stool pigeon! However, it enabled us to leave the place the same day.

Next day we came to Esperanza, headquarters of Suarez Hermanos, the principal rubber firm. Here we found several British mechanics in the service of the firm, well paid to look after the launches. The clerks, Germans to a man, were openly hostile to them.

There was a rapid here which the Indians held in great veneration, hearing in its roar the dancing of the dead. A few days before, a launch had gone over this rapid, owing to a failure of the engine to start when it cast off from shore with a full load of passengers. Its escape was nothing short of miraculous, for strange to say it was not wrecked. Every man on board, except Smith, the English engineer, jumped before it went over. The women shrieked helplessly, expecting at any moment to be capsized and drowned in the maelstrom. By the time it came through the rapid, Smith, who had been calmly working on the stalled engine, had it turning again, and ran the launch to the shore. He was a hero from that time on.

The British mechanics liked their jobs and worked well; their pay was generous and their treatment good; and besides regular duties there were other jobs to be done, such as mending sewing machines, rifles, and so on, which added considerably to their incomes. One of them earned the undying respect of the population by falling, bottle in hand, out of a *batelón* on the Mamoré, going over a waterfall and coming up beyond, where he crawled out, and sat calmly on the bank to finish the bottle!

Another developed an obscure disease that turned his skin almost black and caused an evil smell. One day he failed to appear at work, and the *Mayordomo*, sure that he must have died, promised a couple of Indians a bottle each of alcohol if they would go down to collect the body and bury it. They covered their noses and mouths, put the blackened body in a hammock, and carried it off to the cemetery. On the way the hammock bumped against a tree, and a sepulchral voice from inside said, "Have a care, boys—have a care!" The Indians dropped their load and made off; but fortified by drink, and accompanied by several others, they returned and took up the hammock once more. As they dumped the body at the graveside, the sepulchral voice was heard again, requesting a drink of water. All fled; but after more potations the *peons* again returned, toppled the drooling body into the open grave, and hastily shovelled earth on top until the chance of resurrection was gone!

Shortly after my arrival sixteen Pacaguaras Indians suddenly appeared in a canoe, all in full war-paint. As these braves paddled up the far side of the river Esperanza went wild with excitement. *Peons* shouted—men ran to and fro, all yelling orders at the same time—an irregular fusillade of rifle-fire commenced. The savages paid no attention whatever. The river at this point was six hundred yards wide—about the extreme range for a forty-four-forty Winchester—and with unruffled dignity they paddled along, until some small affluent swallowed them. There were glum faces after the 'Cease fire' when stock was taken of the expenditure of exorbitantly costly ammunition.

Indians often came out on the opposite bank and calmly watched the goings-on at the *barraca*, well aware that there was little danger from rifles. Their appearance invariably created a frenzy in Esperanza, and a waste of cartridges. It was like the noisy bravado of dogs at sight of a cat on a wall.

We accompanied a launch bound for Riberalta on May 18. The

night before we left was made notable by four women and four Indian *peons* who staged a drunken dance after consuming four cases of beer at £10 a case—obtained on credit. Next morning the women received a pick-me-up in the shape of twenty-five lashes each for having been noisy, and were then sent over the river to work in the plantations, a punishment much dreaded because of the Pacaguaras. The men were let off scot free, possibly because they served the firm well by getting themselves deeper into debt.

CHAPTER IX

UNSAVOURY INTERLUDE

A LARGE mail awaited me at Riberalta, and all other thoughts were pushed aside by the welcome news from home, for which I had waited so long. There were newspapers and official communications —and, most important of all, instructions to postpone further expeditions on account of financial difficulties. I was jubilant at this, for besides having had enough of martyrdom for a time, there were maps to complete, reports to be done, and final touches required on the Cobija light railway scheme. Lastly, Riberalta needed a floating dock, and I was asked to draw up a case for it, with estimates. I had no objection to being here while there was plenty to do, and so long as I was paid for it. Inactivity was what I couldn't stand.

No boats were likely to be going up to Rurenabaque for a time, for the Government launch *Tahuamanu* had at last reached a stage beyond repair, and was beached somewhere upstream. With the prospect of an indefinite stay in Riberalta, Dan had put on his Xapury suit and gone on the razzle. As for Willis, his drunken excesses had already landed him in jail. His release was entirely due to bribery and corruption, and he showed his gratitude by leaving me, to set up for himself as a vendor of liquor in a hut on the outskirts of the town, where his own weakness could be gratified at the expense of other addicts. Feo, last but one of my Indians, died.

In spite of the private slave-raiding force kept in the Madre de Dios, the Indians were giving some trouble, and it was, in fact, on that very river that a tame Indian slew with an axe the manager of the Maravillas *barraca*—a fate he probably earned. The Pacaguaras were painted blacker than they really deserved, but as a rule they lost no chance of doing any damage they could. During a trip to the mouth of the Orton with the Bolivian owner of a small rubber property I met a number of them in the forest, and they seemed inoffensive enough when finally they summoned enough confidence to show themselves. They were located by the Indians of our company, who smelt them, the savage having a scent as keen as a hound's. They obviously belonged to the more degenerate indigenes—a small, dark people, with large discs in their pendulous ears and sticks through their lower lips. They brought gifts of game, any pursuit other than hunting being considered beneath their dignity. Degenerate or not, they associated all civilized Indians with the slave raids so frequently practised on their settlements, and would have no truck with them.

There are three kinds of Indians. The first are docile and miserable people, easily tamed; the second, dangerous, repulsive cannibals very rarely seen; the third, a robust and fair people, who must have a civilized origin, and who are seldom met with because they avoid the locality of navigable rivers. This is a subject I intend to enlarge upon in later chapters, for it links up with the ancient history of the continent.

Corruption and inefficiency were the order of the day in Riberalta. A new judge had been appointed, who was also the official butcher—a highly profitable business, as few could afford not to be customers. The soldier of the 2,000 lashes, left to die with bones exposed, had recovered, and was quite cheerful about his ordeal. He had grown very fat—the usual result of a severe flogging, I was told, if the victim survived—and showed no ill effects in his walk, in spite of the fact that his rump had been cut away.

"Here come the cattle!"

It was a *peon* who cried out as he stood on the river bank, watching the approach of *batelónes*. I looked where he pointed, expecting to see beasts from the Plains of Mojos coming in for slaughter by our butcher-judge, but instead it was a human cargo. The owner of a Madre de Dios *barraca* was on the deck of the first boat, and once on shore he stood by to watch his *mayordomos*, armed with formidable whips, herd on to the beach and into a shed about thirty more or less white people from Santa Cruz, whose expressions of abject misery showed only too clearly that they fully realized their predicament. There were not only men in that drooping band, but women also.

"What are these?" I asked a Bolivian Customs officer. "Slaves?"

"Of course." He looked at me, surprised at my foolish question.

"Do you mean to say these wretched people have been brought here for sale?"

"Oh, no, *señor*! It is only forest Indians who are sold openly. These cattle will be handed over for the value of their debts—they are all debtors—and that value is the market value of their bodies. It's a private transaction, you understand, but anyone who wants a man or woman can get one if he's ready to pay the price!"

Was this the year 1907, or had time slipped back a thousand years?

"Only the forest Indians are sold openly!" The brutality revealed by this attitude angered the Bolivian Government all the more because they were unable to stop it, as it angered all right-thinking people. A typical case occurred just before my return to Riberalta—typical of the depraved 'savages' who made up these slavers from the scum of Europe and Latin America.

A slave-hunting force found its way up to a village of the Toromonas, people highly intelligent and by no means difficult to get on with. The chief disliked his visitors, but all the same he had his wife bring *chicha* as a sign of friendship. The head of the slavers, fearing poison, insisted on the chief's drinking first, which he did, and as he stood with raised bowl a shot rang out and he fell dead on the spot. Immediately there was a round-up, and those who were not killed were taken away to the Beni. One woman carrying a new-born child was shot in the ankle, and, unable to walk, was dragged to the river to be towed down stream on a raft behind the launch. When the party in the launch were tired of this, they cut her adrift to reach the shore any way she could. The perpetrators of this ghastly business boasted openly of their doings—proud of their 'victory'! They told how children had been taken by the legs and dashed against trees to kill them. There is no doubt about these atrocities, and it is not an exaggeration on my part. Would that it were! To call such devils 'beasts' is an insult to creatures that are not endowed with human barbarity. Had they been ashamed of this exploit they might have offered as an excuse for it the death of several slavers at a remote village from poisoned *chicha*; instead, they looked on that occurrence as a reason for revenge—and still more revenge.

Many of the Indians who have civilization thrust on them are clever with their hands, and intelligent. At several missions trades have been taught them and they work well; they pick up languages quickly, being naturally imitative, but they soon degenerate physically and morally.

Sometimes the worm turned. Not long before, a party sent out by a Riberalta firm to find labour in the forests were discovered chopped into little bits, floating down river in a large dug-out canoe. From another expedition in the Guaporé only one man returned, quite mad, munching the rotting flesh on a human thigh-bone! It is good to hear of these brutes getting their deserts, and I for one have no sympathy for them.

Not far from Riberalta an Indian labourer shot his *mayordomo* in revenge for some brutality. He was seized, tied up all night face to face with the corpse, and in the morning given one thousand lashes. Hardly a day passed here without floggings, and from where I was lodged I could hear the punishment going on in the compound of the Chief of Police. Generally the victims took it with surprising calm, unless—as occurred in bad cases—the *Sapo Chino* (Chinese Frog) was employed. This contrivance was a framework on the principle of the rack, on which the victim could be stretched out face downwards in such a way that his body was suspended in the air for administration of the lash.

At a *barraca* above Riberalta an Indian was given four hundred lashes, and afterwards thanked his master, declaring that he had been sorely in need of it, and could do good work now! There was in town an old man who when drunk would go to the police station and beg for a beating to teach him how to behave himself. Probably the Indian feels less keenly than the white man—physically. What he feels mentally is anybody's guess. Here in Riberalta he never saw money, nor knew what it was to receive honest treatment, but instead was given the lash for any misdemeanour. Always he was encouraged to drink alcohol.

The lash in a far more serious form was used in the British Isles within living memory—is, in fact, still employed in the penal code, and constantly recommended for more general use. If the victim could choose between the cat of the rubber districts and that of our prisons, there is no doubt about which he would prefer. Responsible for the taming of the West African colonies, we ourselves are in no position to throw stones. To cry out at the atrocities of the rubber boom, while saying nothing of the many cruelties still legally sanctioned in our own country safe out of the public's sight, is to be too narrow in outlook. I must again stress that what took place in Bolivia and Peru was not sanctioned by their Governments, but was the act of individuals outside the range of law and order. Bad as it was, nothing occurred there comparable with the atrocities in the Belgian Congo. The remoteness of a place such as Riberalta is difficult to grasp. There was no telegraph or other communication with La Paz, or any other place, and under the most favourable conditions the capital was two-and-a-half months' journey distant.

The arrival of a new Governor of the Beni gave me the chance to secure some of the money owing to me, by obtaining official drafts on several business houses. He was an effeminate person, very susceptible to flattery, extraordinarily stupid, and he spent most of his time adorning himself. It was ludicrous to see him busily engaged in a room open to public view, decorating his bed and other furnishings with little bows of pink ribbon for the benefit of an unattractive Indian woman with whom he had become enamoured in the hour of landing. As a 'new broom' he was anxious to make a good impression, and knowing that before long his expenditure would be drastically curbed I took advantage of it and acted while there was yet time. His pomposity was overpowering, for he had once been a consul; and he was ever eager to point out that his present position was a come-down for him, fruit of the resentment his ability had created in high places.

When the *surusus* blew Riberalta could be bitterly cold, and one morning there was actually a thin film of ice on the puddles of the so-called roads. On these occasions it rained for three or four days without stopping, and no one possessed enough clothing to keep out the cold. The sudden drop in temperature carried off the cotton-clad Indian *peons* freely, and at this season, too, wakes with drink and dancing were a feature. Among the hordes of the diseased the death roll was staggering, and one by one the earth-eaters vanished!

The labourers and their families were frequently victims of a strange disease which led to an irresistible craving to eat earth. Possibly the underlying cause was an intestinal parasite—earth may have served to deaden internal irritation. At any rate, a swelling of the body and subsequent death was the result. The Indians knew of only one remedy—dog's excrement—but I never heard of anyone recovering. Europeans have been known to suffer from it, but it was usually most prevalent amongst children, whose emaciated limbs and horribly distended stomachs presaged their fate. An Austrian suffering from this strange disease came down the Beni from Reyes. Like a living skeleton, except for his grossly swollen stomach, he was a revolting sight, and in a short time he was dead.

Outside the few offices, no one in Riberalta had any idea of the time of day, for watches were not in general use. A committee of townspeople approached me with the request that I erect a public sundial, and partly for a change of occupation, partly to repay hospitality, I agreed to do so if the necessary materials were supplied. When finally completed and set up in the middle of the square, it was unveiled with pomp and ceremony, a wonderful occasion for speech-making and unbridled drinking. Suggestions were made that a shelter be erected over it to protect it from the weather!

That same night I saw a crowd gathered about the sundial, and crept over to see what they were doing.

"It's a fraud!" muttered a voice. A match flickered. "See! It doesn't tell the time at all. Lend me another match, someone, and let's have another try—or, better still, bring a candle."

"Foreign exploitation!" grumbled another. "That's what it is—British imperialism!"

"No," said a third voice, "it's all right, because this afternoon I saw the time by it."

Sides were taken for and against it, and argument waxed hot. So noisy was it, in fact, that a police official came over to see what the trouble was.

"Fools!" he snapped, on being told. "Don't you know you've got to wait for the moon to come up before you can tell the time by it?"

Three days later the sundial was found completely destroyed. 'Pros' accused the 'Antis' of the act of sabotage; but my own suspicions rested on a dissolute French employee of a local firm who had previously been offered £50 to construct one and couldn't.

The same day I made my first attempt to get away from Riberalta, taking passage for Rurenabaque on a small boat known as a *Monteria*. In spite of my protests, the owner insisted on grossly overloading it, and half a mile upstream it touched a sandbank, capsized, and very nearly drowned the lot of us. The owner salvaged his craft, but refused to go on, and we were forced to return to Riberalta, where I took up my old quarters for another three weeks, despairing of ever being able to leave the detestable place. Riberalta seemed to be playing cat and mouse with me, letting me believe freedom was mine, only to drag me back once more. Again and again the chance of escape would come, only to vanish and leave me more depressed than ever. It was a prison without bars, but no less a prison for that. I could imagine the voice of the place murmuring: "You have come—you will stay—for ever! You may escape—a little way—but my spell is upon you, and return you must—always—to live out your little life here—to die here!"

Some people openly accused the Frenchman of destroying the town's sundial, and it became almost an international problem. Sides were taken; violent anti-French and anti-British demonstrations took place; the local press—a weekly sheet of semi-political trash—plunged into the fray, and published editorials on the subject in the most pompous language. The French Vice-Consul gave a banquet, pointedly excluding all the English and their partisans. This worried me little, but the other English residents felt badly about it, and retaliated with a rival banquet of a highly patriotic character on the following night.

It lasted, I remember, well beyond midnight, and had become musical and maudlin when the oil lamps, in their zareba of fluttering insects, began to show signs of exhaustion. As they flickered and dulled there suddenly came the cry "Cobra!" There was pandemonium at once, and just before the lights went out altogether the shape of the reptile was seen in a corner. Some climbed on chairs, others on tables. A few bold spirits grasped sticks and fiercely attacked the serpent. It leapt and twisted beneath their blows, and then everything was plunged in darkness.

Shouts of advice came from outside, where half the town had gathered. From inside came repeated cries for lights—more lights—quick! The snake might be anywhere. Already one or two revellers were declaring that it had bitten them. At last there came lights, the darkness was dispelled, and the snake turned out to be—you've guessed it—a rope!

In the light of the following morning the faces of the perfidious French and their partisans were knowingly jubilant, but Albion was not to be outdone, and next day, when the Frenchman and several of his supporters had gathered on board the launch *Campa*, bound down river to Esperanza, a red and black snake suddenly appeared on the main deck. A real snake this—not a rope's end!

I have no idea what kind of a snake it was. Possibly it was a harmless coral snake; but at all events there was an immediate stampede over the two rickety planks serving as gangway, and somehow in the struggle the Frenchman was shouldered off into the river. As he came to the surface there was a yell of warning—" 'Ware *piraña*!"—and he screamed with terror as he made for the bank with arms flying like paddlewheels. A group of onlookers pulled him out, but strangely enough he fell back time and time again into the water, crying that the *pirañas* were biting the flesh from his legs! Half drowned, and covered from head to foot with mud, he was at last extracted and carried sobbing to his hut.

The stars must have favoured international friction at this time, for a night or two later a battle royal took place. Bumpus, an Englishman, was entertaining a Peruvian at his house, and celebrating July 28—Peru's national *fiesta*—with beer, most expensive of all local drinks. There were several guests, among them a young Bolivian officer named Zamudio.

At the height of the revels there came demanding admittance a clerk of the Delegation, a useless, foppish creature, who was promptly told to take himself off. Surprisingly enough, he refused to go, and became so belligerent that a fight started, in which he was struck down. His shouts brought a Major, a Captain, and about thirty soldiers from Willis's refreshment saloon close by, and they set on Bumpus—and the Peruvian, who sided with his host. The Major ordered his soldiers to seize Bumpus, who at once responded by punching the Major on the nose. The police arrived, saw a fight was in progress, and stood by to watch with interest. Bottles, chairs, filth of all sorts, flew through the air. Curses and yells brought up more spectators, and betting began. Neither Bumpus nor anyone else knew anything of boxing, and most of the fighting consisted of slapping, swinging of arms, and especially kicking—for, as usual, the air was full of feet. The disorder was quelled only when a portly Colonel appeared on the scene and arrested the Major and Captain. I heard later that a Sergeant and seven men received two hundred lashes each in the morning—a gross miscarriage of justice, as they were only obeying orders.

Perhaps the marked increase in the consumption of alcohol was leading up to the celebrations on August 4, Bolivia's national *fiesta*. Five days of uninterrupted drunkenness ended with military sports held in the *plaza*, where every citizen came to watch, equipped with bottles, glasses, and even kerosene tins full of liquor.

Except for one game, known as the *Rompecabezas* (Head Breaker), the sport was not very amusing, but this one, difficult even for sober folk, was incredibly funny when the competitors were full of *kachasa*. The *Rompecabezas* consisted of a box of triangular section, two yards long, and free to rotate axially on an iron bar set on two posts about seven feet apart. On top of one post was a little seat, and on the other a small flag. The idea was to secure the flag by crossing over the top of the box. Unless a perfect balance was sustained the box turned, and down fell the player.

By this time, desperate at the delays in getting away from Riberalta, I brought pressure to bear on the *Delegado*, or Governor, by hinting of 'official representations', and so on. This frightened him so badly that a *batelón* was produced and placed at the disposal of myself, an employee of the Customs, and the portly Colonel, all of us bound for La Paz. Dan should have come with me, but was in jail at the instance of Willis —of all people—for debts in respect of liquor supplied him. The English came down to see me off, and the garrison turned out for the Colonel, so we put out from shore in a haze of blue smoke from their rifles, and their shouts of farewell kept up till we were out of earshot.

The Colonel was not an ideal travelling companion. He was a half-caste Indian, whose Spanish side was confined mostly to his name, and his only luggage consisted of an antique chamber pot[1] and a dilapidated imitation-leather suitcase. This last was left behind on the beach, and its loss not discovered till we were at a *barraca* twenty-five miles up river, where we had to wait while a canoe went back to fetch it. The Colonel then settled himself in the 'cabin' astern, and there he stayed for the rest of the voyage—forty-five days.

The Customs man was quite a good fellow, but neither he nor the Colonel had brought any food, and consequently relied on my stores, consisting of Quaker oats, a few sacks of hard bread, and some tins of sardines. The Quaker oats did not interest them, but the rest lasted only about ten days, after which they hung round the cooking-pots of the crew, without much success. During the whole voyage I never saw the Colonel wash himself, and the chamber pot was used, amongst other things, for containing food. He was surly, unsavoury, and sickly; and, as he soon broke out in boils all over his body, his presence in the shelter we were obliged to share with him was disgusting. He grumbled at being forced to embark with undue haste, he groused about the lack of variety in my provisions, and both he and the Customs man expectorated constantly, inboard and outboard. In the body of the boat sat a

[1] Ubiquitous possession! This, and the alarm clock, accompany their *Mestizo* owners everywhere.—ED.

Mestiza woman, who amused herself by catching sandflies and *mariguis*, and eating them—the practice of Indians whether civilized or wild. The voyage was one I should not like to repeat.

On the second day we met a *batelón* bound for Riberalta. Its owner, a German named Hesse, immediately recognized in our crew his own *peons*, impressed by the Delegation. He stormed at us and accused us of robbing him, but there was nothing he could do about it, and our pilot merely roared with laughter at him.

At Concepción *barraca* I managed to procure some more food from the wife of the manager, including—a rarity in these parts—English preserves. They were a rarity because British manufacturers resolutely refused to use labels printed in Spanish, and consequently their products were not bought because no one knew what they were.

On the third day out from Concepción a *surusu* caught us and slowed our progress. The air grew bitterly cold; the river was lashed by the wind into fine spindrift till it looked like the ocean in a squall. Forest life lay low, and a sense of gloomy desolation oppressed us. By the time we reached Santo Domingo the sun was out again, and our gloom lifted when Señor Arautz, the manager, loaded the *batelón* with bananas, oranges, and other fresh food.

"I'm sorry for you, having the Colonel aboard," he said, within plain earshot of the subject of his remark. "I know the little so-and-so, and I don't envy you!"

The *batelón* soon caused us anxiety, for its timbers were rotten. The crew's fears were substantiated when on the sixteenth day a snag pierced the bottom, knocking over the woman, who nearly choked on a mouthful of flies. We should have sunk, but somehow the snag was chopped off with an axe, a piece of packing-case was nailed over the hole, and two bailers were appointed to keep down the inpouring water. Half an hour later another and larger tree trunk came through the patch, proving that if lightning never strikes twice in the same place, snags do! Again it was axed, and then all the available clothing belonging to the crew was stuffed into the gaping hole, and a man ordered to sit on it until by good fortune we managed to reach the small *barraca* of Los Angeles. As no one else appeared to be capable of repairing the damage, I secured a length of plank, had the *batelón* hauled out high and dry, and fixed boards inside and out, fastening them with long iron nails and caulking the seams well with *estopa*. It served us for the rest of the voyage, but there were many alarms from the grindings and gratings along the bottom, which terrified the Colonel. He was grateful to me for doing the repairs, all the same—so grateful that on the following day he filched a leg of wild turkey from the crew's cookpot and, after gnawing the best of the meat off it, offered me the rest with a bow.

By the time we reached Cavinas, at the mouth of the Madidi, I was desperately eager to escape from my two cabin mates, whose filthy habits and unclean persons sickened me. The inefficient crew and negligent captain made the journey so intolerable that I tried to procure mules from the Padres of the Mission so as to get overland to Rurena-baque. Alas!—all their beasts were in use elsewhere. There was nothing for it but to continue to put up with the *batelón*—and it was now worse than ever, for the rawhide covering of the cabin's floor had been thoroughly soaked, and the blazing sun drew from it a smell so powerful that it eclipsed even that of the Colonel.

The dry season was at its height, and the river so low that the forests of snags made progress exceedingly difficult. The Colonel had been given a pet monkey at one of the *barracas* we passed. It shared his utensil and added to the filth in the cabin, but he would not hear of putting it outside. Then I discovered that my kettle was being used by both the Colonel and the Customs man, not for boiling water, but for the purpose of drinking from the spout. That upset me; not that I would have refused had they asked my permission—in spite of the Colonel's boils—but they had not even had the courtesy to do that.

With the warmer weather clouds of *mariguis* came back. One advantage of a *surusu* was that it freed us temporarily from the plague of insects; but these, on returning, made up for lost time and nearly drove us mad —all but our lady passenger, who found them a welcome addition to her diet. Everything went wrong. During a violent thunderstorm the monkey fell overboard, while his master shrieked in despair. Before the little creature could be rescued we had chased it a mile down stream, bumping snag after snag in the most reckless manner. Just as the storm was passing there came a report like the discharge of a field gun, and a thunderbolt fell into the river not a hundred yards away, with a mar-vellous display of red, yellow and blue fire. The crew were scared to death, and they had to be fed with alcohol before they were fit to proceed up river again.

No crew will work without alcohol. It drives them as petrol drives an automobile, and when the supply gives out they stop work and refuse to move. Our 'fuel' was kept in a four-gallon can in the cabin— and the smell of it in my kettle suggested that the Colonel was helping himself. I found that we had only just enough to finish the voyage if the daily mileage was increased from the usual crawl to normal speed. I told the captain and suggested that he had better get more work out of his men. He promptly blamed the pilot for the delays.

"That's a lie!" retorted the pilot. "If you weren't always drunk you'd be able to handle your job better!"

A fight should have been the outcome of this, but they didn't come to blows. They had instead a savage battle of abuse, in which the bitterest insult was the epithet '*Indio*', and it ended by one demanding of the

other, "Go on—hit me!" and the retort, "No, no—you hit me!" The
crew seemed likely to join in; the *batelón* drifted down stream without
control, and so the argument had to be suppressed by higher authority.
Shortly afterwards a *batelón* from Riberalta passed us as though we
were standing still, and derisive remarks from the pilot nearly precipitated
the row all over again.

The next mishap was the disablement of one of the crew. In springing
ashore to collect turtles' eggs he stepped on a stingray, which gashed
his foot badly. Perhaps complications were prevented by exploding
gunpowder over the wound—a drastic cure—but for the rest of the
voyage the victim groaned on the floor of the boat. Another man had
two of his fingers snapped off by a *piraña* while washing his hands in the
river after skinning a monkey.

Turtles' eggs were plentiful—so plentiful that the bottom of the
batelón was filled with them for sale in Rurenabaque; but long before
we arrived there careless feet had crushed them into a mess and one
more smell was added to the general stench. To add yet another the
Colonel brought aboard some *chalona*, or dried mutton. Though it was
in an advanced state of putrefaction and swarming with maggots, its
owner prized it highly. For me, it made the cabin unbearable at last, and
I moved my hammock outside, mosquitoes or not.

Fever and influenza broke out aboard, putting nine of the crew out
of action. Short-handed, we struggled on to Santa Teresa, four days
below Rurenabaque, tying up there to await the men's recovery. What
a pleasure it was to go ashore—to escape from the stench of that boat—
to breathe clean air again in the *barraca* of my host!

He gave me more details of the Swiss-German expedition against
the Guarayos in the Madidi, corroborating the story of the atrocities
already related to me. One young girl escaped to the edge of the river
and was there wounded by a bullet. She knelt down at the water's edge
to bathe her face and head, and in that position was ruthlessly butchered.
With the bravery of desperation one of the Guarayos attacked the
expedition single-handed with bow and arrows, but was soon shot
down. I came to know these Indians later; and the abominable way they
were treated by these cowardly brutes filled me with burning indigna-
tion, as it did every decent Bolivian and foreigner in the country. The
perpetrators of the outrage were never punished, I'm sorry to say.

Nothing would induce me to repeat that forty-five days' voyage. At
the time it seemed endless. The 'hoodoo' of Riberalta was not to be
shaken off even by distance. I could almost hear the *Delegado's* farewell
words—vaguely disquieting: "I'm sorry you're leaving us, Major. Your
work has been most valuable to Riberalta. Pity you're not a permanent
prisoner!"

But eventually the day came when it was all over—nothing but a grim memory. On September 24 we arrived at Rurenabaque, where my *Gringo* friends gave me a warm welcome, and the hotel seemed to supply the amenities of a city.

"So you have been among the savages," roared Don Pacifico, the manager. "I know the savages too. I have killed no less than one hundred and thirty in my time—single-handed!" He was a huge fat man, whose little legs could scarcely support his vast weight, and the idea of his killing anyone was ludicrous.

Harvey, the gunman, was a real killer, but no talker. It was only after many drinks that he became at all informative, and when he did it was worth while listening. This silent, red-bearded man was no boaster, nor the man to show off his extraordinary prowess with the six-shooter without good cause. As a genuine Western bandit in earlier days, his life had depended on speed in drawing and sure aim. Like all those brought up before the days of double-action revolvers, he 'fanned' his Smith and Wesson, which means that instead of cocking the weapon and pulling the trigger for each shot, he held the trigger back and worked the hammer at lightning speed with the palm of the other hand. With a price on his head, he dodged the Texas Rangers, and escaped south of the border, blasting his way through Mexico in a haze of gunsmoke, down the Isthmus, and into South America. He knew every mining camp on the West Coast, and his exploits would fill a book.

On one occasion, after holding up a large mining company in a neighbouring republic, Harvey was pursued by a regiment of soldiers. Leading them into a favourable spot, he suddenly turned on them gun in hand and had them 'reaching for the sky' before a rifle could be raised. He took their weapons and tossed them in the river, then dismissed them with a few lusty kicks. Another time he was cornered by twenty soldiers. He shot one down, picked off another who showed his head over a bush, and the rest threw down their rifles and fled.

There was a reward of £1,000 for his capture, dead or alive, in the last country he was in; but Bolivia had no extradition law, and here he was safe. On his way towards the frontier he came to a barricade across the trail with six soldiers behind it, their rifles at the 'ready'. An officer ordered him to surrender, but his reply was a burst of fire. As the officer fell Harvey rushed the barricade with roaring gun. Another soldier fell, and the rest promptly raised their hands.

"I sure was ashamed," he confided to me, "when I 'frisked' them and found that they hadn't so much as a single shell for their rifles. Their cartridge pouches were stuffed with paper!"

Some *callapos* came in from Mapiri, and were split up into rafts for the return, one being procured for me without loss of time. The cheerful crowd at Rurenabaque gave me the usual boisterous send-off, and my crew of three poled the *balsa* away with a fine turn of speed. Not only had I promised them £1 each for a quick voyage, but there were sardines, sugar and unlimited alcohol for them. They earned them, too, by making excellent time in poling, and by towing the craft through the rapids up to their waists in water—a labour I shared with them. We reached Huanay in the record time of four days and a half.

My host, Señor Salamón, had a profound sense of the importance of his position as *Corregidor* of Huanay, and was inclined to offer liquor on the least excuse. It was a gesture of friendliness, but how could he know of my distaste for the stuff? He was garrulous as well as hospitable; he and his charming wife could not have done more for me.

An epicure, Señor Salamón ignored the inflated cost of ducks to provide one for the table every day. For some days before being slaughtered the unfortunate birds were fed on meal soaked in alcohol, and then, while blissfully drunk were plied with the pure liquor, which precipitated what my host called a glorious death. He maintained that this procedure improved the flavour of the meat. I could not agree—but perhaps my appetite was dulled by my recollection of the Colonel's *chalona* and the turtles' eggs!

Here at the mouth of the Tipuani River everyone appeared to be well-to-do; the place had an air of prosperity that impressed me all the more after my long sojourn on the remote frontier. Gold was plentiful. Every time the Tipuani flooded, which was often, it brought down gold and spread it over the sandbank at Huanay, where everyone turned out with pans. No one, however, made a fortune. The river was and still is full of gold, but sudden floods prevent bedrock being exposed long enough to allow access to the metal. As far north as the Santo Domingo mine on the Inambari River, and even beyond, the whole country is full of gold, but prospecting is a dangerous business. I heard of four men who panned a rich stream beyond Santo Domingo. At first they kept careful watch owing to the presence of Indians, but as time went on and nothing happened they relaxed their vigilance. Early one morning the attack came. Three were killed, and the fourth managed to escape badly wounded, leaving behind all the hard-won gold.

There was interesting news of Challana. Ex-Captain Velarde, the Chief, had escaped to La Paz after accepting an offer of £5,000 from a syndicate for the Challana district. When the population got wind of the transaction they cried for the blood of the traitor who had sold them out, but by then he was beyond their reach. Everyone in Huanay knew him. For six years he had been Chief, amassing a tidy fortune during his term of office.

The arrival of a mule train from Sorata raised my hopes of an early departure. They fell when the Colonel arrived from Rurenabaque, for I feared he would officially requisition the animals. I 'shot a line' to the *arriero*. His mules would be commandeered, I told him, and he would get no recompense. Far better hire them to me. I could pay him half in advance.

"Let us say nothing, then, *señor*, but get on our way before anyone finds out that we intend to leave. All will be ready by dawn tomorrow."

They were small animals, and I weighed almost two hundred pounds, but it is amazing what these mules can do. I was noticeably softened by being cooped up for so long on the *batelón*, and it took several days to get back into shape. After two days of mountaineering on the appalling trails, struggling up to vast heights and then slithering down precipitous descents, we came to San José on the Mapiri trail. Here I stayed with Señor Peñaloza, son of an Englishman who had changed his name. He himself looked a Spaniard and spoke no English, but his son had fair hair and blue eyes.

Tales of atrocities persisted even as far out as San José. One concerned a German who worked a rubber estate some years ago near Mapiri. He was a wholesale murderer. Any rubber picker considered useless he shot, giving his victim the privilege of drinking anything he liked before being executed. With lavish promises as bait, he lured 300 *peons* from the Arequipa district of Perus, fed them on watery soup and a cup of coffee each morning, and sent them into the forest to get rubber. They knew nothing of the work, and went sick almost to a man. Yet he would not release them; those who were sickest he shot—forty or fifty of them. The others managed to escape, some to the forest, some to Apolo, from whence they ultimately got back to Peru. This German was charged with the atrocities, yet he was not punished. He surrounded himself with a bodyguard of specially picked *mozos* and piled up a fortune from the work of his semi-starved labourers. I am glad to say that he was eventually shot dead by a vengeful Indian who, biding his time, got him at a moment when the guard's vigilance was relaxed.

At the height of the rubber and gold booms at Mapiri an amateur banker set himself up in business there. Somehow he inspired general confidence, being highly respected as a civilizing influence—a beacon of respectability shining in the darkness of lawlessness. Then he vanished, with 20,000 *Bolivianos* (£1,600), and was never seen again.

How civilized these places seemed on the journey back from the forest! Real bread was the food of the gods; properly cooked meals, served on plates and eaten with knife and fork, were a glorious dream come true. The trip between *Montaña* and *Altiplano*, which fifteen months ago had seemed so hard, was now a pleasure jaunt. True, I felt the cold of the high altitudes keenly, but no more so than the bone-chilling *surusus* of the forests. Sorata with its real houses was like a great city, and La Paz almost terrifying in its amenities and luxuries. On October 17 a bearded ruffian, burned almost black by the hot sun of the tropics and the glare of the snows, came jogging down into the steep streets of the capital on a frisky mule which shied and capered at sight of the carriages and tram-cars. People stopped to point and stare, accustomed though they were to the sight of men from the wilds. A shave, a good dinner, a deep sleep between real sheets, and civilized clothing next morning, transformed me from a savage into a white man again.

I handed over to the President, General Montes, the maps and reports, and was invited to undertake the frontier delimitation with Brazil on the Rio Paraguay. The chance of further exploration was attractive—for this would take me into unknown country—but it would depend on permission from London to continue my services. If the British authorities agreed, I said I would be delighted.

"I have a balance of £800 belonging to the Government, *mi General*," I said. "Shall I hand it over to the Treasury?"

"Please do nothing of the sort," he replied. "It would be inconvenient to return the money now. Do me the favour of accepting half, and credit the other half to the Commission in the Paraguay."

I had forgotten the troubles over money at the start of the expedition to the Beni, and the Government expressed pleasure at the quick completion of the work. Ministers and other responsible officials in La Paz treated me with the greatest courtesy. If I needed cash, the President gave me a note to the Treasury, the Treasury handed me a cheque, and the bank paid me over the counter, all within an hour. I did my best to reciprocate their considerate treatment by preventing all the frontier troubles I could as soon as I got under way with my new assignment. When I think of the months of haggling with an English pay-office over a few shillings or some paltry claim for travelling expenses, I remember Bolivia. My own countrymen are fond of referring to Latin America as 'the Land of *Mañana*'; but with the dilatory officialdom of British Government departments the favourite phrase is 'Next week'!

Ahead of me was the glorious prospect of home. For the present I was satiated with the wild, and my mind was full of the coming journey to the coast; of the lazy sea voyage, and the sight of England, with its funny little trees, neat fields, and fairy-tale villages; of my wife, the four-year-old Jack, and the latest arrival, Brian. I wanted to forget atrocities, to put slavery, murder and horrible disease behind me, and to look again at respectable old ladies whose ideas of vice ended with the indiscretions of so-and-so's housemaid. I wanted to listen to the every-day chit-chat of the village parson, discuss the uncertainties of the weather with the yokels, pick up the daily paper on my breakfast-plate. I wanted, in short, to be just 'ordinary'. To dig in the garden, to tuck up the kids after a bedtime story, to settle down by the fire, with my wife beside me busy at her mending—those were the things I yearned for most. It would be agreeable to me to return and carry out another boundary survey, but if my own Government refused to grant an extension of my services—well, perhaps it wouldn't be so bad after all.

I spent Christmas at home. The well-behaved English winter passed swiftly and evenly, as though South America had never been. Yet deep down inside me a tiny voice was calling. At first scarcely audible, it persisted until I could no longer ignore it. It was the voice of the wild places, and I knew that it was now part of me for ever.

We were standing in the garden at Dawlish Warren on a mild January afternoon, almost spring-like but for the naked trees and black hedgerows. Beyond the sand dunes the restless sea murmured drowsily—the only sound except the occasional rumble of a passing train. Then came another sound. Someone was playing a gramophone in a neighbouring house, and had opened the window to take advantage of the mild air. The record being played was *Estudiantina*.

I was swept back into the forests of the Acre. Before me was the slow-moving river like molten gold in the glow of sunset. The menacing dark-green walls of the forest closed in to imprison me, and I knew that 600 miles of cruel wilderness lay between me and civilization. I was where the only law recognized was that of the whip and the gun, and the only escape the oblivion of drunkenness. A nostalgic pang shot through me. Inexplicably—amazingly—I knew I loved that hell. Its fiendish grasp had captured me, and I wanted to see it again.

On March 6, 1908, I boarded the *Avon* at Southampton bound for Buenos Aires, and was joined on board by Mr. Fisher, my new assistant. My wife and Jack had come to see me off, and when the shore bell rang part of my heart went with them down the gangway to the pier. The agony of another parting was bitter—but something was pulling me—pulling me persistently, irresistibly, far away to westwards.

CHAPTER X

POISONED HELL

A T least once in every man's lifetime death looks him straight in the
eyes—and passes on. In forest travel it is never far off. It shows itself in
many aspects, most of them horrible, but some apparently so innocuous
that they scarcely win attention, though none the less deadly for that.
Time and time again the concatenation of events leads up to the very edge
of disaster, and halts there. The flight of an arrow—an inch of space—a
moment of time—on such insignificant details does fate hang. I can recall
a number of narrow escapes during the Beni, Acre and Abuna journeys.
Each time it could have been death, horrible because sudden and violent
—to our way of thinking, merciless. Yet sudden death, in spite of its
moment of terror and agony, is quickly over, and if we regarded these
matters in a reasonable way it would be considered merciful. Certainly it
is so when compared with a lingering death from starvation. This is
why I consider that never was death so close as in 1908, when we were
caught in the poisoned hell of the River Verde, in Eastern Bolivia.

The first time I saw the big Argentine capital Buenos Aires—
the Paris of South America—it failed to impress me greatly, in spite of
its magnificent shops and avenues. There was an aura of vice about the
place. It reeked of wealth, but the architecture was flamboyant—lacking
in good taste. The noisy streets were clean but narrow, badly laid, and,
apart from the main arteries, congested by horse traffic. It was hardly
improved by the frontage on the estuary of La Plata, and by the flat,
uninteresting country in its environs. The women, following French

modes closely, dressed well; and in no other South American city had I
seen such a high standard of feminine beauty. The vaunted Jockey Club
left me cold. It struck me as a pity that so much money had been lavished
on decorations with so tawdry a result. The quality of the food was
mediocre, in spite of the inflated price of everything.

My first impressions might have been more favourable had the
baggage suffered less in being brought off the ship. Everything was
flung on a long chute to arrive with a crash on the stone wharf. Packing-cases of delicate instruments landed with a sickening impact, despite
my pleas for more care. Every passenger's baggage suffered in the same
way. Elegant hat-boxes were flattened under steel cases; obese trunks
burst their fastenings and vomited feminine garments, which were at
once seized and laughingly displayed by stevedores and porters. I saw one
lady in tears at the wreckage of her wardrobe.

When the tangle of boxes and loose property was sorted out and
removed to the *Resguardo*, it took only the raising of a hat and a polite
word to the Customs officers to get it cleared by a wave of the hand and
a mystic sign made with indelible chalk. Italian brigands then rushed for
it, carried it off, and eventually delivered it to an hotel whose minimum
charge was high enough to threaten the resources of an ambassador!

Why is it that the British Admiralty sends the meanest of its vessels on
goodwill visits to Latin-American republics? They merely provoke
amusement. It is hard to establish an impression of naval superiority
when the visiting ship is dwarfed by the units of the national navy, or
when a month or two afterwards there comes a squadron of United
States capital ships, a crack Italian cruiser, or a German dreadnought.
When we arrived in Buenos Aires H.M.S. *Dwarf* was in port, a tiny
gunboat of no importance. The powers who direct these matters apparently fail to comprehend the fact that our national prestige in these
countries depends entirely on how we impress them, and the presence of
such insignificant warships does more harm than good. The embarrassed
British residents often have a hard task on their hands living it down![1]
There was much joking about *Dwarf*, and more than a few references to
the Falkland Islands—the 'Malvinas', as they call them—Argentina's pet
claim against 'British Imperialism'.

We had brought with us this time a complete set of instruments for
the work, plenty of stores, accessories of many kinds, and champagne for
entertainment purposes. I had, moreover, £1,000 in gold, as a first instal-
ment under the terms of the Government Commission. After two weeks
of lotus-eating in Buenos Aires, we embarked on a river steamer for
Asunción, capital of Paraguay.

[1] The epic of *Ajax* and *Exeter* in the River Plate action dispelled the unfortunate impressions prior to World War II of the apparent superiority of Italian and German warships; and
it is to be hoped that never again will Great Britain fall into the error mentioned above.—Ed.

The Mihanovitch Line ran good, seldom overcrowded steamers. Its vessels ran up and down to Asunción day and night, fair weather or foul, and nothing was allowed to upset the schedule—not even revolution. When the ships were on the move their pilots never slept. They knew the channels by instinct, for no indications were visible, and could tell you the exact nature of the riverbed wherever they happened to be, never confused by the ever-changing sandbanks and seldom grounding their vessels. On arrival in port they slept for forty-eight hours or more, being able in some way to store up sleep by long practice. Their pay was between £30 and £40 a month—not much, considering the work.

At Rosario the River Paraná widens out into an extensive basin, and in the port lay sixty steamers and numerous sailing vessels. This city of 150,000 people does extensive trade, having an active industry, and being surrounded by richly cultivated land. The villas of the wealthy on the outskirts of the town tell of the fortunes to be made.

In four days we were in Asunción, city of chronic revolutions. The walls were pockmarked by bullets; shells from a field gun of ancient pattern had knocked the corner off a building in the main street, and the owner evidently did not consider it worth while repairing. It was a city of Indians and half-breeds, speaking Guarani, the language of 'warriors'. They called themselves warriors with some reason, for they proved it many a time in the war against Brazil, which decimated the male population of Paraguay. Perhaps this explains why the women of Asunción are more forward than elsewhere.

Memories of the war with Brazil are still very much alive, and there is a deep-seated hatred smouldering under the surface, like the feeling of Peru towards Chile.[1] The mulatto soldiers of Brazil and the Guaranis of Paraguay were both capable of atrocities when discipline was loosened. A favourite game was to 'feed the little fishes'. A prisoner of war was tied to a stake about waist-deep in the river and a slight gash cut in his stomach. The *pirañas*, swarming in the Paraguay and its tributaries, did the rest.

At Asunción we were once more close to unexplored South America, for the Chaco is by no means thoroughly known, nor are all its Indians acquainted with civilization. One village of Jesuit origin has been captured, church and all, by Indians, who rigorously exclude civilized men. Exploration would be unattractive in such flat and dry country, I imagine, though on account of the droughts in winter and the floods in summer it would not be easy.

The Chaco Indians still preserve traditions of the white men in armour, whose breasts their arrows were unable to pierce; and the cross is used as a symbol from antiquity—not the Christian, but the Buddhist

[1] All this has vanished now, and the spirit of International Co-operation is growing steadily in South America.—ED.

cross (according to the Japanese Minister in Asunción). In Paraguay there is the tradition of descent from some great race which once colonized the country; but this is not peculiar to them alone, for it is found amongst all the tribes of Tupi origin.

A crowded and dirty paddle-steamer called *Fortuna* took us up the Paraguay River, through country that almost to the foot of the Matto Grosso Plateau seemed flat and uninteresting from the ship. Here and there the Chaco Indians—Lenguas and Chamacocos—had emerged from their haunts to see the world, and work. They seemed harmless enough, but could on occasions be troublesome in their own territories.

In the Paraguay River there is a freshwater shark, huge but toothless, said to attack men and swallow them if it gets a chance. They talk here of another river monster—fish or beaver—which can in a single night tear out a huge section of river bank. The Indians report the tracks of some gigantic animal in the swamps bordering the river, but allege that it has never been seen. The shark exists beyond doubt; as for the other monsters—well, there are queer things yet to be disclosed in this continent of mystery, and if strange, unclassified insects, reptiles and small mammals can still exist there, mightn't there be a few giant monsters, remnants of an extinct species, still living out their lives in the security of the vast unexplored swamp areas? In the Madidi, in Bolivia, enormous tracks have been found, and Indians there talk of a huge creature descried at times half submerged in the swamps.

Mr. Cecil Gosling, who in 1908 was British Consul in Asunción—and first Minister in La Paz after the restoration of diplomatic relations with Bolivia—showed me a queer insect of a greeny-grey colour, rather locust-like in appearance. Its underwings had peacock markings, and the head and thorax were an exact reproduction of a crocodile's! The insect's hideous aspect may have served to frighten would-be aggressors.

I was told of a cave near Villa Rica, in the Alto Paraná, where curious drawings and inscriptions in an unknown language are to be seen. It started me on a train of thought in which scraps of information and stories of ancient traditions picked up from the Indians, rubber pickers, and wandering white men seemed to fit together, forming a pattern with a growing meaning. Could it be, I pondered, that besides the Incas there were other ancient civilizations in this continent—that the Incas themselves sprang from a greater, more widely spread race whose traces, at present unrecognized, might yet be found here and there? What about Tiahuanaco, Ollantaytambo and Sacsahuaman? Those places were not of Inca construction. According to the experts, they existed when the Incas first conquered Peru. Was it possible that in the unknown heart of South America there still lived descendants of the old races? Why not? . . .

The seed had entered. The subconscious mind fertilized it with a legend here and a tale there, till, all unknown to me, its roots were firm. At that time I was fully occupied by the exigencies of the frontier work, and not until that was almost completed did I suddenly discover that the seedling of archæological curiosity had grown and burst into flower.

On the Brazil-Paraguay border grows a plant known in Guarani as *Caa-he-eh*. It is about eighteen inches high, with small aromatic leaves which are several times sweeter than ordinary sugar, and would be worth while investigating. There is another called *Ibira-gjukych*, also a small plant, with leaves that are salty. The convenience of these to settlers in the region may be imagined.

The perfectly contoured columns of mosquitoes are a curious feature of the Paraguay River. A dense, whirling mass of insects anything from thirty to sixty feet in height rises above each bank. At sundown these columns break up, and for an hour make life miserable for everyone in the vicinity. It is during this hour that mosquitoes are at their worst—in other parts of the interior it is the same—but at night, though you are never free from their attentions, their attacks are far milder.

Islands of hills emerging abruptly from the swamps indicated the proximity of Corumba, the Brazilian river port that was our destination. For six months in the year the whole region is one huge lake, except for a few places where the banks are a yard or two above high-water level. Fifteen hundred miles up from the estuary of La Plata the surface of the river in the wet season is less than four hundred feet above mean sea level. That will give you an idea how flat this country is!

The Brazilian Boundary Commission met us on board with much ceremony. The Commander of the garrison was with them, and champagne was produced in the ship's saloon. The town had about twelve hundred soldiers and a small naval dockyard. Some naval officers joined the party, exceedingly nice fellows all of them—quite the pick of Brazil, in fact. The town itself was attractive. There were good hotels, shops, and paved streets, and social life here was a feature of the place. We quickly regretted our lack of respectable clothing, for in our working kit, which was all we had with us, we felt completely out of place. Our Bolivian secretary was to blame. In his nationalistic zeal he had described the town to us as a very backward frontier settlement. I had come expecting something like Rurenabaque or Riberalta, but found instead a well-developed city with smartly dressed people.

The low, swampy country in which Corumba is situated is a paradise for snakes. Anacondas are common. Big ones—luckily rare—were known to seize cattle at times, and even to pick men out of canoes at night. Their usual length was from fifteen to thirty feet, but the really big ones reached quite twice the size—and even more. Their weird cries could be heard at night, which is their normal feeding-time. Brazilians insist that even the poisonous snakes here imitate the cries of birds and small animals to decoy their prey. The people of the district generally carry a small bag of bichloride of mercury in the belief that it keeps snakes at a distance, and every village has a supply of snake serum and syringes ready for instant use.

There was talk of White Indians again.

"I know a man here who has met one," said the British Consul. "They are very savage, and have the reputation of coming out only at night. They're known as 'Bats' for that reason."

"Where do they live?" I asked.

"Oh, somewhere up in the region of the lost Martirios goldmines, north or north-west of Diamantino. Nobody knows quite where they are. Matto Grosso is mostly unknown country. The hilly regions in the north have never been entered, to anyone's knowledge, though many expeditions have gone there, only to be lost. It's bad country all right. Mark my words—it'll never be explored on foot, however big and well-equipped the expeditions. Possibly, in a hundred years' time, flying machines will do it—who knows?"

His words had a significance for me that made them unforgettable.

There is no need to describe a frontier survey. One is much the same as another, and what make it interesting are the incidental happenings, not the tedious routine of the work itself. My predecessor was no expert, and when the Commission met here in the previous year he was incapable of doing the job, in spite of big talk of what he had achieved in Africa. The Brazilians were likable chaps, but not at all anxious to expedite the work—in fact, they looked on any activity with marked distaste. It was up to me to complete it, and I intended to do so without any avoidable delays.

Bolivia had a shoreline and navigation lights at the frontier mark on the Lago de Caceres. Neither soldiers nor *peons* would camp anywhere near this monument for fear of a ghost which disturbed them every night, wandering about the camp and creating the greatest alarm. We were unable to find an explanation for the hauntings, but the evidence certainly appeared overwhelming.

Puerto Suarez, nearest Bolivian village, with its alcohol-sodden population, was a miserable cluster of palm-thatched huts, seven miles from Corumba at the west end of Lake Caceres. For six months of the year it was isolated by floods, and it owed its existence to a nightly contraband trade with the city. Bolivians resented comparisons between its squalor and the comparative luxury of Corumba, and refused to acknowledge any difference between the two places. Puerto Suarez was infested by snakes, the worst of which were the *Cascabel* and the *Surucucu*, or Bushmaster. I can't say for certain that I ever heard these poisonous varieties emit any sounds, but it was firmly asserted that they did—

imitating more or less successfully the calls of birds, as I have already mentioned, in order to attract them.

The *Cascabel* is usually found in 'writhes' of half a dozen together. Their bite is deadly, and death follows on a flow of blood from nose, ears and eyes. The Bushmaster is always vicious, and has been known to hunt a man down. A single bite brings rapid death, but the creature is not content with that—it goes on biting till its venom is exhausted.

By the beginning of July we had completed all the work that could be done in the vicinity of Corumba, and there remained only the adjustment of the frontier far to the north on the River Guaporé. A Commission in 1873 had erroneously taken as the source of the Verde an entirely different stream. The agreed frontier ran along the River Verde, but—here was the hitch—no one had ever ascended it, and its course as shown on the maps was pure guesswork. A proposal was on foot to replace it as a boundary mark by one which would have been prejudicial to Bolivia, and being essentially an explorer—attracted by any sort of risk—I decided to clear up the embarrassing doubts concerning it. Fatal decision! Had I known what I was taking on, the Verde would probably have remained unexplored to this day.

"What about it?" I said to Fisher. "Are you game?"

"Oh, I'll come. Still, isn't it rather unusual for this sort of work—forming a precedent, you know? Surely the contracts don't call for it?"

"If it's not done, the frontier here will always be a bone of contention. I agree that under the terms of the contract there's no obligation to explore the river; but there is the natural desire to round off a job to the best of one's ability, and a personal satisfaction in being the first to penetrate where others have not dared to go. Besides, I'm certainly not going to kick my heels in Corumba for months."

The necessary arrangements were made. We were joined by a Scottish settler on the Bolivian side named Urquhart, and with six *peons* set off up river in the Commission's launch. The Brazilians were delighted. With the river accurately traced there would be no need for complicated and perhaps hotly contested arrangements about a new frontier line. Their fervent blessing was upon the scheme.

A hundred and eighty miles up we came to the cattle ranch of Descalvados, and carts were hired to take us and our provisions overland to the Bolivian village of San Matías, where I hoped to obtain animals for a continuation of the journey. The trip was uneventful except for a scare by a black panther at a place called Bahía de Piedra. Fear of this beast had depopulated the country for miles around, for its ferocity and enormous strength make it more dreaded than the jaguar. Even the value of its pelt—twenty times that of a jaguar's—failed to tempt the local hunters.

As the Prefect in Santa Cruz had, in accordance with presidential instructions, warned the authorities in San Matías to help the Commission in every way, the purchase of animals was greatly facilitated. The *Corregidor* was an energetic, capable man, supported by a *teniente* and a dozen soldiers—but San Matías, oh, what a place that was! The population, mainly Indian, subsisted on alcohol, and cattle raided from the Descalvados lands, and between them and the Descalvados *gauchos* there existed a perennial state of war. A mad Belgian employee at the San Matías end of Descalvados was in the habit of shooting Indians from his verandah for the fun of watching their contortions! The Belgian manager was said to have ill-treated Indians till they fled across into Bolivia. There had certainly been plenty of bloodshed, and everyone here boasted of having killed somebody. One local celebrity distinguished himself by murdering two sleeping men with an axe. Every male inhabitant carried a gun on his hip and a knife hidden somewhere about his person, yet all were hospitable and kindly enough towards us, though usually drunk. Apart from the brigand population, the principal features of San Matías were the limestone caves of Cerro Boturema. All sorts of incredible tales have been told about these, most of them with a ghostly twist, for where human life is not respected superstition is the more marked. There were some pools of insipid water inside the caves that at times were filled with fish and at other times devoid of them, yet there appeared to be no exit.

The weed-grown square of the village was littered with old bottles, empty cans and rotting bananas. Glum-looking Indians squatted dejectedly in the shade of an *adobe* church whose leaning tower stood about ten yards away from the rest of the building. Bolivian whites, apparently with nothing to do, lounged in decrepit chairs set half in and half out of the shade of their doorways. From the 'garrison'—a hut where the twelve soldiers lodged—meaningless bugle calls kept up a simulacrum of military efficiency that fooled no one. So far as I could see, no work was done here. So depressing was the place that I was ready to condone the vast consumption of drink. Our outstanding desire was to get away, and when we left it was none too soon.

The surrounding country looked parched, except for grass pampas where fair grazing was to be had. The uncertainty of life and the local practice of cattle-rustling had prevented its development. Away to the north and north-east was the Serra do Aguapé, where according to tradition there had settled a colony of fugitive negro slaves known as a *Quilombo*. Possibly it still exists there—no one goes into the hills to find out. There were two small *estancias*, Asunción and San José, near the Bolivian frontier, and at the first-named there was a fairly high hill from which could be seen the abrupt precipices of 'The Lost World'— the Ricardo Franco Hills, opposite old Matto Grosso City, seventy miles away. Deer and rhea were common, and the swamps were full of duck. A day or two farther north the tracks of wild Indians were to be seen. In the days of the Empire all this country formed one big cattle ranch belonging to Baron Bastos, but was abandoned long ago.

We reached Casal Vasco, once the Baron's residence, after crossing the Rio Barbados, a stretch of water seventy yards wide, fortunately at its lowest level now and not more than six feet deep. The former magnificence of the old place could easily be judged from the ruins—a feudal stronghold consisting of the shells of several large houses, from the rotted roofs of which bats issued in their thousands at sunset. It was weird—menacing—to see these maleficent creatures etched against a golden sky before dispersing in the gloaming. Some of the great fruit bats, or flying foxes, were so big that they looked like pterodactyls. Half a dozen families of negroes lived in shacks nearby in perpetual terror of savages.

At Casal Vasco we camped for the night only, and then pushed on for an easy day's march of twenty-two miles across the *campos* to Puerto Bastos. It was the spring of the Southern Hemisphere and, except for the perennial green of the palms, the belts and islands of forest dotting the plains were a mass of glorious colour. Never had I seen such wealth of flowers, such beauty as was flaunted that day in the vivid yellows, reds and purples. Brilliant butterflies, themselves more gorgeous than any flower, added to the wonder of it. No painter could have done it justice. No imagination could conjure up a vision equal to this reality!

The carts and animals returned to San Matías from Puerto Bastos, and in a small *montería* we set off down the Barbados River to Villa Bella de Matto Grosso. This long-abandoned city, now nothing more than a dismal collection of ancient but substantial houses and churches, lies on the east bank of the Guaporé, scarcely remembered as the one-time capital of Matto Grosso. A few negroes inhabited patched-up, semi-ruinous houses in the silent streets, apparently subsisting on almost nothing. By day they worked a few small plantations of cane and mandioca; by night they barricaded themselves indoors for fear of the Indians who prowled the streets. Rich gold placers had been worked in the neighbourhood, but these were now exhausted. Then a hideous disease known as *Corupção* had swept over the city, taking such heavy toll of life that the survivors fled in terror. In one of the ruined churches was a marvellous collection of old silver in two huge wooden chests—candlesticks, models of caravels and galleons, boxes, figurines and all sorts of trinkets.

There is something ineffably sad about a ghost town. Imagination pictures the everyday life of the vanished people—their joys and sorrows, their aspirations and pastimes. When human beings abandon a dwelling they inevitably leave behind some shreds of their own personalities; and a deserted city has a melancholy so powerful that the least sensitive visitor is impressed by it. Ancient ruined cities have lost much of it and do not impress in the same way. It is the places abandoned in the recent past that clutch most at the visitor's heart. Matto Grosso City was an outstanding example. It made me think of another—Cobija, once a thriving Bolivian seaport between Tocopilla and Antofogasta on what is now the coast of North Chile. Bolivia's outlet to the Pacific was taken from her in the war of 1879, but the busy town of Cobija was already dead—devastated by a terrible earthquake and raked by tidal waves. The same melancholy broods over the Californian 'ghost towns' of Bonanza days, an emotion perfectly expressed by Debussy in his piano study *La Cathédrale Engloutie*.

In the debris of a church I found the remains of what had once been the bishop's ceremonial chair, a huge thing with a canopy over it. It was not entire, but except for the seat the bits seemed complete, so I collected them together, rolled them up in a canvas, and eventually brought them home to England. It struck me that the chair would make a unique present for my wife, and I saw no wrong in taking it, as its component parts lay rotting amidst the rubble on the church's floor. Its renovation was entrusted to a Dawlish cabinet-maker, and before the work was started I saw the parts unpacked and carefully disinfected, till no remnant of infection could possibly exist from plague-stricken Villa Bella.

No expense was spared in the repair. Seat and back were replaced with fine honey-coloured Morocco leather, and when finished it was indeed a beautiful thing. For a time I had the pleasure of seeing my wife sitting in the great chair of the bishops of Matto Grosso, at the head of the dining-room table; but coincident with its installation she began to suffer from mysterious maladies. One day she said:

"I believe I'm committing sacrilege—I, a Protestant, sitting in the sacred chair of a Roman Catholic prelate!"

I may sometimes be as superstitious as an Indian, but I've experienced more than my share of queer things. No sooner had the suspicion of misfortune been raised than I knew the chair must go. I took a label, addressed it to the Brompton Oratory, South Kensington, London, and despatched the chair without any covering letter of explanation. Let them weave their own story about it, thought I!

Where the chair came from was of course a mystery at the Oratory—and remained so until my wife went there and told the tale. It may be there to this day, and I hope its return to the faith to which it belongs was attended by nothing but good.

Matto Grosso City, surprisingly enough, was at one end of a tele-graph line to Cuyaba—a strategic line installed by the Government. By means of it I managed to dispatch a cable to England, and received a reply within twenty-four hours, though the cost was enormous. It was not easy, for the telegraphist had never heard of England and had to contact headquarters by 'Telegraphone' to find out where it was—moreover, a stranger with a message to send was unprecedented in this lonely place!

The mouth of the Rio Verde was down stream one degree of latitude to the north, and when we came to it guards had to be set at night.

Savages were to be met with on either bank, and were reputed to be bad, while the Guaporé was known to be a river dangerous for its anacondas. The width of the river was anything up to a hundred yards, slow where it was wide and much blocked by thick sudd. This sudd, known as *camelote*, slowed our progress considerably, and at times made it hard to judge the course of the river, for lagoons of it extended into the forest on both sides.

Where there was free water *bufeos* gambolled round the boat. Otters barked at us with excitement, head and shoulders out of the water, and they were answered by frenzied hunting-music from our dogs. Twice we saw Indians on the banks, but they instantly vanished into the bush, leaving us to wonder if the sight was anything more than illusion. At night the saucer-eyed *Nocturno* monkeys roared their challenge, pelting our hammocks with twigs and robbing us of the sleep we sorely needed. Frequently we saw a strange bird, very rare as I was told later, like a huge peacock butterfly when its wings were outstretched in flight. Its name I never learned.

Even if its latitude had not been known, there would have been no difficulty in recognizing the mouth of the Verde, for an old frontier post dating from 1873 still stood in the forest. Here we were in new country with a river of crystal-clear water. Large turtles basked on the sandbanks; fish abounded, and the river swarmed with stingrays, easy to spear and good to eat.

We poled upstream as far as we could, but were soon among hills where rapids began and forced to conclude that boats could go no farther.

"What'll we do now?" asked Urquhart. "Don't tell me we've got to foot it!"

"There's no help for it," I replied. "We must leave all we can't carry on our backs and follow the river's course by land. It's going to be tough, but it's got to be done."

"What about food—we can't carry enough to see us through!" put in Fisher.

"We'll have to trust to what we can find. It's little enough we can take with us because of the instruments, and we can't leave them behind."

Putting in to shore we disembarked, and sank the craft in a pool so as not to attract the attention of Indians. All surplus stores and the instruments that could be left behind were put in two metal cases and buried above high-water mark. Because of its weight, we left £60 in gold in one of the cases. Possibly this is how many tales of buried treasure originate. At any rate, wind of my buried treasure stole up and down the Guaporé, the sum increasing with every telling. The stories pursued me for years. When I last heard of the 'Verde Treasure' it had been magnified to £60,000. At this rate the time may come when it will attract adventurous treasure-seekers from outside—possibly even from the United States or England—and the fruitless search for my sixty golden sovereigns will exhaust the resources of a syndicate. Of course, the glowing accounts make no mention of the fact that we retrieved the buried equipment later. Let the would-be treasure-hunter ponder on the moral of this tale!

The abundance of fish and game at the mouth of the river deceived us. With care our scant food supply might have lasted for three weeks; but *peons* are voracious, and their rations were consumed in a few days. The second day on foot brought us to thick undergrowth where we were forced to cut every inch of the way. Tiny bees, a fifth the size of a house-fly, filled our eyes, noses and ears, and penetrated down inside our clothes till there was not an inch of our bodies free from them. Every now and then cutting would disturb a wasps' nest; or the very aggressive red bees would consider us too close to their preserves and attack not with stings, but by biting our skin and hair.

Follow the river we must. It would have been easier to leave it and detour round the difficult scrub, but the river was the boundary, and it was essential to map it with complete accuracy, or ruin the whole purpose of the expedition.

The river grew bitter to the taste and fish abandoned it. Probably for the same reason there was no game, but in any case the noise we made in hacking our way forward would have scared anything from our vicinity. There was no sign of Indians, and no reason now why there should be, so we relaxed the guard at nights and relied on the dogs to give the alarm should there be any. Rubber trees were plentiful, untouched by the *seringero*.

We started on foot on September 15; six days later the *peons* ran out of food; we others shared out what there was of our supplies, but by the 23rd this had gone too. We found some palmettos and ate the 'cabbages', but they made an unsatisfying meal and even weakened us. On September 25 we saw a turkey—but it saw us first! On the 30th there was the heart-breaking labour of hacking a way through a *tacuara* forest—a kind of bamboo which sends out a tangle of branches armed with wait-a-bit thorns. Next day we found a bees' nest and, very hungry indeed, pounced on it. The honey had fermented and it doubled us up with violent stomach-ache. On October 2 one of the dogs found a bird's nest with four large sky-blue eggs in it. The dog received one as a reward, and the other three did very little except make us more conscious of hunger. On the following day we reached the source of the river, finding there a few *Chonta* palms, with nuts about the size of marbles, and almost as hard.

"Well, we've got here all right," said Fisher; "but how are we going to get back?"

Certainly not by the way we came, I thought. "We'll find a way all right. We don't have to follow the river any more. I expect we can get out over the hills."

"I hope to God we can!" muttered Urquhart.

Fisher said something about, "Leave our bones here, most likely!"

Possibly we should, but we were going to make a fight for it, anyhow.

"That's enough!" I said. "We're going to get out. Pull yourselves together and look cheerful. If the *peons* think we're giving up they'll never have the guts to stick it out. If we've got to die, we'll die walking—see!"

We were starving now—really starving. The tendency to trip and fall showed a growing weakness, yet we still found no difficulty in carrying our packs, weighing now about thirty pounds. The voices of the others and the sounds of the forest seemed to come from a vast distance, as though through a long tube, for the deafness of famine was upon us. Our position seemed absolutely hopeless. Tremendous effort was needed to take observations and make a triangulation connecting the source of the river with Villa Bella, but the work had to be done or our sufferings would be to no purpose—that is, if we ever escaped from this hell! Remembering the game-infested forests of the Guaporé, the *peons* were inclined to be mutinous, and who could blame them? Even had we wished to, it was out of the question to return the way we had come, for observations would not be possible, and we should be held up for certain amongst the lagoons.

Above us towered the Ricardo Franco Hills, flat-topped and mysterious, their flanks scarred by deep *quebradas*. Time and the foot of man had not touched those summits. They stood like a lost world, forested to their tops, and the imagination could picture the last vestiges there of an age long vanished. Isolated from the battle with changing conditions, monsters from the dawn of man's existence might still roam those heights unchallenged, imprisoned and protected by unscalable cliffs. So thought Conan Doyle when later in London I spoke of these hills and showed photographs of them. He mentioned an idea for a novel on Central South America and asked for information, which I told him I should be glad to supply. The fruit of it was his *Lost World* in 1912, appearing as a serial in the *Strand Magazine*, and subsequently in the form of a book that achieved widespread popularity.

In an effort to find a way out in that direction we struck up into the hills, but to our despair found those deep canyons in the mountain-sides impossible to cross. Time and time again we were brought to a standstill at the edge of some ghastly precipice, returning dejected to the starting-point, each time with diminished strength. How long could we carry on was the vital question. Unless food was obtained soon, we should be too feeble to make our way out by any route, and one more expedition would never be heard of again!

The *capataz* of the *peons* was missing, and I suspected that he had laid himself down to die, as Indians will when there appears to be no hope I searched for him, found his tracks, and eventually ran him to earth in the *monte*, or scrub forest, sitting, his back to a tree, weeping like a heart-broken girl.

"Come on," I said, taking his shoulder. "Up on your feet, man! What's the matter with you?"

"Leave me alone!" he wailed, shaking my hand away. "Let me die. I want to die—I can't stand it any longer!"

Kindness is no good in these cases, however sympathetic you may feel. I took out my hunting-knife and jabbed it into his ribs till he cried out and sprang up.

"Oh no you don't!" I said. "You're not going to lie down and die just like that. If you die, you die on your feet—unless you prefer the knife."

He said nothing, but caught his breath with a last sob and staggered off towards the camp, regarding me, no doubt, as a fiend.

I called the party together and told them of my intentions.

"Our only hope is to follow the watershed. I believe it will bring us out. We can't escape by way of the hills, nor by the way we came, so it's our one chance."

There was a groan of dismay, for it meant staking our lives on a mere hope. I called Fisher and Urquhart.

"Better take the *peons*' guns away from them at the first opportunity. To their way of thinking it's going in the wrong direction to follow the watershed, and they may desert. Without guns they won't dare to, for fear of Indians."

Indians were not far away now. At night we saw their fires here and there, but never a savage showed himself. It was bitterly disappointing that they avoided us so obstinately, for we should have welcomed them in the hope of obtaining something to eat.

Again on the move, we encountered another difficulty. The ground was covered with hard, slippery bunch grass on the top of loose pebbles. At every step or two we slipped, and in our weakened condition often fell grovelling. It was then that an almost superhuman effort was required to get up again, for our packs seemed to pin us down. How good it would have been to lie there—just lie and rest! The *peons* had to be driven on with threats and blows, and the effort to keep them on the move stimulated our own flagging energies. I have never struck these people in anger, and the apparent brutality of my treatment now went sorely against the grain, but it was with the sole object of forcing them to make a fight for their lives.

Voracious looks were frequently cast at the dogs, though they were nothing but skin and bones—like ourselves. I had firmly quashed all suggestions that they be killed and eaten. For one thing, I'm too much of a dog-lover; and for another, they might have helped us to find food. Somehow they had managed to keep alive by hunting, though what they found we were unable to discover. They did not appear to be exhausted, yet now they just curled up in the grass, went to sleep, and never wakened. A more peaceful and even beautiful demise could not be imagined. The Indian *peons* wanted to follow their example—to lie down and sleep themselves out of life. Instead, they were goaded on.

It was a miracle that saved us—at least, for me it was then, and always will be, the nearest thing to what we like to call a miracle. On October 13, feeling that we had come to our last gasp, I did what I had never known to fail when the need was sufficiently pronounced, and that is to pray audibly for food. Not kneeling, but turning east and west, I called for assistance—forcing myself to *know* that assistance would be forthcoming. In this way did I pray, and within fifteen minutes a deer showed itself in a clearing 300 yards away.

The others saw it at the same time, and a breathless silence fell as I unslung my rifle. It was almost hopeless range for a violently kicking Winchester carbine; and at the end of one's tether from hunger or thirst the sight is not reliable, nor is it easy to hold the rifle steady.

"For God's sake don't miss, Fawcett!" The hoarse whisper came from close behind me. Miss! As I sighted along the shaking barrel I knew the bullet would find its mark. The power that answered my prayer would see that it did. Never have I made a cleaner kill—the animal dropped with severed spine where it stood!

The *peons* wolfed their portions, skin, fur and all. What a pity the dogs had not survived a few days longer! Our troubles were over. Next day we found a bees' nest full of excellent honey; on the 15th we at last found a way down the cliffs to the forests of the Guaporé, and on the 18th we came to a small negro settlement where coarse sugar made from boiled cane juice was to be had.

Strangely enough, sugar was the thing we had hungered for more than anything else. In our dreams we had gorged ourselves on sugar-coated delicacies, and in the agony of our waking hours discussed repeatedly what sweet things we would most enjoy eating. As you may imagine, we ate far too much head-sugar that day at the settlement—we gorged ourselves on it—we ate till we could eat no more. Nightfall saw us doubled up with agony in our hammocks, groaning with the pain, until relieved by vomiting.

On October 19 we arrived back at Villa Bella, whose sad streets and empty houses cheered us after the utter loneliness of the forest. We had left stores here, and condensed milk and Quaker oats made a considerably healthier diet for us than sugar. As strength came back, it was with a growing realization that we had escaped only by a miracle.

A jubilant telegram from General Pando was awaiting me here.

Anticipating our safe return he sent his congratulations, and asked for an address to which he could send the money owing to us. Little did he guess how close the Verde had come to putting a premature end to our work. The river was explored at last, and its course found to differ entirely from the guesswork of 1873. Its source was in springs, not in a lake as had been thought. Our complete set of observations would enable every mile of it to be accurately mapped, thus saving about 1,200 square miles of valuable country for Bolivia. Our hardships and sufferings were fully justified.

We followed the telegraph line to the Jauru, not too bad a tramp over a fairly good trail, and dropped down from the hills of Aguapé into Porto Esperidião, an *estancia* on the river. Here we procured a large canoe which took us to Caxocira. A hospitable Brazilian fed us well and supplied us with a boat to Descalvados, where we arrived on November 18.

Our reception was chilly. Someone had spread a malicious rumour to the effect that we had complained on all sides of disgraceful treatment last time we were there. We were alleged to have said that any settler would have shown us more hospitality. There was no truth in this, and the propagation of such a lie could only be for the purpose of discrediting us. However, the people soon thawed, and ended by making our stay as comfortable as they knew how.

A launch took us down river to Corumbá, where to our great embarrassment we were hailed as heroes. The Brazilians were full of admiration for anyone who would willingly court a meeting with *bugres*—as they called the savages—and it was impossible to convince them that we had caught no more than a glimpse of any during the whole trip.

Five of the six *peons* died from the effects of the journey. The sixth—the man I had goaded on at the point of the knife—came to me the following year and asked to accompany me again. He was voluble about what he called our 'English stamina', and harboured no ill-feelings towards me. On the contrary, he followed me about with every sign of devotion.

The upshot of the exploration was that both Commissions agreed to proceed in the following year to the source of the Verde under my guidance, while a third Brazilian party ascended the river verifying its course to corroborate my maps. After that we would jointly erect the marks to record it permanently as a frontier point.

CHAPTER XI

UNLUCKY THIRTEEN

IN May 1909 we were back in Buenos Aires, trying desperately to escape up river from a general strike that was paralysing everything and becoming uglier every day. There were leanings towards Communism amongst the Italian workers in the city, and labour disputes were frequent. In this case trouble had broken out when some hothead loosed off a revolver in a crowd, while another pushed his knife into a policeman's horse. Shooting started, there were heavy casualties, and the strike was on.

Food became scarce, shops were barricaded against looters, and blacklegs were lucky if they escaped with their lives. It was not actually revolution, but a sullen atmosphere brooded over the place. The police behaved magnificently, in spite of the surreptitious attacks against them and the ugly practice the strikers had of throwing vitriol in their faces.

River traffic was almost totally suspended, but we managed to secure passage on a Lloyd Brasileiro steamer, the *Ladario,* and even procured carts to carry our baggage to the waterfront, ourselves seated on the top of it, and with an escort of heavily armed police all round us. This line had an excellent coastal service, but the *Ladario* was the worst boat it possessed, and no cabin was available, for it was crowded with lower-class Brazilians. Luckily, on the river steamers one can do without a cabin, for a hammock can be slung anywhere.

Asunción was in the throes of one of its periodical revolutions, and in a state of siege, though Buenos Aires newspapers had given us far too serious an impression of it. However, in due course we arrived at Corumba, where we found that the Brazilian section of the expedition had already gone north.

It took very little time to complete preparations. We had plenty of provisions, and a lighter was chartered to carry the equipment, which included six mules, two horses, twenty-four bullocks and four new carts. A Bolivian official named Pacheco was to accompany us, and there would be also two Chiquitana Indians and four white *peons*.

While preparing to leave we stayed at the Hotel Gatti, and this time had clothes suitable for any social function to which we might be invited —so, of course, we never had occasion to use them. Our host, Senhor Gatti, was the most tactful of men, and he had need to be, for there was an ugly scene in the hotel one night.

A young Bolivian was demonstrating to some Brazilians the old match trick—the one in which two matches are stuck in the end of a matchbox and a third held between the ends and lit, so that it shoots away. One of the Brazilians happened to be sitting in the line of fire, and the missile sped to the point of his nose and stuck there. The Brazilian never thought of brushing the match away; instead, he howled with pain and cursed the Bolivian, while everyone rocked with laughter. At that he seemed to feel insulted, everyone talked at once, and in some mysterious way the matter took a political turn. But for Senhor Gatti's intervention there might have been bloodshed, for at that time every man in Corumba carried an automatic, and scarcely a week passed without fatal gunplay.

The usual practice with a murderer was to lock him up in the calaboose until he could show how much money or influence he had. If lucky enough to possess either or both of these things an 'escape' was arranged across the frontier into Bolivia until the matter had blown over. On the other hand, if he had none, conviction for the crime resulted in thirty years' imprisonment. The system worked well, and no one but the uninfluential pauper had any complaint to make about it. Anyway, he deserved what he got, for indulging in expensive luxuries beyond his means!

There is no capital punishment in Brazil, but it cannot be said that murder is more prevalent in consequence. Shootings in Corumba were usually due to jealousy, drink and differences over international politics; crime for its own sake was almost unknown, for the Brazilian is on the whole a law-abiding person.

Two English missionaries arrived in town, full of zeal to convert the Indians of Matto Grosso. The young Bolivian of the match episode saw in them perfect victims for his practical jokes. He took them out on the hotel balcony one night and pointed out the distant fires all along the flat horizon where small farms stood on the patches of firm ground in the swamp.

"There you are!" he said triumphantly. "Those are the camp fires of savages. They're all around us, watching, waiting to raid the town should an opportunity occur."

"Are they bad Indians?" one of the missionaries asked anxiously.

"Bad? Yes, they're bad all right. Cannibals—every man jack of them!"

That did it. Next day the missionaries departed down river. Actually there wasn't a wild Indian within a hundred miles!

Before we started, a German arrived from the north in a broken-down canoe. He was clad in nothing but a sack, and cursed the country roundly for letting him down. He had been up beyond Diamantino for three months with Bororo Indians as *peons*, hoping to make his fortune in gold and diamonds. Instead, he lost everything.

Another German and an Englishman with the same object had gone upstream in a chartered gasoline launch—we passed them in the previous year—and they too returned empty-handed. Being ignorant of conditions, they had set off confident of success, but sickness, problems of feeding, and lack of experience in forest life had caused their failure. In the vast wilderness north of Cuyaba lack of a reliable map led to the covering again and again of the same ground, so that disappointments were repeated to the point of exasperation.

We left Corumba on June 13, and any hopes we had of escaping ill luck were dashed at the outset by the discovery, after the animals were embarked, that our lighter had started to leak badly. It was too late to repair it, and as the voyage was of only a few days we decided to let it go, but detailed off the *peons* to work in shifts at the pumps. That same night I awoke in the cabin of the launch to hear an ominous bubbling alongside. I dashed out on deck and grabbed an axe just in time to sever the ropes mooring the launch to the lighter as the latter sank with every animal on board. The three *peons* were asleep at the lighter's pumps, and were lucky to escape in the screaming confusion. One or two animals were able to free themselves and swim ashore, but the oxen and all the rest were drowned. The loss to our party was serious, but I decided to go on and trust to luck to secure transport.

With the help of the Belgian manager of the *estancia*, or ranch, at Descalvados, we succeeded in procuring two carts there. While the required oxen were being sought we lived in fair comfort on board the launch, but the atmosphere was thick with the reek of decay and burnt bones, for we had tied up alongside the factory where cattle were killed for the preparation of canned beef. Our *peons* passed their time fishing in the tainted river for *piraña*, those vicious little carnivorous fish that in their teeming thousands make the rivers in the vicinity of slaughter-houses so perilous.

It was here that a short time previously one of the *peons* of the *estancia* fell into the river. The instant his body touched the water swarms of *piraña* rushed at him, and his clean-picked skeleton was recovered next day. The manager told me of a similar case which took place in an *estancia* near Corumba. There was a splash in the river at night, and a sleepy workman woke up and asked, "What's that?" Another replied,

"It's only Ladriguez fallen in the river." The first grunted and went back to sleep. From the unfortunate Ladriguez there came not so much as a scream; he was literally torn to pieces by the *piraña* before he came to the surface!

A red-trousered Brazilian soldier was fishing from a canoe in Corumba Port when the pull of a large fish upset him into the water. He held on to the stern of the canoe shouting, and after some time another canoe put off from shore and came along to see what all the noise was about. Instead of rescuing the soldier, the second canoe towed the first to the beach, where it was found that the soldier was dead, his fingers still locked on the gunnel, and every particle of flesh stripped off his bones from the waist down. The very thought of it caused the greatest amusement for days! There was never any sympathy for victims of fatal accidents. Even the dead man's woman and children shrugged their shoulders and promptly set about looking for a new breadwinner!

It was often necessary for me to swim rivers in order to get a rope across for hauling the equipment over. I had to be very careful to ensure that there was no cut or open sore anywhere on my body, for nothing more was necessary to attract these devilish little fish. When in the water my toes tingled at the thought of them, and when at length I hauled out on the other side, it was with indescribable relief.

Before we left Descalvados a 'dance' was organized in a shed near the launch. *Gauchos*, labourers and their women drank large quantities of alcohol, and reeled through their tangos and *cachuchas* to the thrumming of guitars and lutes. Our own lot, headed by Pacheco, joined in the revels, but came flying back on board about midnight to the accompaniment of a fusillade of revolver-shots. A jealous *gaucho*, gun in each hand, had entered the shed and opened fire at random. One man was killed, another hit in the stomach and a woman grazed. The *gaucho* then took to horse in the approved fashion and bolted for the interior.

The 'dance' was chaos at once! There was no doctor who knew anything of surgery, and some of the Belgian employees operated on the wounded man by probing his vitals for the bullet with a meat-skewer. The victim's groans kept us awake for the rest of the night, and at daybreak he died. A gang went in pursuit of the murderer, but, as was generally the case, he was never caught.

From Descalvados the launch returned to Corumba, and we proceeded to San Matías in the carts. We found that the place had deteriorated since the previous year, and that there had been considerable fighting in the area. In the police station lay a Brazilian feeling very sorry for himself, for he had just received 1,000 lashes for killing a man with a knife. Rattlesnakes had accounted for several of the inhabitants; and a very charming French nobleman whom we had met the previous year at Trinidad, near Descalvados, had been murdered. The place reeked of death, though the people were a hospitable and kindly lot when not engaged in crimes of violence. The conditions under which they lived were such that excuses might be made for them. Less excusable was the action of our two Indian *peons* who vanished with a quantity of stores and two of the best mules from a number I had been fortunate to purchase here.

Shortage of transport forced us to leave a quantity of provisions behind when we left San Matías on July 1. In order to make observations from the summit of Mount Boa Vista we stopped for a day at Asunción, where we heard rumours of the Verde treasure, which had grown to £37,000, and was doing well! A few days afterwards we caught up with part of the Brazilian Commission, engaged in verifying old positions, and were entertained lavishly by them.

We soon left them behind, for we were less hampered with baggage than they; but two days later one of the mules was killed by a rattler, with the result that we were brought to a standstill, as one cart alone could not carry all the supplies. We could not replace the animal, for there were no more habitations of any kind in the vicinity. While we were trying to solve our problem a strange thing happened.

The most beautiful mule I have ever seen, in absolutely perfect condition and complete with brand-new saddle and bridle, walked into camp from the north. As far as I knew, the Brazilian Commission had not lost an animal. Thinking it must belong to some traveller whom we would necessarily meet on the trail, I borrowed it, intending to return it to its owner when we came up with him. However, we met no one, and the mule—literally a godsend—remained with us.

Snakes were a pest in this region. In the dry scrub on one side of us the rattlers swarmed, while the lagoons and swamps on the other side were haunted by *jararacas*. Once my mule gave a flying leap over a rattler that shot out from the scrub—for these animals are very quick to detect small snakes, while apparently unable to recognize the large ones readily. On another occasion my mule was stepping over what we both probably took to be a fallen log across the trail when suddenly the animal stopped dead, shuddering. Looking down, I saw to my horror that the 'log' was part of a large boa constrictor seven or eight inches in diameter. The mule was paralysed with terror, and the rest of the party was well in the rear. I gave a sudden shout, dug in both spurs, and hit the animal a resounding crack on the rump with the flat of the whip. He took off like a rocket, sailed over the snake, and kept going for at least two hundred yards before I was able to pull him up, still shivering with fright. I turned back to warn the others. When I got there it was to find them blazing away at it with Winchesters, but the boa constrictor simply slid off into the undergrowth.

We found the Barbados River considerably swollen and the fording-place, at least a hundred and fifty yards wide, obscured by *camelote*.

The *peons* refused to cross, alleging that there were *bichus* in the river —meaning crocodiles or anacondas—and the cart men supported them firmly. The animals could swim over and the carts would float, but someone must cross first of all with a light rope and pull over the baggage in hide bundles or on a raft. There was nothing else for it. I had to go. As I undressed there was an unpleasant sinking feeling in the pit of my stomach; I remembered that not long before a horse and rider had been taken in the same place.

Once over with the rope it was easy to pull the baggage across. Pacheco couldn't swim and had to cross on a pole, a useful method to know. Any ordinary straight tree-trunk three to six inches thick will do, provided it will float. On one end a short upright pole is tied, and on this one's clothes are placed. One sits astride the other end and paddles with the hands. Balancing is quite easy. One end of the tree-trunk sinks under one's weight, but this serves to raise the other end, with the clothes, well above the water.

The dogs were ferried over in skins, like the baggage. Crocodiles may respect human beings, but will always go for a dog. It is said that they will not attack before midday at the crossings, but after that, and towards the evening, there is some risk. The oxen swam across towing the floating carts, and there were no mishaps.

We found Casal Vasco deserted, for the savages had killed off the men in retaliation for shots that had been fired at them; they had, however, spared the women and children. At Puerto Bastos the carts were sent back; part of the baggage was despatched to Matto Grosso City by boat; and the mules set off overland, a troublesome route that entailed several crossings of the Barbados River. The main body of the Brazilian Commission was occupying the telegraph bungalow in the old city of Matto Grosso when we joined them there, and the following day Commander Oliveira left for the mouth of the Verde with a doctor, an assistant and mountains of provisions.

His expedition was ill-fated. Oliveira fell in the river, became ill with fever and was obliged to return to Villa Bella. The others failed to get up the river. They discovered one of our canoes of 1908 broken and upside-down amongst the trees six miles down stream from the Verde, and they located our trail, but were forced to cross to the Guaporé River, where they remained until a search party rescued them six weeks later.

Commander Lemanha, who was to accompany me, came in from the San Matías trail with six soldiers armed to the teeth. The previous year we had decided to join forces for the overland journey and take with us on donkeys stores for the river party as well. We crossed the river and camped for the night in a small hut in a clearing at the foot of the towering Ricardo Franco Hills.

Suddenly there was a fusillade of shots in the forest, and two breathless soldiers came scrambling back into camp.

"Savages!" they cried. "They're attacking on all sides!"

"How many? Where?" Lemanha shot the questions at them while strapping on his pistol and checking the magazine to make sure it was full.

"Thousands, *mi comandante*," was the reply; "but we have beaten them off—I and Corporal Pereira between us!"

Fisher and I went out to reconnoitre. Shooting at the savages was the most dangerous thing they could have done. It marked us down as enemies at once. But we need not have worried, for no trace did we find of any—in fact the two soldiers had blazed away their ammunition at shadows and nothing more!

The hut was very old and its roof full of snakes and spiders. No sooner were we inside than our legs were covered with the maddening little white ticks known as *garapatas do chão*, and before long we could have torn the skin off from the irritation of their biting. Rather than face that hut for a night we slept in the woods.

The view was magnificent from the top of Ricardo Franco, 2,400 feet above the river, but it was a difficult matter to get the animals up there. One of them fell head over heels down the steep slope and plunged with a sickening crash into a tree. It hung there until we hauled it to its feet; then, apparently none the worse, it sauntered off nonchalantly up the trail.

Once over the top we had to cut a path through a mile or two of thick forest for the animals. It had been adequate for us in 1908, but cargo animals must have a wider trail than men. The cutting was done by Fisher and myself, with a couple of *peons* to help. The soldiers were nervous on account of the Indians—not without reason, for the men were mulattos; and Indians, mindful of past persecutions, will never spare a black man.

We struck our previous trail before long, followed the watershed, and in sixteen days came to the source of the Verde. This time deer were plentiful and quite tame. A week there was sufficient to complete the work and erect the frontier mark; and then, not having enough provisions for a stay of more than ten days, I decided to get back to Villa Bella and, as arranged, leave Lemanha to await the river party.

I gave Lemanha a detailed map of the region, as his bump of locality was not well-developed. We parted in a biting *surusu*, which chilled us to the bone and brought down on the mountains a dense pall of fog that reduced visibility to less than twenty yards.

We decided to retrace our steps by means of the detail map made on the way out last time. It would be an interesting test of its accuracy, for it had been made by compass, and pacing out the distances. Pacing over reasonably easy ground averages 2,000 to the mile, and 2,200 in forest. Surprisingly enough, we found it worked out perfectly, for on the third day we reached the top of the mountain where we had climbed from Villa Bella, and next day re-entered the old city, to find Comandante Oliveira already returned from the Verde and anxious for news of the rest of his party.

I told him we had not seen them. He was reluctant to believe that they had not reached their destination, but finally sent a relief boat down the Guaporé to scout for them. They were found on the left bank, destitute of food and in a bad way. Meanwhile Lemanha waited on up at the source of the Verde until his provisions ran low, and then returned, with great anxiety as to the fate of the river party. It was quite obvious that, but for our journey of 1908, this section would not have been mapped at all.[1]

Oliveira kindly furnished us with provisions, our own stores having been looted, presumably by the negro population. Then, as we had plenty of time, I proposed to Fisher that we entered the forest to the north-east and visited the Parecis Indians. Fisher and Pacheco were against the idea, and so I rode out alone on the plain to the north of the city in the hope of seeing some, as they were usually about. They were there right enough, but too suspicious to come out of the forest or approach within a hundred yards of me; but I was not molested. These same people had massacred every soul in the negro plantation where we ate too freely of sugar after the previous year's journey.

On the trail to San Luis de Caceres a very fine black tiger-cat, about the size of a fox-hound, crossed over in front of us, frightening our mules. Like the big black panther, these creatures are savage and quite impossible to tame. Here we were devoured by ticks, which swarm in Matto Grosso during the winter. They climbed up the legs of the mules, covered the animals' noses and filled their eyes. Hanging in clusters from reeds and branches, they dropped on us as we rode underneath. Every evening we picked anything from a hundred to two hundred off our bodies, leaving irritable little bites that one dared not scratch.

At a hospitable *estancia* on the Jauru I sold the animals and gave the proprietor a saddle in exchange for freighting us to San Luis de Caceres, a small village on the Paraguay River, between Corumba and Cuyaba. He told us of a party that had gone up river to its confluence with another, and had there discovered large nuggets of coarse gold in the gravel.

The river at San Luis is about one hundred and fifty yards wide, and the population of the village was gathered on the far bank to give us an enthusiastic reception, for news of our coming had preceded us. A canoe crowded with men, women and children came over to fetch us, and so

---

[1] After all his sufferings here, my father would have been bitterly disappointed had he known that what he took to be the source of the Verde was not the true source at all. He followed what appeared to be the main stream, but the Verde is a river of many small branches, and one of these opened out into a wide body of water not far from its mouth. The true source was discovered by Col. Bandeira Coelho in 1946, some distance to the south-west of my father's position. Nevertheless, at the time of writing this, the 1909 position still remains the official source.

loaded was it that only two inches of freeboard remained. We took our places in it, and the choppy water, driven by a stiff breeze, came perilously near to slopping over the gunnel; in fact Pacheco, nervous about getting his clothes wet when we were well out in mid-stream, half stood up. The others tried to balance the canoe, the wind blew a gust against it, it rocked, filled and sank, coming up only when freed of its load. Those who could not swim hung on to the waterlogged canoe, and the others struck out for shore. I was wearing heavy boots, and my breeches ballooned out with the weight of water in them; and with the precious records of the trip in the pocket of a coat held high above my head with one arm, I found it no easy task to make shore with the other! One man was drowned.

The population awaiting us had not seen such fun for a long time. Everyone roared with laughter, and the struggles of the drowning man were cheered to the echo. Not the slightest effort was made to help in any way, and when Pacheco, a poor swimmer, just managed to reach the bank and lay there gasping in the mud, there were more roars of laughter.

It was a most undignified entry for an International Boundary Commission, but not a survivor would the *pirañas* have left had a meat-canning factory existed anywhere above Descalvados! I had six half-chronometer watches around my waist—quite a weight to carry—but only one filled with water.

Within a week a river launch arrived, and we went aboard.

"Come this way," said the steward, leading us to the second class where negroes and *mestizos* were crowded amongst their belongings.

"But this won't do," I said. "Where's the first class?"

"First class?" He eyed us up and down disdainfully. Our forest kit was all we had with us, and its condition was pretty bad by this time; moreover, our beards were grown, and our faces and arms scarred with insect bites. On the whole I suppose we must have compared very unfavourably with the passengers in elegant suits, loud ties and billycock hats on the top deck.

"Yes, first class," I repeated.

He went off to fetch the captain, who came back with him, looked us over with frank disapproval, and finally gave his reluctant consent to our being conducted to a cabin. . . .

A new revolution had broken out in Paraguay, river steamers were seized, and we were at a loss to know how to reach La Paz from Corumba. But a tug bound down river with two large lighters in tow came into port, and the skipper was persuaded to make an attempt to get through. Fisher and I took passage with him, slung our hammocks on one of the lighters, and the convoy moved off on the muddy tide.

At night the rats on board that lighter mustered in regiments, held a gymkhana on the deck, swarmed up the stays, ran along our hammock ropes, and chased one another over our bodies. In the light of early morning I woke to see two sitting on my stomach calmly washing their faces. I managed to catch one of them a smack that sent it the whole width of the deck, and its companion, looking rather surprised, ambled away and vanished below.

Sixty miles down stream a Paraguayan Government detachment came aboard—a pompous little major and forty soldiers—and this resulted in our being temporarily requisitioned at Olimpo, farther down, as a troop carrier. Another 200 soldiers boarded the lighters, and the crowding became uncomfortable. But to our relief a launch came up river, and, suspecting it was a revolutionary, 150 men disembarked from the lighters as the launch put in to the bank and tied up. The major vanished into his tiny cabin and locked the door, while his men waited in vain for him. It turned out that the launch was a friendly boat, desiring merely to give us news of the revolutionary position. The soldiers came on board again.

We proceeded warily down to Medanos, an *estancia* of the American Quebracho Company, and as our skipper refused to venture any farther the barefooted and ragged soldiers were forced to disembark. I offered him £100 to berth the lighters and run the blockade, but he refused to take the risk. Then I walked down the left bank of the river and tried to hire a launch from a cattle farm called Terreros, but again was unsuccessful. Trying still farther on I found a Paraguayan sportsman who lent me gratis an ordinary ship's gig, with the sole request that it be left at Puerto Murtinho.

With a large blanket rigged up as sail, Fisher and I continued our journey in the gig, enjoying considerably more comfort than we had known aboard the rat-infested lighter.

"I wonder if we'll manage to reach Murtinho without being intercepted," murmured Fisher, as we reclined drowsily in the hot sun and the gig skimmed along with scarcely a sound. I looked up, and saw a trailing cloud of black smoke beyond the next bend.

"No," I replied. "Trouble's coming to meet us now, by the look of it!"

A fussy little picket boat came into view and altered course to meet us. As it drew closer we saw that sandbags surrounded the deck, and the muzzle of an ancient field gun poked menacingly over the bow. With rifles bristling at every loophole it swung round and came sliding up alongside.

"Who are you?" a man with a megaphone roared at us. We told him, stressing our international importance.

"Proceed to Puerto Murtinho—and no tricks, mind!" came the warning.

We lay over to the breeze as I shifted helm, and astern of us, to make sure we obeyed, the picket boat throbbed along, the sandbags on deck lined with dark faces and the protruding barrels of rifles. It was a major engagement to these cut-throats and perhaps the first great naval victory of the revolution! We were prisoners of war, and on arrival in port the gig was seized and ourselves dumped on board the *Pollux*, a small river steamer serving as temporary prison camp for foreigners.

In spite of its being a Brazilian port the revolutionaries had their headquarters here, and the nondescript troops drilled in the *plaza* without arms. The soldiers in their spare time drank themselves fighting mad and threatened with a wealth of gesticulation to cut our throats.

A huge fellow-prisoner of ours claimed to be a celebrated pugilist who had knocked out the best men on the Pacific slopes of the U.S.A.

"Yes, sir," he boomed. "No man can stand up to me!"

For all his grand talk, when any drunken revolutionary came along brandishing his knife and shouting threats he soon made himself scarce, and we began to suspect his boasting.

"They're after me," was his excuse. "I have a Maxim silencer for a rifle and they know about it. They'll murder me to get a hold of it."

He showed it to us and begged me to accept it as a gift. I still possess it as a curiosity.

A small, drunken Barbadian belonging to the ship's personnel had taken our big friend's measure, and went out of his way to be insulting.

"If that goddam nigger don't pipe down," swore the pugilist, "I'll take him apart!"

Far from piping down, the Barbadian grew more insulting, and finally came out with some unforgivable rudeness or other which the big man couldn't possibly overlook. With a bellow of rage the pugilist tore his jacket off, and, hurling himself on the other, buried his teeth in a black arm and his nails in the little man's face. As he did so he received a neat but hefty blow in the mouth.

They rolled, screamed and clawed on the deck, while the other nineteen prisoners cheered them on, and the revolutionary guards flocked round in joyous anticipation. What a sight it was when at length the tangle was untied and the hefty pugilist rescued bleeding and blaspheming! The enormous shoulders had gone with the jacket, and the great body sloped out bottlewise to an unwholesome obesity. It became the great joke on board, and we heard no more boasts.

The days were not uneventful, though we fretted at the delay. We saw naked refugees from skirmishes up river being ferried across from the opposite side, and corpses floating down stream untouched by *pirañas*, possibly because there was no fresh blood on them. One came down with the forearm and index finger pointing skywards, a weird sight that everybody turned out to see. From the distance we heard spasmodic bursts of rifle-fire, and were positive that the pompous little major was not there!

Two mounted revolutionaries, six-shooters blazing at anything and anybody, came dashing past the wharf one day. They were blind with alcohol and completely irresponsible, and so, after the performance had been repeated on several successive days, the Brazilian police turned out and shot them.

After great difficulty I managed to get an interview with the revolutionary chief, who heard my complaints against the detention of an international commission with great patience and courtesy, and agreed to allow us to depart on the *Ilex*, a Brazilian river steamer that for some reason had a free pass. It was rather sporting of him, as more than likely we should be held up for interrogation by the 'Navy' a few miles below, at Palmas Chicas, and might be considered as knowing too much. Moreover, he warned us that all the baggage might be seized.

The ship was duly hove to, papers were examined, and passengers scrutinized. The chief official, Dr. Cayo Romero, a very distinguished-looking man, boarded us, and evidently knew who we were, for permission to pass was given. The revolutionary fleet consisted of eight river steamers armed with field guns, and forces were strongly entrenched ashore at the English *Quebracho*[1] concern, which had suffered considerably.

Farther on we passed the *Leda*, bound up river with 1,000 Government soldiers armed with machine-guns and modern Mausers. We were told that another 1,000 were going up by land. At sight of these troops the revolutionaries melted away, and the movement collapsed.

The Minister of War at Asunción was anxious for news, and held a banquet for us. As a means of obtaining first-hand information from the front it may not have proved very successful, but every guest seemed to enjoy it greatly, and we all parted on the best of terms.

Pacheco rejoined us at Buenos Aires, and we all crossed to Montevideo and went aboard the *Oravia* for Mollendo, *via* the Straits of Magellan. Pacheco was still dogged by ill luck, for at Montevideo his trousers were stolen during the night, with all his money in the pockets. He borrowed a pair from me, but never took the trouble to return them.

The trip round the Horn is interesting. Of course, a liner experiences little of the hardship that the old windjammers had to contend with. First of all we put in at the Falkland Islands—the 'Malvinas', which Argentina has for so long claimed as her property. My own impression was that no drearier place could exist. Chronic gales sweep the treeless land, and life there must be unspeakably dull.

It snowed all the way through the Straits, and up the coast to Valparaiso the seas were big enough to make even the *Oravia* uncomfortable. One realized what the old-time sailormen put up with by making this passage under sail. A call was made at Punta Arenas, most southerly of Chilean ports, and then with frequent calls we worked up the coast, away

[1] *Quebracho* is a tree with a bark having valuable chemical properties.—Ed.

from Cape Horn weather into warmth again, and the wooded shores gave way to the bare nitrate *pampas*. At last we reached Mollendo, and took train for La Paz.

The President of Bolivia, Dr. Villazon, was good enough to express his great pleasure at the results of the expedition, and invited me to undertake the Peruvian boundary. For this, preliminary exploration of the River Heath would be necessary, and this attracted me greatly, for here too the course of the river was unknown. It had been ascended from its confluence with the Madre de Dios for a few miles, but the savages made it impossible for Peruvians and Bolivians alike to explore it to its source. Meanwhile the frontier question had been left a matter of uncertainty, always likely to produce complications, and there was an effort to compromise in a manner rather to the disadvantage of Bolivia.

This work would mean my retiring from the army, as the War Office would not consent to second me for a period longer than four years. But I had no illusions about the army; it was no profession for a poor man, and any show of initiative was likely to provoke hostility. Promotion was intolerably slow, and I had served twenty years, mostly in the tropics, for a wage less than that of most curates, only to run the risk of being shelved as a major.

I decided to retire, and the War Office took its last kick at me by cutting down a miserable pension on the ground that I had served a foreign government!

CHAPTER XII

GOOD SAVAGE

BEFORE commencing work in 1910 I returned to England, not only because I wanted to see my wife and children, but also to find some assistants to accompany me on the next expedition, which promised to be hard going. How incredibly neat and secure the Devonshire lanes and meadows seemed after the vast expanses of forest and plain—how far removed from those sordid outposts where a man's life was not worth the flip of a finger! The little bushy trees were so tame and friendly, the soft rain so gentle, and the sun's warmth so tempered. The people also—I was accustomed to places where the sight of another man is an event, and here I found myself staring at the well-dressed crowds going to and fro, indifferent to everything but their various occupations! The same impression greeted me every time I returned to England from South America, but always, after a few months of this sheltered existence in park-like scenery, my imagination came to regard it as a prison gate slowly but surely shutting me in.

Even 'Waterside', the big house with its extensive garden at Uplyme, near Lyme Regis, was menacing in its snugness—or should I say smugness? In my joy at being with the family again it seemed at first the very ideal of what a home should be; but alas! after a month or two, thoughts of the wild places—with all their pests and diseases, their misery and discomfort—disturbed the ambient peace and called me back. I would leave, heartsick at another long parting from the home circle, yet deep down inside me something was exulting at the escape from everyday life! Kipling well understood the feeling—his poetry is full of it.

I was lucky to procure the services of two splendid N.C.O.s of the Rifle Regiment, Corporals H. J. Costin and H. Leigh. They proved to be both capable and adaptable, and better companions could not have been found. There was also another soldier, Gunner Todd, a sparring partner of mine in subaltern days; and in addition there was the hope of being joined later by a young officer, a friend whom my wife had taught the art of astronomical observation with theodolite on the roof of a Malta hotel ten years before.

The voyage out was not an enjoyable one, for we had on board a duke and his family who expected more deference than we lowly folk were inclined to give. The 'Holy Family', as we called them, kept a whole side of one deck for themselves and their maids, and were bitterly insulted when some trespasser mistook the maids for the mistresses, and *vice versa*. There was also a representative of the Diplomatic Service who was so impressed by the presence of nobility that he insisted on the passenger list being reprinted so as to include an omitted M.V.O.! The skipper was dazed by the honour done him and his vessel and entirely ignored the rank and file of his passengers, so there was nothing of the customary high spirits found on most British ships. It was with great relief that we transhipped to a coaster in Panama.

We called at Callao, and I made a point of visiting Lima to interview the Minister for Foreign Affairs. I suggested to him the advantages of obtaining British officers to act for Peru in the delimitation scheduled for 1911.

"Perhaps I will ask for them," he told me; "and if I do, is there some prospect of getting any? You seem to think there is."

I knew that there were not many qualified for such work, for military instruction does not include training in surveying. I replied:

"There are those who are only too eager for the opportunity. The snag is locating them; but it's worth a try."

"I'll see about it," he said. "I agree that if we want to get the business done quickly and satisfactorily it's the only solution."

The Bolivian Government had asked me to try to find, while in England, another officer for work in the Chaco, and my hope was that I might be instrumental in establishing confidence in the services of the British so that some political use might be made of it later. Fisher had left me and transferred to the Chaco, but for reasons of his own gave it up and finally went home.

We all dined with the President of Bolivia in La Paz on June 10, and next day left for Tirapata, headquarters of the Inca Mining Company, a mountain village beyond Lake Titicaca. This was our rendezvous with two Bolivian officers desiring the experience of the expedition, Captains Vargas and Riquelme, and a sizable mule train with all sorts of supplies. But this was not all: there arrived a British Regular Army Captain with an ex-Subaltern and N.C.O., to say nothing of a Doctor, and no less than twenty cases of medical supplies together with half a ton of other baggage. How this army was expected to get through wild country I don't know.

Large expeditions are by their very size doomed to failure, for savages think that troops are moving against them and attack with poisoned arrows from cover before their presence is suspected.

The exquisite Captain started off badly by refusing to associate with the three N.C.O.s. In those days the social perspective was very different from what it is today, and the narrow class distinctions to which he had been brought up had not yet been knocked out of him. The Subaltern was of different material—younger and more adaptable. Also, he was keen and ready for anything. The Doctor, too, was a good chap, and his endurance proved later to be greater than his slight physique promised. Before leaving, I sent the Captain's N.C.O. to La Paz to join the Chaco expedition, for trouble threatened unless something was done.

The Inca Mining Company's trail took us up to the lonely Aricoma Pass. Here, even at 15,000 feet, we were free of snow, but all around us towered the white summits, pierced by needles and shoulders of black rock, and there brooded over us the sensation of unfriendliness—I can only call it that—which invariably clings to these Andean heights. The Swiss Alps have peaks as spectacular as any the Andes can show—if not more so—though the altitudes are, of course, considerably lower. Nevertheless, there is a friendly feeling about them—they are domesticated, tamed as an elephant or any great beast might be. In the Andes are things not of our world at all. It is the home of other kind, and stark terror walks beside the lone traveller who invades its solitudes.

The trail dived down into a narrow gorge where in many places a path had been blasted out of perpendicular rock walls. It crossed and recrossed the river on dizzy suspension bridges of wire and rope, so delicate to look at that we hesitated to trust our weight to them. Here and there we saw *vicuñas*, and the gallant Captain couldn't resist slaughtering them whenever opportunity offered. Unfamiliarity with man had made them fairly tame, so the toll he took of the lives of these pretty and harmless animals was sickening. I admit I am biased—I don't like needless killing of that sort!

It happened that we were in a village and that I was absent when the Sub-Prefect of Macusani rode in to welcome us and present his compliments. The Bolivian officers were behind with the baggage, and no one present had as much as a smattering of Spanish. Todd saved the situation by broaching the case of medical supplies containing champagne (!) and launching a first-class drunk. When I came in it was to find that, to keep him out of mischief, the stupefied Sub-Prefect had been tied to a bed in the inn where we were lodging, while Todd, who insisted on calling him George, supplied him with copious draughts of champagne straight from the bottle.

Next morning our visitor had recovered, and took his reception in good part, probably accepting it as just another eccentricity of the mad *Gringos*. The '*Cholo*' of the Andes is accustomed to so much abuse that there is no surprising him by one's behaviour.

Farther down the trail Costin had a narrow escape. We were filing along a rock ledge where the cliff dropped sheer down to the river a thousand feet below. Costin was leading his mule, and stopped to light a cigarette; the mule cannoned into him, and he was knocked over the edge of the precipice. It goes to show how rapidly the subconscious mind can cause deliberate muscular reaction; for as he fell into space Costin's hand shot out and took a firm grip on the stirrup of his mount. The mule, accustomed to sudden emergencies, braced itself in time to take the man's weight; the stirrup leather and saddle-girths withstood the strain; and Costin, an army gymnastic instructor, pulled himself up with one arm to the path before he fully realized what had happened.

Mules always walk on the extreme outer edge of these mountain trails, for when their loads foul the rock walls on the inside the impact hurts their backs. Sometimes a hoof will dislodge a loose stone and slip off the side, and when that happens the rider looks a little green and tries to force a laugh. The peril on the ledges is obvious, but it is even more dangerous to ride over the swinging bridges, for the slats in their flooring give the mule only a precarious foothold; and if a leg goes through the rider is almost certain to pitch into the icy torrent below, whence escape would be nothing short of miraculous.

We crossed the Inambari River and came to Santo Domingo, once said to be the richest goldmine in Peru. It stood on the extreme top of a ridge between two deep valleys where the streams had long been washed for gold. The mine was worked by a syndicate which had bought it from an American for £40,000. The American obtained it from an Indian in exchange for a cow and a calf, a surprising deal in view of the current superstition that to disclose to strangers the location of a goldmine will bring on one so indiscreet the ruin of his family and his own death. The gold mined here ran at eighty ounces to the ton, but I believe the construction of the workings and the improvement of the trail swallowed up most of the syndicate's earnings.

Constant rain made landslides a serious hazard on the trail beyond Santo Domingo. Animal trains freighting rubber up from the Tambopata River had broken the surface into a series of pot-holes that became filled with liquid mud, and into these our mules would place their hoofs with a monotonous plop and a jerk of the body that bounced us on the hard saddles. Above us the mountain slopes vanished in whirling blankets of damp mist, and all the time a relentless rain soaked through our *ponchos* and dripped from our legs. Even the vegetation had a bedraggled look, except for the huge ferns growing luxuriantly in the rocky crevices. Conditions remained unchanged all the way to Astillero, where the Inca

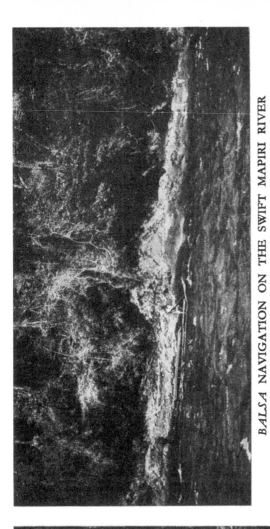

BALSA NAVIGATION ON THE SWIFT MAPIRI RIVER

KACHASA—
THE KILLER!

THE MAPIRI
TRAIL. On these
mountain ledges a
false step means
death

"STARVATION PARTY" AT THE SOURCE OF THE VERDE.
Fawcett is the taller of the two central figures

CHAMACOCO INDIANS OF THE CHACO

THE FRONTIER POST IN THE PICADA DE CACERES.
Fawcett, Fisher and Urquhart running a survey

THE RIVER AND THE FOREST.
It does not matter where—they are all monotonously alike!

THE "LOST WORLD" BORDERING THE GREAT MATTO GROSSO PLATEAU, the account of which inspired Conan Doyle's famous book

Photo by Richard Sasso

THE FRIENDLY ECHOCAS under their shelters

THE SCENE OF THE ENCOUNTER WITH THE GUARAYOS. Friendship is established

Rubber Company had built a small station, in charge of a Scot named Angus.

Two Peruvian officers stationed at Astillero insisted on regarding us as spies sent out by Bolivia to report on the military post at the confluence of the Tambopata and Maldonado Rivers. They toyed with their pistols and murmured angrily until finally we managed to pacify them with the help of champagne from the medical stores. Those supplies were not without their usefulness after all! Tension eased considerably—in fact, the officers became quite talkative when they learned that we were on the way to the River Heath.

"You can't get up that river," one of them asserted. "The savages are so bad that it's certain death! They are in their thousands—not merely a few here and there as on most rivers, but in thousands. Two companies of soldiers tried to make it not so long ago, but so many were killed that they had to abandon the attempt and get back at once. I tell you, you don't see those savages at all—you don't know they're anywhere about until suddenly arrows are flying past your ears, slapping into the canoes and transfixing men right and left! Those arrows are poisoned, too; let one just scratch you and you're done for!"

"What about that German, Heller?" put in the other. "He set off up the Heath with twenty canoes, and forty men on the banks to scour the bush on either side. It made no difference. The attacks came from the forest, and there was appalling loss of life before Heller managed to back off and retreat with the survivors. He had kept going for nine days, but that was the limit. It can't be done, I tell you!"

The gallant Captain looked rather uncomfortable when he heard this, and I fancied he greeted with a certain relief a letter that came through from the President requesting that if I could spare him he should be sent back to La Paz for work in the Chaco region. It was relief for me, too, for the N.C.O.s were so resentful of his treatment of them that they contemplated refusing to go on, and friction in the party was the last thing I wanted. His capacity for the work was open to some doubt, and his rough treatment of the precious half-chronometers had already resulted in damage to one.

We had to wait for some days before a *batelón* could be found to take us to the Madre de Dios, but passed the time in entertaining the station with champagne from the medical supplies. It was out of the question to think of taking these cumbersome boxes with us, so Todd did what he could to ensure that their contents were not wasted, drinking bottle after bottle as though it were lemonade.

News came that the Chuncho Indians were on the warpath below us. They had attacked the rubber gatherers and had caught one, but after stripping him had released him again. There had been no fatalities, and as a matter of fact the rubber people were generally to blame for these attacks, which would not take place if they refrained from molesting the Indians.

The *batelón* had to be returned to Astillero, so Leigh and I took it down to the mouth of the Tambopata. On the way we saw two wild pigs swimming the 500-yard width of the Madre de Dios—a remarkable feat —and bagged them with our rifles to supplement the provisions. We saw little enough of this meat, for the Bolivian detachment at the mouth of the Heath found it much to their liking.

I was able to procure a canoe suitable for the trip, and another *batelón* was to follow after. The Subaltern and one of the Bolivian officers were in charge of the latter; and when at length they arrived at the mouth of the Heath, where we had already been welcomed by the commander, Major Aldasozo, it was with a tale of what might have been a tragedy. The two quarrelled, and the Subaltern smacked the other's face—a deadly insult in South America. That the Bolivian refrained from shooting him there and then I can only call an act of praiseworthy self-control, but, even so, the expedition lost his services, for he preferred to stay with his compatriots in the garrison.

Major Aldasozo was pessimistic about our chances of getting up the Heath.

"It's impossible," he said. "The Guarayos are bad, and there are so many of them that they even dare to attack us armed soldiers right here! We have to be constantly on the alert. To venture up into the midst of them is sheer madness."

"All the same, we'll have a shot at it," I replied.

He shrugged, and then remarked: "Well, if you must go it's at your own risk. I'll tell you what, though—I'll send a few soldiers up with you. I can't spare more than five, but they will help."

He was also able to let me have a canoe; so Leigh, Costin and I took one, and the rest of the party had the other. A third canoe followed with the soldiers and a civilian employee who belonged to the garrison.

The first four days up river were not difficult. Then we arrived at an abandoned Indian clearing on the river bank, and the rapids commenced. The going became harder, and on the banks we saw fresh tracks of Indians. On the sixth day the garrison canoe left us to return to the mouth of the river. Indians were obviously in the vicinity and might attack at any moment, but still we saw no sign of life other than the numerous tracks in the bush at the river's edge. Then, the very next day, we rounded a bend in the river where on a sandbank stood a large Indian encampment.

Dogs barked, men shouted, women screamed and reached for their children, and there was an excited rushing to and fro. The women and children fled to the forest bordering the sandbank, their dogs following so close that they got mixed up with flying legs and brought their owners down yelling and struggling to the ground. The men snatched bows and other weapons from the huts, rushed to canoes lying along the strand, and shoved them into the river with such force that the impetus almost carried them to the opposite bank. We saw them leap from the canoes to the high tree-crowned bank, scramble up in showers of earth and stones, and vanish amidst the foliage; and then their wild jabbering gave way to an ominous silence.

Meanwhile we poled ahead as fast as we could and ran the canoes in on the sandbar, but no sooner had the first man jumped ashore than there was a burst of shotgun fire from the other bank and arrows whizzed between us. Everyone took it coolly enough, though poor Captain Vargas, whose foot must have slipped, fell backwards off the canoe into the river and had to be fished out. The sides of our canoe were quite an inch and a half thick, but I noticed that an arrow had transfixed both sides and stuck out more than a foot beyond. That will give some idea of the force behind them!

We pulled both canoes well up on the shore so that they would not drift away, and then strung ourselves out along the sandbar while arrows smacked into the ground all round us. I raised both arms high and shouted towards the far shore a Chuncho sentence I had learned by heart at Astillero from one of the rubber people. It was probably intelligible to the Guarayos, for there is some similarity between all these dialects; and the practical joker who taught it to me without explaining its meaning would have been greatly amused could he have seen me here, with all our lives hanging in the balance, informing our attackers that we were enemies who had come to kill them! No wonder the arrows flew thicker than ever!

How they missed us I can't imagine, for the river narrowed at this point and there were not more than twenty or thirty yards between us and the Indians. Normally these people are wonderful shots with a bow, and when not excited can lob an arrow up over a tree and down on to a small animal on the other side with the greatest of ease. They had a few guns, too, but having fired these off were too busy to reload them.

I myself saw no arrows at the time, though the others told me afterwards that I had some very narrow escapes. When they are fired at someone else they seem to fly quite slowly, but in the direct line of them they can't be seen.

My peace overtures having proved unsuccessful we moved the canoes to a safer position without any casualties, and then Todd was directed to sit on a log in the middle of the sandbar—just beyond dangerous range —and play his accordion. He was an expert with the accordion, which was one of our principal reasons for bringing him; and as he sat there squeezing out tune after tune, as calmly as though passing a jolly hour in an English pub, the scene must have been ludicrous. Here we were dodging arrows and singing at the tops of our voices, while Todd played away and

L

stamped the time with both feet. Anyone coming on this scene would have said we were all roaring drunk; the cacophony would have caused him excruciating agony! Todd was busy knocking 'em in the Old Kent Road; Costin, eyes rolling and lips quivering with the effort, was asserting at the top of his lungs that we were Soldiers of the Queen; the Doctor was bawling about a Bicycle Made for Two; while as far as I remember my own contribution was 'Swannee River'. Someone—I could not see whom—preferred 'Onward, Christian Soldiers'; and Captain Vargas was doubtless occupied with some gem of Bolivian song.

How long we kept this up I don't know, but it seemed an age. We even forgot about the arrows in time, until all of a sudden I noticed that Costin, still in full song, was voicing, "They've—all—stopped—shooting —a-a-at us!" over and over again. He was right; arrows were no longer zipping past us—in fact, a dark face, eyes rounded in amazement, was peering at us over the top of a low bush. Then another head popped into view—and still another. I should have liked to know at that moment just what the savages were thinking.

We had not fired a shot. To refrain from doing so was the first order I had given as we jumped ashore on the sandbar, for it would have sealed our fate had we retaliated. By this time the savages must surely realize that we had not come with any aggressive intentions, but were concerned only with making friends with them.

The meaningful gesticulations of everyday speech in Latin America have developed into a sign language so comprehensive that an involved conversation can be carried on without a word being uttered. I now walked down to the edge of the water and waved both arms over my head, thereby informing the Indians that I was coming across. Faces were by now peeping out from behind trees, and I hoped my friendly signs were rightly interpreted.

One of their canoes yet remained on the strand, and instructing Todd to go on playing for all he was worth, I sat down in it and asked the Doctor to shove me off. The canoe shot out into the stream, the Doctor climbed in, and at the last moment the Subaltern ran down and joined us. Then we paddled across, while back on the sandbar the mad sing-song continued with more energy than ever.

From the foot of the bank we could see nothing of the savages above, and for all we knew arrows and gunshots at point-blank range might greet our appearance as we clambered up over the edge. Hesitation would only have made the unavoidable more difficult—just as it does when going off a very high dive—and so, followed by the Doctor, I jumped for a hand-hold on the tangled grass and scrambled up.

Two or three brown arms reached down from the thick foliage at the top, grasped my hands and hoisted me over the edge into the midst of a group of forty or fifty Guarayo braves. Then the Doctor was beside me, and we looked round at the intelligent and good-looking faces of these dreaded savages.

Some of them had shot-guns stolen from the rubber pickers, but most were armed only with the great black bows, six feet or more in length, and arrows equally long. A few had arms and faces painted in square patterns with the juice of the *Urucu* berry, and wore shirts of beaten bark with a design across the chest in purple dye. Some wore the long dark gowns which give them a feminine appearance; others were completely naked.

There was much laughing and chattering as they examined our clothing, and then we were led into the forest for about a quarter of a mile, where we came to some more huts and where the *Cacique* of the tribe awaited us. I could think of only one way to show him friendship. I placed my Stetson on his head and patted him on the back. He grinned, and all the surrounding braves roared with laughter—in fact, they laughed at everything, funny or not. Then bananas and fish were produced as gifts for us, and friendly relations were firmly established.

The *Cacique* led me to a large pool where fish of all sizes and kinds were floating on the surface, fin out, beating the water feebly with their tails. They were stunned by the effects of *Solimán* sap thrown in the water —the favourite Indian way of fishing. As the sap is a strong caustic of which the tiniest splash could destroy an eye, there is some danger in collecting it; but it is obtainable almost everywhere, and reasonable precautions have become a matter of habit instilled into the Indians as children. They merely pour it into the water and immediately all the fish in the vicinity become paralysed or stupefied and float up to the surface. The poison seems to have no ill effects on their flesh as food.

The braves collected a number of these fish for us, and then we all returned to the river bank and crossed to the sandbar, where the rest of the party were standing in a rather anxious group. Camp was pitched, and every item of our equipment proved to be of absorbing interest to the savages. They surrounded Todd to finger the accordion, and he, never at a loss in any company, was soon calling them 'Bill' and 'Joe', explaining the instrument in broadest Cockney, and drawing moans from it that sent them off into shouts of laughter. He let one huge, gowned warrior squeeze it for himself; and when a wail emerged, the Indian dropped the accordion as though it were on fire and fell over backwards, while the rest yelled derisively at him. There was no need for a common language, full understanding existed on both sides!

We slept well that night, for no one was required on guard. The expedition always used hammocks covered with long waterproof awnings, slung either between trees or from tripods of canes. There is no bed more restful once one has become accustomed to the curved posture, and I have preferred it even in England.

Six Indians passed the night on the sandbar with us, the only ones of the tribe to be found next morning. The others had apparently gone off into the forest, for all the canoes remained, and the *Cacique* had left as a present for us a number of tooth necklaces. Two of the six Indians volunteered to help us in poling upstream, and I accepted gladly. They were anxious to know whether we were '*soldados*'—the only Spanish word they knew—for soldiers were with reason feared and hated by them. Poor Vargas was in a sweat over this, and begged me not to give him away! The illustration facing page 193 shows these two braves, one dressed in a bark shirt, seated, and the other standing in a red-dyed cotton gown. They have veils I gave them as a protection against the clouds of biting flies which make travel on this river particularly disagreeable.

On the third night after leaving the sandbar the two Guarayos vanished, taking Todd's rifle and ammunition with them. Todd was the sentry and had gone to sleep. His language when the loss was discovered showed only too clearly that henceforth he would have no confidence in Indians! We heard rifle-shots off to the west of us, as though derisively inviting us to pursue. Instead, we proceeded upstream, Todd in a fury that took him several days to shake off, for he realized that he might well have lost his beloved accordion.

On the upper river traces of Indians were plentiful, but we saw none. Their villages are probably well away from the river on the western side, where ground is high, for on the eastern side are swamps extending all the way to the Madidi basin. Snags became a nuisance; the water was low and we had difficulty in passing them. Then, to make matters worse, we came on a series of rapids, one after another, till we thought there would be no end to them.

We saw several canoes upside down on the shore at one place, and passed sandbanks where stood deserted huts built during the dry season. Smoke was seen on top of one high bank, where probably Indians were busy making a clearing, but always they kept out of our way. Now and then we heard voices—a shout or a guttural remark—but neither saw the Indians nor were attacked. Captain Vargas while acting sentry one night claimed to have seen figures creeping up on the camp, but his shots brought no confirmation that they were anything more formidable than shadows.

Fresh food was abundant here. We caught the tasty scale fish called *Dorado*, four or five pounds in weight, and were able to bag a few wild pigs as well. The worst hardship was the peeling of the skin from our feet and legs through their being immersed all day in the river when pulling the canoes over rapids. The skin would come away in patches, and these patches stuck to our socks, making undressing at night a painful business. The Doctor suspected a microbe in the water, but I think the sand was as much to blame as anything. At all events, the only remedy was to rub legs and feet with alcohol every evening and endure the resulting torture as best we could. Luckily we still had plenty of alcohol in the reduced supplies brought with us. *Sututus* were another trial for some of us: these are the grubs of a moth or mosquito which, after hatching from eggs left on the shirt, immediately bury themselves under the skin—usually on the back. The little brutes could not be extracted until the sore they made was 'ripe', and even then it was an art to get them, for on being molested they clung to the flesh with sharp mandibles. Tobacco juice sometimes helped, but killing them under the surface could bring on blood poisoning. Later on, the Indians undertook the cure in their own way. They would make a curious whistling noise with their tongues, and at once the grub's head would issue from the blowhole. Then the Indian would give the sore a quick squeeze, and the invader was ejected. To the Doctor this practice was unorthodox and therefore smacked of necromancy, but when he saw the rest of us relieved from the torture of these pests he submitted to similar treatment.

Going became still more difficult when the river bottom changed from sand to smooth stone, slippery with weed. We slid and cursed, damaged our knees, and constantly fell flat in the water. Had there been any hope of reaching easier going farther up it would not have been so bad, but for all we knew it might get even worse. Still, the trip must be made, and our reward was the valuable geographical data to be accumulated for the first time.

"Savages!" shouted Costin one day as he and I were poling gently up to the foot of a rapid, Leigh having gone back to lend a hand with the second canoe.

"Right there ahead of us, Major!" He pointed to a sandbank a couple of furlongs distant, and I saw eight brown figures regarding us intently.

"Turn in to the shore," I told him. "Quick! . . . Now, wait here in the canoe, and I'll go ahead to see if I can make friends with them."

To carry a rifle would have been to brand myself as an enemy, so I advanced towards them empty-handed and making friendly gestures, half expecting to see them turn and vanish into the forest. Instead of that they spread out in a semi-circle, strung arrows to their bows, and came slowly towards me. It was an awkward predicament, for they seemed hostile, yet self-respect prohibited a retreat. When they were about a hundred yards from me they got excited, and looking back I saw that the other canoe was rounding into view. When I again turned to face them it was to see their backs as they scattered and ran for cover.

I ran after them, but stopped about forty yards from the point where they had disappeared and signalled to them in vain to come out, even using a few friendly words learned from the Guarayos. Then, signing Costin to bring up some sugar and other small articles from the canoe, I held these up to be seen, placed them on a convenient rock, and retreated. The Indians emerged after a short wait and went up to examine the things. Then they stepped back to the forest's edge, laid down their arms, and came up to me. We were accepted as friends.

They belonged to a small tribe called the Echocas, with a large plantation nearby from which they presented us with mandioca, maize and bananas. They gave us fish also, and insisted on helping to drag the canoes up till we came abreast of their big communal hut. We spent the night with them, and were feasted with great hospitality.

Next day we left the canoes with our new friends and set out on foot, carrying the packs, and accompanied for some distance by the Indians. Much to my surprise they showed us where there had been a fight with rubber pickers. It was surprising because I hadn't suspected the presence of rubber pickers on the upper river; in fact we had not expected to meet with any signs of civilization after leaving the Madre de Dios.

I knew we were not far from the Tambopata, and my intention was to cross to that river, do the necessary work, and then complete the circle by building *balsas* and drifting down to Astillero. Food was still plentiful, for in every pool were fish, and we shot two tapirs, finding their beef-like meat excellent. All along were plantations of the Echocas where abundant vegetables and fruit were given to us—in fact, the generosity of these kindly savages was almost embarrassing.

We had reached the hills now, and at night vampire bats became a nuisance. Todd, Vargas and myself were bitten on the head and toes, and Costin on every fingertip of one hand. In the mornings we awoke to find our hammocks saturated with blood, for any part of our persons touching the mosquito-nets or protruding beyond them were attacked by these loathsome animals. It is a mistake to think that man is never molested by them. I actually felt one at work one night. It whirred its wings very soothingly in my face for a while before settling down on me, and I found it quite an effort to brush the creature off, my inclination, I noted with interest, being to sleep and let it have its way. The large and small varieties use the same tactics, and are so dangerous to horses and mules that death often results from repeated loss of blood or from septicaemia.

By September 14 we had reached a point where the river was no more than a brook a foot or two wide, descending from steep wooded hills difficult to climb. After making the necessary observations we turned to retrace our steps until a convenient jumping-off place was reached for the overland stretch to the Tambopata. Before we crossed over, the Echocas met us with more food, and even accompanied us until the Tambopata was in sight. After they left us we struck into a trail which brought us into the clearing of Marte rubber *barraca*.

We found Marte in a state of starvation. In a filthy shed at one side of the clearing lay some thirty Indians in various stages of collapse, putrid with boils and other disorders, while Señor Neilson, the Bolivian of Scandinavian descent who ran the place, had only about a quart of maize left in his stores. This he wanted us to accept. The labourers had existed on leaves and grass for some time, yet on the Heath, just beyond where the rubber gatherers had penetrated, there was food in abundance, for the river was full of fish, and game abounded. Fear of wild Indians kept them away, and one could not fail to see in it the inevitable working of the law of cause and effect. Here were we, who had treated the savages with consideration, plump with the good eating those same people had provided! That the stream over beyond the hills was the Heath, and that the Indians there were disposed to be friendly, were facts quite unknown to these rubber people and surprised them considerably.

Marte was linked to the head *barraca* of San Carlos by a trail of sorts, unfit for animals, but to us much better than no trail at all. It was about thirty miles away, and took us two days to cover. From San Carlos a somewhat better trail led up to Sandia and the *Altiplano*. Before reaching San Carlos we met a foraging expedition of six Echocas, laden with sugar-cane from an abandoned plantation, and they insisted on our accepting a generous supply of it.

San Carlos was in a poor way for food, though better off than Marte. The manager here, an Englishman married to a Bolivian, had had long experience in the rubber industry on the Beni, and I suspect that his methods of treating labourers were learned there. I found out more about this place in the following year. From him we were able to procure a little maize and *chuñu* (frozen potato), but paid a vast sum for it. While the others stayed at the *barraca* to recover from their various ills, Costin and I footed it up the river to its confluence with the Lanza, an important point in the delimitation of the frontier.

Many of the Indian *peons* at San Carlos were earth-eaters, doomed to die after a year or two of this habit. One of its victims had shortly before been sent off sick with a load of bananas and meat to keep him going, but on the way out was caught making three mud pies for breakfast. He died before reaching his destination.

Captain Vargas had suffered rather severely on the trip and was not inclined to make the passage of the river down to Astillero, so he left us here and set off home by way of the Sandia trail. He was an excellent companion and we were sorry to see him go.

Returning to Marte we built three *balsas*, and then embarked for a wild two-day trip down the Tambopata to Astillero—wild, because we shot rapid after rapid, a hair-raising experience in a thirty-mile-an-hour current, where the river, normally a hundred yards wide, would narrow to a half-mile stretch only a fifth of that width, giving to the water a 'venturi-tube' effect. Leigh and I were on one raft, the Subaltern and the

Doctor on another, and on the third Costin and Todd. We came through without mishap, but the others were wrecked several times, and Costin and Todd were actually fished out on one occasion by Chuncho Indians, who fed them, pitched camp for them, and helped to repair their raft. Down the river here were many Chunchos, and above Astillero we passed one of their villages and saw the chief proudly wearing a bowler hat.

Anyone fond of thrills should try rafting down these mountain streams. It takes skill to avoid snags and rocks; the oily current bears you smoothly round the foot of towering precipices; and then suddenly you see that in front the cliff walls narrow and the river drops out of sight. If you are not acquainted with the river—and we were not—there is no telling if ahead is a waterfall or a rapid, but the current is bearing you down on it faster and faster, and when close to the edge you see that it is a steep slope where the water rushes down with terrible velocity. Then you are in it, and there's no time to be frightened!

Poling must be done with great care, particularly in the rapids. The art is to keep close in to the side, and steer away from rocks and snags long before you reach them. The bow man must also avoid keeping the pole directly in front of his body, or it may be driven right through him. Such things have happened!

No trees grow at Astillero, and our *balsas* came in handy for a party waiting to get down to Maldonado. Our Scottish friend Angus gave us a warm welcome, fed us in his rest house on food that seemed luxurious after the scarcity in the upper Tambopata, and procured mules for us. Todd lost one of his socks, and found that the cook had taken it for making coffee! I'm serious—that's what it was being used for. A popular way of brewing coffee in South America is to place it in a bag and then filter hot water through it. Todd's sock was the bag—and though it may have served its purpose excellently, it effectively put us off coffee for the rest of our stay there!

From Angus we had news of the Captain who was sent to the Chaco. On the way up from Santo Domingo he had commandeered the total bread supply of a poor Indian, without the slightest thought of how the man was to replace it, and thrown him the equivalent of a shilling in exchange. He had then tried to expropriate a horse from four Indians, who successfully resisted him. His retaliation was to send a long official report to the Prefect on the insolence of the four men and their combining against him to prevent what, to them, would have been the loss of a fortune! Englishmen generally behave very well in these countries, but such acts as these on the part of one or two take many years for the others to live down. I heard later in La Paz that the Captain had returned to England with the officer who was with him in the Chaco, where their expedition resulted in complete failure. Both these men were decorated for survey work in Africa, and I can only think that the standard for such work in that continent could not have been very high at the time! They were quite unsuited to South American conditions.

We broke up the party in La Paz on October 25. Leigh, Todd and the Doctor went home; the Subaltern took a job with the Inambari Rubber Company, where he was later drowned; and Costin and I stayed on for the following year's work. As Costin remarked:

"It's hell all right, but one kind of likes it!"

CHAPTER XIII

ROOF OF THE WORLD

COSTIN and I were joined by an excellent young fellow named Manley who had worked for me in England. He was a Devonshire man, expert with horses, and proved his worth time and time again— in fact he and Costin were the only assistants I could ever call completely reliable and fully adaptable, and never have I wished for better company.

We set out from La Paz early in April 1911, and crossed over Lake Titicaca to Juliaca, in Peru. This is on the *Altiplano*, but the interesting old Spanish Colonial town was active with the heavy freight movements going on all the time in the yards of the Southern Railway of Peru, for it is a link in the '*Diagonal de Hierro*', the 'Iron Diagonal' of the International rail route now connecting the Pacific coast with Bolivia and Argentina.

Imagine a wide plain stretching from horizon to horizon, bordered by purple mountains and white snow ranges; green with bunch grass, pasture and little patches of tilled land. That is the *Altiplano*. Here, near Juliaca, reed-fringed fingers of water reach in from the swamps at the edge of the lake, the haunt of ducks and other water birds. The native *balsas*, indispensable to the Titicaca scene, lie on their still reflections or skim along under their reed sails, and everywhere are the Indians in their *ponchos* and knitted caps with earflaps, a sturdy, subdued people busy about their own affairs.

From November to May rains lash the *Altiplano*, and where the lightning hits the ground puffs of dust are flung up like shell-bursts. Lives are frequently lost in the cannonading of the thunderstorms, but they are so regular that one learns to know the hours to expect them. It is cold during the wet season at 12,000 feet and over, and the days are raw except when the flying clouds open up and a welcome sun dries the steaming mountain-sides. But the real cold—the merciless, biting cold that can freeze a man to death—comes with the dry season, from May to November, when the thermometer drops below zero at night. In contrast, the temperature in the fierce sun of midday may climb to above 112 degrees without one's realizing how hot it is, so dry is the air. At night the stars are a glory. One sees galaxies which in the denser air at sea level are invisible to the naked eye; and, if the sky is clear, no night is really dark, so great is their illumination.

Our first work was the delimitation of the frontier between Peru and Bolivia where these countries adjoin on the shore of Titicaca, and take it over the mountains from there down to the *Montaña* or forest region at the foot of the *Cordillera's* eastern slopes. The greatest danger was from dogs. I love dogs, and our party was always accompanied by a number of them—making up in character what they lacked in pedigree— but the numerous dogs belonging to the Aymara and Quechua villages in the mountains were trained to attack strangers. Sticks would not keep them off. I once saw a slavering cur being held away at the end of a pole thrust into its mouth, and in spite of the fact that the point was well down its throat, threatening to strangle it and doubtless hurting it severely, it struggled so fiercely to reach the man that it all but succeeded and had to be killed. At length we discovered that by carrying ropes' ends with us the attacks ceased. Those dogs don't mind sticks, but have a healthy respect for ropes' ends, for it is with them that the pups are whipped into discipline.

Caspar Gonzales, a young Bolivian officer, joined us at Juliaca, and we carried out a triangulation survey a degree east to the main *Cordillera* of the Andes, passing nearly three months in these highlands. At night the cold was almost unbearable—regularly down to 22 degrees Fahrenheit inside our tents—and on turning out in the mornings our feet would be so frozen that walking was agony till they had thawed out. After sun-up the heat increased steadily and caused blistering sunburn till we were inured to it. Shaving was out of the question—one's face would have come away with the beard!

The village dogs served as protection for a hospitable folk who could not have been kinder. Sub-Prefects and other dignitaries entertained us lavishly with broths, dried meats and frozen potatoes, and we responded with camp banquets of tea and rum, champagne and Genoa cake. In most places we stopped to pay our respects to the village priest and took a glass of communion wine with him in the manse.

One of our baggage mules known as the '*Chúcara*' ('Shy') was a fine animal but had not been trained for the saddle. Manley coveted this beast as a mount and undertook to break it in. We saddled it without difficulty, and approaching from its blind side—it had only one eye—he got on its back while we held it. We let go and sprang clear. For a minute nothing happened; it stood absolutely immobile. Then the '*Chúcara*' exploded into action, and Manley didn't know what was happening. With incredible suddenness the mule launched itself high in the air, head down between its fore-legs, and Manley shot over its neck to land heavily on his shoulder a good ten yards away! I don't think the most experienced cow-hand could have sat that buck on a saddle without knee rolls. No bones were broken, but Manley was badly shaken and dropped all idea of the '*Chúcara*' as a saddle animal.

Soroche—mountain sickness—took with us the form of chronic stomach-ache, and we made our headquarters at Cojata while this trouble lasted. It was a miserable place, whipped by vicious gales, and during the winter lay under perpetual snow, but it had the advantage for us of being the nearest village to the *Cordilleras*, and from it we went out to do all the necessary work during the days. Evenings were spent in entertaining and being entertained, a very necessary formality in these parts if one is to enjoy the co-operation of local authorities.

Viscachos abound here. These are animals about the size of a rabbit and similar in appearance, except that their bushy tails resemble those of squirrels and their fur is the colour of chinchilla. They jumped about the rocks on the mountain-sides in their thousands and were esteemed good eating by the local people. I marvel that the fur industry has not taken toll of these animals, for the pelt is infinitely superior to rabbit, and they are to be found everywhere in the *Altiplano*.

Pelechuco was our next stop after leaving Cojata. This place contrasted most favourably with the villages on the *Puna*, or high plain, for here was abundance of green, and in spite of being 12,000 feet up geraniums, fuchsias, pansies and roses grew wild and in profusion. The great condor of South America is at its best near here. Señor Carlos Franck, a German-Bolivian with whom we stayed, told us much about them. As is generally known, these are the largest of birds, and the king condor often reaches as much as fourteen feet across the wings. They rarely come down below fifteen or sixteen thousand feet, except to carry off a sheep or—and there are authenticated cases of it happening—a child. Their strength is amazing. A wounded condor has been known to drag a mule along; near Pelechuco a full-grown man was carried about twenty yards by one. But generally they attack the rather small mountain sheep; carry them up a thousand feet or more, and then drop them, to be devoured at leisure.

Carlos Franck, who knew these mountains like the palm of his hand, once came upon a council of king condors. A large ring of solemn birds surrounded two huge black ones and one still larger white one which seemed to be the leader. He had long wanted one of the rare white condors as a trophy and was unwise enough to shoot at it. At once the circle of birds broke up, and two immediately set on him, so that he was forced to throw himself on his back and beat at them with the rifle as they swooped. He escaped, but they followed as he scrambled down the narrow, rocky path on the sheer mountain-side, trying whenever possible to knock him off with their wings into the abyss. He considered himself lucky to have escaped.

In the village of Curva, not far distant from Pelechuco, dwell the peculiar Indian gipsies of South America known as *Brujas* (witches) or *Calahuayas*. Like the Basques in Europe their origin is lost in the mists of time; they wander all over the Andes, are horse doctors, herbalists, or fortune-tellers, and are usually credited with occult powers.

"My daughter, whom you've met," Franck told me, "suffered from hip disease when she was young; in fact she was a cripple. You would hardly believe it, I know, but listen to this story of her cure.

"I had sent her to Germany to see what could be done for her there. Poor girl! She underwent four operations, but was none the better for them, and we despaired of her ever being cured. Then one day after she had come back to Pelechuco one of these *Calahuayas* visited us and offered to cure her for a substantial fee, on the principle of 'no cure, no pay'. I won't go into details of the concoction he instructed me to prepare, for it was gruesome enough to turn your stomach, and if I had not had a firm belief in the powers of these queer people I wouldn't have dared to give it to the child. However, I made it, and administered it as an infusion in water. She, of course, had no idea what it was, and believe me, in a week—in no more than a week!—she was perfectly well, and has remained so ever since."

"And you believe it was the *Calahuaya's* prescription that cured her?" I asked.

"What else could it have been? The child's case was hopeless and even those clever specialists in Germany were unable to do anything for her."

"It sounds fantastic—the sort of thing one would think went out with the Middle Ages."

"Living in these isolated places, very close to Nature and away from the rush and bustle of the outer world, one experiences many things which an outsider might consider fantastic, but which to us are commonplace. I'll tell you another story about a *Calahuaya*, and you can easily verify it, for it took place only last week.

"Have you noticed a solitary hovel down there beside the trail before you reach Pelechuco? You have? Well, it was occupied by a Customs official who lived alone except for a *pongo*, or native servant; and he treated that poor man pretty badly. It's a wonder the *pongo* stayed with him at all; but possibly there was more behind it than we knew. Anyhow, the official caught his servant pilfering, tied him up, slung a rope under his arms and lowered him from the stone bridge in front of the house just above the waterfall. The rope broke; the *pongo* dropped into the rushing mountain torrent beneath, and was carried over the fall and drowned.

"Three nights later, the official was sitting in the hut, with door and windows bolted, when a stone hit the wall behind him and fell to the floor. He jumped up in alarm, and for an instant thought that somebody must have thrown a stone from outside against the building, but there it was on the floor—inside. How could it have come in? Then another stone—a large one—crashed against the table; and immediately there came a shattering noise as a third landed in the midst of his crockery.

"He seized his rifle and flung open the door, prepared to fire at any movement out there in the dark. His radius of vision was small enough, but he had barely time to turn his head when a stone struck him on the forehead. He reeled back with blood flowing from an ugly wound, and slammed the door.

"Next day he came to me begging my help. Together we went down to the *choza* (hovel) and he showed me the stones on the floor—fair-sized river pebbles they were, as big as your fist. I stayed with him until nightfall, and as soon as it was dark the stone-throwing commenced afresh. The pebbles seemed to come right through the boarded window or front wall, and were aimed at the official as though from a great distance. Amazed and, to tell the truth, scared, I murmured, 'It's the Devil that's doing it!' and at once the stones came in directly at me. I was quite unable to explain the mystery, and so incredible is it that I don't expect you to believe that part of the story. I doubt if I would had I not been involved in it as an eye-witness.

"The official could not continue to live there, and for three months the *choza* was unoccupied, but during that time several daring villagers went down to witness the stone-throwing for themselves—and they did! You can question them if you like. Then, only last week, a *Calahuaya* visited Pelechuco and was induced to lay the ghost. He burnt herbs on the threshold and for some hours chanted unintelligible *mantras*, then pocketed his fee and made off. Since that day there has been no stone-throwing, and the official is again living there."

I was not inclined to dismiss Franck's story as a hoax, having heard similar accounts elsewhere. They appear to be genuine visitations of poltergeists, a form of haunting not uncommon in the Andean highlands. The Vicar of Jauja, in Central Peru, told me of his being called in to lay a poltergeist that bombarded a *cholo* labourer and his family in a *choza* on the outskirts of the town. All had been hit by the stones, and one little girl was bruised all over her body. Not the least strange part about it was that the stones or rocks hurled came from a very considerable distance, for they were of a kind not found within many miles of Jauja. The Vicar was quite unsuccessful in putting a stop to the visitation. Not only was he himself rather frightened, but he was up against something not recognized nor provided for in his religion. Eventually the haunting ceased by itself and peace came to the *choza*. No apparent reason for it was ever given.

We were loath to leave Carlos Franck's hospitable roof for the freezing bivouacs of the heights, but in order to pick up various triangulation points northwards along the eastern slopes of the *Cordillera* it was necessary to leave Pelechuco. A farm of his lay on our route near Queara, and here we enjoyed another taste of his hospitality. Here, too, we were serenaded by a large band of drunken Indians who danced outside the house for a whole night and day between intervals of drinking *kachasa*.

The Indian inhabitants of Pelechuco, Muñecas and Apolo saw in the actions of the Boundary Commission working on behalf of Peru an attempt to invade their country, and patriotic fervour was flaming up to create a very delicate situation. We, on the other hand, as representatives of Bolivia, were heroes who had come to repel the invasion, and the clamour everywhere was for arms to avenge the national honour. The fact that the other Commission subsequently destroyed some of the numbered cairns I had erected for plane-tabling made it obvious to us that resentment was not confined to the wholly ignorant.

From Queara we climbed up to the source of the Tambopata, camping at an altitude of 17,000 feet and suffering tortures from the cold. At one spot in the pass we discovered that all the compass needles were completely neutralized within a radius of about half a mile, and suspected a considerable deposit of iron.

Of all the hair-raising trails I have encountered in the Bolivian Andes, that from Queara to Mojos is the worst. The *cuestas*, or ascents and descents, were so steep as to be almost impassable, and in many places sections had been washed away by rain-swollen torrents, leaving great gaps for us to bridge. We lost twelve of our twenty-four cargo mules through accidents during this trip. It was most fortunate that none of the party were killed. There were ledges so narrow that though the animals kept to the very edge of the trail a mule's load would often foul on jutting rocks, and knock it screaming over the precipice. One of them fell hundreds of feet to the river, where it lay dead between two rocks, all four feet in the air and splintered provision-boxes all round it. Another fell a hundred feet, and was caught by its load wedging between two trees. There it hung, high off the ground, unconcerned enough to nibble at everything edible within reach, and as it couldn't be freed we were forced to shoot it.

All the country in the neighbourhood of Mojos is rich in gold and it is difficult to understand why the village itself was abandoned. High above it on the mountain-side was another abandoned village, where the climate was superb and the view incomparable. Not more than five Indian families remained, and there was no activity of any sort, yet it will surprise me if this place does not again become a centre for gold-mining.

Climbing mountains and dropping down into the lush valleys we followed the course of the Queara River to its confluence with the Pelechuco, where it becomes the Tuiche, and then scrambled up a steep trail high above the river to the little village of Pata. There were only four small farms and about a dozen inhabitants, but the *Corregidor* (Headman) made us welcome and accommodated us in a hut where fleas attacked us in legions. There being no water in the village, every drop had to be brought up from the river, 2,000 feet below.

The backward peoples of these isolated hamlets and forest communities consider that every foreign visitor is necessarily a doctor. True, one does acquire certain fundamentals of medicine and first aid, for in the wild self-reliance is a virtue, and this may well be looked upon as a skill where no specialized knowledge is available. Many of the missionaries who penetrate to these parts are qualified medical practitioners, and so it is by no means rare on arrival in a village to be called on to attend the sick. This happened to me in Pata.

A woman of the village was suffering torments from a badly infected hand, and her family begged me to operate on her. Costin held her head and arms in a blanket, Manley looked after her legs and handed me the instruments, and deaf to the muffled screams I went to work. It was perfectly successful, and next day she came to me full of gratitude asking how much she was to pay. Her surprise was unbounded at learning that there was no fee, for these people are not accustomed to receiving any service or favour without extravagant payment being exacted. Her son insisted that the least he could do in recompense was to tell me the secret of a goldmine he had discovered.

In the old Peruvian records of the Province of Charcas this mine is stated to be extraordinarily rich. Its location was lost when in 1780 the *Cacique* of Tungazuque, Jose Gabriel Tupac-Amaru, incited the Indians to rebellion against Spanish rule, and all the mines east of the *Cordillera* were concealed and the trails to them destroyed.

My informant was returning from a local fair and, to avoid trouble with the cargo animals on a particularly bad section of trail, took a short cut up a certain stream—which he pointed out to me. Suddenly he and the two Indians with him found themselves in front of several small tunnels in the mountain-side, which from the overgrown piles of ore at their mouths were obviously old mine workings. They entered and found rusty tools lying on the floor, and moulds into which the gold was poured after smelting. I never found time to visit the place myself, and it seems unlikely that it has been disturbed by anyone else.

Though in the early Colonial days all the existing mines were recorded in detail, very few of those subsequently lost have been rediscovered. Their locations are not unknown, but the Indians hold the secrets and nothing will induce them to speak except in a few cases when information has been given in gratitude for some kindness. In the cruel past torture elicited nothing. How far unscrupulous priests have been successful with the weapons of superstition and terror I can't say, but I rather think the indigene still has a far greater respect for his ancient gods than for the Hell of the Christians.

Tradition says that the Indians piled a big mound over the shaft of the fabulously rich Sunchuli mine. The great mine of San Juan de Oro has never been rediscovered. It lies somewhere about 13° 50' south, between the bends of the Inambari and Tambopata Rivers, and to gauge its possible value one may take as yardstick the 'Olla de Oro' mine on the eastern slopes of Illimani, near La Paz.

David Bricker, an energetic American mining engineer and prospector, had heard of the 'Olla de Oro' and set out to find it. After long and careful search he came to a place where a slight fall of cliff had left a small hole exposed; this he entered by crawling on his stomach, to discover that it was the adit to a mine with no less than twenty-eight galleries. The mine was developed and made a fortune for its lucky finder, for the ore exceeded fifty ounces to the ton.

There has been speculation as to where the Incas obtained their vast hoards of gold and silver. Some consider that it was the accumulation of centuries spent in panning the rivers, while others believe that the extraordinary richness of the mines caused these elsewhere rare metals to be used because they came so abundantly to hand. I incline to the latter belief. The artificial value of gold and silver was created by the Spanish *Conquistadores*, before whose coming the virtues of these metals were their ease in working and their beauty. To this day silver is not considered a rare metal in Peru.

My success as a surgeon brought me another patient, the wife of the *Corregidor*, who as far as I could see was suffering from an internal tumour or cancer. Her husband begged me to operate on her, but in view of my limited knowledge I dared not, for I was afraid that if she subsequently died I should be held responsible. As a matter of fact she did die, only three days afterwards, and I often wonder if it was right to refuse the request.

We left Pata and came to Santa Cruz, another depopulated village; though here the reason was a strange disease which had made its appearance in the last five years. The symptoms began with the vomiting of blood, and ended in death after a high fever. The place lay in the heart of a fine coffee country, and fruit was to be had for the picking, but rattle-snakes were everywhere and a constant danger.

We camped in the doorway of a church far grander than seemed appropriate to such a tiny place, and the few remaining villagers, miser-ably poor though they were, gave us the usual generous reception. We were obviously better supplied than they, and were, moreover, strangers and foreigners, yet these poor ignorant *cholos* were ready to give away the priceless little they possessed in the interests of hospitality. This fine instinct languishes in the sterility of what we like to call civilization, but it is part of the nature of primitive or retarded peoples whom we cus-tomarily regard as a lower form of human life. Surely it is one of the fundamental virtues on which true nobility of character rests, and those who possess it are not to be looked down on.

We filled the children up with chocolate and cakes, and managed to save one of them from a rattlesnake, which served to some extent as a return for the many kindnesses received. Incidentally, an Englishman in Apolo told me that here in Santa Cruz a rattlesnake seven feet long had been killed and found to possess forty-two rattles—this is, I believe, twenty more than the official record! So numerous are these pests that they made coffee-gathering hazardous, and this coffee is in big demand, reputed by experts to be the best there is.

Apolo, our next stop, was once the centre of an extensive Indian population, and was the first forest mission of Old Peru after the Conquest. It lay in the middle of a very fertile plain, yet about five hundred people lived there in dreadful squalor and poverty, no one appearing to do any work. The drinking-water was taken from a dirty stream at a point below that where the inhabitants emptied their garbage and washed their filthy garments. Small wonder that disease was rife!

A Bolivian medical commission was in town trying the effect of '606' on that horrible disease *Espundia*, or Delhi boil. Hearing of this, sufferers had come in from miles around, and the one street swarmed with grue-some victims whose faces had in some cases been entirely eaten away. It is generally supposed to be caused by the bite of a fly infected by some forest beast, as the *tabana* fly is infected by the capibara in the case of *mal de cedera* in horses and the pest in cattle. This does not, however, explain the prevalence of the same disease in the 10,000-foot belt up in the mountains, where it is called '*Uta*'; for a forest fly would be unable to live in the high altitude and harder climate.

I believe '606' was ineffective.[1] If caught in the early stages the disease may submit to strong antiseptics, but the inhabitants of the forest settle-ments have their own ideas about it and resign themselves to its running the full course.

---

[1] It was. The disease is now (1951) being seriously studied by U.S. specialists, and one hopes that soon the '*Uta*', as well as the dreaded '*Verruga*', will be definitely curable.—ED.

It seems that one is destined to meet with Englishmen even in the most isolated places in South America. You might wonder what there is to attract them in such places as Apolo, but a little reflection provides the answer; and in many ways they are to be envied. Their standing in the community is considerable, they live easily and in a fair degree of comfort, and there are few worries to distract them. Their existence provides sure escape from the lurking fear of that heritage of a worn-out financial system—unemployment. I believe the attraction is more in this than anything else. The English peel off the unessentials of modernity very easily—they 'go native' more readily than any Europeans except the Italians; and the more refined their upbringing the quicker the change comes about. There is no disgrace in it. On the contrary, in my opinion it shows a creditable regard for the real things of life at the expense of the artificial. Drink and bad behaviour may often have something to do with it, but it is not uncommon to find that the utmost simplicity in living is sought for its own sake.

We were entertained in Apolo by a cheerful and capable Englishman named Flower, married to a Bolivian, and while we were there his pretty daughter celebrated her birthday with a ball, which we attended in spite of our forest kit. We danced the *Cachucha* to the best of our ability, and cocktails and beer were served so generously that before the party broke up many of the guests were asleep on the floor.

The *Cachucha* is an attractive dance and perhaps some day it may be seen in the ballrooms of London and New York. It represents the flirtations of the cock bird to the hen and can be danced with a coyness that is rather taking. Some of the national dances of South America have been introduced into the northern countries and have met with such popularity that success would be almost certain were the *Marinera*, the *Zamacueca*, the *Cachucha*, and others revived and transplanted from their 'equatorial' setting.

From Apolo we returned to Santa Cruz, where Manley left us to go up to the *Altiplano* and escort down a Biologist from the National Museum at La Paz, who was to join the party for the forest expedition. On their way back they would meet the mules in Santa Cruz and follow Costin and myself, who would by that time have gone on ahead to the Tambopata.

Meanwhile, Costin and I struck off to Boturo on the Tuiche, and proceeded up the Asuriama with the object of attempting a cross-country trip to the Tambopata basin and so to San Carlos *barraca*. It was hard going, for we had to clear a trail ahead of the animals each day, and our crashing advance was liable to be resented by the insect and reptile life hidden in the dense undergrowth. On one occasion we somehow passed a large wasps' nest without disturbing it. Not so the mules, for the leading animal approached too close, and its load caught one corner of the nest. Two wasps alighted on its rump, and all of a sudden the mule shot into the air; boxes scattered in all directions, pack-saddle cinches parted, and it vanished into the scrub, while terrified birds shrieked in the trees overhead to mark its passage. The following mule fared in the same manner—so did the next—and the next! All the rest of that day was spent in tracking down the animals, gathering up the stores and repairing the pack saddles.

On the trail along an affluent of the Tambopata, called the Cocos River, I saw the most glorious butterfly I have ever seen. It was of a yellowish-grey colour with brown markings and orange antennae, and the hind wings had dark brown tails about six inches long with spiral ends. Naturalists may know the species, but never before had I seen it, and never did again. These forests are a paradise for the entomologist, the butterflies are everywhere, and the number of different species is amazing. There must surely be many not yet collected—perhaps entirely unknown.

Heavy rains had swollen the Cocos River, preventing our fording it, and this delayed us considerably, but at length we reached the Tambopata at Playa Paujil, thus connecting up with the work of the previous year. I wanted to make sure of the work here, anticipating possible argument about it later owing to the determination of the Peruvian Commission not to descend the Heath River. It was my intention afterwards to return to the Heath and cross by way of the forest to Ixiamas and from there to Rurenabaque on the Beni, for there had been whispers of Incan remains in that region.

I had by this time heard in several places vague traditions about remains of the ancient civilizations, and my imagination was stirred by them to such an extent that the urge to investigate was becoming more and more insistent. Already I had begun the eliminatory process whereby the location of certain of these remains was after more years of careful study fixed, and had I known then of the document containing the account of Raposo's Lost City of 1743 much time lost in the Bolivian forests might have been saved. Needless to say, I knew nothing about the wonderful mountain city of Macchupicchu, later to be disclosed by Hiram Bingham with the Yale Expedition, in the gorge of the Urubamba north-west of Cuzco. Just as Macchupicchu's location was unknown throughout the Colonial epoch, so may other places yet to be discovered form the basis for many of the legends familiar to the indigene.

From Playa Paujil we reached San Carlos with great difficulty. The general atmosphere at the *barraca* was considerably easier than on the previous occasion. The manager at the *barraca* was jubilant at the un-expected solving of his transport difficulties, for the District Judge of Sandia had come in and proved to be a Peruvian *arriero* who at once signed a contract to freight out all the San Carlos rubber. Man-power, too, usually most difficult to obtain, was to be had for the taking, the

Indians of Sandia being eager to come in with loads in order to escape conscription by the Prefect for service as carriers to the Peruvian Commission, a labour they appeared to dread.

A marked respect towards us on the part of the San Carlos people had mystified us for a time, but was explained by our having successfully brought a raft down a particularly dangerous stretch of river below Playa Paujil, which apparently even the most skilled *balseros* would not attempt. Costin and I—we had been tramping the whole neighbourhood with packs—really had no idea what we were letting ourselves in for when we built a *balsa* and started off in our ignorance downstream. How we ever came through alive I don't know.

The stoicism of the Indian is amazing. A man came in with his left arm gone—blown off by the bursting of one of the rotten gas-pipes sold as guns to the rubber pickers at an exorbitant price. Seeing his arm hanging only by the ragged muscles, he cut it off with his *machete* and stopped the bleeding by holding the stump in hot copaiba oil. His clean recovery suggested that the local belief in the medicinal virtue of this oil is well founded, and indeed it is much used in the forests for application to open wounds.

Generally there is no way to make an Indian cry out or show emotion when he doesn't want to. He seems able to stand any pain, and without doubt the nerve-deadening effect of the coca-chewing habit has a lot to do with it. However, I remember a case in San Carlos when an Indian succumbed to pain and rolled on the ground with yells of agony, and that was after he had stuffed himself full of dry, uncooked rice, followed by a long drink of water from the river. I knew of no remedy in such a case—nothing, that is to say, within my power—but his companions tied his wrists and ankles, spreadeagled him between four convenient trees, and proceeded to literally dig the rice out of him with bits of iron bent up at the end! He survived this treatment, was enough relieved by it to show gratitude, and I dare say exercised considerably greater care in the future.

The Indians are accustomed to alternate periods of scarcity and plenty. When there is plenty their instinct is to eat as long as there is food so as to prepare for the scarcity that is sure to follow. The amount they succeed in getting into themselves is prodigious. I saw my eight Indians on the Acre finish off five pigs at a sitting; but this effort was surpassed by two men in Sandia who ate the whole of a llama in one continuous feast —and the llama in bulk of meat is nearly equal to a donkey!

These forests are not free from occasional hurricanes, which can rip a track some hundred yards wide and many miles in length, felling every tree in a tangle of branches, creepers and scrub. The difficulty in cutting one's way through it afterwards is increased by the ants and wasps, angry at the destruction of their nests and eager to attack. One such hurricane hit San Carlos while we were there. We heard the awe-inspiring roar of the approaching deluge and the crash of toppling trees, and then it was on us, flinging us down blinded and deafened. One of the huts disintegrated and vanished, a wall tilted and fell flat; the roof of the main building began to lift, but all the men and women who were able to do so crawled up and hung on to it while ropes were slung across the top and large stones piled on. Then with a final burst the storm passed and we listened to its thunder as it mowed a path through the forest beyond.

The Biologist came in with Manley at the end of September. He was a disappointed man when he learned how the expedition was to proceed, for instead of being able to travel with the comfort of luxurious equipment —with reference books, collecting-boxes and so on—he was expected to pack on his own back all he needed, plus a share of the foodstuffs and instruments. Mules could not be taken farther, and it was a question of carrying all we could ourselves.

The trail to Marte was particularly difficult on account of the tangle created by the hurricane, and in many places the mud was knee-deep. Bit by bit the Biologist jettisoned his equipment until he had thrown away everything except food, a magnifying glass and a hammock. We carried nothing superfluous, and I remonstrated with him about it.

"I know packs are awkward things to carry," I argued, "but you get accustomed to them in a few days. All this stuff you're throwing away will be needed later."

"Not by me," was his reply. "I don't need these things!"

I shrugged. Maybe he was hardened sufficiently to do without them.

As if to serve as an object lesson to the Biologist, there passed us a string of emaciated rubber pickers, all of them Indians of the *Altiplano*, each with a load of 150 lb. of rubber for San Carlos. Several were suffering from a disease called *Sejtiti*—a species of leprosy contracted in these parts and in the *Yungas* (the warm valleys of the mountains)—and were covered with running sores and soft warts. Their packs were nearly three times as heavy as ours, yet sick though they were they kept going.

Owing to the fever so prevalent at the *barraca* of Marte, we detoured around it, camped in the forest and crossed to the Heath on the following day. The Indians from San Carlos would not go any farther than the river, but carried supplies for us as far as the beach, dumped them there and returned.

We built two *balsas* and set off downstream, Manley and I on one, Costin and the Biologist on the other. We had not gone far before our old friends the Echocas, delighted to see us again, came in with bananas and maize.

The Biologist was inclined to be suspicious of the Echocas, but showed more confidence when by their expert treatment he had been relieved of the many *sututus* under his skin. He attracted more of these unpleasant creatures than we did and was suffering continual pain from them.

"Why not chuck it and go back?" I asked him. "We've barely started yet and the trip is going to be a great deal worse than anything you've yet experienced."

His reply filled me with misgivings, but I admired his pluck.

"Not me," he said. "I've come this far and I'm going to see it through!"

Each of us seemed to attract a particular insect pest. If with the Biologist it was *sututus*, with me it was wasps, and with Costin the monster *tucandera* ants, an inch and a half long. There was an exhibition one morning in front of the Echocas when Costin, pulling on one of his field boots, all of a sudden went mad—dancing, shouting and running in circles. Finally he sat down, tore the boot off, and exposed a toe with a *tucandera* ant clinging to the end with scythe-like mandibles. The Echocas, at first alarmed, burst into roars of laughter. They rocked, they rolled on the ground, they beat one another on the back and guffawed anew, for here was uproarious entertainment put on for their own especial benefit. After that, they frequently requested by means of signs and much laughter that Costin repeat the performance, and even offered him live *tucandera* ants to put in his boots!

CHAPTER XIV

THE TURN OF THE ROAD

BEFORE we set off down the Heath the Majordomo of Marte heard of our presence and came across with a fair-sized party to visit us.

"We're on our way to the plantations you told us about," he informed me. "Now we know of the savages and the food they have there, we feel we must do something about getting supplies, for back at the *barraca* the pickers are keeping alive on nothing but leaves—and we have three hundred pickers to provide for, you know."

"Do you mean Marte is in a state of starvation again?"

"Yes, that's it. When are we not? It's the one thing we can be sure of!" He patted my shoulder and added: "Thanks to you, we now have hopes of being better off than before; but even so, I wish we were as well off as they are at San Carlos."

In this region there are to be found two valuable herbs which merit attention. The first of these is the *Yawal Chunca*, a small bush with leaves ten inches long by three wide, green on the front and a lighter shade behind, with veins and tips of a blood red. Three or four of these leaves infused in a quart of boiling water make an admirable cure for fever. The other is a shrub called *Pando de Coca*, well known to the Indians, who chew it. Its properties are similar to the ordinary Coca, but in a milder form. Neither of these herbs is exploited commercially, but both are in regular use by the people of the district.

With illness and disease so prevalent it is no wonder that herbal remedies are used in the *Montaña* of Bolivia and Peru. In the mountains, too, it seems as though every disorder has its appropriate nature-cure, and the average *cholo* relies almost entirely on herbs except when forced to submit to medical treatment. Colds and coughs yield readily to *Wila Wila*, a plant like Edelweiss, found only at the highest altitudes. In the coastal regions an infallible cure for the most advanced cases of arthritis or rheumatism is the *Sanguinaria Canadense*, or Bloodroot. There are a hundred remedies tor every one I know of, and, of course, the medical profession does not encourage people to make use of them. Yet the cures they effect are often remarkable, and I speak as one who has tried several with complete success. The method of using the herbs is in all the cases I am familiar with to make an infusion in the same way as tea.

Vampire bats swarm on the Heath. They never fail to locate a camp, and at night any exposed part of your person is attacked—in fact, they will sometimes gnaw through the mosquito-net to get at you. There are such myriads of bats in South America—and particularly in the Andean foothills—that the day may come when they may be recognized as having a value for the sake of their pelts. Many have a lovely fur not unlike the mole's in its richness, but of a rosy-brown or sometimes a robin red shading into dark mole. The Incas used bat fur for adorning their garments, and made it unlawful for any but the reigning family to wear it. The vampire bat is a nuisance to human beings and animals alike, and a fortune awaits the enterprising person who commercializes the use of its fur.

We had easy going on the *balsas* to the Echocas' camp. Their big communal hut had been blown down by the hurricane and lay on its side—even here the damage was as marked as in San Carlos. Food was plentiful as usual.

By this time the Biologist—he was a European, by the way—was suffering badly from his sores and from lack of a change of clothes, for those he possessed were stinking. He was beginning to realize how foolish he had been to throw away all but immediate necessities in his pack, and became increasingly morose and frightened. The Echocas had temporarily relieved him of the torture of the *sututus*, but he objected to their methods of extracting these pests, and when a new crop of sores began to appear preferred to use his own remedy—corrosive sublimate. As a result the grubs died inside his skin and left ugly, festering wounds. The bad smell of these and his reeking clothes combined to make him a most unsavoury object, and as we had thunderstorms every day with deluges of rain, he grew worse instead of better.

I was frankly anxious about him. If blood poisoning set in he would be a dead man, for there was nothing we could do about it. By the time we reached the point for the overland crossing I thought him unfit to take to the forest at all; and a few days later I doubted if we could even get him back to San Carlos in time to save his life. Thunderstorms continued, the river was in flood, and to return upstream on *balsas* would mean hugging the bank and pulling ourselves along by grabbing at every branch—far too strenuous a job for a sick man. The only way was to strike up river on foot, and this we did.

Manley went down with fever, but struggled on; and a *sututu* caused a bad sore on Costin's leg. Luckily there was plenty of food to be had, for the Echocas' plantations were everywhere, and they had a custom of "laying" the upper part of a banana tree with the fruit still on it, leaving the fruit thus to ripen more quickly than it would if picked. The chief difficulty was the thorny bamboo, *Tacuara*, which nearly proved too much for ailing men to cut through; but eventually we reached the Echocas' camp again. A new hut had gone up, so there was shelter for us, and maize made a welcome change from bananas.

The kindly savages extracted the *sututus* for us, one nearly an inch long coming out of my back. I had another in the arm which was giving me trouble, and this they removed only after the last resort of dabbing beeswax and a sap of some kind on it. Then they accompanied us upstream, carrying the Biologist's and Manley's loads for them.

I dislike referring to the Echocas as 'savages' and only do so for identification purposes—to differentiate between a domesticated Indian and one in his natural state. These people were primitive, but resembled jolly children more than the generally accepted idea of a savage. There was nothing sly or deceitful about them, and the readiness with which our friendly overtures had been received was plain proof of how unjustified is the general condemnation of all the wild forest people. Friendship once established was binding. Nothing they could do to help us was too much for them. Clean and modest in their persons, as they were kindly in character, I had by this time a warm regard for them, and looked on their inherent nobility as far greater than that of many 'civilized' peoples.

The Echocas knew all the short cuts on the way up to Marte, so their company saved us much time. Even so, I never expected to get the Biologist to San Carlos alive. He was scarcely able to drag himself along by day; at night he slept on the ground, for his hammock had been thrown away long ago.

At the upper plantation we found the Marte foraging party still at work, and they joined us to proceed together as far as their *barraca*.

"Four of my men have already died of starvation," the Majordomo told me. "We've often gone for several days at a time without a bite to eat."

"Why isn't something done about your situation?" I asked. "Surely supplies can be sent down to you from San Carlos?"

"Possibly—but it's a question of the cost. Marte hardly pays enough to warrant the expense, and unless production were very big indeed nothing of the sort would be considered."

Three Echocas were still with us, and food problems never bothered them. When hungry, one of them would go off into the forest and call for game; and I joined him on one occasion to see how he did it. I could see no signs of an animal in the bush, but the Indian plainly knew better. He set up ear-piercing cries and signed to me to keep still. In a few minutes a small deer came timidly through the bush to within a yard of us, and the Indian shot it with bow and arrow. I have seen them draw monkeys and birds out of the trees above by means of these peculiar cries.

The Echocas even stayed with us at Marte for a couple of days, while the sick men recovered sufficiently to go on, and accompanied us as far as San Carlos. Without their help the party—as a party—might never have reached it. The Biologist's sores were attracting clouds of flies by this time, but at the *barraca* they were carefully washed and healed; and by a stroke of luck an *arriero* came in who was able to take him on mule-back to Sandia. We were doubtful if he would survive, but as it happened he did—not anxious, I fancy, to make any more forest journeys.

As soon as Manley had shaken off his fever, the three of us—he, Costin and myself—tramped through the forest to Santa Cruz, where our mules should have been waiting, only to find that the *arriero* had gone off with all but two mangy beasts and had probably sold them, for we never saw them again. To procure more animals from Flower, Costin rode to Apolo on one of the remaining mules. Luck was against him. Apolo had been burnt down and no mules were to be had—in fact *Gringos* were at the moment in bad repute, for Flower was considered responsible for the mishap.

No rain had fallen in Apolo for a long time, so the local church organized a religious procession with prayers for it. Flower—a heretic—laughed at the procession with its blood-drenched effigies of martyrs and its wilting candles; and then one of those candles fell to the ground and started a fire which spread at an alarming speed, caught the tinder-dry houses, and destroyed the place in a matter of minutes—all except Flower's own house, which was roofed with tiles and escaped the holocaust. There could be no doubt of it—his ridicule was the cause of the tragedy!

The two mules served to carry our packs, and thus lightened we set off on foot for Pelechuco. The journey seemed interminable, for under the most favourable conditions it was bad going, but walking we did at least escape the hair-raising ordeal of riding on those narrow mountain trails. When, weary and disheartened, we finally arrived in the mountain village, Carlos Franck welcomed us, and fixed us up with mules for the trip to Cojata. On December 19 we reached La Paz.

The Boundary Delimitation had been the cause of much trouble with Peru, in spite of the fact that Bolivia had ceded to her the land on which boundary marks were arbitrarily put up. There was much dilatoriness which didn't suit me at all. I didn't relish being involved in an international situation so delicate that the two countries were almost at war with each other, so I resigned from boundary work. As far as I was concerned, the President was very cordial and quite understood the situation; and the Minister for Foreign Affairs appeared to be highly amused by it. There had been all sorts of newspaper talk and much abuse on both sides, but in spite of ugly incidents on the border, due to patriotic zeal, a crisis had not come about.

After our withdrawal, so nearly was an Indian rising precipitated that a French Commission was appointed by Bolivia to fix the frontier. It disagreed with the Peruvian findings, and one of the Commission had a row with a Bolivian political officer and challenged him to a duel, which was discreetly refused. In spite of our work of 1910, the only wild section of the frontier, the Heath, was not touched because of its 'savages', but my maps were accepted as official. There was some disagreement at the Tambopata end over the position of the frontier, and the French Commission refused to accept any findings but their own, which were within a minute fraction of our 1910 demarcation. Anyway, I was out of it now and glad to escape, although fond of the actual work of surveying and sorry not to see the delimitation brought to a definite conclusion with full satisfaction on both sides.

When I next met the Minister for Foreign Affairs in 1913 he told me that the Biologist had left Bolivia.

"An expensive matter!" he remarked. "A salary of £500 a year for one beetle, and that a common one. It's too much even for the elastic finances of a West Coast Republic!"

"There is a wealth of scientific data to be had in the *Montaña* all the same."

"Then let someone else pay for it, Major. We've had enough of science for the moment."

There was no return to the army for me. My boats were burnt; but this, on the other hand, allowed me freedom for the private exploration I was itching to make. Even without going farther afield than the mountains and Andean foothills there was a vast amount of research waiting to be done into the remains of the Inca Empire. In the forests north and north-east of Cuzco are many ancient villages and fortresses still to be disclosed and investigated. Macchupicchu's romantic discovery was recent news. But my objective dated much earlier than the Incas, and I felt it was to be sought farther east, in the wilds still unknown. All the superior Indian tribes had traditions of a once great civilization to the east, of a race which may have sired the Incas—and even the mysterious people who left those gigantic remains the invading Incas found and adopted as their own.

In the forests were various beasts still unfamiliar to zoologists, such as the *mitla*, which I have seen twice, a black dog-like cat about the size of a foxhound. There were snakes and insects yet unknown to scientists; and in the forests of the Madidi some mysterious and enormous beast has frequently been disturbed in the swamps—possibly a primeval monster like those reported in other parts of the continent. Certainly tracks have been found belonging to no known animal—huge tracks, far greater than could have been made by any species we know. The anaconda attains greater dimensions there than is generally admitted, but, if reports from reputable travellers are persistently disbelieved, there is no way of proving it. They are dangerous reptiles to meet, and almost impossible to capture because of their prodigious strength—the really big ones, that is.

The savages, too, are not yet known—there are tribes whose existence is not even suspected. The robust, healthy tribes do not live near easily navigable rivers, but retire beyond the range of civilized man. In any case, where their presence is suspected, they are feared and efforts made to avoid them (for my part, I have always sought them!). Perhaps this is why the ethnology of the continent has been built up on a misconception which it will be my endeavour to rectify in a later chapter.

These were some of the reasons behind my resolve to devote myself to exploration in future, and use the information I had already gathered in an attempt to cast some light on the darkness of that continent's history. There, I believed, lay the greatest secrets of the past yet preserved in our world of today. I had come to the turn of the road; and for better or worse I chose the forest path.

Manley was by no means well, and Costin had the beginnings of what turned out to be *Espundia*, eventually cured at the London School of Tropical Medicine; so on January 6, 1912, we left La Paz for home, stopping a few days in the delightful climate of Arequipa.

It is a pity more tourists do not visit this lovely spot,[1] for not only is it in itself an interesting city, but also it is the gateway to Cuzco and the fascinating relics of Incan and pre-Incan civilizations. Indigenous life on the *Altiplano* is undergoing a change, and in another generation or so there may be little left of the colourful pageant of native customs.

Earthquake shocks are frequent in Arequipa—they seem to come with the full moon—and it is by no means rare for the inhabitants to be scared out of their houses in the dead of night. I was told of a recent shock which ended in the greatest hilarity—a panic transformed into general laughter.

The hotels were all full to capacity, and in one of them fifteen ladies

---

[1] The airlines have made Arequipa a popular tourist centre, and those who visit the 'White City' return there again and again! Since P. H. F. wrote those words there have been notable improvements in hotel accommodation here and elsewhere in Peru.—ED.

slept on the floor of a large room on one side while fifteen gentlemen occupied the other side. Among the latter was a corpulent Chilean of phenomenal hairiness—a sort of human doormat! During the night the city was shaken by a vicious tremor. The people rushed into the streets and *plazas*, clad in whatever came readiest to hand. The hotel referred to stood in the main square—the Plaza de Armas—where the biggest crowd congregated, and where the lighting was particularly good.

There was panic as the shocks continued with the low rumbling one feels rather than hears, and against the starry sky the cathedral towers swayed dangerously. Women fell to their knees and raised their arms in supplication, wailing for mercy, uncovering their bosoms and flinging wide their hair. Men crossed themselves and rolled their eyes in terror, striving to keep their feet.

All of a sudden people erupted from the hotel doors—a screaming, struggling mob—and in the rear hobbled the fat Chilean, mouth agape with agitation, his hairy torso covered by a woman's blouse and his ankles fettered in the tangle of a pair of feminine bloomers. At every few steps he halted to reach down, groping for the top of the bloomers so as to pull them up about his bare middle, but each time a new tremor defeated his purpose and drove him forward.

The populace gazed at this extraordinary sight and even forgot its own woe. A roar of laughter went up; at every fresh effort on the part of the Chilean the hilarity increased. Arequipa's sense of humour had come to the rescue and was proof against the worst the earthquake could do! Still laughing, the people returned to their houses. Still laughing, they recounted the episode over and over again next day. And the city continued to shake—but with laughter!

Devastating earthquakes seem to take place only once or twice in a century. I think 1867 was the year of the last serious one here. On that occasion the town suffered heavily and the cathedral towers fell. The south coast of Peru experienced in full force the same catastrophe; a tidal wave wiped out Arica, and in Pisagua Bay—itself the crater of a volcano—a high column of steam rose from the water and terrified the population. The whole of South America trembles periodically in the recurrent but diminishing waves of a vast eruptive age, the history of which can only be found in Indian legend. Even as far inland as the Plains of Mojos in Bolivia the lake known as 'Exaltacion' is frequently shaken by mysterious disturbances, during which columns of evil-smelling vapour are ejected. Their origin is probably volcanic; but it is also reasonably certain that an extensive oilfield of the future will be found in this region. Geologists have made a superficial examination of the more accessible parts of the country, but like the ethnological deductions there is too much theory and too little real knowledge in their reports.

CHAPTER XV

BULLS AND *BULTOS*

L A PAZ was deserted, for its population was flocking to the *Alto* —the high plain above the city—where a murderer was to be publicly executed by a firing squad. Men, women and even the tiniest children decked themselves out in their best clothes, took rugs and sandwiches, and struck off gaily up the steep road, for this was a spectacle not to be missed. Murders and executions were rare in La Paz.

Foreigners kept away, but we were told all about it afterwards. As a matter of fact, we heard little else for many a day. The Judge and the Chief of Police were binding the criminal to a chair, while the firing squad stood by in extreme nervous tension far exceeding that of the prisoner. So nervous were they that their shaking fingers closed on the triggers before the tying-up was completed, and a ragged volley sent bullets whining in all directions. A woman was hit and lay screaming on the ground; another bullet sent the Judge's top hat flying, and a third hit the Chief of Police in the seat! The prisoner cheered, and spat a stream of abuse after the fleeing officials.

The sergeant in charge of the firing squad promptly ordered another volley, aimed at the prisoner, and when this fusillade kicked up the dust round the chair without doing him any injury he began abusing the soldiers. That prisoner was game all right! He survived no less than eight volleys, and his curses only ceased when the sergeant came up beside him and finished the business at point blank range with a revolver.

Several days afterwards the *Alto* was the scene of another spectacle, but this time an aviation display. Two Italian brothers with a name something like Frankelini—I don't recall exactly what it was—were contracted

175

to fly a 25 h.p. aeroplane, and as such a thing had never before been seen up there La Paz was wild with excitement about it. The name of the late Jorge Chavez, Peruvian flying ace, was still fresh on West Coast lips, and it was felt that to bring La Paz up to scratch only the aeroplane was needed.

Unfortunately no one had realized the difficulty of getting an aircraft to take off from ground 13,000 feet above sea level, and the little motor whirled the chain-driven propeller to no effect, except to lumber the flimsy-looking contraption over the ground in erratic runs, during one of which three Indians were killed.

Disappointment turned to abuse—very nearly to violence. The Italians found it discreet to leave the aeroplane and get back to town as fast as they could, and for several days they lay low. When they ventured to appear in public again it was to find themselves mercilessly ridiculed as the two 'Fracasinis'—a clever and typically Creole play on the word '*Fracaso*', which means 'failure'. Nowhere is the art of the nickname more developed than in South America.

Todd, Costin and I had come up from Antofogasta in time to be present when these events took place. It was early in 1913, and we were shortly leaving for the Beni once more in order to explore the Caupolicán, which the collapse of the Biologist had made impossible in 1911. I had hoped to work eastward of Santa Cruz de la Sierra (not the Santa Cruz of the last chapter, but the much larger town farther south), but it was the year in the seven-year cycle when abnormal rains fall in the mountains and the brimming rivers turn all the low ground of the forest region into a vast swamp. Consequently the idea had to be temporarily shelved.

I was impatient to start off on the Quest, for while in Antofogasta my imagination was freshly fired by six queer metal figures which an Indian had brought down to sell. They were about six inches high, and reminiscent of Ancient Egypt. Where he obtained them he refused to say. He had, in fact, already sold them when I heard of them, but I was given the chance of examining them. Without question they were very old, and probably linked up with those things we were about to seek.

To complete the party, I picked up a young Englishman in La Paz who seemed promising. He accompanied us only as far as Huanay, however, for while bathing in the Mapiri River he swallowed a mouthful of water, choked, and lost his false teeth. That effectively prevented his coming with us, for without his teeth he would have starved. At Chiniri, on the way to Rurenabaque, I met our old cook Willis, who had bought a plantation there with the money he made selling drink in Riberalta. I tried to persuade him to join us, but nothing would induce him to do so.

Rurenabaque had not changed at all. The Englishman and the Texan gunman were still going strong; the same parrots chattered on the roof-tops; on their usual perch sat two familiar macaws, one imitating the violin and the other the flute, breaking off in order to greet any stranger with volleys of bad language in Spanish. In spite of the unchanged appearance of the place, there was a difference—Rurenabaque was beginning to feel the adverse effects of the dying rubber trade.

A Texan prospector joined us here; and after giving Todd time to recover from a bout of malaria we crossed the river and struck off for Tumupasa. I was eager to investigate a story about the '*Pozo de Tumupasa*', a hole reputed to be the shaft of a silver mine, but I could learn nothing of its location from the reticent Indians. The priests at the Roman Catholic mission either knew nothing of it or were unwilling to tell me; so we went on to Ixiamas, a pretty little place that might have a brighter future were communications not so bad.

In the church at Ixiamas we saw a very fine collection of plate, and were told that the silver had been obtained locally, but that the location of the mines was now unknown. We were also informed that a diamond rush was on up at the source of the Madidi, so we shouldered our packs and set off to investigate.

The upper reaches of the Madidi pass through deep canyons of soft red rock, subject to perpetual landslides. We found no trace of any mineral-bearing formation, and the 'diamonds' turned out to be topaz— there is no evidence that real diamonds will ever be found here.

Passing through the forest, we came out on the Tuiche at Asuriama, where in 1911 we crossed over to the Tambopata. It is hilly country, and signs of coal and oil are frequently met with. To me, it will always be associated with snakes, for here we had two narrow escapes from *surucucus*, or bushmasters.

I was climbing a steep bank thickly covered with small plants, and put my hand right on the snake. It instantly struck at Ross, the Texan, who was just ahead of me, and he turned like a flash, one hand reaching for the gun on his hip.

"Look out!" I yelled at Costin, and the two of us flung ourselves backwards. Then came a double crack from the Texan's six-shooter, and the bushmaster collapsed paralysed, shot clean through the head.

"Sure was a near thing, that!" murmured Ross, blowing the smoke from the barrel of his weapon and coolly slipping it back in its holster.

Costin and I picked ourselves up. "Did it get you?" I asked.

"Yeah—but I don't know where." He felt his legs and thighs with both hands, then paused for a moment, and drew from a trouser pocket his tobacco pouch. Together we looked at the holes puncturing it from side to side.

"My God!" said Ross, eyes widening. "He did get me! See, his fangs bit on this, and went right through." Swiftly he unbuckled his belt and lowered his trousers. There on his thigh were two dents made by those deadly fangs, but by a miracle of good fortune the skin was unbroken. The venom formed a wet patch on his leg. When satisfied that the snake was really dead, we measured the yellow body with its diamond markings, and found it to be seven feet long.

No one at Asuriama knew whether the Tuiche could be descended in rafts, but as the others in the party were game to take a chance we built *balsas* for the trip. We needed to take food supplies with us, so Costin and I tramped twelve miles up the trail to a sugar plantation where we hoped to buy some. On the way back there was another adventure with a *surucucu*, but this time the narrow escape was mine.

I was leading, and the two of us were loaded heavily with sugar and ducks. All of a sudden something made me jump sideways and open my legs wide, and between them shot the wicked head and huge body of a striking bushmaster. I shouted, half jumped and half fell to one side, and waited breathless for the second attack that I knew was certain to come. Yet it didn't: the brute slithered down to the stream beside the trail and lay there quiet. We had no weapons with us, and as it threatened to attack again when we pelted it with stones, we left it there. It was quite nine feet long and about five inches thick, and the double fangs, if in proportion, would be over an inch in length. Experts claim that these snakes reach a length of fourteen feet, but I have never seen one so big.

What amazed me more than anything was the warning of my sub-conscious mind, and the instant muscular response. *Surucucus* are reputed to be lightning strikers, and they aim hip-high. I had not seen it till it flashed between my legs, but the 'inner man'—if I can call it that—not only saw it in time, but judged its striking height and distance exactly, and issued commands to the body accordingly!

There is every indication that this part of the country was once the ocean bed. The soil and climate would be ideal for vineyards, and were the industry introduced transport would be no great problem. It is fine sugar country too; and gold is to be found here, as in so many other places where the forests and mountains adjoin.

When the two *balsas* were ready we took to the river. All four of us considered ourselves to be experienced raftsmen, but Costin and I took the lead and Todd followed with Ross. Little did we realize what a mad attempt we were making till we entered a canyon with high cliffs a few miles below Asuriama, where the 200-yard width of the Tuiche narrowed to about forty yards, and we encountered one dangerous rapid after another. Our speed increased till we were rushing along on the swift current, and I knew we would sooner or later come to grief.

After a mile of this the water deepened and the current slowed. We gained confidence as the rafts glided easily round a steep bluff, but then our hearts sank as we heard the sinister roar of a waterfall close ahead. I yelled a warning to the other *balsa* and struck down with the pole to turn in shorewards, but the water was too deep to find bottom. The current had us now, and we glided faster and faster towards the edge of a drop that might be anything from a few feet to a hundred.

"Keep her headed straight for it!" I shouted to Costin at the steering oar. Then we slid over the top, and the raft seemed to poise there for an instant before it fell from under us. Turning over two or three times as it shot through the air, the *balsa* crashed down into black depths.

How we came through it I don't know. Costin was up first—a hundred yards beyond the fall—and, not seeing me, thought I was drowned. When I came up gasping, free at last from the tug of the whirl-pools and eddies, it was to find the raft upside-down beside me, rushing at fearful speed towards another bad rapid. Then the stream shallowed and I felt bottom. The current had carried us in close to the rocks at the side, and after a few attempts we managed to find a handhold and pull ourselves out. The *balsa*, driven in with us, wedged itself between two rocks close by.

Looking back we saw what we had come through. The fall was about twenty feet high, and where the river dropped the canyon narrowed to a mere ten feet across; through this bottleneck the huge volume of water gushed with terrific force, thundering down into a welter of brown foam and black-topped rocks. It seemed incredible that we could have survived that maelstrom!

Todd and Ross were warned in time to avoid being caught in the drag of the current and carried over the fall. They portaged the *balsa* and equipment, re-launched it in the swift water below, and were wrecked by the force of the current just beyond where we landed.

All the baggage was securely lashed on the *balsas*, and we lost nothing except my hat; but clothing, instruments and camera were soaked—and the last ruined. It was out of the question to risk another disaster by river, so we abandoned the *balsas* and proceeded on foot to Apolo. Here our friend Flower gave me a hat of sorts to protect my bald head, for in those parts a hat is perhaps the most necessary of all bodily protection.

The worst of bad trails took us northwards to Tumupasa, and from there we cut back to Rurenabaque the changeless. Nothing new had occurred there since our departure except for the killing of a thirty-foot anaconda, caught in the act of devouring a sow. The sow was, of course, dead, but a litter of unborn pigs was saved alive, and the little animals were suckled at the breast of an Indian woman. Pigs were considered more valuable than humans in Rurenabaque!

We heard that up near Tumupasa an Austrian merchant had been murdered by three Indian slaves whom he had maltreated. They first shot him, then knifed him, and to make quite sure about it finished by holding his head under water in the river. Rurenabaque and Ixiamas joined Tumupasa in the hunt for the murderers as soon as the crime was discovered, and the three men were soon tracked down and captured. They received five hundred lashes apiece; but a judge came in from Reyes and ordered five hundred more. After that they were sent off to Apolo by river, but on the trip made their escape into the forest. One was tracked as far as a stream, where all marks mysteriously ceased, and the conclusion reached was that the Devil—or perhaps some beast—had made away with him.

My object now was to reach Santa Cruz de la Sierra, so as to proceed eastwards as soon as the dry season came. On foot the journey was too dangerous as herds of fierce wild cattle roamed the Plains of Mojos. We were warned of the wild bulls, which had killed many foot travellers. On mule or horseback there was little danger. The cattle feared riders and made off at sight. But neither mules nor horses were obtainable, so we went by ox-cart. Carts were safe enough.

The ox-carts of the plains have great solid wooden wheels six feet in diameter on axles of jungle hardwood, easy to replace in case of breakage—or on imported iron axles selling at £12 apiece. Wooden axles are considered preferable, for the high-pitched whine of the wood bearings keeps the draught oxen on the move—they are accustomed to the music of them and move reluctantly if it is missing.

I paid off Ross in Rurenabaque, and Costin, Todd and I set out across the *pampas* in a hired cart bound for Santa Ana. Before we reached Reyes, Costin again got stung on the foot by a big black *tucandera* ant, and owing to the swelling had to ride in the cart, a far more uncomfortable experience than trudging along behind it in the mud as Todd and I did. I doubt if spoked wheels would have stood up to the punishment that cart took as it crashed down into yard-deep ruts or bounded over hidden rocks. To stay in the cart at all, for all its slowness, was a feat!

Reyes turned out to be a collection of dismal Indian huts, with nothing interesting about it except that it once had a mission. It was built on an artificial mound twelve feet or so above the level of the surrounding plain, and except at the entrance a wide ditch encircled it. The place must be very old, for all over these plains are remains of the work of a big and probably ancient population—extensive terrepleins connected in places by miles of causeways. During the southern summer the whole plain is inundated; and these areas periodically under water are known locally as *bañados*.

Near Candelaria the bones of mastodons were recently dug up from close beneath the surface of the ground. Some of these ancient mammals may have existed here until comparatively recent times, and one wondered what monsters might yet be found in the less accessible places. We saw tapirs and rheas in this area, which is one huge sweep of fine pasture, thick with cattle, and with occasional island-like clumps of jungle.

One of the dogs, swimming a small stream near the cart, came within a foot of the jaws of a large crocodile, and strange to say the croc made no attempt to take it. This is most unusual, for, as I have mentioned before, they are nearly always eager to take a dog. The driver got down and poked the brute in the eye with his goad before it would move.

At Potrero we heard talk of some silver mines of fabulous richness in the vicinity of a place called Buena Vista, which with three nearby hills had been captured by Indians. We thought of investigating the story, but decided it was too nebulous to warrant such an extensive detour. In the loft of the little Potrero church were the wooden effigies of two saints, much venerated by the people, and believed to contain in hidden compartments of the bodies some great secret. No one had mustered courage enough to find out, and when we offered to examine them we met with a curt refusal.

While at Potrero we were asked to help an inhabitant who had shot himself through the head with a Browning pistol. As I had no suitable equipment for removing a piece of bone from the man's skull there was little I could do. There were always sick or injured people in these outposts, and all they could do for themselves was to swallow quantities of the quack remedies sold to them by wandering *mercachifleros*, or pedlars, for outrageous sums of money. For snakebite—these plains swarm with snakes of many kinds—they had only one remedy, and that was to kill the snake and apply its flesh to the punctures. It may have worked sometimes, but probably the cure resulted because no snake is at full venom within a fortnight of feeding, and in any case it doesn't always bite badly.

Costin had some adventures with the vicious-looking bulls that wander about here, either singly or in herds. He had gone off with a .22 rifle to hunt wild turkeys in one of the islands of forest at some distance from the cart, and we sighted a large black bull following his scent. We yelled a warning, and he turned to see the bull getting ready to charge. Luckily he had enough start to reach a thicket in a hundred-yard sprint before the bull caught up with him, and regardless of thorns or other deterrents he went head first into shelter. The bull, unable to get at him, prowled round and round, sniffing angrily and pawing the ground, and Costin took shots at the animal's eyes with his pop-gun whenever the chance allowed. Finally he succeeded in blinding it, and while the mad-dened bull hurled itself at the front of the thicket, he escaped out by the back, and came sprinting over to the safety of the cart.

One day I was myself fifty yards behind the others and to my horror saw a big red bull to one side of the trail between me and the cart. It was snorting, lashing its tail, and tearing up the ground—and I was without a rifle, and too far from any tree or other refuge. There was nothing for it but to pass him, so I swallowed the lump in my throat and advanced very slowly, fixing him with what I hoped was a hypnotic eye. It did the trick, and I passed by that bull without being charged. But not for anything would I repeat the experience!

Whenever possible, the local cattlemen lasso these vicious bulls and tie them by the horns to trees to die of starvation. It is cruel retaliation by man on beast; yet you get little mercy from the bulls when caught. One day we were attacked by three bulls, and it was only after one had been killed and the others riddled with bullets that they gave up the attempt to get us. An *estancia* owner of the district told me he had a horse killed under him, and escaped only because the bull continued to gore its dead victim. As elephants often will, these bulls sometimes even try to knock down a tree to get at a man who has taken refuge in the branches. Fortunately, there are fewer to be met with now than formerly, when they wandered in large herds of five hundred head or so, and at breeding time were a serious menace to all the inhabitants of the plains. They go two or three together now, but are more bad-tempered and dangerous than they were because the cows, being easier to catch, have been practically exterminated.

We came to an *estancia* where a child had just been bitten by a snake known as a *Yoperohobobo*—one of the Tachesis family, and a species of *jararaca*—and I was begged to see what I could do to help. The child's skin was hot and dry, and the leg which had been bitten showed the punctures and was greatly swollen. The ligatures already applied above the knee were too tight.

I had with me a small bottle of snake serum, given me by an Argentine woman on board ship during the voyage out. I gave the child two injections of this serum, one in the muscles of the back and the other in the leg above the bite. He was terrified at this, but after about half an hour broke into a profuse sweat and went to sleep. Next morning he was out of danger, much to the amazement of the parents, and they were even more amazed because I did not demand any fee.

We arrived in Santa Ana a day late to witness the extraordinary spectacle of a fight between a domestic bull and a wild bull. They fought on the outskirts of the town, surrounded by hundreds of excited cows stamping and bellowing shrilly from start to finish, and in the end the wild bull won. The vanquished animal lost both eyes and had to be shot.

The raising of cattle is the chief business in Santa Ana, a post on the Mamoré River. It is a neat little place; the well-constructed houses are built on the site of an old Indian village, and the one street is kept fairly clean. Drink is the curse here, as in so many of these isolated places. The inhabitants are always drunk, in the process of getting drunk, or sleeping off the effects of drink!

Here we saw for the first and only time a breed of dog known as the Double-Nosed Andean Tiger Hound. The two noses are as cleanly divided as though cut with a knife. About the size of a pointer, it is highly valued for its acute sense of smell and ingenuity in hunting jaguars. It is found only on these plains.

We took passage on the launch *Guapay* up river to Las Juntas. The east bank of the Mamoré is mainly in the hands of Indians, once tamed by the missions but now wild again—more, I think, from bad treatment than from natural inclination. For the sake of selling them as slaves to the rubber concerns, a white man who spent some years with them was base enough to lead a number of them into a trap. A year or two afterwards he was wrecked near the mouth of the river, was found and recognized by the Indians, and handed over to the women for torture.

A few years ago the Mamoré was not reckoned navigable for launches in the dry season, but when launches were introduced they kicked out a channel for themselves and now operate all year round. Before that, it was not uncommon for boats to be held up by the sandbanks and snags, and then the crews—usually tame Indians or slaves—would mutiny, murder the captain, and make off down river by way of the banks. This part of the country was said to produce a treacherous and cowardly type of native, but considering the abuses they suffered there is something to be said in their defence.

There is a fair-sized lagoon in the River Cusi, between Trinidad and Estrella, where there are still several large villages of wild Indians. At one time these Indians were led by a dour, red-headed Scotsman who had a grudge against civilization and lost no opportunity to express it in raids on the settlements. He was the terror of the countryside until his death. Eighty well-armed Bolivians once marched to attack his stronghold, but their courage gave out on the way, and they turned back. Though not so fierce now as formerly, the Indians still make periodic raids on the settlements, or capture travellers.

The *Guapay* ran aground below Las Juntas, and passengers were sent on by *batelón*. A rain-sodden, miserable and dirty group of huts formed the village, where we were forced to wait for carts to take us on to Santa Cruz. The hut we occupied was separated into two compartments by a screen of laths set well apart, and beyond the partition a man lay dying of smallpox. On entering our compartment, we saw something move in the gloom of one wall. It was big and writhing, and turned out to be a bushmaster. Fortunately we put a bullet into it before it could strike. Yet children had been playing in and outside the hut while it was there!

Before we left this place an old man came in from Santa Cruz with a dozen slaves for sale in Riberalta.

"I'll do all right with them, you understand," he confided, "but they're men—not so profitable as girls. If they was girls, now, I'd be sitting pretty!"

Cuatro Hojas is the real port for Santa Cruz when the river is not too low. From Las Juntas to Cuatro Hojas we rode the cart through a region of swamps at the edge of thick forest, and the trail was in a sea of mud so deep that the animals wallowed in it up to their bellies, and the wide-spaced eight-foot wheels of the cart alone made it possible to get through. It felt like riding a punt in the open sea during a gale, with violent jolts thrown in. There were snipe everywhere, and we shot enough with our ·22 rifles to give us a welcome change from the eternal canned food. There were also ticks—the *bichu colorado*, a tiny red one; and the *garapata do chão*, most venomous of them—and their bites kept us scratching.

At Cuatro Hojas another cart joined us, with a widow from Santa Cruz and two pretty and clever children. They were not hers—she had found them dumped on her doorstep and adopted them, although she was very poor. They were obviously half European. She told me that not so long ago unwanted babies were left by night at the doors of the church in the *plaza* at Santa Cruz to be devoured by the scavenging pigs that roamed freely in the streets. To stop it, the authorities had to banish the pigs—there was no holding up the supply of unwanted children!

Costin came floundering and cursing up to the cart one morning.

"It's after me!" he shouted, quite unnecessarily, for only about ten yards behind him was a huge black bull. If any wild cattle were around, Costin was sure to attract them. We emptied our rifles into it, and after a time it shook its head angrily, turned, and lumbered off into the swamp.

All round Santa Cruz is good cattle country—good country for crops too—but communications are so bad that it has not been developed. Indifferent mule tracks retard the progress of the place, which is a pity, for the soil is so rich that it could become the garden of Bolivia. The city has 20,000 inhabitants and 2,000 houses; it lies at 1,600 feet above sea level, in a delightful climate, and its fields produce three crops of maize in the year. Some day it will come into its own, but at present it is notable for incredible poverty, and, perhaps in consequence, a low standard of morals.

In the jail, where he had lain for two years, was an Englishman named Walker, about to be executed for his share in a brutal mass murder accompanied by robbery. For the sake of a considerable sum in gold, he and a German had killed every member of a convoy except for a woman who escaped and gave the alarm. Walker then shot the German to get his share. Since his capture he had escaped twice, but was recaptured on each occasion, once only a few paces from the frontier where he would have been safe—and brought back to Santa Cruz. Having met him years before in Rurenabaque, I went to the jail to see him. He told me that his trial was absolutely fair, and admitted that he deserved the fate that would be his in a day or two. When the time came he faced the firing squad with perfect composure, in front of the whole population of the town.

Todd was very ill, and before we could go east from here it would be necessary to return to La Paz and arrange for his passage home. We decided to stay in town a month to feed up and recuperate for the arduous trip up to Cochabamba; and rather than stop at the hotel, which was quite good but too noisy with drunks, I rented a house for next to nothing. Santa Cruz was not a particularly interesting place in which to stay. The streets were of sand, and in wet weather became a series of small lakes, crossed by means of unsteady stepping-stones. It had a cinema—in the open air—and the lurid melodramas so worked the audience up that a guard with loaded rifles had to be present at every performance. The people are very fair-skinned compared with the *cholo* predominating in the mountain districts, for here one finds Spanish blood as pure as anywhere in South America.

As the rest of the party preferred the hotel to the house, I was glad of the chance of bringing all the geographical work up to date. An *arriero* out of a job offered to cook for me, so he moved into the back premises while I slung my hammock in the large front room. The furniture consisted of a table, two chairs, a bookshelf and a lamp. There was no bed, but that didn't worry me, for hammock hooks are always found in the houses of these parts.

The first night I bolted the doors and wooden windows, and the *arriero* went out behind to his sleeping-quarters. I climbed into my hammock and settled down for a comfortable night's rest. Lying there after blowing the light out, waiting to sink into sleep, I heard something brush along the floor. Snakes! thought I, and hurriedly lit the lamp. There was nothing; and I told myself it must have been the *arriero* moving on the other side of the wall. No sooner had I put out the light than the brushing sound resumed, and a fowl scurried across the room, squawking noisily. Again I lit the light, wondering how the bird could have got in, and again I found nothing. The moment I put out the light for the second time there was a shuffling over the floor, like a crippled old man dragging himself along in carpet slippers. This was too much. I lit the lamp and kept it burning.

Next morning the *arriero* came to me, looking scared.

"I'm afraid I must leave you, *señor*," he said. "I can't stay here."

"Why not? What's the matter?"

"There are *bultos*[1] in this house, *señor*. I don't like it."

"Nonsense, man!" I pretended to scoff. "There's nothing. If you don't like being out at the back alone, move your things in here. There's more than enough room for the two of us."

"Very well, *señor*; if you let me sleep in here, I'll stay."

That night the *arriero* rolled himself up in his horse-blankets in a corner, and I, climbing into my hammock, put the light out. The moment we were in darkness there was the sound of a book being thrown across the room, its leaves fluttering. It seemed to strike the wall above me; but a light showed nothing, except the *arriero*, buried under the blankets. I put the light out, and the 'fowl' returned, followed by the 'shuffling old man'. After that I left the light burning and the hauntings ceased.

On the third night darkness was greeted by loud raps on the walls, and, following that, the crashing of furniture. I lit the lamp, and as usual there was nothing to see; but the *arriero* heaved himself up from his blankets, unbolted the door, and without a word fled into the night. I closed and bolted the door again and settled down, but no sooner was the light out than the table seemed to be lifted up and hurled down on to the brick floor with great violence, while several books flew through the air. When I lit up, nothing appeared to be touched. Then the fowl returned, and after it the old man, who came in to the sound of an opening door. My nerves are pretty good, but I had had about all I could stand of this, and next day left the house for the hotel. The noisy drunks there were at least human!

Enquiries disclosed the fact that no one would live in the house because of its evil reputation. The *bulto* was reputed to be the ghost of someone who had buried silver on the premises—a treasure nobody ever had the temerity to seek.

My 'poltergeist', though noisy, was, I think, less unnerving than the thing which haunted another well-known house in town—at any rate for one unversed in the ways of ghosts. Here the ghost was said to lean over anyone in bed in a certain room, to paw the victim with a bony hand, and puff a foetid breath in his face. Several occupants of that house had gone mad, and the place was now abandoned.

Todd was sent up to La Paz, and I wired home for another man to replace him. Then Costin and I set off for the mountains to look into

[1] *Bultos* means literally 'bundles', and is, I think, an expressive term for a ghost. I heard it first from locomotive-shed workers on a mountain railroad in Peru. The night shift came to me one day and asked for their hours of duty to be changed so as to avoid returning to their houses—beyond the town—in the darkness before dawn. They complained that every morning, when passing a shoulder of the cliffs surrounding the place, a *bulto* came out from the rocks and chased them. I asked them what the *bulto* looked like. "Like a sack with short legs," they said. I had to refuse their request, and they avoided further encounters with the *bulto* by waiting in the shed till daylight, or riding up to their houses on an outgoing freight train.—ED.

mining conditions north of Cochabamba. On the way we passed through Samaipata, a rather broken-down place, but with a future, for it lies at 5,300 feet up and enjoys an agreeable climate. Not far from the village are some Inca ruins, the most south-easterly settlement these ancient people have left. It was probably built by the Inca Yupanqui for his military expeditions to the east, for there are the remains of a palace, ruined baths, and a shaft or tunnel said to be the entrance to a treasure chamber. The place might be worth excavating, for village ploughs have turned up golden llamas and other relics. As far as I could find out, the only attempt ever made to explore the shaft was abandoned on the investigator's equipment being stolen, yet, I was told, half-way down is a passage branching off the shaft into the hill. The shaft has well-worn steps in it, cut out of the solid rock, and my impression is that it may have been a mine.

The Cochabamba trail follows in places the bed of the Rio Grande, and during the rains is often impassable. Where it runs through one or two narrow canyons it could even be dangerous were a cloudburst to take place above, as often happens in the Andes. On the whole the route is rather barren, but not unattractive, and the giant tree cactus found here gives the scene an almost surrealist look.

Life is colourful in Totora, a fair-sized Indian mountain village, but there is no pretence of cleanliness. In the dilapidated *tambo*, or rest-house, we shared a room with a number of sheep and pigs—and also their vermin.

Passing the 11,000-foot summit of the trail, we dropped down into the Cochabamba valley, and at Pucara heard the shriek of an engine whistle—the first since we left La Paz. It is a sound that above all others heralds one's return to the world of everyday, after months of primitive and lonely existence in the outposts—a thrilling sound eloquent of home and reunion with family and friends. When we drew nearer, the fussing exhaust of a switching locomotive and the crash of couplers was like music in our ears. It was only a steam tramway we found here, but to us it was magnificent!

We rode into Cochabamba in the tram; through the fertile country-side, well wooded with blue gums and thickly populated by the mountain Indians. As a city, Cochabamba is probably the best in Bolivia, for it has an ideal climate and is not too high. It is a branch railhead of the Antofogasta–Bolivia Railway, and may become a place of great importance—it certainly would, in fact, were road or rail communication established with the productive Santa Cruz country.

We ate a great deal of strawberries and cream and many other temperate zone fruits which for so long we had not tasted. Friends entertained us, took us out to the refreshing baths at Calacala, and proudly showed us the beauties of their city. They may well be proud of it, for it is beautiful and its situation is superb, set as it is in a bowl of the mountains with snow-covered peaks to the north. But for the popular fashion of dressing in unrelieved black the streets would be gay, for the buildings have plenty of colour and the *plazas* are decked out with flowers.

There is one unpleasant thing about Cochabamba, and that is the *Buichinchas*, or blood-sucking cockroaches, vile insects which enter the houses at night if windows are left open and gorge themselves on the sleeper. There are fleas, of course—in South America it is hard to escape them—but no one worries much about them, and in any case there comes a time when even the freshest-blooded foreigner ceases to feel them.

There was an establishment here at this time that made two very tasty drinks I have never found elsewhere. One was called *Viña Raya*, so named, I suppose, for its lightning strike and potency. The other, known as *Coca*, was made from a distillation of specially selected coca leaves in alcohol, with other ingredients added, and I don't recollect ever tasting anything quite so good. In colour and consistency it is like green Chartreuse, but its flavour is entirely its own. A wineglassful allays the pangs of hunger and adds to endurance, besides being an excellent stomachic. Anyone lucky enough to obtain the recipe and produce it in Europe or the United States would, without a doubt, make a fortune. I took a dozen bottles home with me, but, alas, they did not last very long!

At the junction of the Sacambaya and Inquisivi Rivers, not far from Cochabamba, is a ruined Jesuit mission where a big treasure is said to be buried. Sacambaya was the most accessible of a series of thirty-eight gold-mines worked in the area by Jesuits, who established at each mine a mission, and made use of Indian labour in bringing up the mineral.

When the Jesuits were banished from South America all these gold-mines were in full production, and the shipment of gold to Rome had been suspended for some time so that the priests might amass enough wealth to purchase a section of Bolivia and turn it into a Jesuit colony. On learning of their impending expulsion, however, all the gold was gathered at Sacambaya, where a tunnel was prepared by six Indians—a tunnel which took over a year to excavate, and which included thirty-eight alcoves. The treasure of each mission was deposited separately, and it took six months to close up the tunnel, for it was carefully filled in and a large egg-shaped stone placed in the entrance to the shaft. The six Indians were killed to ensure that secrecy be kept, and the eight priests returned to Rome, where seven were put to death and the eighth imprisoned.

The surviving priest was released years afterwards and returned to Bolivia, where he had a daughter—for most country priests have un-recognized wives. This girl either married or became the mistress of an Englishman, and told him the secret of the treasure. The secret was passed on by word of mouth, till some descendants of the couple decided to look for the treasure. They went to Sacambaya, identified the clues, found the skeletons of the six Indians, and set about excavating.

While this was going on a Cornishman came on the scene, and managed to force himself into partnership. The discoveries made suggested they were on the right track, but quarrels broke up the partnership, and the Cornishman continued the search alone. I had the story from him. He asserted that he found the tunnel, with clear traces of lime, charcoal, and bits of monks' clothing. Then his funds ran out.

"Did you ever try again?" I asked him.

"Yes—but not at once. There were people who knew I held the secret, and I was railroaded to jail on a charge of holding up a mail coach. I suppose they wanted me out of the way, so as to have a shot at the treasure themselves, but if so they were disappointed, for in a year I was out again. I went back to Sacambaya and started digging where I left off, but my cash ran out and I had to stop."

"You need capital for treasure hunting. It's an expensive game. Usually more money goes into the diggings than ever comes out!"

"That's true enough, Major. As it happens, I got four or five Englishmen interested, and we formed a syndicate for another try. We were fourteen days up there, but I gave up when I found that those men didn't like hard work. We quarrelled, of course. They wanted Indians to do the digging, but I wasn't having any, for the secret would have been out. It was for us to do all the work, and good men would have done it. With a half-dozen Cousin Jacks I'd have had that treasure up in a week, for there's no miner like a Cornishman, I tell you!"

"What happened after that?"

"Oh, we broke up, you understand. They went to England, and one of them claimed his share in the syndicate to be worth £40,000. The case came up in the London Bankruptcy Court."

"Why are you telling me all about it?"

"Well, for this reason, Major. If you're interested and want to come in on the business—and if you've a bit of capital you'd like to invest in a sure thing—we'll form a partnership. You strike me as a straight shooter, Major, and I know you're not afraid of work. What do you say?"

"Um! ... I'll go up there and have a look at the place first. It's on our way when we leave here."

CHAPTER XVI

A PREHISTORIC PEEP

STRIKING off into the mountains north of Cochabamba, we spent some useful time looking into mining prospects in the district, and came by a roundabout way to Sacambaya. There is no difficulty in reaching the place, either from Cochabamba or from Inquisivi, a mining village three leagues upstream, for it is open country, and there are several farms in the vicinity. Some broken walls represented what was once the Jesuit mission, and not far away I found six or eight open holes, and others that looked as if they had been dug only to be filled in again.

The treasure is reputed to be worth half a million sterling—if it exists, which I am inclined to doubt. There may be some evidence for it in the traditions of the place; but since the story of my Verde treasure I have been suspicious of these tales of buried hoards. And yet—a certain Bolivian of the district whose circumstances were very modest became a man of great wealth in a remarkably short time. He never explained his good fortune, but it was said that he had made a number of furtive visits to Sacambaya.

My opinion is—if a treasure really exists there—that the attempts to locate it have not been carried out very intelligently. Anyone who knows all the clues would find it a simple matter to settle once and for all if a tunnel is there or not. The Cornishman told me he found the tunnel, but I saw no trace of it though I made a careful examination. The pits that were dug looked like shafts intended to strike into a tunnel, but it was obvious that they had not done so.

There was nothing I could do about it, for I had no capital to spare, and while I was sure of the Cornishman's sincerity, the place disappointed me. It didn't 'feel' as though treasure was buried there, and I am inclined to give some weight to such impressions.

Being hard up, the Cornishman subsequently left for Rio de Janeiro, where he worked, I believe, for the Light and Power Company. I was unable to get in touch with him again, and think he must have died there. Further attempts may be made to find the treasure, for the secret is shared by the members of the syndicate, and there are always adventurous people ready to take part in a treasure hunt, even though they ruin themselves in doing so.

From Inquisivi we crossed the mountains to Eucalipto and took a train from there to La Paz. I had already wired home for another man to replace Todd, and was expecting Manley to arrive shortly. Meanwhile I had some business to do in the capital, including preliminary talks about a scheme I was preparing for a motor-road from Cochabamba to Santa Cruz.

I calculated that on an average 150 loaded mules passed each day between these two cities, even in the wet season; but animal transport, besides being slow and inefficient, was totally inadequate for the potential traffic of vegetables, fruit and timber from the 'Garden of Bolivia' to the *Altiplano*. A railroad seemed the obvious answer, but there were certain drawbacks. The terrain was difficult and construction would be costly, but the principal obstacle would be maintenance of the permanent way in the narrow, torrent-swept gorges. A motor-road, however, by reason of its greater flexibility in grading, could avoid the dangerous locations, and in the event of interruption by landslides and washouts would take less time to open up again, and require smaller permanent labour forces. Even in 1913 the development of road haulage was easy to foresee, though I admit there were difficulties that never occurred to me. I saw with the eye of imagination huge lorries hauling useful lengths of cut timber from the forests of the interior, which can supply a suitable if not superior wood for every industrial use we know; but axle loadings on fills and bridges, tyre wear and tear, and curve negotiation on mountain roads, were matters of which I had no experience. I saw only the possible advantages of road transport and the disadvantages of railroads. Rail traffic has since proved itself to be the most efficient method of handling bulk freight—particularly in times of national emergency—and its sense of duty to the public is incomparably greater than that of wildcat trucking concerns.

I was enthusiastic about the idea of a motor highway, and the Government authorities who listened seemed to feel strongly about it too. It looked probable that they would guarantee a return on the construction cost, and I anticipated no great trouble in raising capital locally. Alas, the war[1] came, and my scheme was shelved.

[1] The 1914 war, of course.—ED.

Christmas, 1913, was spent very quietly in La Paz, and afterwards we returned to Cochabamba by rail, *via* Oruro. Then we hired mules, replenished stores, and set off for Santa Cruz, a difficult journey at this time of the year when the wet season is at its height and rivers frequently in flood.

We were all but trapped in one of the narrow gorges when there was a cloudburst in the mountains above us. I realized what might follow and kept my eyes open for a way up the side of the canyon. Luckily we came to a spot where the mules could find a foothold, and struck upwards away from the valley floor—not an instant too soon. There came a dull roar from the gorge, and turning we saw a wall of water twelve to fifteen feet high leaping and foaming below us, carrying away everything in its path. A minute or two earlier we would have been caught, for as it was the last animal barely cleared the tumbling boulders and brown spume.

We were held up for a day or two in Totora, which gave us a chance to learn something of the native customs there. One of these is for the husband of a woman in childbirth to go to bed with his head tied up, and stay there, moaning and groaning, for four days. Meanwhile the woman delivers the child with the facility usual to these Indians, and attends to her poor husband, feeding him on a tea diffused from maize, while the neighbours gather round to sympathize with the agonies a cruel Nature inflicts on an unfortunate father! This ludicrous custom is not confined to Totora—it prevails amongst backward peoples in many parts of the world.

On reaching Santa Cruz I developed what must have been enteric fever, and for some days felt very miserable. The spartan cure of sitting naked in the hot sun for hours finally baked it out of my system; but then came an annoying attack of *Susu*, which is a kind of contagious conjunctivitis very prevalent here on account of the dust and dirt. My eyelids swelled badly and broke out in styes. I was able to cure it with the contents of the medicine-chest, but only because the attack was slight. It was rather unusual for me to be laid low in this way, and I was heartily ashamed of myself.

The disease most fashionable in Santa Cruz is what they call there an 'Espasmo', or stroke. Rheumatism is an 'espasmo de aire' (air stroke), and fever of any kind an 'espasmo del sol' (sunstroke). Any ill, from indigestion to Yellow Jack, becomes an 'espasmo de'—something or other! So poor are the people of the town that the few doctors earn a meagre living. Disease is usually left to run its own course—all of which goes to show how necessary is a State medical service. In the interior of Bolivia and Brazil there is no other way in which the treatment and prevention of disease can be carried out to the benefit of those who most need it.

Sooner or later these countries will come to it—and so will every other that considers itself civilized.[1]

Living in Santa Cruz is as cheap as anywhere, and in spite of their poverty the people are hospitable and uncomplaining. For the equivalent of 30s. a month I rented a new and well-built house (without a *bulto* this time!); and all the food we could eat—including meat, bread, milk, fruit and vegetables—cost us only 1s. 6d. a day each. No wonder there have been foreigners unable to tear themselves away from the place! Land was selling at about £80 the square league, and it struck me that here was an excellent opportunity for a colony of industrious foreigners, ready to develop the unlimited resources, carry out city improvements, and build feeder roads to bring produce in to a central distributing point.[2]

The young women of Santa Cruz are for the most part very pretty, but morals are lax. In the streets one intercepts looks of unblushing boldness, and at night it is by no means uncommon to hear soft taps on the door or shutters and a voice enquiring if the *señor* desires anything! Never was this so noticeable as during the three days of carnivals, when all pretence of respectability was relaxed and men and women gave themselves up to an orgy of drink.

With the carnivals came earthquake shocks, and the houses were violently shaken, causing much alarm but little real damage. We ventured into the streets at the risk of being pelted with eggs filled with ink or paint, or having buckets of dirty water emptied over us from the overhanging balconies. It was all a huge joke to those who enjoyed the licence of those mad days, but we were glad when it was over and King Carnival solemnly interred in the cemetery.

As soon as my old friend Manley arrived from La Paz we said good-bye to our many friends in the town, saddled up, and set off towards the Brazilian frontier. The country all about was still showing the effects of the rainy season, which in 1913 extended well into August, and the rivers were abnormally high. The Rio Grande had to be crossed in *pelotas*—a sort of coracle made by tying up rawhides at the corners—and the current made even those dangerous. Then we passed through uninteresting forest for thirty-six leagues, to where a small detachment of Bolivian soldiers kept the wild Indians in check. The whole region of the River Parapiti to the south, and between the River Piray and Rio Grande to the north, is in the hands of the Yanaiguas Indians, who sometimes attack

[1] In the Peruvian *Montaña* the Inter-American Co-operative Public Health Service—known as SCISP—provides the inhabitants with a medical service they have never before enjoyed. It is a recent development there; whether Bolivia and Brazil now have the same facilities I cannot say.—ED.

[2] This has been tried more than once in the *Montaña* regions of the Pacific republics, and little success has come of it. The chief trouble is that even an energetic colonist like the German or North Italian succumbs to the enervating climate, and, when lassitude sets in, prefers to 'go native' and do nothing. Nature keeps him supplied with the necessities of life, and there's nothing he need worry about!—ED.

travellers. We passed through without meeting any, and came to El Cerro, a hill with a small cattle ranch and about fifty Indian labourers.

Beyond El Cerro we dropped down into palm country, where the Palmares Lake stretched far and wide in extensive *bañados* during the rains. We followed a dry track quite ten feet below the late high-water mark to El Cerrito, another cattle ranch. This *estancia*, covering two square leagues, could easily carry 5,000 head of cattle, yet it was bought for £240—a good example of what the best land in the province cost at that time.

It was a dry and dusty stretch from here to San Ignacio, but the country looked rich in minerals. In the hills to the north there is gold at an ounce and a half to the ton. The mines were originally worked by Jesuits. Neglect and decay brood over the whole region, for isolation has killed it; and San Ignacio—capital of Chiquitos Province—is an impoverished village where a largely Indian population of 3,000 lives a hand-to-mouth existence.

Carnivals had not yet finished in San Ignacio—in fact, the New Year celebrations had never really ended. In most of the shabby houses we heard the tinkle of guitars to the drone of dismal voices, and the smell of *kachasa* was thick in the air. Here and there a drunk lay sprawled against a step or wall, or flat on the ground like the victim of a massacre. Not a dog barked or a bird cried; it was as though the place were subsiding into the coma that precedes death.

We were on the edge of what is perhaps the worst snake country in South America, and the loss of human life from this cause is awful. A number of people assured us most emphatically that in this region was a snake about three feet long which telescoped into itself before striking. As though to modify the account of what sounded to me like an anatomical impossibility, they added that it was not very poisonous. I should like to have seen one, but never did.

The real indigenes of Chiquitos were a fair-complexioned people who lived in pit dwellings—holes in the ground about twelve feet in diameter, approached by a long sloping tunnel and entirely covered over with branches and palm fronds. The Morcegos Indians of Brazil still live in this way—genuine troglodytes—an ugly, intractable people impossible to deal with.

In the low-lying forest beyond San Ignacio we trudged for six days through *bañados* of mud and water—where during the rains the land is completely inundated. Rising straight from the ground, the buttressed trunks of cottonwood trees towered ghostly white, until the interlacing branches overhead, heavy with moss beards and parasitic creepers, formed a ceiling penetrated only here and there by a pin-point of daylight. In the gloom between the huge boles were the dull whitish rubber trees struggling upwards for a peep of sunlight.

In the woods of the temperate zone the trees are dark-trunked, and the unobscured bark shows its interesting texture in a myriad scales; but here in tropical America the boles are smooth and of an almost luminous pale colour that can be distinguished even in the dark. Everywhere the vine-like tangle of undergrowth creeps over the open spaces of the ground, embraces the trees and any shrub sturdy enough to support its weight, and climbs with deadly intent towards the high-flung jungle terraces where the sun's light blazes, and where orchids flame in a riot of colour. From above, net-like, hang the lianas, as though some monstrous spider had spun a web of living fibre to trap man and beast in unbreakable meshes. From the ground rise the leafy vines in a wave of green, breaking through the cover of palm and bamboo.

Here and there, where some strangled forest giant had fallen dead to rot in the mud beneath, daylight reached down into a clearing where a papaw or cabbage palm stood erect and graceful, like some beautiful nymph of the glades. The step from death to disintegration is swift in the forest. The trees live out their lives and fall unheeded, to become the home and food for swarming insects. The perpetual damp, and spreading fungus, rot the dead timber to a stinking pulp, crumbling it away till it becomes part of the mud that absorbs it. There is none of the dry, cushioned earth you find in the northern woods—it is all mud, except on the islands of high ground, and through a blanket of straggling leaves and matted grass your feet sink monotonously with a sucking noise, so that leg muscles ache with the unrelieved effort of freeing the boots for every pace forward.

Where the forest fell back at the edge of open ground we looked over flat swamp, broken in places by little islands a few feet above the general level, crowned with thickets of bamboo, *tacuara* and scrub. On one of these islands—a fairly large one—was a miserable *estancia* called San Diego, inhabited by people as gloomy as the outlook from the rotting cane door. The place crawled with snakes, for all these islands in the swamp formed refuges from the floods, and inside the ranch house no less than thirty-six —all venomous—had been killed in three months. In the thatched roof they could be heard rustling day and night.

Two leagues beyond San Diego we struck into the San Matías– Villa Bella trail, already familiar to me. The carts we had brought from San Ignacio being unable to cross the swollen Barbados River, we were forced to camp as close as possible to Casal Vasco and fire off quantities of rifle ammunition to attract attention from the other side. On the third day a negro appeared on the far bank, who turned out to have been with the Brazilian Commission of 1909. He returned to Casal Vasco and brought up a canoe to ferry us across.

"You wouldn't get far if you tried to swim this river, *señor*," he said as we paddled from shore. "People have been seized by crocodiles here."

He gasped when I told him that I had swum it in 1909.

"It was a miracle they didn't get you. A white man has far less chance than a coloured man with those *bichus*—anyone can tell you that!"

"But I'm told they won't attack man before midday."

"Yes, *señor*, that's what they say—but there's more than crocodiles in these rivers. There are anacondas too, and they don't wait till after lunch to attack! The Guaporé is worse for anacondas, perhaps; it's not too safe to pitch camp even on the shores of that river in some places."

He went on:

"One party I was with camped on any convenient *playa* (beach) where the hammocks could be slung. One of the men liked to sling his away from the others—said he could sleep better if he didn't have to listen to our snoring. One night we heard a sort of stifled shriek—cut off as though a man's windpipe were being squeezed—and we all tumbled out and ran down with rifles to where this man had slung his hammock. Someone brought a lantern, and in its dim light we saw a sight I shall never forget, for a huge anaconda had the hammock ropes in its mouth and several coils wrapped round the man inside, hammock and all. We blazed away at it, and after a time it freed its prey and made off into the river. The man was quite dead, *señor*—he hadn't an unbroken bone in his body!"

In Matto Grosso, where anacondas abound, there is a curious superstition that any man who is bitten by one and escapes is thereafter immune to the bite of any poisonous snake. In the Brazilian *sertão*, or wilds, it is believed that a little bag of bichloride of mercury carried on the person will prevent snakes from attacking. The natives doggedly cling to these ideas, and any argument brings the reply, "*Senhor*, I have always lived in the *sertão* and I know these things."

Casal Vasco, where the population had been slaughtered by savages, was again inhabited by a few blacks, and we were lucky enough to procure a boat to take us to Puerto Bastos, where Antonio Alves, an old friend of Boundary Delimitation days, sold me a fine canoe for the rest of our river journey.

The squalor, ruins and dilapidation of Villa Bella were unchanged, but as we entered the grassy street a black-and-white torpedo shot out of a house straight for my chest. It was a fox terrier I had left here with a broken leg in 1908, and the frenzied lickings of a darting tongue told me I was not forgotten.

To avoid the pilfering Indians who prowl the silent streets of Villa Bella by night, we camped on the far side of the river, where we were visited by a crocodile, a jaguar, a tapir, and some pigs—and a number of night monkeys, which announced their presence by uncanny howls.

Game is plentiful on the upper Guaporé, for there are few people to disturb it. Eleven days of hard paddling brought us to the Mequens River, where there was a German rubber *barraca*, and here we met Baron

Erland Nordenskiold, who with his plucky wife was engaged in investigating the more accessible Indian tribes of the Guaporé. It says a lot for this attractive young Swedish lady that she was ready to tramp in the forests with her husband and wade swamps for days together in order to meet some distant tribe.

About twelve miles away to the east were hills, which the Baron considered it would be rash to visit.

"There are sure to be large tribes of savages there," he observed, "and they are almost certain to be dangerous. I've heard something from the Indians we have visited. They all speak of cannibals somewhere in that direction."

"They say the men are big and hairy," put in the Baron's wife.

I laughed. "We'll know soon, for it's there we're going," I said.

"Most rash!" muttered the Baron. "Frankly, I won't expect to see you again. You're doing a most foolhardy thing."

Weighed down by heavy packs, we left the Rio Mequens and for two days waded through the soft mud of extensive swamps until we came to a sluggish river emptying into them. We followed up this river, and some days after reached grassy plains forming the first hills of the Serra dos Parecis. This part of the country is so beautiful that I could well understand why, scattered through the forests, there are hermits of many nationalities, preferring a life alone in the wild to a penurious and uncertain existence in civilization. Rather than pity them for losing the amenities we are accustomed to consider so necessary, we should envy them for having the wisdom of knowing how superfluous such things really are. Perhaps they are the ones most likely to find the true meaning of life.

Climbing the *Serrania* we came again to forest, where the undergrowth afforded little obstacle to our progress, and where the huge rubber trees, some as much as twelve feet in girth, showed no signs of regular tapping. True, some had been clumsily hacked, but we could see that it was not the work of a company *seringero*. It looked as though white men had never been here before, but the traces of Indians were obvious.

We found some delicious fruit in these woods. What it was called I don't know, I had never seen it before. It had the peculiarity of being nearly all stone and very little pulp, but the little it had tempted us to eat one after another. There was another fruit which we decided to try after noticing that insects seemed to enjoy it. It was about the size of a pomegranate and looked palatable, but the after-taste was astringent, and what we swallowed made us violently sick, leaving us giddy for some time.

It was three weeks after we entered the forest that we came to a wide and well-used trail crossing our own at right angles.

"Savages!" I said. "The village must be quite close, for that's a trail in everyday use!"

"What about the one we're following?" asked Costin. "It's pretty well used too. Might be either of 'em, if it comes to that."

I looked at both, and couldn't decide which was most likely to be the right one.

"Tell you what, Major; let's toss for it," suggested Manley.

I searched for a coin and after some time located one in the corner of a trouser pocket.

"Heads we go on—tails we take the other path."

I flipped it up, and the three of us bent over where it lay half-hidden by a dead leaf. Tails was showing.

"Come on, then—we take the new trail."

We followed it for two or three miles, passing several plantations, and suddenly daylight broke upon us in full force at the edge of a large clearing. With great caution we peeped out from the undergrowth, and there in front of us, on a wide space of smoothly packed earth, were two large huts shaped like beehives. They were quite forty feet high in the centre and a hundred in diameter, but only one door could be seen in the nearer one—perhaps thirty feet away.

As we watched, a naked copper-coloured child came out of the hut, a nut in one hand and a little stone axe in the other. He squatted down on his haunches before a flat stone, laid the nut on it, and then started to hammer on the shell with the side of the axe.

I forgot my companions and all else as I gazed on this scene. The curtain of time was drawn aside to reveal a glimpse of the distant past —a prehistoric peep—for just so would the neolithic child have looked and acted when man was beginning his ascent of the ladder of evolution. The primeval forest, the clearing, the hut, all were exactly as they might have been countless thousands of years ago! Then the nut broke, the child gave a little grunt of satisfaction, and, laying down the stone axe, popped the kernel into his mouth.

With a mental effort I brought my mind back to the present, and gave a low whistle. The child looked up, his jaws ceased to move and his eyes rolled; two arms came out of the darkness of the hut's interior, grabbed him, and pulled him inside. There was an excited jabbering, the rattle of bows and arrows, and smothered screams. It's no use lurking in the forest once your presence is known to the savages, so I came out of cover, swiftly crossed to the hut, and slipped through the low entrance to crouch down beyond in the darkness of the wall.

When my eyes had accustomed themselves to the gloom I saw that the hut was empty but for an old woman, who stood watching me from amongst a number of high earthenware urns under the centre pole. There were other doors on the far side, through which the occupants had fled. The explanation dawned on me—we had arrived when every man was away in the plantations, and the women and children but a moment ago in the hut were by now racing off to give the alarm, leaving only the ancient crone who was too old to escape.

The old woman muttered to herself, and then bent to continue the work she was doing when the excitement began—the brewing of maize beer over a fire. I signalled to her that I was hungry, and, obviously terrified, she took up a gourd and came hobbling over to me, still muttering. The gourd was filled with very tasty food, whatever it may have been, and I took it out to the others, who were still waiting in the scrub at the edge of the clearing.

The sky had clouded over, and with a thunder in the foliage above, torrential rain began to fall.

"Come on inside with me," I shouted. "We may as well be in there as out here."

Together we entered the hut, and when the gourd of food was empty I took it over to the old woman to be refilled. It was while we were eating the second helping that the men came in. They slipped in by various entrances not previously noticed, and through the doorway beside us we could see the shadows of more men outside, probably surrounding the hut. All the men carried bows and arrows. A man, whom I took to be the chief, stood beside the old woman listening to her excited tale of what had happened. I went over to him and tried to convey to him by signs that we were friendly and only wanted food, explaining that we had already had some. He stood perfectly still as I approached, and gave no indication of understanding what I was trying to tell him. I went back to the doorway, took some small gifts from the pack, and returned to hand these to him. He took them without any kind of acknowledgment, but the women came over to us with gourds full of peanuts. Our friendship was now accepted, and the chief himself sat down on a curved stool and shared the peanuts with us.

I found out later that these people were the Maxubis, that they had twenty-four villages and numbered over two thousand. They were not very dark, but of a bright copper colour; rather small, and with a tint of red in their hair. The men wore shells and sticks in their ears, pegs through their nostrils and lower lips, and armlets of seeds and carved *chonta* wood. On ankles and wrists they wore rubber bands tinted red with *urucu*, and in these we perceived the answer to the mystery of the tapped rubber trees. The women wore no ornaments, and their hair was short, while that of the men was long, a curious reversal of our own custom. I believe that these people, like many others in Brazil, are the descendants of a higher civilization. In one of the Maxubi villages was a red-headed boy with blue eyes—not an albino.

Our destination was yet much farther towards the east, and we stayed with the Maxubis only long enough to learn a little of their language and their ways. They are sun-worshippers, and one or two men in each village are on duty every morning to greet the sunrise with musical voices, chanting a weird and haunting song in what I should say was the pentatonic scale—similar to the *yaravi* of the mountain Indians in Peru. In the utter silence of the forest, when the first light of day had stilled the night-long uproar of insect life, these hymns impressed us greatly with their beauty. It was the music of developed people, not the mere rhythmic noise beloved of the true savage. They had names for all the planets, and called the stars '*Vira Vira*'—curiously suggestive of the name '*Viracocha*' by which the Incas knew the sun.

They had a gentle courtesy in their manner, and their morals were beyond reproach. Their feet and hands were small and well formed, their features delicate. They knew the art of making pottery; they grew tobacco, and smoked it in small-bowled pipes or in cigarettes rolled in maize leaves. In every way they indicated a fall from a state high in man's development rather than a people evolving from savagery.

Scattered over the vast expanse of unknown South America are tribes like this one—a few better organized, and some even clothed—utterly refuting the conclusions arrived at by ethnologists, who have only explored the rivers and know nothing of the less accessible places. At the same time there are real savages, ugly, dangerous, and treacherous.

Never had we seen peanuts such as those grown by the Maxubis. It was their staple diet, and the nuts in their pods were between three and four inches long. The taste, as well as the nutritive value, was excellent, and it would be hard to find a more convenient food to carry on a journey —as we learned later. At meals, every man helped himself from a communal bowl filled with these huge peanuts, while the women ate apart and kept the men's bowl replenished.

In about ten days we could exchange ideas with the Maxubis in their own language, and it was then that they told us of a tribe of cannibals to the north—the Maricoxis. "*Vincha Maricoxi, chimbibi coco!*" they said— to give you a sample of their speech. "If you visit the Maricoxis you will be food for the pot!" A gruesome pantomime accompanied the warning.

The information obtained from the Maxubis was useful and interesting, and after visiting several of the nearer villages we took our farewell of them and set off towards the north-east where the Maricoxis were said to live. We entered entirely trackless forest—probably no man's land avoided by Maxubis and Maricoxis alike—and on the fifth day struck a trail which looked as if it were in regular use.

As we stood looking from right to left, trying to decide which direction was the more promising, two savages appeared about a hundred yards to the south, moving at a trot and talking rapidly. On catching sight of us they stopped dead and hurriedly fixed arrows to their bows, while I shouted to them in the Maxubi tongue. We could not see them clearly for the shadows dappling their bodies, but it seemed to me they were large, hairy men, with exceptionally long arms, and with foreheads sloping back from pronounced eye ridges—men of a very primitive kind, in fact, and stark naked. Suddenly they turned and made off into the undergrowth, and we, knowing it was useless to follow, started up the north leg of the trail.

It was not long before sundown, when, dim and muffled through the trees, came the unmistakable sound of a horn. We halted and listened intently. Again we heard the horn call, answered from other directions till several horns were braying at once. In the subdued light of evening, beneath the high vault of branches in this forest untrodden by civilized man, the sound was as eerie as the opening notes of some fantastic opera. We knew it was made by the savages, and that those savages were now on our trail. Soon we could hear shouts and jabbering to the accompaniment of the rough horn calls—a barbarous, merciless din, in marked contrast to the stealth of the ordinary savage. Darkness, still distant above the tree-tops, was settling rapidly down here in the depths of the wood, so we looked about us for a camping site which offered some measure of safety from attack, and finally took refuge in a *tacuara* thicket. Here the naked savages would not dare to follow on account of the wicked, inch-long thorns. As we slung our hammocks inside the natural stockade we could hear the savages jabbering excitedly all around, but not daring to enter. Then, as the last light went, they left us, and we heard no more of them.

Next morning there were no savages in our vicinity, and we met with none when, after following another well-defined trail, we came to a clearing where there was a plantation of *mandioca* and papaws. Brilliantly coloured toucans croaked in the palms as they picked at the fruit, and as no danger threatened we helped ourselves freely. We camped here, and at dusk held a concert in our hammocks, Costin with a harmonica, Manley with a comb, and myself with a flageolet. Perhaps it was foolish of us to advertise our presence in this way; but we were not molested, and no savage appeared.

In the morning we went on, and within a quarter of a mile came to a sort of palm-leaf sentry-box—then another. Then all of a sudden we reached open forest. The undergrowth fell away, disclosing between the tree boles a village of primitive shelters, where squatted some of the most villainous savages I have ever seen. Some were engaged in making arrows, others just idled—great ape-like brutes who looked as if they had scarcely evolved beyond the level of beasts.

I whistled, and an enormous creature, hairy as a dog, leapt to his feet in the nearest shelter, fitted an arrow to his bow in a flash, and came up dancing from one leg to the other till he was only four yards away. Emitting grunts that sounded like "Eugh! Eugh! Eugh!" he remained there dancing, and suddenly the whole forest around us was alive with these hideous ape-men, all grunting "Eugh! Eugh! Eugh!" and dancing from leg to leg in the same way as they strung arrows to their bows. It looked like a very delicate situation for us, and I wondered if it was the end. I made friendly overtures in Maxubi, but they paid no attention. It was as though human speech were beyond their powers of comprehension.

The creature in front of me ceased his dance, stood for a moment perfectly still, and then drew his bowstring back till it was level with his ear, at the same time raising the barbed point of the six-foot arrow to the height of my chest. I looked straight into the pig-like eyes half hidden under the overhanging brows, and knew that he was not going to loose that arrow—yet. As deliberately as he had raised it, he now lowered the bow, and commenced once more the slow dance, and the "Eugh! Eugh! Eugh!"

A second time he raised the arrow at me and drew the bow back, and again I knew he would not shoot. It was just as the Maxubis told me it would be. Again he lowered the bow and continued his dance. Then for the third time he halted and began to bring up the arrow's point. I knew he meant business this time, and drew out a Mauser pistol I had on my hip. It was a big, clumsy thing, of a calibre unsuited to forest use, but I had brought it because by clipping the wooden holster to the pistol-butt it became a carbine, and was lighter to carry than a true rifle. It used .38 black powder shells which made a din out of all proportion to their size. I never raised it; I just pulled the trigger and banged it off into the ground at the ape-man's feet.

The effect was instantaneous. A look of complete amazement came into the hideous face, and the little eyes opened wide. He dropped his bow and arrow and sprang away as quickly as a cat to vanish behind a tree. Then the arrows began to fly. We shot off a few rounds into the branches, hoping the noise would scare the savages into a more receptive frame of mind, but they seemed in no way disposed to accept us, and before anyone was hurt we gave it up as hopeless and retreated down the trail till the camp was out of sight. We were not followed, but the clamour in the village continued for a long time as we struck off northwards, and we fancied we still heard the "Eugh! Eugh! Eugh!" of the enraged braves.

Later we turned east, and for some days went on through the forest, always watching for signs of Indians, and always listening for the threatening note of a horn. We knew how easily they could track us down, and had no illusions about our fate if they caught us. At night our dreams were filled with hideous faces under lowering brows, and great grinning lips drawn back from stained, filed teeth. Manley's nerve began to show signs of breaking, Costin was jumpy, and I myself was feeling the strain. We had to admit that we were in no condition to reach our goal, and so with reluctance decided to turn back. The experiences we had just come through, following on those of the previous year, had taken too much out of us. We needed complete rest—complete relaxation from the strain of being always on the alert.

We gave that wasps' nest of a village as wide a berth as our calculations of its position would allow, and returned to the Maxubis, striking the original village with perfect accuracy. Our arrival coincided with the funeral of a warrior who had been hunted down and shot by a Maricoxi foraging party, and I wondered if the two events might be thought by superstitious tribesmen to be connected. There was no definite animosity shown, but I fancied I detected a slight coldness, and a few suspicious glances in our direction.

The dead man's entrails had been extracted and put in an urn for burial. The body was then cut up and distributed for consumption by the twenty-four families of the hut he had occupied, a religious ceremony not to be confused with cannibalism. Finally the hut was freed from the ghost of the deceased by the following elaborate ritual:

The chief, his second-in-command, and the medicine man sat down in a row on their little stools before the largest entrance of the hut, and performed movements like those of squeezing something down each limb, catching it as it emerged at fingers and toes, and throwing it at a palm-leaf screen about three feet square. Beneath the screen was a half-gourd partly filled with water, with herbs of some sort floating on the surface, and every now and then all three of them would carefully examine the screen and the water under it. This was repeated many times, and then they went into a trance, and for about half an hour sat immobile on their stools, eyes rolled up into their heads. When they came to, they first rubbed their stomachs, and were then violently sick.

All night long they sat on their stools and chanted singly or in chorus a series of three notes, descending in octaves, with the words, repeated over and over again, "Tawi-Tacni, tawi-tacni, tawi-tacni." In response, the families inside the hut joined in a chorus of lamentations.

These ceremonies lasted for three days, and the chief solemnly assured me that the dead man's ghost was within the hut and visible to him. I could see nothing. On the third day the proceedings reached a climax; the screen was carried into the hut and placed where the light from the doorway fell on it; the people dropped to their knees and lowered their faces to the ground; the three headmen discarded their stools and crouched in great excitement before the entrance to the hut; and I knelt down beside them to watch the screen at which they were all gazing intently.

Inside the hut, to one side of the screen, was a closed cubicle where the dead man had slept, and the eyes of the headmen turned towards this cubicle. For a moment there was absolute silence, and in that moment I saw a dark shadow emerge from the cubicle, float towards the centre pole of the hut, and there fade from sight. Mass hypnotism, you say? Very well, let's leave it at that; all I know is that I saw it!

The two chiefs and the medicine man relaxed, broke out into a profuse sweat, and fell prone on the ground. I left them and returned to my companions, who had not been present at the ceremony.

In three villages which we visited after this event our arrival coincided with a *tapi*, or ghost-laying ceremony. There was the same singing, but I was not allowed to witness it, for there were growing suspicions that the deaths were due to the baneful influence of our presence. They construed my work with theodolite in the environs of the villages as 'talking with the stars', and were ill at ease about it. There were only three of us, and kindly though these people appeared to be there was the possibility that superstitious dread might turn to anger against us. It was time we moved on.

Before we departed I learned that the Maricoxis numbered about one thousand five hundred. To the east was another tribe of cannibals, the Arupi, and another and more distant tribe to the north-east—short black people covered with hair, who spitted their victims on a bamboo over a fire, and when cooked picked off pieces to eat—a human barbecue, in fact. I had heard rumours of these people before, and I know now that the stories were well founded. The Maxubis obviously considered themselves to be civilized, and spoke of the surrounding cannibals with great scorn. They had a careful system of guards on the borders of their territory where unfriendly tribes lived, and the 'sentry-boxes' we saw—common to all these Indians—were screens from which arrows could be fired.

Loaded with string bags of peanuts, stone axes, and bows and arrows —the weapons were real works of art—we left the Maxubis and turned south-west towards Bolivia. Game was scarce; it was one of those periods when for some reason or other animal and bird life goes elsewhere. Once we managed to shoot three monkeys, but a roving jaguar walked off with two of them, and we kept going on a diet of eight peanuts a day each. Perhaps that saved us from excessive prostration, for it is a fact that while a vegetable diet, if sufficient, endows one with plenty of strength and energy, under conditions of semi-starvation meat induces a feeling of great lassitude.[1]

It was not easy going, and we were very hungry men when eventually we struck a rubber-gatherer's hut on the bank of a small stream. Here we stayed for two days, fattening up on rice and *charque*.

[1] The chief of the Maxubis, enchanted by the photographs my father showed him of the family in England, gave him a large string bag of the giant peanuts for us children. This was brought home intact—not even the pangs of starvation had induced my father to broach it —and I feel ashamed now to recall the nonchalant way in which we youngsters ate them. I still have the bag; and a few of the nuts were preserved as curios, but unfortunately the termites destroyed them later in Peru.—Ed.

I shall never forget our first breakfast in that hut. Beside us, under the shade of the hut's eaves, a man was dying of earth-eating—an emaciated creature whose stomach was greatly swollen. To those who knew the symptoms the case was obviously hopeless, and our *seringero* host was wasting no sympathy on him. All the time the victim kept up a monotonous groaning, and ejaculated, "*Senhores*, I'm in agony—*aie*, what agony!"

"You've got to die in about half an hour," said the *seringero* in answer, "so why all this fuss? It spoils the breakfast of the *senhores*!"

"*Aie!*" wailed the dying man. "I'm in agony—*aie*, what agony!"

Suddenly a woman snatched away the mosquito-net. The man was dead. A wasp settled on his nose, which twitched feebly, but there was no sound from him. Within an hour the body was buried, and probably forgotten. I wondered why he had been born—what object was served by his passage through childhood to a life of hopeless misery, and finally to a lonely, agonizing and unwept exit. Surely it was better to live as a beast than in so degraded a human condition as this? Yet—there *is* a reason! I don't know why I was so impressed by the event; I had seen many men die in this way. The twitching of the dead nose stuck in my memory; and I remembered once seeing a llama, in the process of having its throat cut, flicking away a persistent fly with its scut of a tail, as though nothing untoward were taking place.

Burial was not the last of the dead man. The *seringero* insisted that at night his ghost walked. Everywhere in the interior it is taken as a natural occurrence that the ghosts of the dead walk for a time after death; the people of the wilds are close enough to Nature to know things which are hidden from us.

We continued downstream, and eventually met another rubber gatherer, Don Cristian Suarez, who had carried out some notable explorations in the Chaco, and was now settled temporarily on the Guaporé. He entertained us as well as his short supplies allowed, and I found him a most interesting and enlightened man—not by any means the lowly *peon* usually engaged in tapping rubber.

"I might have made my fortune in the Chaco, *señor*," he said one evening, as we sat round the fire where he was smoking the balls of *goma*. "The trouble with me is, I can't stay in one place. There was a friend down there with me, and he used his brains—not like me. I just take things as they come along. That fellow knew a thing or two, and he bought on credit a large area of cattle land in the Santa Cruz district. Then he went down to the North Chaco and Parapiti country, where the Yacanaguas and other Indians have large herds of cattle. He took a toy cow with him—a little thing which walked in a sort of jerky way and nodded its head when you wound it up. He told the Indians that this was a great spirit, and knew all their thoughts. He would turn on an Indian suddenly and accuse him of thinking of something bad, telling him he would die for offending the spirit in the toy cow. When the Indian was ready to pass out from fear my friend would say, 'If you don't want to die, I'll propitiate the great spirit for a hundred head of cattle—delivered at Santa Cruz!' The Indian always accepted eagerly, and my friend then spoke mumbo-jumbo to the toy cow, which nodded its head. Soon he had the best-stocked ranch in Santa Cruz, and all for the cost of the toy and no more! He had brains, I tell you."

Like Suarez, all the *seringeros* we met were kindly and hospitable, and it was only at the German *barraca* that the possibility of exploiting travellers overshadowed other considerations. We weighed ourselves while there, and found that since leaving England Manley had lost twenty-nine pounds, Costin thirty-one, and myself fifty-three—yet we felt none the worse for it.

Vast quantities of *camelote*, or sudds, held us up on the river between here and Porvenir, on the Paraguá. On the way we witnessed a fight between a manatee and a crocodile. One doesn't expect much fighting ability in the humble sea-cow, but it whipped the crocodile decisively.

After we had stayed five days at Porvenir a bullock-cart came in from San Ignacio, and we used it for continuing the journey. Three days of rough forest track brought us to the first *estancia*, and the going became easier. Much travel by cart is done in the very early hours of the morning, and this one had room only for our packs—we ourselves walked beside it. At every *estancia* we touched scarlatina was raging, and men were dying like flies. At San Ignacio, which we reached at the beginning of September 1914, there was an epidemic of it. It was here we heard that war had broken out in Europe. A German told me; and in spite of our being officially enemies he lent me enough money to take us up to Santa Cruz —for all I had left was £4—merely requesting that the loan be repaid to his representative there.

We could get only one mule in San Ignacio, so we loaded it with our packs and provisions, and footed the 231 miles to Santa Cruz. As we had just covered 250 miles on foot with the cart, it seemed nothing to complain of—in any case, our minds were full of the war and its possible repercussions on our families and friends in England.

Two weeks of walking, ten hours a day, brought us to Santa Cruz. On the way our daily food consisted of two hard biscuits in the morning, and sardines with sugar in the evening—yet it agreed with us! In the city the Germans were jubilant. After an orgy of beer-drinking, they tore down the bulletins on the British Vice-Consul's door and paraded the streets singing patriotic songs. Many had already left for Europe and the front, only to find on reaching the coast that no German ship was available to take them. We also were anxious to get home to do our bit in the war, but it took eight days to procure animals, and another ten days to reach Cochabamba.

In Cochabamba we met Baron Nordenskiold again; and he confessed that he was surprised to see us return. The Huari Indians, whom he had visited, had also spoken of hairy cannibals to the north-east; but savages have little idea of judging distances, and their talk often gives an impression of contiguity quite unfounded in fact.

We passed through La Paz, crossed Lake Titicaca in the *Inca*, and arrived at the coast in time to see Admiral Cradock's ill-fated squadron steaming to its doom off Coronel. After that, Englishmen had a thin time in the Pacific ports, especially those in Chile where the German influence was strongest, till the tide turned with the Battle of the Falkland Islands. It was an adverse period in the war, and on our way home we found New York without lights, for German raider submarines were already at work in American waters.

By the beginning of January 1915 we were absorbed into the great armies to be.

CHAPTER XVII

THE FRONT DOOR

THERE'S reason in the old saying, 'See Rio before you die'. I know of no other place to compare with Rio de Janeiro, and it is my hope to live there some day—if such good fortune should be mine. If financial success rewards this exploration work we shall build a family home on the slopes of the mountains overlooking that glorious harbour, so that the dispersed family can forgather there every year at Christmas, and my wife and I can end our days in what must surely be one of the world's most beautiful situations. I like the people, too, and if this dream comes true I shall be grateful to be accepted as one of them. My present work is in their country, and nothing could please me more than to spend the rest of my life in the service of Brazil.

A certain amount of interest was aroused in England by my work, but financial support was not forthcoming. Perhaps the objective was too romantic for hard-headed conservatives, who much preferred to play safe and back expeditions to Mount Everest and the good old Antarctic. I don't blame them. The story you have read in the opening chapter is not easy to accept as fact; but that is not all—what has not been told is stranger still! Men of science had in their day pooh-poohed the existence of the Americas—and, later, the idea of Herculaneum, Pompeii and Troy. You might argue that those great discoveries had confounded the incredulous, and this should have been in my favour. As a Founder's Medallist of the Royal Geographical Society I was accorded a respectful hearing, but to get the elderly gentlemen or the archæologists and museum experts in London to credit a fraction of what I knew to be true was a task altogether beyond my powers.

I came out of the war convinced that as a world power Britain was on the wane, and I saw Europe only as a place to avoid. Many thousands must have come through those four years of mud and blood with a similar disillusionment, which is the inevitable aftermath of war, except for the very few who gain materially by it. I had lost heavily; for the war caused me to drop the threads of a new activity; and to pick up those threads once more would be difficult. I left the army with a noble gratuity of £150 a year, but it had cost me double that to come home with Costin and Manley, and to return again would take every penny I could find after the family was provided for.

Costin, who had been with me some of the time, came through those years as a Lieutenant of Artillery, but had married, and was no longer available for further exploration work in South America. Manley survived the war, but died of heart disease shortly afterwards.

From under the clouds of post-war depression I looked towards the Americas and saw in them the only hope of our civilization. North America had already taken a place at the head of our western nations; but, to me, the focus was on the Latin-American republics, which, stimulated by inflated wartime markets, were beginning to forge ahead. At all costs we must leave England, I thought, and give the children an opportunity to grow up in the virile *ambiente* of the New World. They were still of school age, and my eldest son was nearing the climax of his school career, but this was not the only education they needed. The decision to leave was taken, and the roots were severed. Our house at Seaton— whither we had moved from Uplyme—was rented, and there was little to sell up. With all that could be moved, my wife and children would leave for Jamaica, and I for Brazil.

When the President of Brazil, Dr. Pessoa, visited London, he was good enough to give me an audience, and listened with interest to what I had to tell him. I heard later that his Government was at the moment unable to subsidize any investigations; but this was by no means through indifference. Brazil was now in the shadow of the financial crisis, and all inessential expenditure was cut to a minimum. Perhaps I should have more success, I thought, in Rio, where I could make contact with the ministers concerned with affairs in the interior. Unquestionably I would stand a better chance on the spot.

In February 1920 I arrived there. I lost heavily on the exchange, for on arrival I had to change pounds sterling into *milreis* at only slightly over twelve to the pound; and later, when I was forced to exchange back into sterling before returning to England, it was at forty to the pound. Rio was not a cheap city to live in, especially as I was forced to stay in hotels; and I was never free from anxiety about what might happen if my efforts failed to raise funds for the expedition. I stayed first of all at the International Hotel, high up in Silvestre; but as it was fast becoming a sanctuary for Germans I left it, though with regret. Prejudice on my part, no doubt; but the war was a tragedy of the recent past—a wound far from healed—and I was not yet able to regard Germans with a completely open mind. The fact that before the war I had met and been befriended by many Germans was forgotten—or overshadowed, rather, by the illusion of what we knew as patriotism. Anyway, it was a change for the better, for Sir Ralph Paget, the British Ambassador, invited me to stay with him at the beautiful Embassy residence.

The time I spent in Rio lengthened out to six months, but on the whole it was a delightful experience in spite of my anxieties. From the Embassy roof there was a perfect view in all directions, and when it comes to views Rio is incomparable. Below, the wonderful Beira Mar avenue passed under the ridge and entered the suburb of Copacabana, beyond which it extended through suburb after suburb along twelve miles of exquisite coastline. In the evenings we often motored along this highway to return after dark, when one of the most wonderful city lighting systems in the world suddenly flashed out into full glory, throwing a carpet of shimmering reflections over the still waters of the bay. How drab and gloomy our worn-out English cities appear after such beauty as this! One could not be bored here. There was the unceasing activity of the harbour—the arrival and departure of liners, the fussing bay steamers racing like giant water-beetles to and from the state capital of Niteroi—the thronged avenues and gaily dressed people—the great sandy beaches which even the thousands of bathers could not crowd. If anything was required to complete the picture it was yachts. There was none, but some day they will come, for it is a wealthy place. I see it as the capital of civilization in embryo.

In the tropical and sub-tropical belts of South America the climate is becoming cooler in summer. From May to September there is no more delightful temperature than Rio's, and were it not for the fact that its season clashes with the northern summer I feel sure that there would be an enormous annual influx of visitors. Nobody who has not seen Rio can realize what a paradise it is—front door of a vast hinterland whose illimitable resources cannot be truly estimated. The Brazilian has reason to be proud of it. He has the finest of all harbours, landlocked by picturesque and lofty mountains, and in this perfect setting has built himself a jewel of a city, abounding in wealth, in luxurious hotels, magnificent shops, wide avenues and superb boulevards.

I was able to talk with the President again, and he listened to my proposals with the courtesy and quick intelligence typical of South American ministers. I was heard also by members of the Cabinet, but achieved no success till the British Ambassador added the weight of his influence to my requests. Then the Government consented to subsidize an expedition. I would receive no pay, but they agreed to give a good salary to an officer in our Air Ministry at home, who was anxious to accompany me.

I was conscious of a certain laxity in entering the palaces and parliaments without tail coat and top hat, but, to tell the truth, such garments were not in my possession. The memorable horror of them still lingered from drab days at Westminster School; and later, when I came up against the regulation forcing young officers to be so clad when approaching the Gods of Whitehall. The time had been when strict observance of such a convention was necessary in visiting South American presidents, but the formality was now waived, and this seemed to me an indication of the broader outlook spreading through the continent.

I cabled the officer to come out and join me. The Embassy cabled the Foreign Office, and the Brazilian Government cabled their Ambassador in London. But the officer had changed his mind, and I was now faced with the problem of finding a companion out here. It seemed impossible to get men of the right sort in Rio, but the editor of a British paper in São Paulo, anxious to help, advertised for 'bright young men'. It hardly indicated what was required, but the response was so great that I had hopes of finding at least one amongst the many impossibles. They besieged the Embassy, lay in wait for me in the streets, and showered me with letters and recommendations. Most of them had jobs, but the irresistible glamour of exploration tore them from their occupations regardless of the security they would be sacrificing. I regretted having to disappoint so many, but not one was apparently fit for the work.

When almost desperate, I met a huge Australian who was hanging about for a job. 'Butch' Reilly, six feet five in height and broad as a barn door, claimed to be a major and a V.C., a bronco-buster, a sailor and several other things.

"And what's more," he said, "I own twenty thousand acres of stocked farm in Australia. You can't teach me anything about a horse—or a ship!"

In a recent prize-fight Butch had lashed into his antagonist, an American pugilist, with such enthusiasm that there was no stopping him with gong, seconds or referee. It took the combined efforts of many onlookers to separate the two, who were determined to settle the matter by knockout either in or out of the ring. A man like Butch should be well able to stand up to forest travel, and I engaged him gladly.

The Government promised me two Brazilian officers; and General Rondon, the well-known explorer and engineer who had accompanied the Roosevelt expedition to the Rio Duvida, was kind enough to make the necessary arrangements for them to come. Everything done that could be done, Butch and I left for São Paulo on August 12, after a farewell from the cheeriest and most hospitable colony of British folk in all South America.

In São Paulo the British colony entertained us and helped us in every way possible. They even presented us with pistols and ammunition—gifts of doubtful value, but accepted none the less gratefully. While there, we visited the Butantan Snake Farm, where we were given a quantity of snake serum in case of accidents. This well-managed institution is of inestimable benefit to dwellers in snake-infested areas, and should have its counterpart elsewhere in the world. For years, not a single case of snakebite, treated with the serum produced there, has failed to recover even after reaching a desperate stage. Bushmasters, *jararacas*, the deadly rattler, and practically every known variety of Brazilian poisonous snake is on view here, and utilized for the manufacture of serum. There is also a valuable non-poisonous snake called the *Musserau*, a shiny black reptile four to six feet long, which feeds on poisonous snakes and is therefore worth breeding. The attendants at Butantan treat all the snakes with the nonchalance born of long experience in handling them, and though to the onlooker their seeming recklessness is mad, they well know what they are doing and just how far they can go.

The train journey from São Paulo to the Paraguay River was dusty and tedious, over a roadbed that must be the worst constructed and least efficiently maintained in the whole republic. It is quite usual for the train to be derailed once or twice west of the Parana River, and the continual rocking never lets the passenger forget the imminent perils. During our journey we were fortunate, for only one derailment took place, and that was because a brakeman threw the switch under the engine as we were coming out on the single track main line after letting another train pass by. The most memorable episode of the journey was the loss of my precious Stetson out of the train window through Butch's carelessness—and good Stetsons are not to be replaced in the hat shops of the outposts!

We went up river by steamer to Corumba, a town that had altered much for the better since 1909, for its traders and cattlemen had cleaned up tidy fortunes during the war. Here a telegram awaited me. It said that the Government was forced to cancel the services of the two officers owing to the financial crisis and the heavy expenditure occasioned by the visit of the Belgian King and Queen. This was serious news, but I felt better when another telegram came from a friend in Rio who knew of my difficulties and was sending up a young man—a *Gringo*—to fill the gap by joining the party in Cuyaba.

The river was very low, and from the steamer on which we left Corumba we were forced to tranship to a launch for the rest of the way up to Cuyaba. We found this place impoverished and backward, and, in spite of its being the seat of the Matto Grosso government, inferior in every way to Corumba. The population was distinctly mulatto, and very poor, principally because it was so exploited by the local merchants; and what little money the people had left the municipality and the Church annexed. The astute, energetic Bishop of Matto Grosso, who was also the

President, was not the man to let his Church suffer, and the numerous priests and monks fostered a profound ignorance and fanatical superstition in the faithful, which kept them meekly subjected to the yoke. Altogether, the place was very primitive, but there was a service of Ford cars that handled the traffic on the mile and a half of road linking town to river port, and raced to and fro all day with radiators boiling and clouds of dust smothering their intrepid passengers.

Cuyaba was founded as the centre of a great gold industry, and both gold and diamonds have been washed out of rivers and soil in the area. Here, and at Diamantino to the north, dredgers worked the streams, but the business failed to pay off expenses and the boom collapsed, leaving the place little better than a ghost town. After heavy rain, gold nuggets are still occasionally picked up in the main *plaza*, and the whole environment of the city itself has been turned over. To the west is San Luis de Caceres, mentioned in previous chapters; to the north Rosario and Diamantino, both in a state of decay; east, to the borders of the State of Goyaz, there is nothing but scattered diamond workings and a few tiny settlements with their plantations. For agricultural purposes the soil in this region is poor, and disease is very common. The general poverty may be ameliorated in some measure by the railway now under construction to link up with the North-Western at Aguas Claras, near the River Parana, but I cannot see how it can ever pay.

The new member of the party arrived after we had been in Cuyaba a month, a cheerful and neat young man who bubbled over with good intentions. He told me his full name, and added, "Call me Felipe." Whenever anyone asked him his name he would finger a long sausage-like roll of colourless hair on his brow and reply, "Call me Felipe"—so Felipe he was to everyone.

"I suppose you've been told something of our objective?" I enquired.

"Oh yes; I've heard about that. Mighty interesting too! I sure am glad to get a chance to see new country where there might be birds no one knows of yet. I'm mighty keen on ornithology, Colonel."

He spoke of little else, and in a week or two nearly had Butch and me discussing trogons and other things we had never heard of before! His effervescence was stimulating, but, unfortunately, once out on the trail away from Cuyaba he relapsed into anxious silence and stayed like that until nearer civilization again.

My intention was not to return by way of Cuyaba, but to spend at least eighteen months in the forest and come out eventually on one of the big rivers. At General Rondon's suggestion I would load two horses and two oxen, and take them beyond the point where we would have to give up our riding animals. There would also be a limit for the oxen, from which point we ourselves would carry what equipment was indispensable. The objective could be reached in the spring, after seeing the wet season out with the Indians. That was the idea, but it remained to be seen how my two companions would stand up to it!

Two days after Felipe's arrival we left Cuyaba.

Butch, the horse expert, proved to be a stranger to the saddle. His big talk had by this time prepared me for the disillusionment, and I was not confident about his ability to stand hardships after the mad round of women, gambling and drink he had been following. My remonstrances were always met by the same excuse.

"A real man's got to have his fling, and I'm flesh and blood like the rest!"

Our departure was witnessed by a large proportion of the town's population, for events such as this relieved the daily monotony. Butch mounted clumsily, teetered on the saddle for a moment, and then fell off on the other side. He tried again, with similar results. The third time his horse rose to the occasion and caught him, and amid the cheers and jeers of the onlookers we ambled away, Butch hanging on with grim determination. After a mile or so he felt safe enough to talk.

"These ain't horses like I know 'em," was his observation. "I ain't used to this kind of horse, and I'm not accustomed to a saddle. Back home down under I always ride bareback."

We never moved out of a walk, for this was the usual pace of the cargo animals, but Butch fell off four times in two days, once into a stream. His seaman's vocabulary meant nothing to his patient little horse, but when he began to shower vicious kicks on the animal it was time to stop him.

"I've been at sea too long," was his mumbled excuse. "Must have forgotten a lot I knew about a horse."

On the third day he developed serious organic weakness, and though scared of returning alone, at length succumbed to my arguments that if he valued his life he had better go now, while he could. He left without apology or regret, and was concerned only about the pay coming to him. As he heaved his great debauched body on to the horse's back, he turned to me and said:

"Don't worry, Colonel; I won't give you a bad name when I get back."

That was the last we saw of him, but I heard later that he reached Cuyaba on foot, the little horse having been lost on the way. The tale of his lonely journey he kept to himself. One way and another he cost me £600; and as a trusting missionary in Cuyaba handed over to him a bundle of my clothing to deposit for me in Rio, he added this to his gains. I was now left with Felipe only, and was by no means sure of that young man's stamina.

We were most hospitably received everywhere as we headed north. Little *estancias* put us up, and provided us and the animals with food, all offers of payment being emphatically refused. At one of these places we

were told that the dreaded Morcegos lived only ten days' journey to the
north. These Morcegos—the 'Bat' people—are reputed to be savages of
the most barbarous kind, ape-men who live in holes in the ground and
come out only at night.

"I know a *mouço* now living near Cuyaba who was with them," my
informant said. "He went on an expedition up the Xingú River—ten
of them in all—and nine were killed. He escaped, but the Morcegos caught
him again, and because one of their women had taken a fancy to him
they allowed him to live. They held him for a long time, but eventually
he got away by day, climbing a tree and swinging from tree to tree to
keep his trail from being found by the savages. They tracked him to the
tree all right, but lost him there, and couldn't figure out where he'd
got to."

At the ranch of Colonel Hermenegildo Galvão I was told that an
Indian chief of the Nafaqua tribe, whose territory lies between the Xingú
and Tabatinga Rivers, claimed to know of a 'city' where the Indians
dwelt, and where there were temples and baptismal ceremonies. The
Indians there spoke of houses with 'stars to light them, which never
went out'. This was the first but not the last time I heard of these permanent lights found occasionally in the ancient houses built by that
forgotten civilization of old. I knew that certain Indians of Ecuador were
reputed to light their huts at night by means of luminous plants, but that,
I considered, must be a different thing altogether. There was some secret
means of illumination known to the ancients that remains to be rediscovered by the scientists of today—some method of harnessing forces
unknown to us.[1]

Soon we were not far from the edge of civilization, where savages
are occasionally seen. Here, near the head-waters of the Rio Cuyaba, is
good cattle country, but anacondas are so numerous as to be a pest.
Nearly every waterhole has two or three of those monsters in it, and
streams are dangerous to approach carelessly. The Indians of the region
attack them fearlessly, springing into the waterholes a dozen together,
and stabbing the snakes to death with their knives. They look on it as
great sport, but the principal motive is that anaconda meat is considered
good eating.

One *Morador*—as the small settlers are called—told me of a curious
adventure with a bushmaster. He went down to a stream one day to
wash his hands and have a drink, and while squatting on his hams beside
the water felt a tap on his shoulder, first on one side and then on the

[1] In view of recent developments in atomic research there is no reason to dismiss the
'lamps that never go out' as myth. The world was plunged into a state of barbarism by terrible
cataclysms. Continents subsided into the oceans, and others emerged. Peoples were destroyed,
and the few survivors who escaped were able to exist only in a state of savagery. The ancient
arts were all but forgotten, and it is not for us in our ignorance to say that the science of ante-
diluvial days had not advanced beyond the level we have now reached.—ED.

other. He turned round, and to his horror saw the head of a large *surucucu* swaying about in the air above him. Instantly he flung himself into the stream and swam away as fast as he could. The snake made no attempt to attack or follow, yet these creatures are deemed so aggressive that they will hunt a man down. Perhaps the aggressiveness is confined to the breeding season.

We headed north into unknown country, through coarse open grass and occasional low scrub, often so boggy that extensive detours were necessary to make headway. We climbed precipitous ridges, up narrow tracks made by the tapirs, and dipped into the northern forests, where for a while the country is low-lying. It rained incessantly—the rains were early in 1920—and violent thunderstorms broke over us day and night. It seemed as though the elements were trying to drive us back, for, had we but known it, we were a month too late for this section of the trip. Ticks made our lives even more of a misery, for they swarmed everywhere, and the worst were the fiendish *garapatas do chão*. Microscopic flies covered our faces, penetrated inside our clothing from morning till sunset, stayed there all night if there was a moon, and would be found in little heaps in the hammocks when morning dawned. Their bite was not severe, but it irritated like a rough woollen vest, only much worse. I myself was hardened to these things, but Felipe suffered considerably, and his morale dropped lower every day.

We had with us two dogs. One was a large red, nondescript animal bequeathed to Felipe by Butch; the other a delightful, long-bodied, sturdy any-sort-of-dog answering to the name of 'Vagabundo', a stray I had picked up in Cuyaba. This hound was remarkably intelligent, very good-natured, and his greatest use to us was as a warning when wasps' nests were on our path. He had a sure attraction for wasps, and these insects, varying from the size of a housefly to monsters an inch and a half in length, were with us all the way.

The oxen had a habit of leaving the trails if they could, to crash through the undergrowth on one side. The cargoes on their backs cannoned into wasps' nests, and the angry occupants would wreak vengeance on any living thing in the vicinity. Vagabundo, busy with attractive smells in the scrub close by, invariably took the brunt of the attack, and when we heard a fearful howl of agony we knew a quick detour was advisable. The wasps might leave us alone, and certainly made no impression on the oxen, but Vagabundo would be singled out every time.

Felipe was terrified of the wasps, and wore himself out in mad acrobatics to beat them off. I couldn't blame him, for I have yet to meet the man who can stand forty or fifty stings on face and neck without panicking—and these wasps, the small ones at any rate, go for the eyes.

The red dog seemed to be in a state of chronic hunger, and developed a taste for chewing the rawhide ox harness at night. Under the constant rain the leather stank like carrion, and handling it made scratches fester till Felipe became convinced that blood poisoning was inevitable. But these rawhide cinches were essential, for without them we could not load the animals, and then where would we be for food?

"Somehow we've got to stop that dog chewing the cinches," I remarked innocently enough.

Felipe brooded on this, and one day the red dog was not to be found. "It's no use looking for him, Colonel," he said; "I've shot him!"

This shocked me considerably, for nothing could have been farther from my mind than to destroy the dog. On expeditions like this dogs are not only cheerful companions, but invaluable as sentinels.

We had been on the trail for six weeks when one of the oxen lay down and would go no farther. A week later Felipe's horse somehow managed to drown itself in the night. My horse had long ago been relegated to cargo, and Felipe was now obliged to join me on foot, which he loathed. From that time he began to break up. Stiff legs made him apprehensive of some peculiar muscular disease from which he had suffered as a child; then came a spot on the lung, which he had always known about but thought wouldn't matter. He suspected his heart of giving out. Then he took to lying on his back on the ground with pains in his head, moaning in a sepulchral voice, "Never mind me, Colonel; you go on—just leave me here to die!" Finally he developed a sort of got-it-all-over disease, such as the British Tommy sometimes gets when parades become too irksome. How could I face real danger with such a cripple? I couldn't send him back alone, for it was almost certain he would lose the way, and I was not prepared to take such a responsibility. There was nothing for it but to take him back and give up the present trip as a failure—a sickening, heartrending failure!

We camped in very dry forest, and found ourselves short of water— in fact, for thirty-six hours we had no water at all. The *piums*—those tiny biting flies—tortured us unceasingly, and wasps and bees were a plague. The two remaining animals were failing, and driving them made the journey more difficult than ever. Luckily the ox kept on the move, and served as a good guide for us, as it seemed to sense the best routes to take, but the horse was hard to urge along. It managed to get itself bogged, and we only succeeded in extricating it with the help of the ox. Next day it collapsed, and had to be shot.

Transferring to our own backs as much as we could carry, we pushed on, always tortured by those flies and wasps, our legs and feet an agony from the chafing of wet boots. Then, while crossing a stream, the ox collapsed in the water and was drowned. Loaded heavily, struggling as best we could through long grass covering slippery clumps and loose, rolling stones—tripping and stumbling as we went—we covered the last three or four days and came to the nearest outpost. It was the hardest going or all, but Felipe homeward bound was becoming less fatalistic and could even take an interest in birds again.

The Manager at the post fed us well, and we rested there a day or two before going on.

"You've just missed a troop of soldiers returning to Cuyaba," he told us. "You might have gone with them."

There was a long walk ahead of us yet, but nothing to what we had just done.

"They say it's bad country you've been in," remarked the Manager. "Twenty years ago a troop stationed here went in with their Colonel and very few came out. The Colonel went mad. They ran into the Morcegos on the left bank of the Araguaya. Lucky for you none were around where you went!"

He told me canoes were to be had four days' trip away, and lent us horses to take us there—an unexpected help. But the horses were unable to ford the swollen Tabatinga and were sent back, so on we went on foot, carrying the packs. Felipe developed serious symptoms on this part of the journey, including sunstroke, but before the next post was reached he had recovered sufficiently to whistle. From post to post we went on, always receiving great hospitality and help, and finally reached a place where it was possible to get transport for Cuyaba. Our feet and legs were by this time in such a state that further walking was out of the question. Felipe was at the end of his tether; and a bad leg had troubled me for some time, giving me so much pain at nights that sleep was difficult. By the time Cuyaba was reached we were both feeling better, and Felipe had recovered most of his high spirits.

Two days later we sailed for Corumba, leaving Vagabundo in his old haunts to await our return in February. Owing to a rivermen's strike, the launch to Corumba was more crowded than usual with the *élite* of Cuyaba society. These people, crowding the tiny upper deck, were horrified—shaken to the core of their respectable souls—by the sight of Felipe removing shoes and socks and inserting a charge of vaseline between his skinny toes! Such a thing was considered the very acme of bad breeding. It took me a long time to live it down, for, as Felipe's companion, some of the shame fell on me, and I was destined to be close to these people for a month or two. Was he my son? Was he my countryman? How could I associate with such a boor?

Felipe went on his way to Rio, undertaking to return with a fresh supply of stores for the next expedition. I should have liked to go too, but could not afford it, so in the meantime decided to stay in Corumba, which I preferred to Cuyaba. My intention was to go in again the following February, but without animals and by water. I hoped to find another companion to share packs with us, and by doing the greater part of the journey in a canoe it should not prove too much for either of them. How they would shape when we made contact with the Indians was anybody's guess.

The British Consul in Corumba, an ex-officer of the Brazilian Navy, had a good library which he invited me to use. This, and the local cinema, saved me from boredom, and occasionally an Englishman came into town from some *estancia* down river to relieve the monotony.

I returned to Cuyaba in the middle of February, and a wire came from Felipe to say that he had promised Mother to be back by Christmas! Supposing him to be already on the way up, I could do nothing about this —but surely few explorers on the eve of departing on a risky venture have received such a communication! As it happened, he didn't arrive till April, and in the meantime I kicked my heels in that deadly dull town, compared to which Corumba is a metropolis.

Easter was celebrated by one of those amazing processions to be seen at certain times of the year in every provincial town in South America —and in some capitals. It was headed by priests in robes and acolytes swinging censers, followed by the most villainous-looking blacks in town—also robed—carrying on their shoulders wobbly erections representing saints and martyrs. There was a Christ, horribly gory; and a Virgin Mary, bedecked in tinsel crown and spangled garments, her halo a child's circular tinplate railway track. These figures rocked precariously, threatening to fall from their heaving platforms as step by step the procession shuffled forward over the cobbles and open drains. Behind the black penitents—all of them delinquents expiating thus the sin of a multitude of petty crimes—came a straggling band, strong in the percussion section but dreadfully weak in the others, and playing a rousing march to which not one of them attempted to keep step. In the tail, and lining the sidewalks, came the whole population of Cuyaba, bareheaded and devout.

As the procession crossed the stone bridge on the main road to the river the shadow of the Virgin's effigy was cast on the filthy surface of a little beck that carried the sewage away from the town. At once scores of eagerly waiting negroes plunged in and greedily lapped up the foul water in the belief that their ailments would be miraculously cured. That they often were shows the power of their faith!

The foreign population of Cuyaba consisted of a drink-sodden English beachcomber—you find them everywhere—a few Italians, and two American missionaries with their wives. They seemed content enough, for the missionaries were full of zeal, the Italians were busy amassing fortunes, and the beachcomber could procure all the booze he wanted at infinitesimal cost. It put my own impatience and boredom to shame, and induced me to open my dwindling purse to the beachcomber, who, on seeing me cross the *plaza* one day, heaved himself up from his bench and came staggering over to cadge. This human derelict's vision focused on my riding-breeches; he reached out to feel the material, and then burst into tears.

"Boxcloth, by God, sir!" he muttered. "I ought to know it. I was once a cavalry major in India!"

CHAPTER XVIII

FEELING THE WAY

"WHAT on earth induced you to buy stores of this sort, Felipe?"
I asked, keeping my irritation back with an effort. "You must
have known perfectly well what would be needed!"

Felipe lit a cigarette, rested his posterior on the table, and enquired,
"What's wrong with them?"

What's wrong! Everything was wrong! It was quite obvious that he
had not troubled about the supplies till the last moment, and had then
bought up what happened to be at hand, without stopping to consider if
it suited our purpose. After all, he had done a trip with me; there was no
excuse for bringing rubbish such as enormous bradawls for repairing
boots, and medical supplies enough to cure every disease in the pharma-
copoeia! There was hardly an item that was of real use to us. Here he was
—two months overdue—with quite different stores from those I listed for
him when he went to Rio, and with a formidable bill for extras, as well as
a shameless claim for personal expenses.

I was on edge from the delay. Cuyaba was deadly enough in itself, but
the worst part of my stay there was the intolerable idleness, and the
knowledge that the time at our disposal for reaching the Indians before
the rains set in was being frittered away. My low funds were causing me
anxiety, too, though living here was fortunately not costly in comparison
with most places of its size. I paid only eight shillings a day in the hotel,
a modest enough charge. The food was good and there was plenty of it;
there were also facilities for a bath—which I had daily once the charcoal
for the kitchen stoves had been removed—but the place was disgracefully
dirty, and I objected to tarantulas and lizards in the bedroom!

Every evening Cuyaba society gathered in the park—a place no bigger than a smallish garden, where a band played on Sundays, and the town's young folk walked round and round its pavement at sunset, girls in one direction—four or five abreast—and youths in the other, ogling and passing remarks to them. It is the regular routine that you will find in every provincial town in South America, and scoff how you like, if you stay a few years in these countries you'll find yourself going down to the *plaza* every evening to watch, if not to join, the promenade.

There was a cinema, too, where twice a week sentimental Hollywood dramas or Western serials were shown. The performances were carefully timed to avoid interference with the evening promenade, and when darkness had fallen, and the ping of mosquitoes was in the air, the young people strolled up to the little theatre to take their customary seats on the rickety chairs and start a grand game of passing notes to one another under cover of the darkness, while the town's children yelled themselves hoarse at the doings of the awful villain in the film.

I was reluctant to start on another expedition with Felipe as sole companion and, during his absence, sought another man to accompany us. The only one I could find was an ex-R.A.F. officer who asked to come in an unpaid capacity, and I was disappointed to discover that he was a degenerate. I had to admit to myself that the trip would have to be dropped—besides, without proper supplies it was out of the question. Though convinced that the intended route was the right one for the objective, I decided to go up to Bahía and investigate certain interesting rumours in the Gongugy area. The animals and stores were sold, and we departed for Rio. No doubt it could be called failure, and the taste of it was sour in my mouth. I longed for the day when my son would be old enough to work with me—it seemed impossible to find anyone out here able to stand up to the inevitable hardships. Had it been possible to obtain in Brazil the necessary navigating instruments, light enough to be included in one man's equipment, I think I should have set out alone. Later on, that's what I did.

It occurred to me that my principal objective might be reached by a route through the State of Goyaz, and any return to Matto Grosso thus avoided. The Gongugy country was still in possession of Patajoz Indians, who were the terror of the few settlers there, but I had no apprehensions on this score, as past experience had shown that the savage was invariably painted blacker than he deserved. Rock inscriptions had been found there; in the forests of the River Preguiça fine ceramics were discovered, and an antiquated silver sword-hilt; near Conquista an old man returning from Ilheos lost his ox at night, and following the trail through the *mato* found himself in the *plaza* of an ancient town. He entered through arches, found streets of stone, and saw in the middle of the square the statue of a man. Terrified, he ran from the ruins. This—the sword-hilt

JULIACA, 1911. Costin, Manley, the *Comisario* of Police and Fawcett

Top left:
THE BRIDGE WHERE THE *PONGO* DIED, PELECHUCO

A REST ON THE UPPER HEATH

FAWCETT WITH TWO GUARAYO BRAVES. Amongst the savages of Western Amazonia it is not always easy to distinguish men from women. These two Indians are warriors

CAMP BESIDE A SAVAGE HUT ON THE HEATH

ACROSS THE PLAINS OF MOJOS BY
BULLOCK CART

A STREET IN SANTA CRUZ DE LA
SIERRA, as it used to be. The town is now an
important link in the International air route
between Lima and Rio de Janeiro

FAWCETT IN THE *PATIO* OF THE
HAUNTED HOUSE AT SANTA CRUZ

A *BALSA*
ON THE
TAMBO-
PATA

Above: COSTIN IN FRONT OF THE MAXUBI *MALOCA* (communal hut)

Left: A HYMN TO THE SUN BESIDE A LONELY MATTO GROSSO RIVER. An ethnical riddle of the forests, he plays a reed flute similar to the Peruvian *quena*, and he calls the stars *"Vira Vira"*

Photo by Richard Sasso

Below: THE MAXUBI HEAD PRIEST, holding a stone axe

and the town—made me think that perhaps the old man had stumbled on the 1753 city, though its proximity to the settlements did not tally with Raposo's account of the long journey back to Bahía. There was talk of an old castle—reputedly 'Incan', not far from the Rio de Cobre—once containing statues, but now much damaged by treasure-seekers.

I took Felipe with me to Bahía, for he was already paid in advance up to the end of 1921, and we reached it on May 3. It was the original capital of the Brazils and the centre for the African slave trade. An attractive place, with a bright future because of its unlimited resources and fine climate; but the population is negroid or mulatto, quite distinct in every way from the people of Rio, to which city it bears something of the relation of Brighton to London. It has an excellent service of street cars, fine roads and innumerable churches. Foreigners of all nationalities swarm there, for business is active. Fruit is abundant, shops are impressive, the hotels are good, and there are many cinemas. The better-class Brazilian families are rather aloof, but the ordinary people, and the officials, are generally courteous and friendly. The place is quite healthy, though once yellow fever was prevalent. The people give me the impression of being intensely superstitious, and it is said that *Macumba* (voodoo) is freely practised by the negroes, who are often consulted as soothsayers in spite of the energetic attempts of the police to put a stop to it.

A British naval captain, who vouched for its truth, told me a story about the Bahía *feiticeiros* that is worth repeating.

In 1910 an English whaler put in to Bahía for stores and water after a disastrously unsuccessful voyage, and to distract himself from his troubles the skipper went to a local bar for a booze-up. He was sitting alone, making good progress with a bottle of whisky, when a friendly Brazilian who spoke English came up and asked if he might sit down for a 'gam'. The skipper waved him to a chair, invited him to help himself to the whisky, and the two were soon deep in talk, during which the story of the unprofitable voyage was told.

"Tell you what, *Capitão*," the Brazilian said, "you come along with me and I take you to a *macumba* man I know, who tell you something to help you."

"Nonsense, man!" scoffed the captain. "I've little faith in that sort of thing."

"Never mind, *Capitão*; you come anyway. You not be sorry."

"Och! What's the good? Come, drink up and have another."

"One more, and then we go seek the *feiticeiro*, no?"

"All right, then, if you want to. The bottle's empty anyway."

The skipper might have thought better of it had he been perfectly sober, but there was enough drink in him to make him venturesome, and it promised to be a new experience. The Brazilian led him through narrow streets of poor buildings to a house where, after much knocking and mysterious exchange of passwords, they entered and found the *macumba* man.

"I know why you came to me, *Capitão*," said the witch doctor in Portuguese, which the Brazilian translated. "You sail next Monday and go south-east. Five days out you will see a big whale. Leave it alone. Next day you will sight a school of five. Attack these and you will get all the oil you want. I have said." Rising with great dignity the *feiticeiro* condescended to take a fee, and without any word of acknowledgment showed them to the door.

The captain was sceptical about it when the ship sailed on the following Monday, but the Saturday afterwards a huge bull whale was indeed sighted. At once the *macumba* man's instructions were forgotten in the excitement, and the boats pulled away to the attack. The mate was the first to get fast to it, but no sooner did the whale feel the harpoon than it turned on the boat, smashed it to smithereens, and drowned the mate and two seamen. Then it sounded and was seen no more.

Next day five whales were sighted and again the boats put out, but before they could approach near enough all five sounded and escaped.

The skipper returned to Bahía to report the mate's death to the Consul, and while in port ran across his Brazilian acquaintance, who persuaded him to visit the *macumba* man again. When they entered the house it was to find the witch doctor in a towering rage.

"You did not do what I ordered!" he thundered at the crestfallen captain before the latter had a chance to speak. "You attacked the bull whale, which was myself." The *feiticeiro* jerked away his shirt and disclosed a fresh wound on his shoulder. "Your mate's harpoon did that! Don't expect anything but ill-fortune for the rest of the voyage!"

Not another whale did the ship sight, and after a disappointing voyage reached home with empty holds. . . .

We left Bahía in a steamer of the Navigacão Bahiana, and crossed over to the river port of Nazareth, where a train took us up to Jaguaquara, the temporary railhead. We found this to be a dirty and insanitary little village just recovering from a violent epidemic of Yellow Jack. Senhor Roberto Grillo, a kindly and prosperous merchant whom we met here, lent us mules for the trip to Jequie on the Rio de Contas.

Jequie is the centre of a considerable area of country exporting to Bahía large quantities of cacao, tobacco, coffee, cotton and medicinal products. It is extraordinarily beautiful country, but sparsely populated, with Italian immigrants. The town is fairly new, for the old one was washed away by abnormal floods in 1914, which did incalculable damage in the south of the state.

We met here an old negro called Elias Jose do Santo, once Inspector General of the Imperial Police, but now engaged in retailing alcohol on the outskirts of the town. An Imperialist to the backbone, he was exceed-ingly dignified and grand, and was at pains to make frequent mention of Dom Pedro, bowing low each time he did so. Felipe had recently acquired a habit of bowing, possibly learned from a correspondence course for foreign salesmen, and his technique was reminiscent of the music-hall comedian. To see these two idiots bowing low to each other at every sentence exchanged was almost more than I could stand without explod-ing. They looked like a couple of sea-cows courting! For my edification the old man donned his ancient uniform with magnificent golden epaulettes and monstrous shako, and became a striking figure, though pathetic when his present status was contrasted with his former import-ance. He told me wonderful stories of the Gongugy basin—of fair-complexioned Indians with red hair, and a *Cidade Encantada*, or Enchanted City, drawing the explorer on and on until, mirage-like, it vanished.

His was not the only such story. The Aymorés, or Botocudos Indians, farther to the south, preserve a legend of the *Aldeia de Fogo*—the Fire City—so called because its houses are roofed with gold. The legend is connected with a long-forgotten past, and neither a *Cidade Encantada* nor an *Aldeia de Fogo* has any real existence in these parts.

Why should it be supposed that the ancient cities, if they exist at all, must necessarily be in the region where the traditions about them are heard? Time and time again I have found that the Indian has no conception of distance and gives one the impression that something actually remote is relatively near. The Indian child may hear from his mother of a wonderful city 'over yonder', and grow up to believe that it is somewhere just beyond the limits of the tribe's movements. Yet the tale may have been passed down from generation to generation, from a remote past when the tribe was part of a nation, before cataclysms drove the people into a nomadic existence. To hear tales of an ancient city in the vicinity of certain Indians, and then to find that nothing of the sort exists, must not be taken as evidence that the traditions have no grounding in fact. Time means less to the primitive peoples than it does to us. They can trace their ancestry back for thousands of years when we can seldom trace ours for hundreds, and occurrences dating from antiquity are related as recent happenings. This is one of the greatest difficulties in locating the old places, and to ignore it is to lose both time and confidence.

All this beautiful country—in fact, the whole state—suffered from the '*Politica*'. Brazilians are extremely patriotic and like all Latin peoples take their politics very seriously, without necessarily having a knowledge of the art of government. But the '*Politica*' must not be confused with politics, for there is a difference. A man who has won considerable wealth and local importance may secure a following, arm them, and proclaim himself a '*Chefe Politico*', or holder of all local votes. If not accepted as such and given the official position the title involves he sets to work to

destroy all opposition. A kind of local civil war results; there is considerable loss of life, much burning, looting, shooting and general destruction.
It is this system that too often hinders development of the vast natural
resources, and denies the Republic the prosperity it deserves—but will, I
am sure, achieve in time.

Waiving any offer of payment for the transport to Jequie, Senhor
Grillo found us mules for the next stage of the journey to Boa Nova. It
seemed the most suitable jumping-off place, and on leaving there we
would at once be in the *catinga*, that low thorny scrub occupying the
greater part of the state south and east of the São Francisco River. It is
difficult to negotiate, very dry, and full of rattlesnakes. Where there is
water a few settlers find a precarious living, but other areas known as
chapadas are pure desert, with low bush, high above sea level. Beyond
are the great forests of the Gongugy and Pardo Rivers, stretching across
to the Jequitinhonha, well-watered country with splendid timber. It is in
these forests, surrounded by plantations and constantly encroached on
by Brazilian settlers, that the remains of the once great indigenous
population finds its last sanctuary.

The forest of the Gongugy is amazingly fertile. On the western side
its agricultural products are brought in to the weekly markets of Boa
Nova, Poçoes, Conquista and Verruga, while to the east a very profitable
cacao industry finds its outlet at Ilheos. In the north, near the confluence
of the Gongugy and the Rio de Contas, an American lumber company
has a potentially valuable concession; but to southwards the Patajoz
Indians hold the forests and the northern bank of the Pardo, facing the
several *estancias* on the other side of the river between Verruga and
Jacaranda. West of the Jequie-Verruga trail and north-west of the Rio de
Contas is a region of *catinga* where in many places there is no water, or
so little that the land is useless for agriculture, though valuable minerals
are to be found in plenty.

We reached Boa Nova in three days and found it a clean little place,
relying for its supplies on the weekly market and the dry goods purchased
at exorbitant prices by the planters. As in other places, it was the middle-
man who made the profits. We were entertained by a hospitable merchant
who undertook to see that I obtained animals and anything else needed
for the expedition.

There was no information to be gleaned about the Gongugy, for no
one here knew it, yet just east of this village lay the fringe of the forest,
and the people subsisted mainly on its products. In Brazil I often came
up against this complete ignorance of local topography. Beyond their
own particular area all is a mystery which they take no trouble to penetrate, though they are ready to believe any rumour about it.

Couro d'Anta

CHAPTER XIX

THE VEIL OF THE PRIMEVAL

"I BELIEVE we're wrong in coming here," I said to Felipe. "It isn't a convenient point for entering the Gongugy region."

"What do you intend to do, then?" he asked anxiously.

"Go back to Boa Nova, so as to get further south, and see if an entry from that direction is more promising."

"Do you mean we must return the way we came?"

We had crossed high hills covered with *catinga* before plunging down into the thick forest creeping up the mountain-side as it did on the eastern slopes of the Andean *Cordillera*. Finally we reached Baixa de Factura, last *estancia* on the river, where the Gongugy was only ten inches wide and its source about eight leagues away. Between here and Boa Nova ran a long narrow plateau about 3,000 feet above sea level, where the cold was uncomfortable at times, and it was this plateau that Felipe disliked. The idea of returning that way was not at all to his liking, for he felt the cold keenly and was afraid of that spot on the lung he often mentioned.

My object was to find the best route to enter the *Mato Bruto*, or forest still not wrested from the aborigines. Baixa de Factura had suffered many attacks from savages in the past—its remarkable collection of bows and arrows was proof of it—but it was not at the edge of unknown country. Settlers had penetrated here, and something was known about it.

I asked our host if he knew of any tales about a lost city in this area.

"I know only that there is one," he told me; "but over at the *fazenda* of Pau Brasil de Rio Novo, four leagues away, there's a man who knows where it is—and could direct you to it."

227

This was exciting news. Next day we departed and made for the *fazenda*, where we were well received, but it turned out that the story was untrue—nothing was known of a lost city.

We returned to Boa Nova, where it was raining hard and abominably cold, spent the night there, and next day pushed on to Poçoes, a small decaying village where only the fleas thrived. Beyond Poçoes is Conquista, where we arrived on market day, and the inhabitants of the district, clad in all kinds of weird costumes, were pouring into town with stocks of pineapples, oranges, peanuts, native sweets and boots. The main trade —coffee, cacao and cotton—was not done in the market but direct with the merchants in exchange for cloth, ammunition and tools. It was a place that prided itself on being up to date; the people felt that electric light and an inferior movie house functioning once a week put them on a higher level than any rival community in the neighbourhood.

They could talk of only one thing—precious stones! Aquamarines and tourmalines are fairly common from just south of here far into the state of Minas Gerais, and a stream of hopeful people flowed into town to have stones examined and valued. They were all very careful to prevent others from seeing what they had found, but there was little need for this secrecy as very few of the stones were of value. Occasionally good ones were brought in, mostly of the blue kind, and infrequently the rarer green stones.

We put up at the hotel belonging to Dona Ritta de Cassia Alves Meira, whose romantic-sounding name was no obstacle to her running a clean, comfortable little place. Once the market was over and the stalls cleared away Conquista relapsed into a state of somnolence which lasted till the next market day, for the half-caste Indians thronging the streets with their goods were from outside the town, and when business was finished they loaded up their ponies and faded away overnight.

I woke at half past six in the morning and looked out of the hotel window. The sun was up but not a soul stirred. Then a black woman in a white dress and shawl brilliant with aniline dyes came out of the church just opposite, blew her nose with her fingers, spat thoughtfully on the steps, and went inside again. A few minutes later there appeared at the top of the street a small black boy sitting on the extreme tail-end of a barebacked donkey, which he urged along in a gallop by firing at it a stream of disgraceful language. The clatter roused sleepers in many houses; doors opened and tousled heads appeared at the window grills. Little by little Conquista came to life.

My *arriero*, an indolent but aristocratic-looking scoundrel who had committed several murders, was not easy to wake, but finally I succeeded, and after breakfast we set off again. We descended from the plateau by a slippery mud path to the basin of the River Pardo, and arrived at the *estancia* of Morro de Gloria, where the proprietor urged us to stay the night and advise him about some aquamarine crystals. He concluded that as a foreigner and a traveller I must be an expert in gems. I am not; but I have picked up odds and ends of knowledge in many subjects during my travels, and explorers are—or ought to be—a bit of everything.

Another 'lost city' story was told to me here—about a half-breed of the Rio de Peixe who crossed the Gongugy not far from Boa Nova and lost himself in the forests of the Serra Geral to the east. He climbed a hill to look for familiar bearings, and saw on a plain not far off an old city with an arched entrance. He was near enough to distinguish Indians outside the walls and in the streets, and prudently retired as quickly as he could. This story was interesting, for it sounded as if the man had stumbled on the city of 1753; and after going on as far as Verruga I decided that the way into the forests by Boa Nova was probably the best after all.

At an *estancia* a few miles beyond Morro de Gloria a huge crystal of fine colour weighing about two hundredweight had just been extracted from the top of a large quartz boulder not three yards from the trail. For a long time it had been in full view of passing travellers, but no one had previously thought of taking it from the matrix. It had a bubble in the middle, and the finders, thinking this was a diamond, broke half the crystal into small fragments to reach it. I heard later that the remainder sold for sixty *contos*, or about £2,500.

There is a tale of a Negro who discovered on the bank of the Jequitin-honha River the point of a crystal showing above the ground. He dug it up and found that it weighed a quarter of a ton, and sold it to a German for £100. The German loaded his treasure in a canoe, and set off down river, bringing it eventually to Germany, where it sold for something like £9,000. There is big demand in Germany and the U.S.A. for these crystals, which are used in the manufacture of cheap jewelry.

At Verruga those stones were the sole topic of conversation, and the unending search for them had impoverished the district. I had the greatest difficulty in gleaning a little information about the Indians in the region, but eventually learned that they were mostly to be found north-east of the lofty Couro d'Anta Mountain. They had dark skins, and one of their chiefs had a black beard—an unusual thing with these normally beardless people. Another chief was renowned for his big feet, said to be over eighteen inches long. These Indians have a distinctly negroid appearance, and are descended from the real negro aborigines of South America, with a mixture of Tupi-Carib blood. In the forests of the Gongugy the Indians, fewer in number and lighter in colour, are obviously of a different race.

On leaving Boa Nova once more we took a north-easterly route to the forests skirting the foot of a lofty mountain called Timorante. A rich goldmine is said to have been abandoned here for lack of capital to work it, and investigation might have been worth while if other interests had not urged us on. We reached the Gongugy, at a place where unmistakable signs of coal and oil were to be seen, and followed the bank down river, from *estancia* to *estancia*, until the last one was reached at the confluence of the Rio de Ouro. There was great excitement here, for Indians from the forest to the east had come out on the bank of the Gongugy and let fly with arrows, killing a child. The ranchers promptly joined together to form a punitive expedition, and entered the forest in pursuit of the Indians. They found a small aboriginal settlement, and massacred all the inhabitants they could find, except for one young girl, who, together with several parrots, they brought back with them. I am glad to say the girl later escaped. Settlers on the edge of wild country did not regard the Indians as human beings—it was the same in Brazil as in Bolivia!

The rumours that attracted me so strongly seemed to focus on the Rio de Ouro; but no one on the Gongugy appeared to know anything about this river, except that the *estancias* near its confluence were perpetually subjected to Indian raids. Even the east banks of the Gongugy and Nova Rivers were left entirely to the Indians.

At the ranch called Barra do Rio de Ouro we sent our animals back to Boa Nova, for we were now going to continue on foot. The local Brazilians were horrified at the idea—to them it amounted to suicide for only two men to venture into those dangerous forests!

Carefully prepared maps of the regions already visited gave me a number of cross bearings from the heights we had passed, and extensive though the forest might be there was little chance of our losing ourselves. Trails came to an end a day up from the ranch—at any rate, in the neighbourhood of the river. With his pack on his back Felipe was again reminded of his lung weakness. My heart sank. We had barely started, and the old complaints were beginning already! Then he developed something wrong with his heel, and when five days later, following a new trail, we struck an isolated cattle ranch, it was necessary to stay there for a day or two while he recovered.

On leaving the ranch we made for a high, bald-topped hill known as 'Cerro Pelado'. So far, we had found settlements scattered here and there, but no signs of Indians—it was not, as I had been given to believe, unknown country. From the summit of the mountain another plantation could be seen to the south-west of the Rio de Ouro, and taking a bearing on it we set off in that direction.

At the foot of the 'Cerro Pelado' I killed a large bushmaster inside a hollow tree stump, not aggressive but watchful and ugly. At Felipe's suggestion, we took a number of cutlets from its carcass, though it is considered one of the few snakes which don't make good eating. These snakes were very plentiful here, and there were three varieties, equally poisonous—the one known as *Surucucu*, the *Surucucu Pico de Jaca*, and the

Surucucu Apaga Fogo, or 'Fire Extinguisher'. The last mentioned are attracted by fires, and forest men are so much in fear of them that they never keep their fires alight at night. These snakes will coil up on the ashes of a smouldering fire, and when clearings are burnt for planting, several may afterwards be found burnt to death. They are said to have an extremely keen sense of hearing; and have been known to reach a length of fourteen feet with a diameter of seven inches.

A rancher told me he once sent a messenger to a neighbouring *estancia,* and as the man—a mulatto—did not return, a search party went out to look for him. He was found dead on the trail, with a large *surucucu* coiled round his thigh. The snake had bitten the man all over his body, striking again and again until it was tired and its venom exhausted.

At the next homestead a man and his wife were expecting us.

"We knew strangers were coming, for the fowls had been putting their heads together," they said. "When they do that it always means someone will arrive before nightfall."

The man told me of strange snakes called '*Salamandas*' (not to be confused with the salamander lizard). I had heard of them before, and was inclined to confuse them with the *Surucucu Apaga Fogo,* but he described them as large yellow reptiles as much as twenty feet in length, with dark cross-markings, and they were to be found in these forests. Possibly they form a species of large bushmaster—I never met with one, which is perhaps just as well, for he said they were particularly vicious.

I went into the woods with him to see if we could bag a monkey, and as we passed a tree with a hole in it about ten feet from the ground we heard a thin, shrill whining noise. My host clambered into the tree well above the hole, and emptied his shotgun into the cavity. Like a jack-in-the-box a *surucucu* shot out into the air, fell to the ground, and scuttled away into the undergrowth. Had either of us been within reach we would surely have been bitten; as it was, the shock was unpleasant. I now had evidence of the truth of the story that these reptiles whine when sleeping —it reminded me of anacondas which give voice to melancholy wails by night, a weird sound I have heard scores of times.

A trail ran eastward from here to Ilheos. To the south and west the forest was in the hands of the Indians, who occasionally came out to gather *mandioca* from the plantation but otherwise did not molest the settler and his wife. He claimed to be the last settler on the Rio de Ouro, and beyond his ranch was virgin forest—certainly there was no trail in that direction. It was that way we turned on leaving our hospitable friends.

Signs of Indians met us everywhere, mostly in the form of booby-traps made of pointed sticks placed in a manner intended to catch an unwary raider at the height of the stomach. I could imagine a man falling victim to one only if he were running blindly at night, for normally they would have done little more than prick the skin if a walker failed to see them in his way. Perhaps they were poisoned, in which case a prick or scratch would do the trick. Another form of trap we occasionally found had sharp pointed stakes just protruding from the ground, and ahead of them a canted spear hidden in the bushes, upon which the barefooted victim was presumably intended to fall.

Our settler friend was wrong in believing his plantation to be the last, for on the fifth day after leaving him we ran across another trail, which we followed to a fine plantation where we fed with gusto on sugarcane. A mile beyond was an *estancia* whose owner welcomed us with *mandioca*, maize, eggs and chickens. He seemed surprised at Felipe's low bowing, and I couldn't blame him. The bowing custom was becoming an embarrassment to me, but I hadn't the heart to tell Felipe to stop it.

I was by this time exasperated at finding trails and settlements where absolutely wild country was expected. So ignorant were the *moradores* of everything beyond the confines of their own plantations that in all sincerity they claimed to be the most remotely situated. The awful mystery of the Rio de Ouro burst like a bubble. True, the settlements and homesteads were separated by considerable distances. These people, like the frontiersmen of the United States, had pushed steadily into the wilds, each carving out a clearing for himself which became his whole world, but ignorant of the fact that others were doing the same thing on either side of him. Mention of neighbouring plantations always surprised them; they imagined themselves to be completely isolated.

It seemed now that we might really be at the last outpost, for not only were there no trails in the direction of our intended route west-south-west but from the *morador's* hut we often saw Indians come out on a rise beyond the plantation and shoot arrows in our direction. The idea of our going on alone into the midst of these savages was considered madness.

No sooner had we started out than it began to rain. It was the period of the new moon, and the rain kept up for several days, making our progress a misery. Even one heavy shower a day in the forest will make keeping dry impossible, and to be constantly in wet clothes has a depressing effect on morale. Felipe, apprehensive about his health, moaned all the time, and I myself felt my enthusiasm evaporating. But we plodded on, and except for the futile little sharpened stakes found no trace of Indians for three days. Then we came upon trails, good for a while, but petering out in the forest—a ruse favoured by the savage to confuse enemies.

One day we were going through the forest steadily and quietly, thinking of nothing in particular, when the sight of an Indian hut on a high bank ahead stopped me dead.

"Look out!" I whispered to Felipe. "Don't move. They haven't seen us yet!"

A savage was standing beside the hut, sharpening the point of a stick, and near him was a short hammock in which another savage was swinging. For a minute we watched them without moving, and then cautiously slid behind a tree and made off to the side in order to approach the hut by a more circuitous route under cover of the undergrowth. When we came to the spot on the high bank it was to find nothing. There was no sign of a hut there or elsewhere! Never have I had a clearer vision in my life than this, and can offer no explanation of the phenomenon.[1]

Next day, following a badly defined trail, we came into an old camp by a small stream where there were eight low huts—nothing more than shelters—and about them a litter of broken *cusi* nuts and large snail shells. The camp had the appearance of having been occupied by about sixteen people two or three days earlier. Trees in the vicinity were in places clumsily hacked, showing that the Indians had knives, probably stolen from the Gongugy settlers. Half a mile farther on was another camp, older and larger, with the same litter of nut and snail shells. The *cusi* nuts, found everywhere on the Gongugy, grow on a tall palm in clusters of several hundred, and have an extremely hard shell or husk containing from one to three nuts, twice the size of an almond and rich in oil. The taste is similar to coconut, and the Indians of this region evidently esteem it highly as a food. Near the camp was an empty bees' nest with a large hole hacked in it; presumably honey formed part of their diet too. Apparently the large snails made good eating, but where the Indians found them we were unable to discover, for we ourselves never saw any, or we should have sampled them.

Following other abruptly ending trails we came to a brook running through magnificent forest, and went on upstream till a third camp was reached, probably some months old, but with a number of well-made huts, in one of which we camped. Half a mile on was another camp, but again no Indians to be seen. I had great hopes of meeting them, for there was no lack of evidence that we were in their midst, but either intentionally or by accident they avoided us. The country here is cut by numerous streams with lofty ridges between them, most difficult to climb owing to their steepness. It seemed likely that the chief habitat of these Indians was in the flatter country to the north of where we crossed. Probably in any case they were not numerous.

A few days later we cut into what was obviously a trail made by

---

[1] Perhaps the clue lies in the fact that he was thinking of nothing in particular at the time. The mind, not otherwise occupied, was able to 'tune in' to the wavelength of a thought—a memory—which registered itself on the senses as definitely as an actual vision. After all, what we call 'sight' is the interpretation our brain puts on a message from the organs of vision, and if the message is relayed to the same place from another sense the result might be to give the impression of seeing something not actually there. I wonder how many of us experience this without knowing it! Many ghost stories might be explained thus. The vision mentioned here may not have been seen by Felipe—we are not told. Even if it was, the impression can be 'received' by two as well as by one.—ED.

civilized man, and following it along we came from the south-west into a settlement on the Rio Buri, an affluent of the Rio Novo, which is itself a tributary of the Gongugy. We had traversed the forest. On the Rio Novo were two or three other settlers, one of them a Senhor Marcelino, who was a sincere Baptist, and who offered, in addition to the hospitality of his house, prayers and hymns played on a wheezy harmonium.

Felipe's spirits showed much improvement when we came again to the settlements. The continuous rain we had had all the way across the forest was enough to depress anyone, and the gloom in the dark caverns under the huge forest trees weighed heavily on both of us. The long beards of moss hanging from nearly every branch lent an air of solemn mystery to the woods, and gnarled limbs seemed to be waiting above ready to grab us. We didn't starve, for there were monkeys, quail and partridges; and Felipe shot a sloth, which proved, however, to be poor eating. Nor was the going difficult—what made the crossing a nightmare was the atmosphere of the forest. There was disappointment also. We had seen no Indians, and found none of the fine houses with lights that never go out, which according to hunters on the Ouro existed in this area. My hopes that something of interest might be found in the Gongugy had now evaporated. Nevertheless, it is country eminently suitable for settling, it is not unhealthy, and it offers great possibilities for timber exploitation, for in the whole state there is no finer forest.

A good trail took us over a high ridge and down into the valley of the Rio Colonia, where at one time there was a village, now completely wiped out by the Patajoz Indians. Two days later we came into the Verruga–Ilheos trail at Bahía Branca. I had wished to cross this trail and go on to the Rio Pardo in the hope of visiting the black Tapajoz Indians—if they could be found—but Felipe was failing and developed so many ailments that I thought it wise to continue to Verruga.

Colonel Paulino dos Santos, a well-known political man of substance who owned a ranch at a place called Duas Barras, was horrified at the idea of two *senhores* walking on foot, and insisted on providing mules to take us to Verruga. As the mud on the trail was becoming ever deeper and more adhesive, this courtesy was welcomed, and the rest of the trip was done in comparative luxury. Felipe's spirits soared!

At Verruga we stayed with the same man who accommodated us on our previous visit, and not content with this kindness he found us mules to cover the first part of the Rio Pardo section.

Crossing the Pardo at the 'ghost' village of Caximbo we followed a good trail down the south bank of the river leading through many *estancias*, all of them beginning to recover after the destruction by floods in 1914. We turned off at the high mountain called Couro d'Anta, which dominates the surrounding country. I was anxious to climb to the top to take a series of bearings, and we rode into the plantation of an old Negro called Vasurino who agreed to guide us to the top. At one time the Jesuits had a mission at the foot of the mountain, but since its abandonment the Indians permitted no settlers to stay on the north bank of the river where it was situated.

It took us two days of hard climbing to reach the summit, but the magnificent view more than recompensed us for the trouble. The forest was spread out under us like a map—a dark green carpet broken here and there by little clearings and the distant gleam of streams winding crazily in and out of view. Far away to the north we could see the 'Cerro Pelado'; to the east were the hills of Salobro where a diamond industry once flourished and where lies the source of the Una River. Bahía Branca and our trail from Verruga were perfectly clear. Had there been any 'lost cities' down there in that forest, they might well have been seen from here. To the south-west was the mysterious rock of Maquiqui, rising like a gigantic monolith from the forest half-way to the Jequitinhonha. Many superstitions centre about it, particularly amongst the Indians.

There were traces of Indians all over the mountain-side, and Vasurino told me they often came up to the summit in order to watch the *estancias* on the south bank of the river. The woods on the steep slopes were rich in *poalha*, better known as Ipecacuanha. It is prized locally as a medicine, and was without doubt so used long before its efficacy as an emetic was known in the outer world.

In a picturesque bend of the river, two days' journey on, we came to Angelin, half *estancia*, half village. Here there is a cave about three hundred yards long, converted into a church by two priests who lived in it for many years. It consists throughout of alternate strata of limestone and sandstone, and the numerous stalactites give the interior an impressive appearance, much as the great organ pipes do in an ordinary church.

"How about taking to the forest again from here?" I said to Felipe. "It's a good spot to go in from, and we can't be very far from the black Indians."

Felipe said nothing. Of late he had taken to whistling, sure sign that he was anticipating an end to the wilderness, but the look of martyrdom that spread over his face and found expression in his drooping shoulders at my suggestion warned me that it was useless to expect him to support the idea.

The good folk of Angelin offered us mules for the next leg of the journey; and one day's going down river brought us to Novo Horizonte, a miserable huddle of huts on the bank. Close to this place, in the bed of the river, lay the remains of the fine village that had existed prior to the 1914 floods. Here we put up and, as usual, not one of our hosts would consider taking any payment. It was almost an insult to offer it! Rich or poor, it was always the same, and the only return I could make beyond profuse thanks was the familiar 'Dius lhe pague'—'God will repay you.'

At Jacaranda a fat black mammy was our hostess in the dirtiest hotel I have ever seen—and that's saying a lot! It was quite a flourishing little town of 300 houses, the river port for the Salobro diamond field. These workings were at one time rich, but are now said to be exhausted. They have changed hands several times, but since slave labour was given up have not been very profitable. As in all the Brazilian diamond fields it is hard to say where the diamonds come from. They are washed in river beds, and have been found embedded in conglomerate, but it is probable that originally they came from volcanic pipes, for the whole of this side of the country has been turned up by earthquakes now forgotten. Eastern Brazil was once an active volcanic region, and craters can still be recognized.

The bristles of the *piasaba* palm, found in great quantities near Jacaranda, are used in the manufacture of brushes, and form a large part of the region's trade. Farther up river can be seen enormous clearings marking the sites of former villages of the Aymoré Indians, none of whom now exist north of the Jequitinhonha. An ugly, negroid race, they still hold the coastal ranges and forest of the state of Espirito Santo, and remain independent and unmolested.

The trip from Jacaranda to Cannavieiras was made in a large canoe with a leaf shelter serving as cabin. In an atmosphere altogether too thick for me, Felipe and three Brazilians stowed themselves away inside this cabin, but I preferred to sit on the roof throughout the journey, in spite of lashing rain and thunderstorms, soaking clothes and bitter cold.

The smell of the ocean greeted me thrillingly when in the early hours of the morning we came to Cannavieiras, and as day dawned the masts and spars of several sailing vessels were etched on the bright copper of a clear sky. There is little to be said about the town, my chief impressions being dirt, grassy streets and numerous Italian traders.

Felipe was to return to Rio de Janeiro from here, for the further investigations I planned could be done better without him, but he chose to accompany me as far as Bahía in a Brazilian seventy-ton coasting schooner whose captain was willing to take us for the sum of ten shillings each.

Vaccination certificates were necessary for landing in Bahía, and we were forced to seek out a doctor willing to provide these with or without the operation. The doctor's consulting-room was open to the kitchen, and full of screaming children, dogs and flies. A family gathering was in progress, and the doctor, in shirt-sleeves, waved a knife and a bottle of vaccine in time to the thrumming of banjos and guitars. He sterilized the knife carefully, and then laid it down on a filthy chair while he washed his hands. As he performed the vaccination his alcoholic breath settled about me in a suffocating cloud. Felipe then submitted to the same rites, and we were given the certificates, on which the doctor lavished all his art of penmanship in providing the inevitable *rubrica*, or complicated series of squirls, under the name. Chickens scuttled from under our feet as we opened the door and emerged into the street.

Cannavieiras is an inconvenient port to navigate. Across the entrance there is a shallow bar which with an on-shore wind is dangerous to cross. The *Vitoria*, as the schooner was called, ran aground on the way out of the estuary, causing a delay just sufficient for the skipper to take on board a last-minute cargo of green hides in a highly odorous condition. There were five deck hands, a cook, a boy, two pigs, two dogs, two turkeys and two women passengers who, like Felipe, were sick from start to finish of the voyage.

The schooners have no stays to the masts, and if they take the risks the *Vitoria* did it is a marvel how they complete a trip without coming to grief! We crossed the bar, tacking out to sea in the face of a heavy surf and stiff breeze, and at the most critical moment the main halyards carried away. Felipe and the women were in their bunks dead to the world, but on deck there was bedlam. Men rushed to and fro shouting utterly un-heeded instructions to everyone else; the seas came over green, and the pigs protested at the top of their lungs as they were rolled over and over into the scuppers. We just managed to weather the shore end of the passage, and by a miracle escaped a wicked ledge of coral exposed between rollers on the beam. Thanks to the energy of the giant mulatto captain the ship was brought under control, and the rest of the voyage accom-plished without excitement.

On arrival in Bahía, Felipe left me, and I heard later that he was married shortly after returning to Rio. I picked up my mail at the Consulate and crossed the harbour to Cachoeira and São Felix, two towns facing each other a little way up the Rio Paraguassu, where a railway serves the interior as far as the diamond fields. The terminus at that time was Bandeira de Mello, and here I put up at the hotel of Dona Lydia, one of the best and cleanest I have met with in Brazil, and with a most generous table—a really delightful refuge from the dirt and discomfort so general in the small places.

At Bandeira de Mello I chartered mules as far as Lençois, one of the chief centres of the Bahían diamond industry, at the western end of the mountains of conglomerate which stretch away south to the great Sincora range.

Thousands of *garimpeiros*, or diamond washers, spend their lives turning over gravel day after day in what is generally a vain attempt to find precious stones—a labour of soul-killing monotony, and an existence in the most abject poverty. Diseases of all kinds are prevalent, and if temporary prosperity should favour some fortunate worker it is soon destroyed by the '*politica*'. Occasionally small diamonds are found, exquisitely coloured but rarely exceeding half a carat. Blue, pink, green, wine, white and brown stones are all turned up from time to time, and a single find is enough to keep the *garimpeiros* at their work year after year. Wherever water is to be found in or near the mountains of conglomerate, there the *garimpeiros* will gather to scratch over every vestige of gravel and wash it for diamonds. The buyers are the people who make the profits, for the market in gems at Lençois is so favourable that diamonds are often brought up from the workings in the south for the sake of the higher prices they fetch there.

I don't think the diamond industry here is yet played out, for it is quite likely that other fields may be discovered, and the matrix may one day be found. Diamonds have been washed from river gravels over an area extending from the Atlantic coast to the extreme west of Matto Grosso, and from the Eleventh Parallel to the south of São Paulo. When the pipes are discovered—and they must exist—the fields of Brazil will once more cut out the industry of South Africa, for the superiority of the Brazilian stone is outstanding.[1]

I bought two mules, one for the saddle and the other for cargo, and set off alone into the interior. I was away in all three months; and once I was accustomed to travelling alone I found it less difficult than with one or more unsuitable companions. Loneliness is not intolerable when enthusiasm for a quest fills the mind. The chief disadvantage seemed to be that were I to find anything of scientific or archæological value there would be no witnesses to support my word. But the main object was to penetrate the veil of the primeval—to eliminate false clues and make sure of the right route, and then an expedition could be organized for the discovery.

I found enough to make it imperative to go again. The hints that follow may be sufficient to indicate the extraordinarily interesting nature of the research. With the right companions, the right organization, and knowledge of the right way to go, it can, I am confident, be brought to a successful conclusion. I have probed from three sides for the surest way in; I have seen enough to make any risk worth while in order to see more, and our story when we return from the next expedition may thrill the world!

---

[1] P. H. F. is talking here of the ornamental stone, and not the industrial kind. As personal ostentation decreases in our changing world, the value of the diamond consists more in its usefulness for industry, and whether Brazil can ever compete with South Africa in this respect I am not qualified to say.—Ed.

CHAPTER XX

IN THE DAWN

THE story of South America prior to the arrival of the European can only be inferred from archæological remains and geological changes —and, with reservations, from the traditions of the indigenous peoples. Not one of these sources has been exhaustively studied. Official archives, as well as those of the historical societies, and the missions which did such splendid work in their day, could have yielded data that may now be lost. Ethnologists have reported in detail on the habits, conditions and languages of the Indians of the rivers, but errors have come about because no intensive study has been made of the wild people of the interfluvial regions.

The geographical form of the continent has completely changed during comparatively recent times. We know that the Andes are still in process of modification; they constitute the western volcanic area, with many active and inactive volcanoes. On their loftiest summits, above the ever-receding snowline, marine fossils may be gathered. In the neighbourhood of Cerro de Pasco, Jatunhuasi, and other elevated places in Peru, 14,000 feet above sea level and high above the timber line, the presence of abundant coal testifies that what is now the roof of the world was once low-lying carboniferous jungle. The bed of the ocean between the Bay of Panama and the Galápagos Islands is still littered with the trunks of trees. In the eastern foothills of the Andes, about 15 degrees south latitude, masses of lacustrine clay may be found, rich in fossil limpets. Practically the whole eastern foot of the Andean *Cordillera* for 10 degrees in longitude is a vast carboniferous deposit, once under water.

From the Gulf of Guayaquil to as far south as Valparaiso there is a ledge from 30 to 300 miles wide, lying between the ramparts of the mountains and the Pacific Ocean. This ledge is a desert where little or no rain falls. The few rivers are small, and in their vicinity are belts of productive soil, but beyond is nothing but sand, damped for half the year by the pall of the *Camanchaca*, or 'Scotch mist', which is created by the ice-cold Humboldt Current sweeping up the coast from the Antarctic, and scorched by the tropical sun for the rest of the time. Between the Coast range, of older formation, and the more recently created *Cordilleras*, is the *Altiplano*—the great Andean plateau—once the bed of a huge lake that has now dwindled into Titicaca, Poopó, Coipasa and many small lakes scattered along under the snows.

The warm air currents from the eastern forests precipitate heavy rainfall on to the *Cordilleras*, and this drains down into the irregular courses of the network of mighty rivers making up the affluents of the Amazon and the smaller Paraguay. Above the existing beds of the mountain torrents, and cutting them more or less at right angles, are the auriferous channels of an ancient river system, clear evidence of the sweeping changes brought about by time and seismic disturbances. Evidence of these changes is everywhere—there is no need to call attention to it in more detail.

Trovessart was probably right in concluding that at the end of the Tertiary epoch the two Americas were not joined together, and that Brazil was a huge island. Farther west was another island, now the Pacific coast, which—if we can infer anything from the area of comparatively shallow soundings—stretched as far out as Easter Island, in the south. North of the present River Amazon a third island may have extended northwards into the Caribbean Sea. Between these islands were branches of the ocean, and the Caribbean joined the Atlantic to the Pacific.

It is not too much to infer that in the Pacific a great continent, or group of large islands, was breaking up contemporaneously with the changes building the Americas into their present masses. The remains to be found in the Marquesas and Sandwich Islands, the Carolines, Tahiti, Pitcairn, and dozens of others, form a convincing argument in favour of it; and according to Hooker there are seventy-seven species of plants common to New Zealand, Tasmania and South America.

There is a curious granite belt about three degrees in width extending from Trinidad Island, in 21° south, through Vitoria and Rio de Janeiro, and across the continent. In the Parana and Paraguay Rivers it is visible in the form of sugarloaf bosses rising abruptly from water or dry ground. It becomes huge mountains in the Bay of Guanabara, and it is these granite masses that make Rio de Janeiro and—on a smaller scale —Vitoria the most picturesque harbours in the world. They are evidence of the vast seismic activity that changed the eastern side of Brazil as ruthlessly as it did the Pacific coast. Minas Gerais has numerous extinct craters and active hot springs, and while now there are no living volcanoes, it was once the centre of a very extensive volcanic area. On the upper reaches of the Paraguassu and Rio de Contas, in Bahía State, are ragged mountains of conglomerate, rent into fissures which have become the beds of small rivers, in the gravels of which diamonds are found. To the north-east of Lençois are low rolling plains where the great bones of antediluvian animals are scattered in an abundance that suggests some sudden catastrophe. Caverns in the limestone, so plentiful in this part of the state, no longer carry streams. There are considerable deposits of saltpetre and chloride of sodium here; and farther east, on the coast north of Bahía City, coal and bitumen are to be found.

The Danish naturalist Peter William Lund wrote:

"The nature of the Central plateau of Brazil shows that it formed part of a vast continent when the rest of the world was still submerged under the ocean, or rose in the form of islands of small extension. Brazil ought therefore to be considered as the most ancient continent on our planet."

Recognizing these facts and with further enlightenment from the archives of the South American republics, with their wealth of little-known record and tradition, it becomes possible to make some conjectures concerning the continent's history before the Conquest.

Mexican tradition tells us that in the remote past there came to Cholula from the east a Toltec (i.e. wise and artistic) people, who became the great and prosperous nation responsible for the construction of the cyclopean architecture preceding that of the Aztecs. These Toltecs may have had another name. There were, for instance, the Olmecs and Xicalancas, who claimed a great antiquity and were said to have been the destroyers of the last of the giants.[1] For the sake of simplicity I call them Toltecs. Giants also figure in Peruvian tradition. The Muyscas and Puruays of Colombia and Ecuador preserved the tradition of Bochica, who lived for 2,000 years and founded their civilizations, as Quetzalcoatl did that of the Aztecs. He, too, came from the east. A branch of these same people occupied an island to the south, extending from what is now Guatemala westwards beyond the Galapagos, and southwards to 20° below the equator. East-central Brazil formed a fourth island from about 9° to 25° south latitude, extending from the Paraguay River to some 5° beyond the present Atlantic coastline. The people whom I am generically calling Toltecs had colonized this island from another island whose savage aborigines were of a black or dark brown colour, in a very

[1] To the reader interested in these fascinating legends I recommend G. C. Vaillant's authoritative work, *The Aztecs of Mexico.*—Ed.

advanced stage of degeneracy, and of whom I shall have more to say later on.

All these Toltec peoples were delicately featured, of a light copper colour, blue-eyed, probably with auburn hair (see Short's *North Americans of Antiquity*), and were accustomed to wear loose white habits or coloured robes of fine texture. Even today the glint of henna can be seen in the black hair of the copper-coloured tribes of South America, in spite of the mixture of blood—as in the case of the Maxubis—and I have seen members of these tribes with blue eyes and pure auburn hair, although they have had no contact with any fair-haired modern peoples, or even with the dark-haired Spanish and Portuguese.[1] To the degenerate autochthones the Toltecs were superior beings. They constructed great cities and huge temples to the sun; they used papyrus and metal implements; and were accomplished in civilized arts undreamed of by the inferior races.

In Mexico, and the southern island where South America's Pacific coast now lies, these people were adept in the use of ideographic and hieroglyphic writing. García, in his *Origen de los Indios del Nuevo Mundo e Indias Occidentales*, states that the ancient Peruvians made use of paintings and characters, an art not shared by the later Incas. In Brazil it may be assumed from inscriptions still existing that possibly by reason of communication with our Middle East, or possibly as an inheritance from an older civilization, a phonetic alphabet had replaced the glyphs.

No tradition exists, nor is there any evidence to suggest that there was communication between these three colonies, until we reach the dawn of historic times. It may be that the Brazilian civilization goes back far beyond our imagining, or that the links have perished. Their evolution or devolution in geologically recent times may have been directed along separate lines by the isolation enforced by vast distances, extensive swamps infested by venomous and terrifying reptiles, and forests inhabited by fierce, intractable savages. Chinese tradition suggests the possibility of the Pacific coast having been in communication with Asia; while inscriptions point to the probability of the Brazilian island having had commercial relations with the Orient.

The *Popul Vuh* says:

> "The black and the white men lived happily, and soft and delightful was the language of these people. They were strong and intelligent. But there are in places under the Moon men whose faces are not seen. They have no houses. They wander as unintelligent as the mountains, insulting the people of neighbouring nations."

[1] Such Indians found amongst the tribes of the Upper Xingú since 1930 have been categorically stated to be infused with 'Fawcett blood', and I have been presented with 'nephews' regardless of facts. I hope these words will reach the eyes of those who see in every light-complexioned Indian youth, or albino, a 'son of Jack Fawcett'!—ED.

Does this refer to the troglodytic aborigines predating the Toltec colonization?

Upon this portion of the world there fell the curse of a great cataclysm, preserved in the traditions of all its peoples, from the Indians of British Columbia to the Tierra del Fuegians. It may have been a series of local catastrophes, spasmodic in character, or else sudden and overwhelming. Its effect was to change the face of the Pacific Ocean and to raise South America to something like its present form. We have no modern experience to gauge the extent of human disorganization resulting from a calamity which built a continent out of islands and created new mountains and river systems. We only know that the destruction of one big city may shake a nation to its foundations.

It does not require much stretch of the imagination to surmise the gradual disintegration and degeneration of the survivors after the cataclysm with its fearful death roll. The Toltecs split up into separate groups, each fighting for its own survival. We know that both the Nahuas and the Incas founded their empires upon the ruins of an older civilization. In the northern continent, outlying Toltec settlements, in what are now California, Arizona, Texas and Florida, seem to have relapsed into barbarism. Not only were the cities of the cliff dwellers later inhabited by the Otomis from the north, but tradition ascribes to the Caribs (or degenerate Toltecs) a character of extreme savagery.

Among all ancient peoples education was mainly confined to the priests, who belonged to the ruling caste or were intimately associated with it. They were custodians of the records and traditions. A calamity that shook the whole world and razed to the ground ancient America's mighty stone cities in all probability wiped out the priesthood as well as masses of the lay population. Many centuries must have passed before reconstruction produced anything like another advanced civilization. Trade must have ceased, for there is a tradition that the Atlantic Ocean was deemed unnavigable owing to the violence of its storms, and this not on the American side but on the European. The Pacific was probably the same. There can be little doubt that a cataclysm of such dimensions produced tidal waves and minor catastrophes throughout the world, for everywhere are to be found traditions of a deluge.

The Toltec civilization was in ruins and the remnants of its people scattered far and wide. It was long reported that even in Upper Canada buildings similar in character to Incan architecture had been found, but this has not yet received confirmation. Tiahuanaco, centre of Toltec culture in the south, was levelled to the ground and practically buried in the upheavals when the Andean plateau was raised, and the greater part of Titicaca emptied through the gap south of Illimani. Tiahuanaco must at one time have been a city on an island in the greater lake. It could not have existed where it is today in relation to the level of the lake, for, though drying up at the rate of a foot every ten years, the lake is yet higher than the ruins. The remains of the great city cover an area of about a square league; and at the time of the Conquest natives attributed the building of Tiahuanaco to white, bearded men long before the time of the Incas.

The cities of the interior were grievously damaged, though not to anything like the same extent as Tiahuanaco. Between them lay an immense area of low country, freshly emerged from the bed of a sea or lake, and probably for a long time inundated by rivers which overflowed from the torrents cascading down the sides of the new mountain range, on which exceptional meteorological disturbance deposited far more snow and rain than fall today. Over this swampy region there soon grew an impenetrable mass of high, coarse grass, and an entanglement of swamp scrub where lingered far beyond their time of extinction elsewhere reptiles of ferocious and gigantic species. Communication with the outer world had ceased —the surviving communities believed themselves to be all that was left of the world. Their traditions suggest this.

It was during this period of confusion and slow reconstruction that refugees from Polynesia arrived on the coast of Chile. These were the Tupis, a yellowish light-brown people, who even at the time of the Conquest still held the tradition of an origin in the Pacific. The name 'Tupi' means 'parent, or original stock'. They settled and multiplied in Chile and southern Bolivia, and spread as far north as Ecuador in a belt seven degrees wide. In the south they were the Araucanians, in Bolivia the Aymarás, and in the warm valleys east of Peru became known as the Antis, the name 'Andes' deriving from them.

The art of tattooing, common to the Polynesians and Melanesians alike, was brought by them to the continent and practised by all the Tupi tribes. According to Padre d'Evieux, who travelled much in the interior of Brazil during the sixteenth century, this tattooing was superbly executed, on the men all over their bodies, and on the women from waist to knee. The Patagonians and Tierra del Fuegians were presumably branches of the Tupis also. Even today the Tierra del Fuegians carve their wooden deities in the facsimile of the Easter Island images, a significant fact apparently missed by the ethnologists.

Contemporaneously with this influx from Polynesia, immigrants flowed into the northern continent by way of the Behring Straits and Aleutian Islands, the last arrivals being the Kitans, about A.D. 600. Buckle, in his *History of Civilization in England*, notes the presence of the 'Tscktschi' on both sides of the Straits. Even if the existence of the Americas was forgotten by the growing nations of Europe, it was certainly not forgotten in China and Japan—nor, probably, by the Polynesians and Melanesians. The Chinese termination *Tsin* occurs frequently in Mexican place names. The mythical voyage of Hoei-Chin to 'Fon Sang', 20,000 *li* to the east, is ascribed to A.D. 458—probably not the only voyage of its kind, for a small junk has sailed to England. In the ruins of Yucatan and Guatemala figurines with distinctly Mongolian features have been dug up. About 1920, the Chinese Minister to Mexico identified characters on the base of the great pyramid of Teotihuacan with ancient Chinese words for Sun, Eye and City. Quechua Indians and Chinese can understand each other's language, and the same is said of the Otomi tongue. The later Inca method of recording events by means of *Quipos*, or knotted cords, was common to China and Tibet, and supports the presumption that communication across the Pacific had at one time existed.

The result of the northern immigration was an increasing pressure on the more habitable latitudes of the continent, and the pushing back of the Toltec elements to the Mexican plateau, where some of the family tribes were forced into the warmer regions of Yucatan and Guatemala. The magnificent architecture of Uxmal, Palenque, Chichen Itza, and many other remarkable relics owe their existence to this. But although these migratory movements were definite, they were also slow, and there exists a record of a Toltec migration to Tlapallan which took over a century to complete.

In the light of recent discoveries—or rather re-discoveries—in Colombia, there seems to be little doubt that the movement continued southwards, with accompanying degeneration imposed by the loss of civilized environment. The many remains of stone-built settlements connected by paved roads to be found in that country show little of the meticulous craftsmanship of the Isthmian relics. However, they do show what will later be recognized as important—windowless houses with narrow entrances, their interiors free from the grime associated with every cooking or illuminating agency known to us except electricity!

It is not yet clear what happened to the Central Brazilian colony after the partial destruction of its cities, but the probable function of these as sea ports had abruptly terminated, and without doubt a large proportion of the populations perished. The survivors appear to have been isolated for a long time in the midst of swamps—those, that is, who were unable to escape to the east in boats, as did some who may later have become the Tapuyas. A few may have escaped to the north; but it is likely that the majority were isolated in the ruins of their cities. Extant records, dating from the time of the Conquest, refer to the appearance of these people. Physically they were a fine race, differing little from the Mexicans, Muyscas and Peruvians. Descent from a white race was a tradition they all preserved. The Molopaques, found in Minas Gerais in the seventeenth century, were fair-complexioned and bearded; their manners were elegant and refined; and their women are said to have been 'fair as the English, with golden, white, or auburn hair'. They are recorded as having 'delicate features of great beauty, small feet and hands, blue eyes, and fine smooth hair'—and this was after an inevitable mixing of blood with that of the brown-skinned Tupis. They were not anthropophagous.

The Mariquitas were a fine people too, whose women fought like the Amazons. They had women chiefs; and it is not improbable that the *Amazonas*—the almost legendary women warriors of the Amazon—were of this race. Tribes with women chiefs exist today, and preserve a singular nobility of bearing which contrasts sharply with that of the miserable folk commonly supposed to be the remains of the indigenous population.

The Tapuyas were skilful workers in precious stones, and possessed many finely cut ornaments of aquamarine and jadeite.

On many occasions the early explorers of the interior reported glimpses caught here and there of clothed natives of European appearance. They were glimpses only, for the people had an almost uncanny knack of disappearing. These reports have not so far been substantiated, but they cannot be airily dismissed. Our destination on the next expedition—I call it 'Z' for the sake of convenience—is a city reputed to be inhabited, possibly by some of these timid people, and when we return the question may finally be settled.

Some of the Tapuya tribes, differing in appearance and customs, existed at the time of the Conquest. Among them were the Tabajaras, the Guajajaras, Tymbiras, Potiguaras, Caetés, Guaitacas and Teremembes. Through scarcity of food, or mixture with cannibal neighbours, a few had become cannibals.

At the time of the great cataclysm the Brazilian island was inhabited by an autochthonous race of negroid troglodytes, dark-skinned if not black, hairy, brutal and cannibalistic. Remnants of these people still exist in remote parts of the interior and are greatly dreaded. They have been known to the Spanish as the *Cabelludos*, or hairy people; and to the Portuguese as *Morcegos*, or bats, from their custom of hiding during the day and hunting by night. The Indians on the fringes of civilization call them the *Tatus*, or armadillos, from their way of burrowing in the ground. Where there are caverns in the cliffs they occupy them, but prefer to dig holes in the ground, about twelve feet in diameter, roofed over with branches, leaves and soil. Their holes are approached by long, sloping, covered passages. The same kind of dwelling was used by the Chiquitana of Bolivia, mentioned in Chapter XVI, and both these races were probably contemporary with the pit-dwellers of the British islands. The Morcegos have a very acute sense of smell, enabling them to hunt down men and animals with the greatest facility, and it may well be this that is responsible for the seemingly telepathic knowledge of a stranger's presence—a sense shared by many forest Indians. On our way to 'Z' we shall have to pass through the territory of these people, and I shall welcome the opportunity of studying them.

The rising of the Andes and the difficulty of feeding a constantly augmenting population impelled large numbers of the Tupi tribes in the west and south-west to emigrate. They spread north-eastwards by way of Cochabamba and the plains of Santa Cruz, following the courses of the Rios Grande, Mamoré and Madeira, and eventually possessed themselves of the Amazon estuary and the lands north as far as the Orinoco. Meanwhile, Carib hordes passed through the islands of the Caribbean and landed on the shores of Venezuela, spreading southwards and coming face to face with the Tupis in the basin of the Orinoco. Constantly reinforced by fresh hordes, the Caribs overwhelmed the Tupis, absorbed some tribes, massacred others, and drove the survivors across the river. They were not known as Caribs until later, but probably as Aruacs, and other tribal names. 'Carib' is a name of Quechuan origin meaning 'man of energy, brave'. In Hebrew it is 'Cari', hence possibly 'Carini' or 'Guarini'—a warrior—a name later adopted by the Carahybas ('Descendants of Caribs') or Carijos, who settled in and around Paraguay. Their legends of a great deluge helped to identify them with the people of Mexico and the Antilles.

The Carib invasion did not stop on the northern bank of the Amazon, but continued to spread southwards into the forests and higher lands of Para and Piauhy, where it met the concentrated resistance of the Tupis, aided probably by the Tapuyas. A Carib war then began which lasted for centuries and involved Tupi tribes from the remotest corners of the continent. The Antis, for instance, anxious to participate in anything bellicose, but probably wearied by the constant warfare with the Incas, moved to Matto Grosso and occupied the land at the sources of the Guaporé and Jauru Rivers. The Caxibis and Mundurucus of the Tapajoz may be descendants of these people.

The Caribs are stated to have been a bright copper-coloured race showing a strain of white descent. Whether the white was peculiar to the Toltec races, or originated in the legendary migration of Madoc and Eric the Red, is a problem not likely to be solved. Their more advanced elements were known as *Caribocas*—that is, descended from a white race. They practised cannibalism and appalling barbarities.

There now enters a tradition recorded as extant among the Bolivian Indians at the time of the Conquest—a tradition significant to all who attempt to probe the secrets of unknown Brazil. It is to the effect that the Musus—the Toltec people of the Brazilian colony—hearing of the barbarity of the Carib invaders, surrounded themselves with their most savage subject tribes whom they put under orders to kill all who attempted to enter the country, and in this manner cut themselves off from the outside world. It is apparently from this time onwards that the knowledge of their existence became legendary among the remoter Indians of the interior— although, according to reports of the Franciscan missionaries, for some time annual pilgrimages were made even from as far afield as the Bolivian

Caupolicán, to pay homage to the 'Emperor of the Musus', or, as he was sometimes called, 'The Grand Paitití'. The pilgrims brought back with them pearls, amber and metal implements, not only astounding the Spaniards but also raising their greed for treasure to fever pitch. It was the first hint of the fabulous Ambaya or Manoa, and it inaugurated a vain search that cost numerous lives and millions of money; but to it may also be attributed the early exploration of the river system in the Amazon basin. The geographical knowledge thus gained was far from complete, but in the long run it was worth more than the treasure of Paitití. Even today knowledge of the rivers is not complete—one has only to see their dotted courses on any good map to realize this.

CHAPTER XXI

THE VEIL DESCENDS

DURING the many centuries that rolled by while these events were taking place extensive changes were occurring in the topography of the interior. The new river system was establishing itself, and surplus water drained from the swampy areas as the extraordinarily heavy precipitation in the mountains diminished—or, perhaps, as the low ground slowly rose. Indeed, it is probable that the lands newly emerged from the sea floor continued to rise imperceptibly, giving more ground for settlement to the augmenting indigenous population. One passes over in a few sentences periods of time that would stagger the imagination, referring to vast geographical changes as though they came about from one year to another. It is as well to remember that such changes are going on everywhere even now. Here, a coastline is being yearly eaten away by the sea; there, a village once on the coast is now a mile or more inland. Mountain ranges are slowly rising or sinking; always there is change—gradual change—taking place; but it is only in relation to one man's brief lifetime that the change is not apparent. The 11,000 years said by Plato to have passed since the last of the Atlantean islands submerged could be spanned by the lifetimes of only 110 centenarians. An eye-witness account of the disaster could be passed on from father to son down to the present day with only 184 repetitions! More credence may be given to what may sound mythical if this is borne in mind.

There was a gradual diminishing of the stormy conditions and heavy rainfall which must have accompanied the declining spasms of a terrestrial upheaval of such magnitude that a continent was formed by it. A dry season permitted more freedom of movement, and forests grew on the rich soil left by the inundations.

As the interminable Tupi-Carib war dragged on, the racial characteristics of Tupis, Caribs, Tapuyas and autochthones were undergoing modification. In the case of the first three, it was the custom to absorb the women of a conquered tribe, and as long as the Caribs were victorious over the Tupis they gradually changed under the influence of the proud Tupi women, who claimed blood superiority as the 'original stock'. In the course of time the Caribs became half Tupi, and adopted the mythology, language and customs of the people they were conquering—and who in turn conquered them. The tide of battle turned when there were no longer hordes from the north coming in to replace casualties. The Caribs were driven back to the Amazon and retired northwards, a number of them escaping south to Goyaz, but, soon ejected from there, they retreated farther south until ultimately they settled in the basin of the Parana and were known as the Carijos.

This assimilation of one another's characteristics among Caribs, Tupis and Tapuyas made identification of these tribes almost impossible, even at the time of the Portuguese discovery of Brazil. To attempt any classification by language appears to be hopeless. The *Lingua Geral*, or Tupi, was of course spoken by all Tupi tribes, but a multitude of dialects modified it. The Caribs had adopted much of it as their own, and presumably some of the Carib speech had infiltrated into that of the others. Adding to the complexity of the situation, other and smaller tribes were driven to mix with the autochthones, owing to a decrease in their own women, who were carried off by more powerful tribes. The result of this can be seen in the negroid Aymorés or Botocudos of Espirito Santo. But there are other tribes who preserve the negroid appearance and cannibal habits, notably to the east of the Guaporé—I referred to them in Chapter XVI. This blood taint spread more in some places than in others, and accounts for the confusing differences in colour reported by travellers.

The Tupis were a yellowish light-brown race; the Caribs a red, or light copper; the Tapuyas—some of them, at any rate—more of a warm ivory. At the time of the Conquest, the fairest-complexioned Indians were accustomed to staining their bodies with the juice of the red *Urucu* berry, and other dyes, in order to simulate the appearance of Tupis. The Tupis themselves used dyes calculated to accentuate their yellowish complexion, with the idea of appearing fairer than they actually were; and it was in this way that a certain confusion arose amongst chroniclers. It seems that in accordance with the Tupi tradition of being an 'Original Race', yellow was esteemed a sign of nobility.

It is difficult today to realize how dense were these indigenous populations, even in the sixteenth century. Tupis and Tapuyas shared the Atlantic seaboard, but more than half the total area of Brazil, Peru and

Bolivia was occupied by Tupi tribes in thousands of villages. The Jesuits calculated no less than 700 different 'nations' in the Amazon basin—and their knowledge was by no means complete. Conquest by force of arms did not destroy the 'nations'; but the contagious diseases of the white man wiped out many of these people who were unable to develop resistance to them.

The wars of the Tupis, Caribs and Tapuyas did not cease with the coming of the Portuguese. An era of intertribal warfare set in that has persisted to the present day amongst the survivors; and during the struggle for European national supremacy in Brazil the Tupis allied themselves with the Portuguese because the Caribs sided with Spain, and the Tapuyas with the French. All three of the Indian races backed the wrong horse, as it turned out—a parallel to what happened in Mexico and Peru.

It must be remembered that so far only those tribes or 'nations' have been recognized that happened to occupy lands adjacent to the navigable rivers. The many large tribes with thoroughly developed organization who dwelt at least a week's forest travel from the nearest point to which boats or canoes could be handled are still unknown—or, at all events, known no more than they were in the sixteenth century. Speaking broadly, Tupis occupied the whole of the West up to the limits of the Incan Empire; Caribs held the North; Tapuyas shared the East with autochthonous mixed tribes who were also to be found throughout the interior. A fragment of an unknown race, probably Toltec and related to Incas and Mexicans, found sanctuary where a combination of natural obstacles and deep-rooted superstition left them undisturbed. The occasional appearance of some of these people on the neighbouring rivers seems to have ceased with the multiplication of the rubber pickers. The earliest migrations of the Tupis must have come under the influence of these people, for nearly all the tribes in contact with the missions in the sixteenth and seventeenth centuries possessed the tradition of having once been dominated by a 'White Race' expert in the arts of civilization.

When the greater Tupi-Carib war drew to a close, the Incan Empire dominated the West. Possibly there had been many Inca dynasties, but latterly they had broken up into small principalities, each with epochs of domination, such as the Chimus of Trujillo, and the Muyscas of Colombia. The Incas inherited fortresses and cities built by a previous race and restored from a state of ruin without much difficulty. Where they themselves built with stone—in the regions where stone was the most convenient material, for in the coastal belt they generally used *adobe*—they adopted the same incredibly accurate mortarless joins that are characteristic of the older megalithic edifices, but made no attempt to use the huge stone masses favoured by their predecessors. I have heard it said that they fitted their stones together by means of a liquid that softened the surfaces to be joined to the consistency of clay.[1]

Their empire extended roughly from Quito to Valparaiso and far enough east to cover the foothills of the Andes. Inca remains are to be found in the forests of the Huallaga and upper Marañon, and an outpost on which a good deal of architectural skill was lavished exists at Samaipata, in Bolivia (see Chapter XV). Tradition has it that the Inca Yupanqui fitted out an army to descend the Amarumayo River—later the Paucar-tambo, and now the Madre de Dios—and attack the 'Emperor of the Musus', but he failed to reach his objective. At the farthest point of his venture he erected two stone forts to commemorate the march, and these have yet to be discovered by explorers. Apparently he retired with his troops by way of Santa Cruz and Cochabamba, utilizing or building the Samaipata fortress as a base. The tradition is plausible. The retreat followed the natural and easy watershed between the Amazonian and Paraguayan river systems. The casualty list on this invasion was probably heavy enough to deter any further enterprise in that direction; but the tale of it—and the tempting objective—must have inspired Pizarro to commission his brother to make the attempt. Traditions about the place, preserved by the Carib tribes through the Tupi strain, led many explorers

[1] "I don't believe it!" said a friend who had been a member of the Yale Peruvian Expedition that discovered Macchupicchu in 1911. "I've seen the quarries where these stones were cut. I've seen them in all stages of preparation, and can assure you the fitting surfaces were worked by hand and nothing else!"

Another friend of mine told me the following story:

"Some years ago, when I was working in the mining camp at Cerro de Pasco (a place 14,000 feet up in the Andes of Central Peru), I went out one Sunday with some other *Gringos* to visit some old Inca or Pre-Inca graves—to see if we could find anything worth while. We took our grub with us, and, of course, a few bottles of *pisco* and beer; and a *peon*—a cholo—to help dig.

"Well, we had our lunch when we got to the burial place, and afterwards started in to open up some graves that seemed to be untouched. We worked hard, and knocked off every now and then for a drink. I don't drink myself, but the others did, especially one chap who poured too much *pisco* into himself and was inclined to be noisy. When we knocked off, all we had found was an earthenware jar of about a quart capacity, and with liquid inside it.

" 'I bet it's *chicha*!' said the noisy one. 'Let's try it and see what sort of stuff the Incas drank!'

" 'Probably poison us if we do,' observed another.

" 'Tell you what, then—let's try it on the *peon*!'

"They dug the seal and stopper out of the jar's mouth, sniffed at the contents and called the *peon* over to them.

" 'Take a drink of this *chicha*,' ordered the drunk. The *peon* took the jar, hesitated, and then with an expression of fear spreading over his face thrust it into the drunk's hands and backed away.

" 'No, no, *señor*,' he murmured. 'Not that. That's not *chicha*!' He turned and made off.

"The drunk put the jar down on a flat-topped rock and set off in pursuit. 'Come on, boys —catch him!' he yelled. They caught the wretched man, dragged him back, and ordered him to drink the contents of the jar. The *peon* struggled madly, his eyes popping. There was a bit of a scrimmage, and the jar was knocked over and broken, its contents forming a puddle on the top of the rock. Then the *peon* broke free and took to his heels.

"Everyone laughed. It was a huge joke. But the exercise had made them thirsty and they went over to the sack where the beer-bottles lay.

"About ten minutes later I bent over the rock and casually examined the pool of spilled liquid. It was no longer liquid; the whole patch where it had been, and the rock under it, were as soft as wet cement! It was as though the stone had melted, like wax under the influence of heat."—Ed.

of the Orinoco, including Sir Walter Raleigh, to seek 'El Dorado'; and both Spain and Portugal sent in scores of private and official expeditions.

After his river journey from the Orinoco to the Amazon, Humboldt expressed the opinion that "the story of El Dorado resembled those myths of antiquity which, travelling from country to country, have been successively adopted by different localities". This reminds one of the warship of a certain South American republic which was sent out to find the small volcanic island of Trinidad, failed to do so, and reported that it had been submerged! The fact is that El Dorado was not to be found in the region north of the Amazon—nor was travel on the rivers the way to reach it.

Chile has a tradition of the Ciudad de los Césares—'City of the Caesars' —which is very like that of 'El Grán Paitití'. In this story, however, the city, inhabited by cultured people of a high order, is said to lie in a hidden valley of the high Cordilleras. When I heard it told in Northern Chile, the secret valley was placed down south in the Aconcagua direction; when I heard it in the south the valley was reputed to be somewhere north. The city is paved with silver and the buildings roofed with gold. The inhabitants lead an existence of blissful isolation under the benignant rule of an enlightened king; and there is some magic property about the place that makes it visible only to a few chosen seekers from outside, and invisible to all undesirable adventurers. Many people, even in modern times, are said to have set out in search of the Ciudad de los Césares, never to be heard of again.

My own opinion is that this place really exists. The tradition is old, and it seems to me reasonable to suppose that in pre-Conquest times the fame of the golden city of Cuzco—sacred city of the Incas—might have been carried down to the south by the chasquis or native runners, losing nothing in the telling. Within the Incan Empire only official travel was permitted—the Indian serfs did not move from one place to another any more than did those of feudal England. Visits from indigenes beyond the frontiers of the Empire would have been unthinkable, even if the intending visitors could have found the time from the never-ending struggle to live. Nor would the headmen of these communities—where everyone worked for the common good—have allowed members of their villages to wander off simply to gratify idle curiosity. The stories told over the evening fires by the chasquis would be woven into impressive tales, becoming in time an integral part of their folklore, and thus the tradition of the marvellous Ciudad de los Césares could be built up. Even the romancing of imaginative minds could hardly exaggerate the wonders of ancient Cuzco, where the Inca, supreme spiritual and temporal dictator, conserved a civil discipline with almost savage severity, but with results that for the people were unquestionably beneficial.

It is pretty certain that the Indians so frequently stated in the early days of discovery to be 'fair as white people' were not Tupis, or connected with Carib tribes who emulated the appearance of Tupis, for the women are definitely asserted to have neither painted nor tattooed their bodies.

Another circumstance adding to the general ethnological confusion is that large tribes forced to emigrate westwards, as often happened, were unable to keep their numbers together with the meagre food supply to be found in the forests or taken in raids on smaller communities. The tribes split up, separated, and proceeded in different directions. That is probably why the same tribal name turns up so often in widely distant areas. The Aruacs are no doubt the same people who are called the Arawaks in the West Indies; and it is significant that a tribe called the Nahuas should be found on the Amazon.

The most developed of these tribes preserved the marks of a superior civilization, and were not savages, any more than they are today. They had organized government; they worshipped a god. The Tupis adored Tupan, God of Thunder; the Tapuyas and Caribs alike worshipped the Sun and the Serpent. I have told of the dawn hymn to the Sun, chanted in wonderfully harmonious song by men of the Maxubis. The higher tribes built well-constructed houses around a square, with a sanitary system which not only puts to shame any civilized village of the interior today, but was far ahead of that common in England a century ago.[1] They were monogamous and observed marriage ceremonies. Only the chiefs were permitted more than one wife. Marriage was the basis of family life, and children were carefully brought up, and educated for tribal vocations. The children paid the greatest respect to their parents, venerated their ancestors, whom they knew as *Tamoin*, and cultivated a pride in noble birth. The man was *Apgaúa*, the woman *Cunha*. Polyandry was unknown, and a strict code of morality was enforced under pain of death. Diseases were few.

The less advanced tribes lived in *Aiupas*, separate shelters which were crudely built, and located at caprice. They were reckoned by their more developed relatives as 'savages'. In common, however, with all the Tapuya tribes they were quick to learn and adapt themselves to the civilization of the Portuguese. Both the higher and the lower tribes had chiefs of villages, answerable to a supreme chief. They also had a nobility, which served only as warriors and would not demean itself by doing

---

[1] The Incan mountain resort of Macchupicchu, built on the top of a rocky pinnacle above the Urubamba River north of Cuzco, had running water in every house. A spring at the highest level was led through a conduit into the Inca's house, and then down to the houses on the level next below. From there the water passed down till the lowest level was reached, after which it emptied over the crag and fell to the river two thousand feet below. As this running water may have carried off sewage, the Inca would have been the only one to enjoy it fresh. The others—in descending order of importance—would receive it in a state of growing pollution, till the humble people at the lowest level had it full strength! I may be wrong—perhaps sewage was disposed of otherwise, and this water used for drinking and bathing.—Ed.

THE ENIGMA OF SOUTH AMERICA'S ANCIENT CITIES HAS
NOT YET BEEN SOLVED. The one of which this building forms part
is in Peru

ON THE WAY UP TO THE KATANTIKA PASS. Delimitation of the
Bolivian-Peruvian frontier, 1911

Photo by Richard Sasso

INSIDE A KALAPALO *MALOCA*, MATTO GROSSO. A seven-foot bow and a sheaf of arrows stand ready to hand beside the hammocks. The chief's wife and bairns are unconcerned at Brian Fawcett's presence.

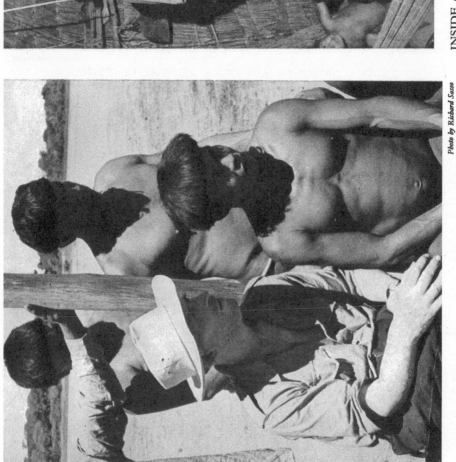

Photo by Richard Sasso

BRIAN FAWCETT WITH COMATZI, CHIEF OF THE KALAPALOS

Above: JACK FAWCETT AND RALEIGH RIMELL AT DEAD HORSE CAMP

Left: BRIAN FAWCETT WITH TWO HUSKY YOUNG KALAPALOS. Yarulla, who stands full-face, was once said to be a son of Jack Fawcett. However, it is well known that his father was Izarari, and he is heir to the chieftainship

Photo by Brian Fawcett

INDIAN WOMEN
OF THE XINGÚ

Photo by Brian Fawcett

Photo by Brian Fawcett

THE *CAXAMORA* TREE. It was reported that on this tree the Kalapalos marked the heights of the three members of the lost Fawcett party in 1925. The knife sticks in the trunk at the lowest point in one of the marks, while six-foot Major Norwood Eggeling, U.S.A.F., helps to measure the height of the knife from the ground. Looking on with great interest is the Kuikuro Indian, Narro

Photo by Brian Fawcett

THE GRAVE BESIDE THE LAGOON. The supposed remains of Col. Fawcett were found in this shallow depression by Orlando Villas Boas in 1951. Investigations carried out in January 1952 proved that the bones belonged to no member of the Fawcett party. The Xingú Indians never bury their victims

manual labour. There is in fact every reason to see in the appearance and customs of these people either the degeneration of a superior civilization or the after-effects of long domination by a highly civilized power which had been suddenly withdrawn. Many of the customs relating to the treatment of Mexican and Incan royalty were also found among the advanced tribes.

In 1661, Fernando Dias Paes penetrated the forests of the Parana, and near the hills of Apucarána found the powerful tribe of the Guayanão. This nation was governed by three kings, living in adjoining palaces, and each with a defined share in jurisdiction. The chief king was known as *Tombú*, and was distinguished by a 'coat of arms' over the portico of his palace, consisting of three macaws perched on a branch. When one of these birds died or escaped it was immediately replaced, and a good deal of superstition centred about them in the minds of the populace. The supreme king was general master of all ceremonies, and appeared in public on a chair supported on the shoulders of the four chief princes of the kingdom. At sight of him his subjects prostrated themselves, kissed the ground, and remained in that position until the *cortège* had passed.

The second king was named *Sondá*, and the third *Gravitay*. These may have been generic rather than personal names. By some feat of eloquence or sheer power of personality Fernando Paes induced these three chiefs to accompany him to São Paulo with a large following. *Gravitay* died before setting out, and bequeathed his authority to a favourite general. This made the others more desirous of migrating, and eventually a large body marched to the city, at that time a rising settlement and headquarters for all Portuguese enterprise in the interior. *Sondá* died on the way, and the tribe put itself entirely under *Tombú*, who reached São Paulo with 5,000 subjects of both sexes. They erected their dwellings on the banks of the Rio Tiete, in a very fertile valley, and grew maize and other produce for the city's markets.

Tombú was soon disillusioned by civilization generally and Christianity in particular, saying that the law was not good that God should fail to punish a transgressor on the spot. He stoutly resisted baptism and practised his own religion and code of morality, though his subjects all adopted Christianity. After some years *Tombú* was taken ill, and on his deathbed sent for Fernando Paes and expressed his desire for baptism. He was baptized under the name of Antonio, given the last sacrament, and —as the historian unctuously remarks—gave up the ghost a pious Christian. No sooner had this happened than the tribe abandoned everything and melted away into the forest.

According to our conventional history, Brazil was discovered in 1500 by the Portuguese navigator Pedro Alvares Cabral, and visited later in the same year by Vasco de Gama. Further expeditions were sent in 1501 and 1502, but it was not until 1526 that a fleet set out to establish the discovery and start a colony there. This colony was greatly assisted by our old friend Diego Alvarez, with whose adventure the first chapter opened, and in this he was aided by his Indian wife Paraguassu, whose name was later given to the largest of the rivers opening out into the Bay of São Salvador.

The territory of Brazil was placed by the Portuguese Government under the direction of hereditary captains, who swore the oath of allegiance to the crown, and colonized the land at their own expense. This system proved to be unsatisfactory, and it was replaced in 1545 by crown supervision. Francisco Pereira Continho, incumbent of the captaincy of Bahía, was wrecked on the island of Itaparica, in the bay, and he and his companions were seized by the Tupinambas and devoured. The same fate overtook the first bishop sent out from Lisbon; for being at daggers drawn with the Governor of Bahía he and numerous companions determined to lay their grievances before Dom João III, but were wrecked on the shore of Alagoas on the way home, and eaten by the cannibal Caetés.

From the earliest days of the colony slavery was forced on the Indians, and the Portuguese raided the nearest tribes to round up slaves under circumstances of the greatest brutality. Once captured, the wretched Indians were converted to Christianity by the Jesuits, and compelled to work by exploitation of their superstitions. The Government then formed what was known as a 'Board of Conscience', which decreed that the colonists might keep in slavery only such Indians as were captured in rightful warfare, or those who sold themselves, or were sold, into bondage. This led to endless evasion and abuse.

Once obstacles to the uncontrolled enslavement of the Indians had been raised, the traffic in black slaves from Africa commenced, and as many British slavers enriched themselves by it as continental Portuguese.

It is interesting to note that the Aymorés or Botocudos, who held the coastline from Ilheos to Vitoria, in Espirito Santo, were the chief enemies of the colonists, and that even today they preserve their independence in the mountains and forest between that state and Minas Gerais.

In the year 1600 Bahía, the capital, boasted a population of 2,000 whites, 4,000 negro slaves and 6,000 tame Indians. In 1763 the capital was transferred to Rio de Janeiro. Rio had been in French hands from 1555 to 1567, and in 1710 and 1711 the French made other attempts to capture Brazil. A fleet sent out by the Dutch in 1630 took Pernambuco, and this place was held by Holland for thirty-one years. Brazil was regarded by the European countries as a rich prize; and it is remarkable that Portugal was able to keep her foothold there against the Spanish, French and Dutch.

The epoch of the *Bandeiras*, or 'Flags', lasted from 1561 to 1700, and their principal function was to capture Indians for the slave markets. The officially or privately sponsored expeditions did not entirely cease with the close of the seventeenth century; even after that date *Bandeiras* were formed occasionally, sometimes for the purpose of locating mines, as was that of 1753 headed by 'Raposo', which found the ancient city.

The aborigines, deprived of their lands and subjected to ruthless treatment, attacked the colonists fiercely for some years in reprisal. Defensive measures gave way to active attempts on the part of the colonists to exterminate their enemies altogether, and the Indians were massacred wholesale. Mamelukes—Indians drawn into the net of European civilization—were largely employed for this purpose, a service vigorously opposed by the Jesuits. It was the protection afforded by this Order to the Indians that aroused the ire of the Marquis of Pombal, under King José I, and was the principal cause of their expulsion from Brazil in 1760. After the Jesuits left, the war against the wild Indians continued with more activity than ever, for slaves were profitable—in fact, a renowned Brazilian writer, Raymundo Pennafort, has observed:

"Brazil owes to its poor indigenes the conquest of the country and the construction of its cities and villages—and to them the fact that it was able to defend itself in earlier days from French, Dutch and English—in return for which they were treated with harshness and cruelty, their possessions confiscated, and every vestige of their national heritage taken. The indigenes merited from the colonists more than extermination by steel and fire, and every other means that it was possible to employ against them."

It is on record that a governor of Bahía, despairing of being able to stamp out hostility by force of arms, sent natives suffering from smallpox among the indigenes, and by this means exterminated them not in hundreds, but in thousands, and hundreds of thousands—a terrible example of early bacteriological warfare.

Before condemning the Portuguese for these brutalities we must remember that at that time every European nation with overseas possessions was actively engaged in the business of slavery, and the British, while using African Negroes for labour in the colonies of North America, were not above sending out political prisoners from the mother country to the appalling conditions of slavery in the West Indies. After all, slavery with the Anglo-Saxon nations has not yet been extinct for a hundred years. At the height of our mealy-mouthed Victorian righteousness we supported it! It is said, too, on good authority that the domestic slave in Latin-America was treated far better than his counterpart in the U.S.A. Voices condemning the system were not lacking in Brazil, and much was said advocating fair treatment for the Indian.

It is likely that intertribal warfare, raging since the Tupi-Carib war, carried off as much of the indigenous population as the bullets of the European conquerors, but the most ruthless destroyer was, and is, contagious disease.

The slaving expeditions of the *Bandeiras* gave place almost entirely to the search for minerals by 1693, but it still involved war with the indigenes, who were generally shot at sight, as in many places they are today. They in their turn lost no opportunity of killing their oppressors. Then on the heels of the search for gold and diamonds came the rubber boom. Many of the tribes had long used rubber for their ornaments, and the idea was seized and made use of in Brazil in the same way as the Indian use of coca was adopted in Bolivia and Peru, and tobacco in North America. The advent of the rubber picker, the quinine bark hunter, and the ipecacuanha, or *poalha*, seeker disturbed the privacy of hitherto untouched rivers and forests, and encouraged further exploration. All this made it difficult for the Indians. They died in their thousands from common colds and influenza—even today, in places where the trading instincts of the forest people cause them to crowd round one too closely, it is only necessary to sneeze and the mob will disperse.

What had taken place in Brazil was repeated in Bolivia, and to a lesser extent in Peru. In Peru the tribes were not so vulnerable as those inhabiting the wide *pampas* of Bolivia, for the almost impenetrable forest covering the whole of the hinterland gave them added protection. Padre Armentía, who later became Bishop of La Paz, stated that during his residence in the Caupolicán from 1870 to 1883 no less than 60,000 Indian lives were sacrificed to rubber!

The gradual extinction of the Indian, and his confinement as an independent element to ever-narrowing sanctuaries, has continued to this day—and has, incidentally, created a labour problem as fresh areas are opened up for exploitation. In the more accessible regions, if not wiped out altogether, he has been brought to his undoing by the missions, losing his independence and cultivating a taste for *chacta*, or cane alcohol.[1]

Most notable of early Peruvian expeditions to the forests was that led by Gonzalo Pizarro in 1541. Hernando Pizarro was attracted by Atahualpa's accounts of the Empire of Paitití, with the palaces and wealth of Manoa, where the forests gleamed with gold and were scented with vanilla. There are some circumstances of this expedition less familiar than the bare story told by Prescott in his *Conquest of Peru*. Orellana, the first to cross the continent, left Pizarro in order to procure food, and followed down the river banks with a fairly strong party. He reached Omagua, where an advance party had seen many well-clothed Indians in

---

[1] This was true enough when these words were written in 1923, but now there is in the countries referred to a complete change of attitude. The enlightened policy of today is to win the Indian over by friendship and aid, and to extend to him full recognition of citizenship on equal standing with others. It may take generations to eliminate the inborn animosity and suspicion, but tolerant recognition of this is being made.—ED.

canoes, and these Indians, friendly at first, became antagonistic and began to disappear. Their going took away all chance of obtaining supplies. The first clumsy boat was built here, and the party went on downstream to Aparia, where a larger boat was constructed. Consistent cruelty to the Indians drove the native population into hiding, and created unnecessary hardships. Medina says that before he reached the Solimões, or main Amazon River,[1] Orellana intended to return to Pizarro, but was thwarted by starvation, and a strong river current which made it a difficult matter to travel upstream. At the very idea of return his seventy men mutinied, so he was forced to go on. Father Carbajal has written the story for us. At Aparia women helped them with the building of the boat, but later became hostile—owing, no doubt, to the brutal treatment meted out to them by the European scum. Asked the reason for this, a friendly Indian said that they were the Amazons, who lived at seven days' journey in the forest.

Those women were unmarried, the Indian told the Spaniards, and had been many times in his country. He knew seventy of their villages by name, and there were many more besides. Their houses were of stone, and good roads connected village to village, roads that at certain points were closed and guarded so that none could enter without paying toll. The women mixed with men now and then, at which times there were large gatherings to attack a great monarch who lived not far off, and whose men were seized, carried off to the Amazons' villages, and after a time permitted to leave unhurt. If the women bore male children these were killed, and if daughters they were brought up with great care and taught the arts of war. There was a queen named Coñori; the country was full of gold and silver, and all the principal women used eating-vessels of these metals, the inferior ones using wood, except in the case of cooking-pots, which were of clay.

The story is not to be summarily dismissed. The Paranatinga Indian who told it is hardly likely to have invented it. The *Amazonas*, according to the Jesuit Father Gili, were also known as *Aikeambenanas*, or 'Women Who Live Alone'. Such women—also called Amazons—were known in Greece, curiously enough, as 'Women Without Breast'; and a similar tribe, with the same custom of cutting off one breast, dwelt at one time in Assyria. It is certainly not generally known where the South American *Amazonas* lived, and their district has not been penetrated by the explorer as yet.

The collection of these facts and suggestive traditions must surely interest archæologists and persuade them that there is more to be found in Brazil than is commonly supposed.

---

[1] *Solimões* was the native name of the Amazon. It s the same as Soliman, or Solomon, and is suggestive of the tradition that the ships of Kings Solomon and Hiram of Tyre made voyages every three years to a secret destination. Semitic names are rather common in the Amazon Valley, and many of the characters in known rock inscriptions there have more than a little similarity to the Phoenician.

The existence of the old cities I do not for a moment doubt. How could I? I myself have seen a portion of one of them—and that is why I observed that it was imperative for me to go again. The remains seemed to be those of an outpost of one of the bigger cities, which I am convinced is to be found, together with others, if a properly organized search is carried out. Unfortunately, I cannot induce scientific men to accept even the supposition that there are traces of an old civilization in Brazil. I have travelled much in places not familiar to other explorers, and the wild Indians have again and again told me of the buildings, the character of the people, and the strange things beyond.

One thing is certain. Between the outer world and the secrets of ancient South America a veil has descended, and the explorer who seeks to penetrate this veil must be prepared to face hardships and dangers that will tax his endurance to the utmost. The chances are that he will not get through, but if he should—if he is lucky enough to run the gauntlet of savages and come out alive—he will be in a position to further our historical knowledge immeasurably.

CHAPTER XXII

THE DARKEST CONTINENT

IT has been said that the civilizing of Brazil was more the work of the Jesuits than of the Government; and the same might be said of Peru, which included what is now Bolivia, though here the self-sacrificing labours of the Franciscan order must also be given credit. The Jesuit priests were skilled in mining, agriculture and the sciences, and expert in many trades. Their good work must not be obscured by their unfortunate interference in local politics and the wealth they amassed. They were openly against slave labour, but by playing on the superstitions of the Indians were able to procure for their own use labour so cheap that it was practically the same thing. They established missions throughout the main Amazon Valley, on the Tapajoz, the Araguaya, the Tocantins, and the Guaporé, and amongst the Parecis of Mattc Grosso, as well as over the whole southern part of the continent beyond the Tropic of Capricorn. A chain of missions stretched from Inquisivi in Bolivia, down the River Bopi and on the Secure, to as far east as Santa Rosa, in the Province of Santa Cruz. Where the Jesuits didn't go, the Franciscans did. Every one of the thirty-eight Jesuit missions in Bolivia was engaged in gold-mining. They chose places adjacent to the rivers, and left undisturbed the Indians who lived at any distance from the banks. Whether or no the Indians who came under their influence gained any advantage from being 'civilized' is a matter of opinion, but I doubt if they themselves thought so.

The *Bandeiras* in the extreme north of Brazil, particularly in Parahyba and Sergipe, were made up not only of troops to garrison forts, but also of missionaries to pacify the Indians and persuade them to obstruct the predatory bands of French, Dutch and English who were becoming interested in the continent they had ignored until too late. The east bank of the São Francisco River was settled in this manner, and so too were the wilds of Bahía and Minas Gerais. Indian villages were frequently converted into mission centres, but where there were no minerals or other sources of profit the missionaries left the Indians to themselves.

It was not until the last quarter of the sixteenth century that missionaries penetrated the forests to the east of Peru, following down the River Ucayali and entering the Caupolicán of what is now Bolivia. Except for the ill-fated expedition of Gonzalo Pizarro in 1541, organized exploration of the forests did not commence until about 1560, and even then was undertaken spasmodically and with little worthwhile result. The conditions in the forests under the Andean foothills were utterly different from those found by the Portuguese in the low-lying and more populated region of the Atlantic coast. As the historian says:

> "Easy as it was to conquer the Empire of the Incas, this was not so as regards the region east of the Andes (known commonly by the designation of *La Montaña*) owing to the impenetrable forests which cover its surface. There these men of iron had to struggle against obstacles such as an almost impenetrable growth, aided at times by human beings as barbarous as Nature herself. Wide and rapid rivers, torrents capable of destroying anything which resisted them; hungry wild beasts; gigantic and poisonous reptiles; insects no less dangerous and more troublesome than the reptiles; inaccessible mountains, on whose slopes every pace carried its risk, now of going over the precipice, now of being bitten by a venomous serpent or by one of the millions of equally poisonous ants, should any plant be seized to save a fall; limitless forests, immense lagoons, swamps; torrential rains, inundations of enormous extent; constant damp, and consequently fevers which attack a man in a thousand forms; and boils painful and dangerous. To all this add an absolute lack of food. But even these circumstances were incapable of stopping men so audacious."

In one important respect the historian exaggerated. Between Cuzco and the south of Peru there were four recognized trails constructed by the Incas for military purposes. Over these, narrow and difficult though they were, the early explorers crossed the *Cordilleras* and descended to the forests with large trains of saddle and cargo animals. In the Caupolicán province of Bolivia was a paved road ten feet wide, now long overgrown, leading from Carabaya to the Beni margin of the Plains of Mojos. On the Plains of Polopampa—as Apolobamba was called—travelling was easy, but before and beyond them the trails must have been narrow—

adequate for an Indian on foot, but extraordinarily difficult for animals. Even today the Andean trails, improved though they have been, are mostly suitable for pedestrians and agile mules only, and always with some considerable risk. Away from the trails the historian's description is not exaggerated—and the forests have changed little in 400 years.

Fired by an Indian slave's account of the riches of the Kingdom of Ambaya, Hernando Pizarro sent Pedro de Candia on the first of the forest expeditions in 1535. The next was that of Pedro Auzures, who in 1539 entered by way of Camata with considerable cavalry, came up against the Maquires in the Plains of Mojos, and lost most of his men before finally beating a retreat to the *Altiplano* through Cochabamba.

These efforts were followed by innumerable attempts to find the Kingdom of the Musus, and under its various appellations of Ambaya, Paitití, Emín, or Candiré, its reputed wealth continued to arouse Spanish avarice. Though the ventures failed to win fabulous riches and found only disaster, yet as a result of them missions were established and some knowledge of the geography of Peru's hinterland was gained. In 1654 Fray Tomás Chavez revived waning enthusiasm by reporting that he had been taken from Mojos in a hammock carried by Indians for a march of thirty days, followed by twelve days of canoe travel, and then twenty-one days by land, to Paitití, where the fame of his medical knowledge had reached the Emperor of the Musus. He stated that it was more thickly populated and richer in gold than Peru and all the Indies!

Similar tales of its wonders were told by a Portuguese named Pedro Bohorques in 1630, and in 1638 by an obscure person called Gil Negrete. "In the province of Paitití are mines of gold and silver, and great store of amber," they said. It may well be that these men were merely gratifying their vanity by claiming as personal knowledge the stories heard from the Indians.

However much romance may have coloured the tales, the fact remains that the legendary existence of a highly civilized remnant of an ancient people persisted amongst the indigenes of the continent; and these traditions can be heard today from the Indians of the remote places rarely visited by a white man. There is a remarkable similarity in the accounts, which makes it reasonable to conclude that there is a basis of truth in them.

In 1679 the Spanish Government officially protested against the expenditure of so much money on an objective that since Pizarro's time had been attempted by seventeen expeditions, not counting those equipped by private enterprise. But it needed time and constant failure to shake the belief in the story—and meanwhile it was proving a potent factor in the exploration of the Amazon basin.

Exploration of the Madeira River by the Portuguese commenced in 1716, and of the Guaporé in 1760. These joined up with the limits of

Spanish penetration, and the two nations arranged a recognized demarcation of the spheres of their respective influence. To preserve Portuguese
interests and to protect a garrison from the attacks of the Araras,
Pacaguaras, and other hostile tribes which swarmed in the open forests
of this section, Fort Principe de Beira was built in 1783 near the confluence
of the Guaporé and Mamoré Rivers. It still stands intact, and there is some
talk of reoccupying it.

While adventurers were seeking the elusive *El Dorado*, more practically minded colonists of Peru were taking advantage of the abundant
slave labour to operate the rich placers of Carabaya and the *Altiplano*,
and the numerous mines that supplied the Incas with the bulk of their
treasure. The immensely rich silver mountain of Potosi attracted much
attention, and it is said that over one hundred million pounds sterling
worth of silver formed the Royal Fifth in a single century. At Puno, on
Lake Titicaca, rich silver mines were also worked. So plentiful was the
metal that even the Indians possessed feeding utensils made of it, and
for the shoes of horses it was found cheaper than iron.[1] Lima, capital
of His Most Catholic Majesty's possessions in the New World, was
fabulously wealthy by the end of the seventeenth century. I quote an
eighteenth-century chronicler:

> ". . . But to give some idea of the wealth of that city, it may suffice
> to relate what Treasure the Merchants there exposed about the Year
> 1682, when the Duke *de la Plata* [Marquis de la Palata.—Ed.] made
> his entry as Viceroy: They caused the Streets called *de la Merced*, and
> *de los Mecadores* [Mercaderes.—Ed.], extending thro' two of the
> Quarters (along which he was to pass to the Royal Square, where the
> Palace is) to be paved with Ingots of Silver, that had paid the Fifth
> to the King: they generally weigh about 200 Marks, of eight Ounces
> each, are between twelve and fifteen Inches long, four or five in
> Breadth, and two or three in Thickness. The whole might amount to
> the Sum of eighty Millions of Crowns."

The immense treasures of the Incas looted in Cuzco and elsewhere,
and the huge production of the mines under slave labour, created the
Buccaneers of the Spanish Main and Pacific. Up to the time of the Wars
of Independence, when the yoke of Spain was thrown off in the third
decade of the nineteenth century, the Pacific coast was never free from
semi-piratical brigs, ultimately hard-headed 'Down-Easters' masquerad-

---

[1] But not so good! During World War II it came within the province of the editor, then a
locomotive engineer in Peru, to find, for use in bearing metals, a substitute for tin, scarce
because all supplies were being shipped to the U.S.A. Tests were made with silver—not as a
substitute, but to see what could be done with it industrially—and the conclusion reached was
that while it looked pretty when made into plates and dishes, or even in the locally popular
form of chamber pots, in the field of railroad engineering it was valueless. A pity, because
there was so much of it.—Ed.

ing as respectable raiders under letters of marque, or else making no pretence of disguising their intentions. The people of these countries had no illusions about the adventurers—they had suffered too frequently in the past from raiders such as Drake, Spilberg, Jacob the Hermit, Bartholomew Sharp and Dampier. Even our venerated Lord Anson is classified by them as nothing more than a pirate. It is interesting to note that the last *Armada*, or treasure fleet, left the Peruvian port of Callao in 1739 bound for the Isthmus of Panama, where treasure would be taken overland for reshipping on the Atlantic side. Anson's raid on the Pacific coast frightened the treasure ships into the Guayas River and up as far as Guayaquil, where they stayed for three years before returning to Callao with the bullion still on board.

So rich were the goldmines beyond the *Cordilleras* that no trouble was taken to extract the metal except in a most primitive way. Fine gold was ignored. In 1780–81, during the Indian rising led by José Gabriel Condorcanqui—Tupac Amaru—every Spaniard and employee east of the Andes was massacred, trails were destroyed, and every possible trace of the mines obscured. In the archives are records of the names and production of these mines, few of which have been rediscovered. Indians may know of their whereabouts, but nothing will make them talk; for in their hearts they cherish the belief that one day the Inca will return to claim his hidden treasure and his ruins, when the last vestige of Spanish rule has disappeared from the continent.

In the power of their conquerors the lot of the Indians fell from bad to worse. Under the system of *Repartimientos* they became slaves to be sold together with the lands where they lived. The *Peonage* system left them little better off, even if nominally free—they still changed hands with the land. But the Aymarás of Bolivia are of different stuff from the docile Quechuas; they are more independent, and even walk with a truculent air. It is not wise to enter without their consent some of the Aymará villages east of Lake Titicaca. Today there are 800,000 Indians in Bolivia, as against 700,000 cholos (mixed Indian and Spanish blood), and the same number of whites—and the Government keeps a respectful eye on them. The Aymará of the mountains is physically rather a fine man. Even under the rags and humility of the Quechua smoulders a latent fire, and in spite of his apparent zeal for the Catholic Church he preserves his ancient ceremonies, conducting them in secret in the mountain fastnesses. The beautiful emblem of the Sun still appeals to him more than the hypocrisy of the priests and the sanguinary images in the *adobe* churches. Not that all the priests are hypocritical; for while many of those to be found in out-of-the-way villages are ignorant half-castes or even Indians, greedy and vice-ridden, there are also men of the highest type, especially amongst the members of the French missions and the virile, abnegating Franciscans.

With the suppression of the Jesuits in 1760 the status of the Indian in Brazil became that of an animal, and he was hunted for the value of his labour. The importation of large numbers of Negro slaves and the acquisition of a growing army of Indians produced an extraordinary number of half-castes. It was the same on the western side of the continent. Portuguese and Spanish colonists of the best blood mixed freely with both, and the Negro in turn mixed with all the different tribes of the civilized indigenes. A very difficult social problem was created when slavery was abolished and the half-castes were placed on a level with the free population.

Brazil is by no means homogeneous except in its intense patriotism. The Negro is not regarded as an equal by the whites, and while there is freedom and a measure of *camaraderie* among all classes, there is below the surface as much class distinction as in any other part of the world. Indian blood is tolerated, and in some cases considered a matter for pride, just as in the U.S.A. The result is curious and interesting. Every Negro woman is so conscious of her colour bar that she spares no pains to disguise it, and when she can will mate with someone lighter in complexion than herself. This, and the selective preferences of the well-to-do classes, are breeding out the Negro, while preserving his valuable immunity to tropical diseases. More and more Europeans come to the country, marry locally, and produce—in the upper classes, at any rate—very good-looking children. Eventually there will be a fine and vigorous race free from the inherent weaknesses of inbred nations.

In the seventeenth century Brazil suffered much from lawless and independent communities of escaped Negro slaves, who were either joined by women of their own race or obtained them by raiding Indian tribes. These communities destroyed settlements and *estancias*, and were guilty of appalling atrocities—for under the influence of the liquor known as *pinga* the Negro, and particularly the Negro-Indian *mestizo*, becomes a wild animal.

Not many years ago, in the Lençois district of Bahía, an Englishman was unwise enough to knock down one of the *Caboclos*, or half-castes, for some trifling offence. The man said nothing, but went to his shack and sharpened the *faca*, or triangular-bladed stiletto with which insults are unhesitatingly avenged. He openly acknowledged the intention of knifing his *patrão*—and he did; and not even the certainty of thirty years' imprisonment could stay him. He had been struck, and that was enough!

Although many thousands of Negroes live in both Bolivia and Peru, they are a negligible element in the population. For the most part the half-castes in these republics are the product of the European and the Indian, though it is hard to find just where black blood ceases. These half-castes are capable of even worse excesses than the full-blooded Indians, if driven by the maddening cane alcohol called *chacta* in Peru, *kachasa* in Bolivia, and *pinga* in Brazil.

Except in the capitals and big towns—where a cosmopolitan element produces a certain general aloofness—there is not a dwelling or village, however poor, in any one of these countries that does not dispense the unstinted hospitality I met with so often in my journeys in the interior. This is particularly the case in Brazil, where it may be counted on if the ordinary rules of courtesy be observed. No people possess less racial prejudice, or are more kindly disposed towards the stranger. But Spanish and Portuguese alike attach great importance to etiquette; and it is desirable for the foreigner to know the language. Some say these languages are easy to learn. To acquire a smattering of grammar-book talk may not be difficult, but that is not enough. Nor is it enough to reach the point of understanding either language rapidly spoken by a provincial. The necessary standard is the ability to tell a good joke, make witty remarks, and discuss philosophy and the arts. How many foreigners take the trouble to aim at that objective? The staccato and slangy pronunciation acquired by a child may be beyond the powers of an adult, but South Americans ignore the lack of this, and even shortcomings in grammar, so long as conversation is witty and intelligent. Conversation is the breath of life to them, and fifteen minutes of 'chawing the fat' with a *peon* about Plato or Aristotle will do more to build up mutual esteem than years of good intentions without the ability to express them. It is always a matter of surprise to Americans and Europeans to find how profound can be the conversation of even the humblest South American.[1] On the other hand, as elsewhere, the conversation of high and low can be woefully uninformed about elementary matters, as we shall see in a moment.

What annoys the people is a suggestion of superiority—and who can blame them? It is difficult to keep a straight face when an educated lady asks, as I was once asked in Bolivia, "Did the *señor* come from England in a canoe or on muleback?"

"No, *señora*," was my reply; "I came in a steamer carrying about a thousand people."

"Oish!" exclaimed she. "Was there no danger from currents and rapids?"

A dignitary at San Ignacio, Bolivia, hearing of the *Titanic* disaster, said to me out of the maturity of his river experience:

"Heavens, man! Why don't they keep near the bank? It's far safer. Those big canoes in mid-stream are always dangerous!"

A gentleman in the same village took much pride in the possession of a horrible oleo-lithograph representing a storm, a lighthouse, and a

[1] I can vouch for this being no exaggeration. The greatest mistake a foreigner can make in these countries is to insist on hustle and bustle without ever taking time out to chat with the workmen under his authority. I myself learned to converse with them because I liked them, and my reward was a priceless store of tales, legends and titbits of knowledge, to say nothing of the pleasure derived at the time. Besides the need to learn the *colloquial* language, it is worth while stressing the importance of abundant reading in that language, the ability to write it well, and—sooner or later it will be necessary—to make a speech in it!—ED.

fantastically rough sea. He was frequently asked if it was the *Cachuela Esperanza*, a well-known rapid in the Beni.

Once when I asked the postmaster in a provincial town in Peru what was the postage to England, he took the envelope, turned it upside down and sideways, scrutinized it with the most ludicrous attention, and then asked, "Where's England?" I explained to him as best I could. "Never heard of it," he said. I explained in more detail, and tried a different approach. Finally light dawned. "Oh! You mean *London*. England's in London, then? Why didn't you say so at first, *señor?*"

It sounds terribly ignorant, no doubt, but what about the society lady in London who asked if Bolivia was 'one of those horrid little Balkan states'? Another titled lady, who is now a big figure in politics, asked me in all seriousness if the people in Buenos Aires were civilized and wore clothes! Apparently she imagined that the people of one of the world's finest cities were wild Indians—with perhaps here and there a *gaucho*, armed to the teeth, galloping along unpaved streets and lassoing turbulent cattle! Even the passport official of a great bank slipped up badly when in 1924 my youngest son, about to leave for Peru, applied for a passport. He enquired whether Peru might be in Chile or Brazil!

Many parts of the interior, in all these countries, are isolated from the world by weeks of atrocious mule trails, and consequently there is no check to inbreeding and superstition. In San Ignacio, for instance, the people when ill cover up mouth, ears and nose, so that the spirit may not escape. Nearly everywhere more faith is placed in the miraculous power of wax images than in expensive medicines. There are villages where in-breeding has practically wiped out the men, but it is interesting to note that the women seem to improve in physique by it. When men from outside visit these places they have to be careful, for there is no feminine modesty!

Many foreigners consider the Indian an animal, incapable of any feelings beyond instinct. Even after four centuries of utter debasement and cruel treatment as serfs, I have always found them readily responsive to kindness, and I know them to be highly capable of education. There are Indians who have enriched themselves and become important national figures. They have started as *peons*, and in spite of almost insurmountable obstacles have risen to become owners of land, mines, ranches and businesses. I have met many such men in the course of my wanderings. In the countries they inhabit direct taxation is practically non-existent, indirect taxation is low, and personal liberty is unchallenged by over-legislation.

The curse of the Indian is *kachasa*—too often the only means of temporary escape from hopeless servitude—and he can obtain it on credit. The Indian is not the only one to drink himself into stupor; practically everyone in the interior, including the European, does so. It debases a man physically and morally, and accounts for nine-tenths of what crime there is—which isn't very great. I am not blaming them and am certainly not going to repeat teetotal dogma. Some people fated to live under similar conditions would prefer suicide!

I hope these chapters will have made clear what I am looking for, and why. The failures, the disappointments, have been bitter, yet always there has been some progress. Had I still had Costin and Manley as companions it is possible that instead of writing an uncompleted manuscript I might now be giving to the world the story of the most stupendous discovery of modern times.

There has been disillusionment too. After the Gongugy expedition I doubted for a time the existence of the old cities, and then came the sight of remains that proved the truth of at least part of the accounts. It still remains a possibility that 'Z'—my chief objective—with its remnant of inhabitants, may turn out to be none other than the forest city found by the *Bandeira* of 1753. It is not on the Xingú River, or in Matto Grosso. If we ever reach it we may be delayed there for a considerable time—an unsuccessful journey will be a rapid one.

Our route will be from Dead Horse Camp, 11° 43' south and 54° 35' west, where my horse died in 1921, roughly north-east to the Xingú, visiting on the way an ancient stone tower which is the terror of the surrounding Indians, as at night it is lighted from door and windows. Beyond the Xingú we shall take to the forest to a point midway between that river and the Araguaya, and then follow the watershed north to 9° or 10° south latitude. We shall then head for Santa María do Araguaya, and from there cross by an existing trail to the Rio Tocantins at Porto Nacional or 'Pedro Afonso'. Our way will be between latitude 10° 30' and 11° to the high ground between the States of Goyaz and Bahía, a region quite unknown and said to be infested by savages, where I expect to get some trace of the inhabited cities. The mountains there are quite high. We shall then follow the mountains between Bahía and Piauhy to the Rio São Francisco, striking it somewhere near Chique-Chique, and, if we are in fit condition to do so, visit the old deserted city (that of 1753) which lies at approximately 11° 30' south and 42° 30' west, thus completing the investigations and getting out at a point from which the railway will take us to Bahía City.[1]

---

[1] This is the route my father set out to follow in 1925. Experts in Brazil maintain it is impossible to do it, and inasmuch as he never returned they may be right. The area where he believed 'Z' to lie has in recent years been regularly flown over by domestic airlines, and no trace of an ancient city has been reported. Moreover, this part of the country is not unknown— and I can hardly believe it was unexplored at the time he wrote. It is true that remains of incalculable age have been found thereabouts—on the borders of Goyaz and Bahía states—but no city. But for over a century one has been known in the state of Piauhy, and called '*Sete Cidades*', from its seven citadels.

I have personally investigated the bearings he gives for the 1753 city, and can state authoritatively that it is not there.—ED.

I have talked with a Frenchman who for some years occupied himself with tracking down the legendary silver mines, associated indirectly with the deserted city (for it was in looking for these Lost Mines of Muribeca that the 1753 *Bandeirantes* found it). He claims to have been all over the region I propose visiting, and states that it is populated by civilized settlers wherever there is water—that there is no real forest in that area— that no ruins can possibly exist there! He asserts that he discovered a peculiar, weather-worn formation of sandstone which from the distance looked very much like old ruins, and that this is what the *Bandeirantes* of 1753 actually saw, inventing the rest of their tale in the fashion of those days. When I told him of the recorded inscriptions (he had neither seen nor heard of the document left by 'Raposo') he had no answer—and in any case, various essential points did not tally with his arguments. The inscriptions on the ruins, and the 'jumping rats' (jerboas) cannot surely have been a mere invention.

Frankly, I have little confidence in the Frenchman. To have been *all over* such a region is hardly possible. There are sandy areas devoid of water; cliffs bar the way; even a single valley may remain hidden for centuries, for exploration has never been systematically carried out, although the lure of diamonds in this region has in the past disclosed the safe and accessible places. My impression is that there is an inner area bordered by a waterless belt that has discouraged expeditions. The Frenchman had an alcoholic breath, and I cannot consider drinkers fully reliable. I was told, too, that he had never been away for more than two or three weeks at a time—far too short a period for prolonged investigation.[1]

The late British Consul at Rio, Colonel O'Sullivan Beare, a gentleman whose word I would not have dreamed of doubting, gave me as nearly as the wretchedly inaccurate maps of the region would allow the location of the ruined city to which he was taken by a *Caboclo* in 1913 (mentioned in Chapter I). He never crossed the São Francisco—his city was well east of it, twelve days' travel from Bahía. The São Francisco has been associated with legends of White Indians for centuries, and it is possible that the two clothed whites seen by 'Raposo's' advance party were somewhere between the mouth of the Rio Grande and Chique-Chique. Since then, encroaching civilization may have kept them in their valley beyond the dry belt.

There are curious things to be found between the Xingú and the Araguaya, but I sometimes doubt if I can stand up to that journey. I am growing too old to pack at least forty pounds on my back for months on end,[2] and a larger expedition costs a great deal of money and runs

---

[1] Nevertheless, from what I myself have seen, I believe the Frenchman was right. I have heard much in Bahía about this Frenchman's travels, and he really did penetrate unknown regions of the state.—ED.

[2] He was fifty-seven when he wrote this in 1924.—ED.

greater risks—besides, all the men who go *must* be picked men, and there is probably not more than one in a thousand who is fit for it.

If the journey is not successful my work in South America ends in failure, for I can never do any more. I must inevitably be discredited as a visionary, and branded as one who had only personal enrichment in view. Who will ever understand that I want no glory from it—no money for myself—that I am doing it unpaid in the hope that its ultimate benefit to mankind will justify the years spent in the quest? The last few years have been the most wretched and disillusioning in my life—full of anxieties, uncertainties, financial stringency, underhand dealing and outright treachery. My wife and children have been sacrificed for it, and denied many of the benefits that they would have enjoyed had I remained in the ordinary walks of life. Of our twenty-four years of married life only ten have been spent together. Apart from four years in the Great War, I have spent ten in the forests, yet my wife has never complained. On the contrary, her practical help and constant encouragement have been big factors in the successes so far gained, and if I win in the end the triumph will be largely due to her.

EPILOGUE

by

BRIAN FAWCETT

Have I named one single river? Have I claimed one single acre?
  Have I kept one single nugget—(barring samples)? No, not I!
Because my price was paid me ten times over by my Maker.
  But you wouldn't understand it. You go up and occupy.

RUDYARD KIPLING.

T

I

THROUGH THE VEIL

IT seemed in 1924 as though funds for the final expedition would never be forthcoming. Disappointment followed disappointment, while ever just beyond reach was the glowing image of the Great Objective—the ancient cities of Brazil. Funds were low—so low that it was a problem how the family could keep going in even a modest way—yet it was necessary to preserve an attitude of preparedness and be ready to move at a moment's notice.

Ever since his return to England late in 1921 my father's impatience to start off on his last trip was tearing at him with ever-increasing force. From reticent he became almost surly—yet there were also times when this dark mantle was laid aside, and he was again a jolly companion to us children.

We—that is, my mother, my brother, my younger sister and myself —who in 1920 set out for Jamaica, never, as we thought, to return to England, were back again in under two years. Disillusionment hastened our departure from Jamaica. The island was not, as had been hopefully expected, like Ceylon; living conditions were difficult for the white minority and educational standards were poor, and so there was another frenzy of packing and an exodus to California, which had for many years been a sort of dream Mecca. Several reasons, not the least of them the high cost of living, necessitated our departure from Los Angeles after only a year, and in September 1921 we landed at Plymouth, where a month later we went to meet my father on his arrival from Brazil.

A house was rented in Exeter for a while, and then we moved out to a dilapidated but roomy place at Stoke Canon, in the direction of Tiverton.

Here we stayed till the family broke up. I was the first to go, leaving for Peru on a railway appointment. My father and brother were the next to leave. Plans had suddenly come to a successful conclusion, and off they went to New York. My mother and sister left for Madeira, where they stayed for some years before going to reside on the French Riviera, and then in Switzerland.

It was during our stay in Stoke Canon that the present book was written, and from my father's lips I heard many of the anecdotes and ideas he records. I realized too late that had I shown more interest I might have been told much more that now I would give anything to know. That's usually the way of it. At the time my enthusiasm was concentrated on locomotive engineering to the exclusion of everything else.

My father would get up at an ungodly hour of the morning to make breakfast for me before I set off on a bicycle to the engineering works in Exeter, where I was serving a grimy but interesting apprenticeship as moulder's helper in a foundry. He could turn out as good a breakfast as anybody, and his acceptance of the task with silent humility only became significant to me years later when I recalled the circumstances of that period. He did it to ensure more rest for my mother, and because he would not consider my doing it for myself.

Though the time spent in Stoke Canon must have seemed to him like a jail sentence, there were bright moments too. Cricket, ever his joy, took him and my brother—both exponents of the game up to county standards—far afield in the season, for they were much in demand.

I saw him for the last time in March of 1924, when the Liverpool train pulled out of St. David's station, Exeter, and his tall figure was lost beyond view from the carriage window. As I was whisked northwards on the first stage of the long journey to Peru I fully expected that we should meet again in a few years in South America.

"I was up in London for a week on expedition matters," he wrote in May 1924, "and it may be that things are now fixed up satisfactorily. Probably the whole business will be done in the U.S.A., and if so the results will go there too. But the Royal Geographical Society has unanimously endorsed the expedition, so at least it has scientific backing.

"Jack and I may go *via* New York in June, where Raleigh will join us. He is as keen as mustard. It will be a comforting feeling that we are all in the same continent."

But it was not yet to be. Arrangements took much longer to make, and in the meantime he and Jack 'went into training'. Rudiments of the Portuguese language and some experience with theodolite work were instilled into Jack; and they went vegetarian in preparation for what might make an otherwise hungry expedition less difficult to bear. Physically there was little training required. Jack's six feet three inches were sheer bone and muscle, and the three chief agents of bodily degeneration

—alcohol, tobacco and loose living—were revolting to him. Jack made a cult of physical fitness, and the only domestic chores he never complained of doing were those requiring an exercise of strength.

At school it was always Jack who distinguished himself in games, in fights, and by standing up to the severe canings of the headmaster. In his scholastic work too he could excel when the subject interested him. I, three years his junior, followed him in my humble way, true member of the unimportant but not contemptible rank and file. Bullied into a stupor during my first term, it was Jack's ready fist that ultimately brought me respite—but thereafter he made me fight my own battles and only took part when the odds weighed too heavily against me.

At home it was Jack who formed and led the gang—Jack who kept a log book in which to record all the mischief that could truly be classed as anti-social. His able and willing lieutenant was Raleigh Rimell, son of a Seaton doctor. Raleigh was with us most of the time during these school years at Seaton. He was a born clown, perfect counterpart of the serious Jack, and between the two there sprang up a close friendship which led to the Adventure of 1925.

During the Great War (of 1914–18) we were too young to be drawn into the army, but not too young to get hold of a horrifying assortment of firearms, with which we made so free that the authorities honoured us by nominating a special constable to follow our trail and bring us within reach of the law! I'm afraid we led the poor man a miserable life, and it ended up by our trailing the constable with intent to work mischief on him. The police never pounced; we continued to shoot inoffensive starlings off the roofs of the town's houses, and even made targets of the enamelled collection-plates on pillar-boxes. Raleigh was summoned on this charge and made to replace a broken plate at the cost of ten shillings. Whenever he passed that pillar-box he would polish the plate with his handkerchief and say, "This is mine, you know!"

When we went to Jamaica, Raleigh was already there, working for the United Fruit Company on a coconut estate at Port María. Jack was employed as a cow hand on a big cattle ranch up in the Montego Bay area, on the other side of the island, but occasionally they met. Raleigh went to California ahead of us, but we saw nothing of him there, for when we arrived he had moved on. Jack, between intervals of doing nothing, worked as a chainman to a Riverside surveyor and as an orange picker. A clever but untutored draughtsman, he also did some art work for the *Los Angeles Times*. The glamour of the movies bit him for a time—as it does most of the impressionable people who visit Hollywood—and he made perfunctory attempts to land extra parts under Betty Blythe and Nazimova, two stars whose names are no longer familiar but who at that time were at the height of their fame. He might have broken in, for he lacked none of the necessary looks, but a friend who was acting as technical director in the making of an exotic picture that never saw the light—*Omar Khayyám*—warned him off before the celluloid octopus grasped him in its fatal rentacles. Actually, the nearest he ever came to the movies was when a property-man hired his cricket bat, because of its authentic appearance, for Mary Pickford to use in *Little Lord Fauntleroy*. Apart from the cash received, he was awarded a letter of thanks and a signed photo from the star.

Towards the end of 1924 arrangements for financing the expedition were made, and a friend of my father's went off to New York in advance to raise the money and have the business concluded by the time he and Jack arrived there. When the two of them landed in the U.S.A. it was to find that this 'friend' had squandered in a glorious drunk lasting six weeks $1,000 of my father's and $500 of Mrs. Rimell's (which he got hold of from Raleigh's mother on the plea of a wildcat mining syndicate). Needless to say, he had not succeeded in raising a cent, and only £200 were recovered of the funds entrusted to him.

My father now set to work to raise enough for the expedition; and this he managed to accomplish in a month by arousing the interest of various scientific societies, and by the sale of newspaper rights to the North American Newspaper Alliance, which nominated him a special correspondent.

"We are going to have a thoroughly good time going out, and in Brazil until we vanish into the forests for three years or so," my father wrote me in September 1924, before leaving England. "I fancy Jack and Raleigh will enjoy it. On the expedition, no one else will be with the party, except two Brazilians up to a certain point only."

Then, towards the end of January 1925, he wrote from on board S.S. *Vauban*, of the Lamport and Holt Line:

"Here we are, with Raleigh, approaching Rio. Personally I find the voyage rather tiresome, but Jack is thoroughly enjoying it. . . . They were very hospitable and sympathetic in New York, but the position was of course difficult. However, we are now in the same continent with you and on the way to Matto Grosso, and with at least forty million people already aware of our objective.

"Given facilities at Rio in the Customs, etc., we shall leave for Matto Grosso in about a week, and Cuyaba about April 2. Thereafter we shall disappear from civilization until the end of next year. Imagine us somewhere about a thousand miles east of you, in forests so far untrodden by civilized man.

"New York tried us badly. It was extremely cold, under a foot of snow, and the winds were bitter. Jack haunted cinemas—which were on the whole very poor—and chewed masses of gum. All three of us took our meals at an Automat."

Now Raleigh speaks in a letter to me from Rio:

"On the voyage down I became acquainted with a certain girl on board, and as time went on our friendship increased till I admit it was threatening to get serious—in fact, your father and Jack were getting quite anxious, afraid I should elope or something! However, I came to my senses and realized I was supposed to be the member of an expedition, and not allowed to take a wife along. I had to drop her gently and attend to business. I sympathize with you if you get sentimental once in a while.

"Jack said to me the other day, 'I suppose after we get back you'll be married within a year?' I told him I wouldn't make any promises—but I don't intend to be a bachelor all my life, even if Jack does! . . .

"I have wished several times that *you also* were coming on this trip, as I believe you would help to make it even more interesting and cheerful. I am looking forward to the actual start of the expedition into the forest, and I think Jack shares the same feeling. With an objective like ours, it requires too much patience to remain long in one place. The delays in New York were almost more than we could bear. . . ."

While in Rio de Janeiro they stayed at the Hotel Internacional, and did the rounds of sightseeing and sea-bathing. Jack was not greatly impressed, and wrote:

"I would not live in Rio or any other town here if I had a million a year, unless I could come for only a month or two at a time! I don't care about the place, though of course the surroundings are magnificent. Brazil seems frightfully cut off from the world somehow. I must say the people are awfully decent everywhere, and help in every way."

Expedition kit was tried out in the 'jungle' of the hotel garden and found satisfactory, and in February 1925 they set off, going first to São Paulo. From Corumba Jack wrote a lively account of the trip as seen through the eyes of an enthusiastic youth of twenty-one:

"We have spent a week in the train from São Paulo to Porto Esperança, fifty miles down from Corumba, and are glad to get this far at last. The train journey was interesting, in spite of the sameness of the country we passed through, and as we were lent the Line Official's private car, privacy was ours all the way. In this respect we were lucky, for from Rio to São Paulo, and from there to Rio Parana, we had the private car of the President of the railroad.

"Most of the way was through scrubby *mato* forest and grazing land, with a good deal of swamp near the river. Between Aquidauana and Porto Esperança I saw some quite interesting things. In the cattle country were numerous parrots, and we saw two flocks (or whatever you call them) of young rheas about four to five feet high. There was a glimpse of a spider's web in a tree, with a spider about the size of a sparrow sitting in the middle. In the River Paraguay this morning there were small alligators, and we are going out to shoot at them.

"On account of the passports left behind in Rio we might have been held up when we landed here this morning, but apparently there will now be no bother, and we sail for Cuyaba tomorrow on the *Iguatemi*, a dirty little launch about the size of a naval M.L. There will be a large crowd of passengers, and our hammocks will be slung almost touching one another.

"Mosquitoes were pretty bad from Bauru to Porto Esperança, but last night on the Paraguay there were none at all. The food is good and wholesome here, and much more sustaining than in Rio or São Paulo. One eats rice, beans—big black ones—chicken, beef, and a sort of slug-slime vegetable, something like a cucumber in texture, egg-shaped and the size of a walnut. Then comes *Goiabada* (guava cheese), bread and cheese, and the inevitable black coffee. Macaroni is also a favourite dish. All this is consumed at one meal.

"The heat is pretty stifling here at present, but not so bad inside the hotel. We are fed-up with these semi-civilized towns, amiable though the people are, and want to get through our time at Cuyaba as quickly as possible so as to start off into the forest. When Raleigh and I are unusually fed-up we talk of what we will do when we revisit Seaton in the spring of 1927, with plenty of cash. We intend to buy motor-cycles and really enjoy a good holiday in Devon, looking up all our friends and visiting the old haunts.

"Our river trip to Cuyaba takes about eight days, and we shall probably have all our mules ready for fattening by the middle of March. We leave Cuyaba on April 2, and it will take us six weeks, or perhaps two months, to reach the spot Daddy and Felipe got to last time. To reach 'Z' will probably take another two months, and it may be that we shall enter the place on Daddy's fifty-eighth birthday (August 31).

"Aren't the reports of the expedition in the English and American papers amusing? There is a lot of exaggerated stuff in the Brazilian papers too. We are longing to start on the real journey, and finish with these towns, though the month in Cuyaba will probably pass fairly quickly. One thing I only realized today is that we have crossed Brazil and can see Bolivia from here—and the places where Daddy was doing much of his boundary delimitation work.

"We had a fine send-off from São Paulo by a number of English people, including members of the diplomatic and consular corps. Before we left there we visited the Butantan snake-farm, where Senhor Brasil, the founder, gave us a talk on snakes—how they strike, how much poison they eject, the various remedies, and so on. He presented us with a whole lot of serum. An attendant entered the enclosure where the snakes are kept, in beehive huts, surrounded by a moat, and with a hooked rod took out a bushmaster. He placed it on the ground, reached down, and caught it by the neck before it could do anything. Then he brought it over and showed us the fangs, which are hinged, and have spare ones lying flat with the jaw in case the principal ones are broken. Senhor Brasil let it bite on a glass saucer, and a whole lot of venom squirted out.

"Last night saw the end of Carnivals, and all the inhabitants were tearing up and down in front of the hotel, on the only bit of good road. They made the deuce of a row, and were all in home-made fancy dress, some costumes being quite pretty. The custom during Carnivals is to squirt scent at you—or ether, which gets in the eyes and freezes them. The heat is awful today, and we drip with sweat. They say that in Cuyaba it is cooler. This morning we were talking to a German just in from Cuyaba, and he told us they have over a hundred Ford cars there now— not bad for a place two thousand miles up river! He also said he came down on the *Iguatemi*, the boat we go up on, and that the food is good, but the mosquitoes are bad. I hear that in the new park they have a couple of jaguars in captivity, so I think I'll go and see them.

"The lavatory arrangements here are very primitive. The combined W.C. and shower-room is so filthy that one must be careful where one treads; but Daddy says we must expect much worse in Cuyaba.

"We have been exceedingly lucky to get passages, and to have all our luggage put on board the *Iguatemi* intact. It will be terribly cramped, but no doubt interesting going up river. The country we have seen so far has a dreadful sameness about it, though not in this respect as bad as the Mississippi.

"We have decided not to bother about shaving between here and Cuyaba, and already I have two days' growth on me. Raleigh looks like a desperate villain, such as you see in Western thrillers on the movies."

February 25, 1925. "We are now nearly two days out of Corumba, and reach Cuyaba next Monday evening, if we haven't died of boredom before then! The boat is supposed to carry only twenty people, but fifty passengers are crowded on board. We travel about three miles an hour, through rather uninteresting swampy country, but today the monotony was broken by the sight of hills. We sleep on deck in hammocks, and it is quite comfortable except for the mosquitoes, bad enough up to now, but expected to get worse tonight when we enter the São Lourenço River. The first night was so cold that I had to get up to put on two shirts, socks and trousers. The monotony is appalling, and there is no room for exercise of any sort. Cuyaba will seem like Heaven after this! . . .

"Most of the passengers are 'Turks' (which means here a citizen of any of the Balkan countries) and run small shops in Cuyaba. Their women jabber incessantly, and whenever a meal is imminent gather round like vultures. The smells on board are pretty bad. Every now and then we stop at the bank to take on wood fuel for the boiler, counting with great care every stick as it comes in overside.

"At present the banks of the river are scrubby *mato* with in the background some rocky hills about eight hundred feet high. There are a few alligators to be seen, and everywhere along the edge of the river any amount of cranes and vultures. Owing to the congestion on board it is out of the question getting the guns out to shoot at the alligators."

February 27. "Daddy says this is the dullest, most boring river journey he has ever made; and we are counting the hours of the three more days yet to be spent before Cuyaba is reached. We are still in swamp country, though no longer in the Paraguay River, for we entered the São Lourenço the day before yesterday, and the Cuyaba River last night. The São Lourenço is noted for its mosquitoes, which breed in the extensive swamps, and on Wednesday night they came aboard in clouds. The roof of the place where we eat and sleep was black—literally black—with them! We had to sleep with shirts drawn over our heads, leaving no breathing-hole, our feet wrapped in another shirt, and a mackintosh over the body. Termite ants were another pest. They invaded us for about a couple of hours, fluttering round the lamps till their wings dropped off, and then wriggling over floor and table in their millions.

"We saw some *capibara* today. One of them stood on the bank not eighteen yards away as we went past. It is a tragedy that the whole of this country for hundreds of miles is absolutely useless and uninhabitable. We go up river at a walking pace—so slowly that today we were overhauled by two men in a canoe, who were soon out of sight ahead.

"There is no entertainment in staring at the river bank, for it has altered in no way since we left Corumba. There is a tangle of convolvulus creeper and wild banana-like dock leaves—with *onça* (jaguar) holes, worn bare with use, coming out to the edge of the water. Behind, and towering above, are thick trees of various sorts, extending about twenty yards back, and then the swamps begin, stretching as far as the eye can see, broken only by isolated clumps of swamp trees like mangroves. Occasionally there is to be seen a fœtid pool, lurking-place of anacondas and nursery of mosquitoes. Sometimes the swamp comes right up to the river and there is no bank at all. There are many vultures and diving birds like cormorants, with long necks which make them resemble snakes when swimming. The *jacares* (alligators) live only where there is bare mud or sand where they can bask.

"Heavy rain has fallen today and the temperature has dropped to about the same as an English summer. The weather is supposed to grow cooler now anyway, as we are nearing the dry season. Daddy says he has never been in this region in the really dry season, and thinks it probable that the insects will not be as bad as they were in 1920.

"A new pest has come aboard today. It is the *mutuca*, a sort of horse-fly with a nasty sting. We smashed many, but Daddy and Raleigh were stung. All of us are of course covered with mosquito-bites.

"What we miss a good deal is fruit, and none can be obtained till we reach Cuyaba. Otherwise the food is good. Lack of exercise is annoying, and in Cuyaba we intend to make up for it by having a good long walk every day. As a matter of fact, we have had almost no exercise since leaving Rio, except for a fairly long hike up the railway track while we were held up for a day or two at Aquidauana. I do 'press-ups' whenever I can, but so crowded are we that even this is not easy.

"Raleigh is a funny chap. He calls Portuguese 'this damn jabbering language', and makes no attempt to learn it. Instead he gets mad at every-one because they don't speak English. Beyond *faz favor* and *obrigado* he can say nothing to them—or is too shy to try. I can now keep up a fair conversation provided the person I am speaking to answers slowly and distinctly. They mix it with a lot of Spanish here, owing to the proximity of Bolivia and Paraguay."

March 4. "Cuyaba at last—and not so bad as I had been led to expect! The hotel is quite clean, and the food excellent. We are feeding up now, and I hope to put on ten pounds before leaving, as we need extra flesh to carry us over hungry periods during the expedition. The river journey took eight days—rather a long time to be cooped up on a tiny vessel like the *Iguatemi*, and confined to the same spot on the same bench. Yesterday we went for a walk in the bush, and joyed at the freedom to take exercise. Today we go shooting for the first time—not at birds, but at objects put up for practice.

"We called on Frederico, the mule man, but he is away until Sunday. His son says there will be no difficulty about getting the twelve mules we require. The *sertanista* ('guide' is near enough) Daddy wanted has died; and Vagabundo has gone into the *sertão* with someone else, which is a great pity, for I've heard so much about that dog that I wanted to see him. There is an American missionary here who has a lot of back numbers of the *Cosmopolitan* and other magazines, and we are going along tonight to swap books with him. . . ."

March 5. "Yesterday Raleigh and I tried out our guns. They are very accurate, but make a hell of a row! We expended twenty cartridges, which leaves us 180 for future practice.

"I hear that on leaving Cuyaba we have scrub country for a day's travel which will bring us to the plateau; then small scrub and grass all the way to Bacairy Post; and about two days beyond that we will get our first game. In the first day or two we may be able to photograph a gorged *sucuri* (anaconda) if anyone can direct us to one in the vicinity. . . ."

April 14. "The mail has come in—the last we shall get, for on the 20th we leave. The heat here is something like Jamaica at its very hottest, but Raleigh and I go out daily to a stream on the Rosario road and stay in the water for an hour or so. It's not very refreshing, for its temperature is about the same as the air, but the evaporation in drying off afterwards cools us down.

"I have tried to get some sketching done here, but the subjects are so commonplace that I can't put any pep into them, and the result is they are not worth a damn! What I am always looking for is a really good subject, and then possibly something worth while will be produced. When we reach the place where the first inscriptions are to be seen I shall have to sketch, for all those things must be carefully copied.

"You would be amused to see me with a fortnight's growth of beard. I shall not shave again for many months. We have been wearing our boots so as to break them in, and Raleigh's feet are covered with patches of Johnson's plaster, but he is keener than ever now we are nearing the day of departure. We seem to be a hell of a time waiting for animals, but it is all the fault of Frederico and his lies. It was hopeless trying to get anything done with him, so we are now dealing with another chap called Orlando. I think the mules arrived today. The two dogs, Chulim and Pastor, are getting very *bravo*, and rush at any visitor who dares tap at the door.

"There was some rather bad shooting at Coxipo, a league distant. A fellow named Reginaldo with six companions, all of whom we saw leave Gama's Hotel here in the morning, were waylaid by a gang with a grudge against them. There had been a quarrel over gunplay and drink in the Casamunga diamond fields, and they met at Coxipo and shot it out. Reginaldo and one of the bandits were killed, and two others seriously wounded. The police went to work on the case after a few days, and over a cup of coffee asked the murderers why they did it! Nothing more has happened. . . ."

Extracts from my father's letter of April 14:

"We have had the usual delays incidental to this continent of *mañanas*, but are due to get away in a few days. We start with every hope of a successful issue. . . .

"We are all three very well. There are two dogs rejoicing in the names of Pastor and Chulim; two horses and eight mules; a polite assistant named Gardenia, who has an unrestrained appetite for advances—or *providencias*, as they euphemistically call them here—and a hard-working negroid *mouço* who answers to everyone's call. These two men will be released as soon as we find traces of wild Indians, as their colour involves trouble and suspicion.

"It has been abominably hot and very rainy, but things are settling down now into the cool and dry season.

"Jack talks a fair amount of Portuguese, and understands a modicum of what is said to him. Raleigh cannot acquire a blessed word!

"A ranching friend of mine told me that since a boy he and his people have sat in the verandah of their house, six days north of this, and listened to the strange noise coming periodically out of the northern forests. He describes it as the hiss, as it were, of a rocket or great shell soaring into the air and plunging again into the forest with a 'boom-m-m-boom-m'. He has no idea what it might be, but I think it is probably a meteorological phenomenon connected with high volcanic areas, such as mystified people at Darjeeling, where discharges of artillery were heard between monsoons. Other parts of this lofty region give out 'booms' and snoring sounds, to the terror of the people who hear.

"My ranching friend tells me that near his place there is in the River Paranatinga a long rectangular rock pierced with three holes, the middle one being closed and apparently cemented at both ends. Behind it, somewhat carefully concealed, is an inscription of fourteen strange characters. He is going to take us there to photograph it. An Indian on his ranch knows of a rock covered with such characters, and this we also propose to visit.

"Another man, who lives up on the *chapada*—the high plateau just north of this, which was once the coastline of the old island—tells me he has seen the skeletons of large animals and petrified trees, and knows of inscriptions, and even foundations of prehistoric buildings, on the same *chapada*. It is, of course, the border of our region. One wide grassy plain near here has in its centre a great stone carved in the shape of a mushroom —a mysterious and inexplicable monument.

"The intermediate building between 'Z' and the point where we leave civilization is described by the Indians as a sort of fat tower of stone. They are thoroughly scared of it because they say at night a light shines from door and windows! I suspect this to be the 'Light that Never Goes Out'. Another reason for their fear of it is that it stands in the territory of the troglodyte Morcegos, the people who live in pits, caves, and sometimes in thickly foliaged trees.

"Some little time ago, but since I first drew attention to Matto Grosso by my activities, an educated Brazilian of this town, together with an army officer engaged in surveying a river, were told by the Indians about a city to the north. The offer was made to take them there if they dared face the bad savages. The city, said the Indians, had low stone buildings with many streets set at right angles to one another, but there were also some big buildings and a great temple, in which was a large disc cut out of rock crystal. A river running through the forest beside the city fell over a big fall whose roar could be heard for leagues, and below the fall the river seemed to widen out into a great lake emptying itself they had no notion where. In the quiet water below the fall was the figure of a man carved in white rock (quartz, perhaps, or rock crystal), which moved to and fro with the force of the current.

"This sounds like the 1753 city, but the locality doesn't tally with my calculations at all. We might visit it on the way over, or, if circumstances permit, while we are at 'Z'.

"My rancher friend told me he brought to Cuyaba an Indian of a remote and difficult tribe, and took him into the big churches here thinking he would be impressed. 'This is nothing!' he said. 'Where I live, but some distance to travel, are buildings greater, loftier, and finer than this. They too have great doors and windows, and in the middle is a tall pillar bearing a large crystal whose light illuminates the interior and dazzles the eyes!'

"So far we are getting a lot of rain and it is very hot. I don't remember perspiring so much for many years—yet it is only 80 degrees in the shade. . . ."

Jack takes up the tale again:

Bacairy Post, May 16, 1925. "We arrived here yesterday after a rather strenuous journey from Cuyaba. We left on April 20, with a dozen animals; the horses in fairly good condition, but the mules thin. It seems that the place where they were sent to be fattened up had half-starved them instead, so as to make a few extra milreis!

"At the start we went very slowly on account of the animals, and camped the first night about two leagues from Cuyaba. During the night an ox collided with Raleigh's hammock, but apart from pitching him out no harm was done. The second night we camped three leagues on, and bathed in quite a good stream. The third night was spent in the higher *chapada* country, where we were in terror of the Saube ants eating our equipment. Next day we lost the way for the first time, having to retrace our steps some distance and camp on a side trail. Fortunately we cut the main one next day, and on reaching the house of a *morador*—a man who lives on the trail—we asked the distance to the Rio Manso. He told us four leagues, so we decided to make it that day—but it was about seven leagues, and darkness had fallen before we reached there.

"Daddy had gone on ahead at such a pace that we lost sight of him altogether, and when we came to a place where the trail forked we didn't know which to take. I spotted some marks made by a single horse on the larger trail, so we followed it and eventually arrived at the Rio Manso in pitch dark, to find he was not there! I discargoed at once and sent out Raleigh and Simão, one of the *peons*, to fire shots in the hope of getting a reply. Meanwhile we camped and made tea in the pitch dark, and when the others returned without him we thought he must have put up for the night with a *morador*. Next morning we sent out more signals but they were unanswered; then, as we finished breakfast, he rode in after spending the night on the ground.

"We stayed in camp next day to rest ourselves and the animals, but were plagued with *garapata* ticks the whole time. Ticks of all sizes swarmed on the ground, and Raleigh was bitten so severely that his foot was poisoned. Next day we crossed the river on a *batalão* and camped in a deserted place where a *morador* had lived, finding there any amount of oranges.

"To cut things short, we missed the way again, and Raleigh gloomed all the way to the Rio Cuyaba, which we found impossible to cross owing to rapids and the weak condition of the animals. A fording-place was found higher up, and we had to unload the animals and make them swim across, sending over the cargo in a canoe we found there. Raleigh could do nothing because of his bad foot, so Daddy and I attended to the cargo, while the *peons* looked after the animals. After a difficult passage we finally reached the house of Hermenegildo Galvão, where we stayed five days to feed up. I found that between Cuyaba and here I had gained seven pounds in weight, in spite of far less food. Raleigh has lost more than I gained, and it is he who seems to feel most the effects of the journey.

"Five days after leaving Senhor Galvão's place we reached the Rio Paranatinga, only to find that the Bacairy village was deserted and the canoe on the other side of the river. Someone had to swim over and get it, so I went—though I was scared stiff of things in the river, and felt rather like that time in Jamaica when Brian and I were chased by a shark. We camped in the village, and next day swam the animals over, and did the cargo in the same way as on the Cuyaba River. One league beyond we had to do it again, to cross a boggy stream; one league beyond that the whole back-breaking business had to be repeated. By this time we were absolutely fagged out, so we camped, and came into Bacairy Post yesterday morning.

"It is nice and fresh here, and just beyond the hills—about four miles away—is absolutely unexplored country. The schoolhouse has been put at our disposal, and we get our meals from the head of the Post, a decent fellow named Valdemira.

"Shortly after we arrived, about eight wild Indians from the Xingú —stark naked—came in to the Post. They lived about eight days down the river, and occasionally visit this place for the sake of curiosity and for the things they are given. There are five men, two women, and a child, and they are living in a hut by themselves. We gave them some guava cheese yesterday, and they liked it immensely. They are small people, about five feet two inches in height, and very well built. They eat only fish and vegetables—never meat. One woman had a very fine necklace of tiny discs cut from snail shells, which must have required tremendous patience to make. We offered her eight boxes of matches, some tea, and some buckles, and she readily swapped. The necklace will be sent to the Museum of the American Indian in New York."

May 17. "Today we took some photos of the Mehinaku Indians which will of course go to the North American Newspaper Alliance. The first showed four of them with their bows and arrows, standing near a small stream by a strip of jungle. I am standing with them to show the difference in our heights. They just come up to my shoulder. The second picture shows them preparing to shoot arrows at fish in the water. The bows are bigger than the ones we had in the house at Seaton, and are over seven feet long, with six-foot arrows; but as these people are not so powerful, I can easily draw the bows to my ear.

"Last night we went to their hut and gave them a concert. I had my piccolo, Valdemira his guitar, and Daddy his banjo. It was a great success, though we were nearly choked with smoke.

"These Mehinakus tell us by signs that four hard days' travel to the north live the Macahirys, who are cannibals, and not over five feet tall. They may be the Morcegos, but I doubt it, as they use arrows, which the Morcegos have not yet come to.

"About three weeks' journey from here we expect to strike the waterfall mentioned by Hermenegildo Galvão, who heard about it from the Bacairy Indian Roberto, whom we visit tomorrow. It is entirely unknown to anyone, and Roberto was told of it by his father, who lived near there when the Bacairys were wild. It can be heard five leagues away, and there is to be seen an upright rock, protected from the waters, which is covered with painted pictures of men and horses. He also mentioned the watch tower, supposed to be about half-way to the city."

May 19. "A nice fresh day for my twenty-second birthday—the most interesting I have had up to now!

"Roberto came over here, and after being primed with *Vinho de Cajo* told us some interesting things. He says it was the ambition of his life to go to this big waterfall where the inscriptions are, and settle there with his tribe, but now it is too late. Also, there are Morcegos and Caxibis there, and he is scared of them. We obtained the location from him together with a description of the country. The waterless desert is only one day's journey from end to end, and after that we come into grass country with no *mato* at all. His uncle talked about the cities, and he alleges that his very ancient ancestors made them. We leave here the day after tomorrow, and five days will see us in unknown country. I shall be glad when the *peons* leave us, as we are getting sick of them.

"You may be interested to hear what we eat while on the trail. At half past six in the morning we have one plate of porridge, two cups of tea, and one third of a cup of condensed milk; then, at half-past five in the evening we have two cups of tea, two biscuits, *goiabada* or sardines, or one plate of *charque* and rice. Here we have been able to buy any amount of *farinha* and sweet potato to help out the rice, and I do the cooking of it. We are also able to get some bones and a little *mandioca*. There are plenty of cows belonging to the Post, so fresh milk is obtainable in the mornings.

"We have clipped our beards, and feel better without them. I must be even heavier here than I was at Hermenegildo's, in spite of the journey, and I have never felt so well. Raleigh's foot has nearly healed, and Daddy is in first-rate condition. What we now look forward to is reaching Camp 15 and getting rid of the two *peons*.

"By the way, they say the Bacairys are dying off on account of fetish, for there is a fetish man in the village who hates them. Only yesterday a little girl died—of fetish, they say!"

May 20. "The photographs for N.A.N.A. have just been developed and there are some very good ones of the Mehinaku Indians, and of Daddy and myself. It is hard to develop successfully here as the water is so warm, and we were lucky to find the temperature of one stream as low as 70° Fahrenheit.

"Raleigh's other foot is swollen. He rubbed it or scratched it one morning, and in the afternoon when he took his sock off to bathe the skin came off with it, leaving a raw place. Now it has started to swell— and he has a raw place on his arm, too. What will happen when we really meet insects I don't know! There will be plenty of walking in about a week, and I hope his feet will stand it. Brian could have stood it much better, especially as we have had no hardships.[1] Daddy was saying today that the only ones he has had with him who were absolutely fit all through were Costin and Manley. Both of us are feeling damn good.

"Next time I write will probably be from Para—or 'Z' maybe!"

To Jack it was a grand adventure—the very thing he had been brought up to do, and kept himself fit for. My father's letters were more matter of fact. To him it was routine stuff, and his eyes were focused on the objective lying ahead of them. He speaks again:

Bacairy Post, Matto Grosso, May 20, 1925. "We reached here after rather unusual difficulties, which have given Jack and Raleigh an excellent initiation into the joys of travelling in the *sertão*. We lost our way three times, had endless bother with mules falling in the mud of streams, and have been devoured by ticks. On one occasion, being too far ahead, I missed the others. Returning to look for them, I was overtaken by the dark and forced to sleep on the open *campo* with saddle for pillow,

[1] Big-brother stuff! He may have been the most muscular, but I was ever the stronger constitutionally.—ED.

thereby being covered with minute ticks which gave me no rest from scratching for over two weeks.

"Jack takes it well. He reached here stronger and fatter than he was in Rio. I am nervous about Raleigh's being able to stand the more difficult part of the journey, for on the trail the bite of a tick developed into a swollen and ulcerous foot, and of late he has been scratching again till great lumps of skin have come away.

"To Jack's great delight we have seen the first of the wild Indians here, naked savages from the Xingú. I have sent twenty-five excellent photographs of them to N.A.N.A.

"I saw the Indian chief Roberto and had a talk with him. Under the expanding influence of wine he corroborated all my Cuyaba friend told me, and more. Owing to what his grandfather had told him, he always wanted to make the journey to the waterfall, but is now too old. He is of the opinion that bad Indians are numerous there, but committed himself to the statement that his ancestors had built the old cities. This I am inclined to doubt, for he, like the Mehinaku Indians, is of the brown or Polynesian type, and it is the fair or red type I associate with the cities.

"The Bacairys are dying out like flies of fever and fetishism. Every malady is the work of a fetish! Without question it is the finest opportunity for a missionary if only one with medical experience would come, for he could contact the wild Indians and tame them.

"Needless to say, I was cheated over mules and pretty well everything else. It was unfortunate that the man supposed to provide them failed me, forcing me to get them at very short notice from another—and in Cuyaba commercial honesty is not dreamed of! They turned out to be so bad that it was necessary to buy mules on the way, and for this purpose—as well as to cure Raleigh's foot—we stopped five days at the *fazenda* of my friend, Hermenegildo Galvão. The *peons* are useless too, and, on account of the wild Indians, are terrified at the prospect of continuing north.

"Jack is pretty good at Portuguese now, but Raleigh still has only two words. I prefer Spanish, but Portuguese is more important for Brazilian developments, and of course I am pretty fluent.

"A letter will be sent back from the last point, where our *peons* return and leave us to our own devices. I expect to be in touch with the old civilization within a month, and to be at the main objective in August. Thereafter, our fate is in the lap of the gods!"

Finally comes the last word from him, dated May 29, 1925, and sent back with the *peons*. After this not another thing was heard from them, and to this day their fate has remained a mystery.

"The attempt to write is fraught with much difficulty owing to the legions of flies that pester one from dawn till dark—and sometimes all through the night! The worst are the tiny ones smaller than a pinhead, almost invisible, but stinging like a mosquito. Clouds of them are always present. Millions of bees add to the plague, and other bugs galore. The stinging horrors get all over one's hands, and madden. Even the head nets won't keep them out. As for mosquito nets, the pests fly through them!

"We hope to get through this region in a few days, and are camped here for a couple of days to arrange for the return of the *peons*, who are anxious to get back, having had enough of it—and I don't blame them. We go on with eight animals—three saddle mules, four cargo mules, and a *madrinha*, a leading animal which keeps the others together. Jack is well and fit, getting stronger every day even though he suffers a bit from the insects. I myself am bitten or stung by ticks, and these *piums*, as they call the tiny ones, all over the body. Raleigh I am anxious about. He still has one leg in a bandage, but won't go back. So far we have plenty of food, and no need to walk, but I am not sure how long this will last. There may be so little for the animals to eat. I cannot hope to stand up to this journey better than Jack or Raleigh, but I had to do it. Years tell, in spite of the spirit of enthusiasm.

"I calculate to contact the Indians in about a week or ten days, when we should be able to reach the waterfall so much talked about.

"Here we are at Dead Horse Camp, Lat. 11° 43′ S. and 54° 35′ W., the spot where my horse died in 1920. Only his white bones remain. We can bathe ourselves here, but the insects make it a matter of great haste. Nevertheless, the season is good. It is *very cold* at night, and fresh in the morning; but insects and heat come by mid-day, and from then till six o'clock in the evening it is sheer misery in camp.

"You need have no fear of any failure. . . ."

Those last words he wrote to my mother come to me like an echo across the twenty-six years elapsed since then.

"You need have no fear of any failure. . . ."

THE NEW PRESTER JOHN

IT was in 1927, when I was stationed up in the Mountain Section of the Central Railway of Peru, that a call came from Lima saying that there had arrived in town a French civil engineer named Roger Courteville, who claimed to have come across my father in the state of Minas Gerais, Brazil, a month or two earlier.

I rushed down to Lima and met M. Courteville, who told me that he and his wife had crossed from Atlantic to Pacific by car, *via* La Paz. When coming through the *sertão* of Minas Gerais, he said, they met seated by the wayside an old man, ragged and sick, who on being questioned replied that his name was Fawcett.

"Did he say anything else?" I asked.

"He seemed confused, and not all there—as though he had come through terrible hardships."

M. Courteville was anxious to persuade me to contact the North American Newspaper Alliance, raise funds for an expedition, and return to find the old man.

"I didn't know anything about Colonel Fawcett till I reached here," he explained. "Had I known we could have brought him with us. Anyway, it shouldn't be hard to find him if we go back—there are very few *Gringos* in that district."

I was sceptical, but reluctant to dismiss the story in case it might be true. After all, it *could* be! However, N.A.N.A. thought otherwise, and no funds were forthcoming. It was not yet the heyday of the big, well-financed, and top-heavy 'rescue' party, with movie apparatus and two-way radio.

The following year N.A.N.A. organized a big expedition led by Commander George Dyott (whom I met in Peru in 1924) to investigate my father's fate, and it left Cuyaba in May, 1928. They made across country to the Kuliseu River, coming to a village of the Nafaqua Indians. In the hut of the chief, Aloique, Commander Dyott saw a metal uniform case, and the chief's son wore round his neck a string with a brass tag bearing the name of the maker of this trunk, Silver & Co. of London.

Aloique said the trunk was given to him by a *Caraíba* (white man) who had come with two others, younger, and both lame. The three had been taken by Aloique to a Kalapalo Indian village on the Kuluene River, after which they crossed the river and continued east. For five days the smoke of their camp fires was seen, and then no more.

The Dyott expedition returned with no proof of anything—not even that the Fawcett party had been there, for while the uniform case, identified by the maker, had belonged to my father, it was one discarded by him in 1920. It was Commander Dyott's belief that my father had been killed; but I have given the evidence, and leave it to the reader to judge. We of the family could not accept it as in any way conclusive.

The next expedition to solve the mystery was led by a journalist, Albert de Winton; and in 1930 it reached the same Kalapalo village where de Winton believed the Fawcett party was wiped out. He never came out alive, and nothing was proved.

There was a sensation in 1932 when a Swiss trapper named Stefan Rattin came out of Matto Grosso with a tale that my father was a prisoner of an Indian tribe north of the River Bomfin, a tributary of the São Manoel River. He claimed to have spoken with him, and this was his statement:

"Towards sunset on October 16, 1931, I and my two companions were washing our clothes in a stream (a tributary of the River Iguassu Ximary) when we suddenly noticed we were surrounded by Indians. I went up to them and asked them whether they could give us some *chicha*. I had some difficulty in communicating with them as they did not speak Guarany, though they understood a few words. They took us to their camp, where there were about 250 men and a large number of women and children. They were all squatting on the ground drinking *chicha*. We sat down with the chief and about thirty others.

After sunset there suddenly appeared an old man clad in skins, with a long yellowish-white beard and long hair. I saw immediately that he was a white man. The chief gave him a severe look and said something to the others. Four or five Indians left our group and got the old man to sit down with them a few yards away from us. He looked very sad and could not take his eyes off me. We sat drinking all night, and at dawn, when most of the Indians, including the chief, were sleeping heavily, the old man came up to me and asked me if I was English. He spoke English. I answered, 'No—Swiss.' He then asked, 'Are you a friend?' I said, 'Yes,' and he went on. 'I am an English Colonel. Go to the English Consulate and ask them to tell Major Paget, who has a coffee farm in the state of São Paulo, that I am a captive here.' I promised I would, whereupon he said, 'You are a gentleman,' and gave me a handshake.

The old man enquired whether I had any paper, and took me to his tent. Several Indians who were watching him followed us. He showed me four blocks of wood on which he had made rough sketches with a sharp stone. I copied these as best I could. I then noticed that the backs of his hands were badly scratched and I sent one of my companions to get some tincture of iodine which we had brought with us. He put some on his hands, and when the Indians saw this they took it away from him and started to paint themselves with it.

The chief and most of the others were still fast asleep and I was able to ask the old man whether he was alone. He said something about his son sleeping, and began to weep. He did not mention anyone else, and I dared not ask more questions. He then showed me a gold locket which he wore at the end of a chain round his neck. Inside was a photograph of a lady wearing a large hat, and two small children (about six to eight years old). He wore four gold rings; one with a red stone, one with a green stone and a lion engraved on it, one very thin one with a small diamond, and a snake ring with two red eyes. He is a man of about sixty-five, approximate height five feet eleven inches, and powerfully built. He has bright blue eyes with a yellowish tinge, chestnut eyelashes and a small scar over the right eye. He looked very depressed, but appeared to be in full possession of his faculties. He seemed to be in good health—neither too fat nor too thin.

Soon after sunrise we got back to our two mules and left the camp. About fifty Indians followed us until noon. I did not like to ask questions, but I tried to find out from them what the old man was doing there. All they said was, '*Poschu demas*,' which apparently means 'bad man'. We travelled for six days in a southerly direction and . . . I made my way to Barreto *via* Goyaz. . . .

I never heard of Colonel Fawcett until I arrived at Barreto."

The above is the official declaration made to the British Consul General in Rio de Janeiro; and later Rattin was cross-examined by the Brazilian authorities.

Credence was given to the report principally because of the mention of 'Major Paget'; but this to me was unconvincing. My father's great friend was Sir Ralph Paget, at one time H.B.M.'s Ambassador to Brazil, but Sir Ralph had long been back in England, and before I left for Peru I remembered my father visiting him at Sittingbourne, Kent. I believe Rattin was speaking substantially the truth, but the identity of the old man I cannot accept.

My father's beard would be mousy-grey, not yellowish-white, and if he had long hair it had grown surprisingly on a head remarkable for its baldness from an early age. Why should he speak English to Rattin—who knew so little of it that the above declaration was made in German? The logical thing would have been to converse in Portuguese, in which both were presumably equally fluent. The old man said his son was 'sleeping', and wept. Both the remark and the emotion are utterly unlike my father. I don't think he ever had a locket like the one Rattin describes —certainly he never wore such a collection of rings. The height given is short. My father was *well* over six feet—but the statement is not positive anyway. His eyes were not blue; they were steel-grey, and at times almost greenish. His eyelashes were not chestnut; they were mouse-coloured. When he left England he had no scar over either eye. And why—why did the old man not tell his name?

The regions bordering on civilization, where the 'degenerate tribes' —as my father calls them—live, are often visited by white men—prospectors, hunters, fugitives, naturalists, botanists, and so on. Rattin himself was wandering there! It is quite possible that some white man was indeed held prisoner by these Indians, but there are many reasons for doubting that it was P.H.F.

Rattin made no financial demands, nor sought publicity. He discouraged any attempts to organize an official rescue expedition, and set off himself to bring back the old man. "The English Colonel will reward me afterwards," he said.

He was never heard of again—but on his way in he passed by the ranch of Senhor Hermenegildo Galvão, my father's friend. On July 8, 1932, Senhor Galvão writes to my mother, referring to the 'top-heavy' expeditions I have previously mentioned:

"These expeditions are considered as scientific ones, but are composed merely of adventurers who, while saying that they are looking for your husband, make it a sort of picnic and do not take it seriously. In such a case is the Swiss trapper Rattin, who, arriving recently in Cuyaba and advised of the direction in which Colonel Faucetti went, took an entirely different direction, leaving Cuyaba *via* Rosario, then Diamantino; and from this last city of Matto Grosso he left for the Arinos River, where he embarked in a canoe with his two companions. This river is a tributary of the River Joruena, which is the principal tributary of the great Tapajos, which is itself a tribu- tary of the Amazon. This expedition can in no way give any true notice about your husband. . . .

Colonel Faucetti . . . when he was about to make this last expedi- tion . . . informed me of the course he was to follow, and as I have observed that all who come here to look for him do not follow that route, and that when they do follow it do not make any attempt to find out the real truth—nor try to find out from the Indians of these regions anything about it—I have resolved to place myself at your disposal to take charge of an expedition to find the whereabouts of the party. . . ."

In June 1933, the Secretary of the Royal Geographical Society delivered to my mother a packet containing a compass belonging to a theodolite, identified by the makers as being part of an instrument supplied to my father in Devonshire on February 13, 1913. The compass was in a very well-made case of some South American wood, and inside the lid was a note with these words:

"*Theodolite Compass*. Found near the camp of the Bacairy Indians of Matto Grosso by Col. Aniceto Botelho, late deputy of that State, and given by him to the Inspector of Indians, Dr. Antonio Estigar- ribia, who presented the same to Frederick C. Glass (missionary), on April 14, 1933. The case was made by Dr. Estigarribia."

Mr. Glass sent the compass to Mr. A. Stuart McNairn, of the Evangelical Union of South America, resident in London, and so it came into the hands of the Secretary of the Royal Geographical Society.

Now the significance of this find lies in the fact that there is no record of P.H.F.'s having been in contact with the Bacairys until the last trip, when as you will remember he spoke with Roberto, a Bacairy Indian, about the waterfall where the inscriptions are. Roberto told him that his tribe lived 'very far to the north', possibly on my father's intended route.

The compass was in perfect condition and obviously had not been exposed to the weather for any length of time. There were also indications that it had been in the possession of someone who understood these instruments. The conclusion reached by my mother was that P.H.F. himself placed this compass in the path of Colonel Botelho, whom he knew to be in the vicinity, with the object of its being found and identi- fied. The message intended to be conveyed to her was that the work was done and P.H.F. was ready to come out with his proofs—possibly a great slab of stone with inscriptions—and needed a small escort to help him. He discussed such a possibility with my mother in 1924.

My own opinion is that it was left in the region on the return in 1920, when the death of cargo animals forced the jettisoning of all but essential things. It might have been left as a gift at one of the posts where hospitality was given to my father and Felipe, or it might have been found by curious Indians examining the recently abandoned camp sites.

In July 1933 there came the narrative of an expedition to the Kuluene River by Virginio Pessione. It was sent to the President of the Royal Geographical Society by Monseigneur Couturon, Administrateur Apostolique, of the Salesian Mission in Matto Grosso.

"... We arrived at the 'Rancharia' estate, situated on the left bank of the Rio São Manoel, an affluent of the River Paranatinga, where we spent the night. Here we learned of the existence of an Indian woman of the Nafaqua tribe of the Cuycuru, accompanied by her son and another Indian of the Kalapalo tribe who had been staying at the estate for about a year.

We were informed by the owners of the house that this Indian woman, after learning a few words of Portuguese, made it understood that she wished to tell of the existence, for several years, of white men in the midst of the Aruvudu tribe, one friendly to her own. Next morning we had the opportunity of listening to this woman's story, she making herself understood by signs, and with the help of a Bacairy Indian employed on the property, who spoke Portuguese.

Before her son was weaned, she said, there came down the River Kuluene by canoe to the village of her tribe, *three White Men*. One of them was old, tall, with blue eyes, bearded and bald; another a youth whom she gave us to understand was the son of the first; and the third a white man of greater age. We saw the woman's son, said to be still at the breast at the time of the arrival of these men at the village, and judged him to be about nine or ten years old. Touching our hands, and by signs and half-formed words, she gave us to understand that the eldest of the white men wore on the right hand a large ring—very large—and another slender ring on the index finger. He whom she called the son of the eldest wore on his head a colonial helmet similar to the ones we were wearing; and the old man—Father *Carayba*, as she called him—wore a felt hat like Senhor Becerra's (the owner of the house). She said she saw them constantly, whenever she visited the Aruvudu tribe, and about a year ago they were alive and well.

The white men spoke all the languages of the friendly tribes, and the *Carayba*—he with the long white beard—is now chief of the Aruvudus, and his son married to the daughter of the chief Jeruata. When she last saw them, said the woman, the son's wife was carrying a male child, completely naked, and still quite small, with blue eyes (she pointed to the blue jeans of one of the persons present) and hair the colour of maize (she indicated some maize which happaned to be in a corner of the room).

The *Caraybas*, she went on, spend their time on a small piece of arable land, and hunt and fish. In particular, they go from one village to another, and are in the habit of gathering together the children and drawing pictures on the sand. This last information reminded us that in the neighbourhood of the rapids where the Kuluene flows past spurs of the Serra Azul we had seen marks cut on the trees as though with a stone implement—marks which resembled letters of the alphabet, and which looked as if they had been carved about two years previously. She said the *Carayba* chief and the other white men were greatly esteemed by the tribe, and well looked after. When asked why the white men did not escape, she replied vaguely that there were no more bullets for their guns, and added more intelligently that where they lived there were very fierce tribes in the neighbourhood—Suyas and Cayapos—and that even the friendly Indians would kill them if they attempted to leave, for they were always watched and followed wherever they went. . . ."

The woman was then asked how civilized people could best reach them, and replied with a lengthy explanation accompanied by much pantomime. It was necessary to pass through many tribes before reaching the Aruvudus. The narrative concludes:

> "Explaining and making signs in this way, she beat her foot on the ground and declared impetuously that the white men were in safety, and still remained there. Each of us in turn made her repeat it several times, and each time she gave the same precise information, particularly at the point when she insisted that the white men were still with the Aruvudu tribe. . . ."

There are points about this report that certainly indicate that these white men might be my father, Jack and Raleigh. 'Gathering together the children and drawing pictures on the sand' would not only be the easiest form of expression for two artists, as were my father and brother, but I well remember Jack's inability to pass over a clean stretch of sand without finding a twig or a splinter and scribbling on it! Their taking to a canoe might have been forced on them by the persistence of Raleigh's lameness after the last of the animals had been given up. In the description of them given by the woman are two discrepancies. My brother did not have a sun-helmet—all three of them wore Stetsons. Also, Raleigh was not of 'greater age' than Jack, though prolonged sickness could have made him appear so. Anyway, these discrepancies are not of much moment. It is too much to expect perfect accuracy from the woman, and there is room for misunderstandings in communication carried on mainly by signs.

I have heard it said that the wild Indians like to hold a white man captive. It enhances their prestige in the eyes of neighbouring tribes, and the captive, usually well treated but closely guarded, holds a position similar to that of a mascot. White travellers usually have a fair working knowledge of medicine, which is of service to the tribe. Also, a man of strong personality might persuade the Indians to regard him in due course as their leader. I knew such a case in Peru, where an Englishman became almost a local king, with authority over a wide area. Naturally, the Indians are unwilling to allow their mascot, doctor and leader to leave!

Mr. Patrick Ulyatt returned from Matto Grosso in 1935, and in a letter to my mother said:

"While I have yet no proof and do not desire that you should feel that I have, I still maintain the belief that one of your husband's party is alive. I am only going by vague informations garnered in the Matto Grosso. I cannot support anything and for the moment I prefer to keep my own counsel. To which my brother is in agreement. It is interesting to add, however, that I believe even more firmly now in your husband's Lost City than ever before. . . .

"*I must go back*. Perhaps it is hard to understand. We went through much misery, but *I must go back*, even if I go alone. . . ."

He and his brother Gordon set off up the Jamari River, a tributary of the Madeira, and worked over towards the Rio Machadinho. They nearly walked into a camp of Boca Preta Indians; and then found themselves surrounded by savages, who refused to allow them to proceed farther, and let them escape only after the Ulyatts had given them all their packs and had departed with nothing but rifles, carried reversed as a sign of peace. These savages were concerned with preventing the Ulyatts from passing through them. Why? After many adventures they were lucky enough to emerge once more, and even resolved to go back. Mr. Ulyatt said that the rubber gatherers, who were bushmen, knew quite a lot about my father, though they did not know who he was, and that the area where he was believed to be was ringed round with unfriendly Indian tribes.

On February 13, 1944, I received a long-distance telephone call from São Paulo. At the other end of the cracking, spluttering wire was Senhor

Edmar Morel, journalist of the *Agencia Meridional*, who told me that he had with him an Indian boy named Dulipe, in reality a white boy, and *son of my brother Jack*. I was in Lima, Peru, at the time, and what with the noise on the wire, due to bad weather, and the dim sound of Senhor Morel's unfamiliar Portuguese, I found it most difficult to understand all that was said to me, but what I did get was that the boy was all ready to be put on the next 'plane to Peru as soon as I accepted him! He had brought the boy out from the Kuicuro tribe in the Xingú region, where definite proof had been obtained of the wiping out of my father's party.

I was not at all ready to swallow this, for it was not the first I had heard of Dulipe. In 1937 my mother received a long letter from Miss Martha Moennich, a missionary just arrived out from the Xingú, who sent a batch of excellent photographs of a 'white boy' named Duh-ri-pe with the Kuicuro tribe.

"In the spring of 1925 the party of three started for the Xingú headwaters from Cuyaba," wrote Miss Moennich (she was talking of my father's party). "They made their way over the Central Plateau to the Kuliseo River *via* the Paranatinga. By canoe they continued their nine days' river journey down to the first Indian village—the Nafaquas. Here the Colonel left his army pack trunk with Chief Aloique, and travelled overland, northward to the Kuikuro Indians on the Kuluene River, taking only bare necessities along with him. . . .

Raleigh Rimell died soon after entering the Xingú from fever and insect bites. The Colonel and Jack stayed with the Kuikuro tribe a year, and the Indians treated them well (as far as could be expected by so primitive a people who had nothing to offer). In the meanwhile a little son arrived in the jungles, and though the Indian mother and Jack have passed away, the little offspring was being taken care of by his Indian foster-father and jungle relatives as best they could.

After that the Colonel and Jack determined to go on to the 'River of Death' (Rio das Mortes) in a last search for their objective. Leaving the Kuikuros they walked over to the Kalapalos south-eastward where a group of Indians escorted them some days beyond the Kuluene River. When their food supply of *mandioca* and beans ran out the Kalapalos begged the two men by signs to return to their village, indicating that it was a hopeless effort to venture into a region that would mean inevitable death. They, too, had become emaciated and couldn't go on. However, still dauntless in spirit and in spite of their weakened condition through untold privations, father and son went on—no food, no medical aid, no replenishing of clothes, etc. Then came the fatal moment. I, and my three friends, discerned by the dramatic demonstration of our Waura Indian that the murderous deed was not enacted in a spirit of treachery (as it would have been had the savage Cayapos and Caxibis handled the situation) but due to a sentiment of mingled pity and provocation; of pity, the Indians realizing that death inevitably awaited them, and of provocation because they did not comply with their well-meaning appeal.

Our party of four have been with the Kuikuros and some of us have walked over to the Kalapalos. In fact, we contacted nine of the eleven tribes. We walked where the Colonel walked, sat where he sat. . . .

As to the little boy: he is pure white and ruddy. His body is frail and his blue eyes have suffered from the strain of the tropical sun. In his dual nature there are conspicuous traits of British reserve and of a military bearing, while on his Indian side, the sight of a bow and arrow, or a river, makes him a little jungle boy. . . .

Rev. Emil Halverson first discovered the little boy in 1926 when he was a baby in arms. In 1934 we saw him again. . . ."

In the photographs Miss Moennich enclosed the boy certainly looks like the son of a white man, but the screwed-up eyes and colourless brows are those of an albino. Albinos do exist amongst the savage tribes—and, according to P.H.F., so do 'white' offspring with blue eyes and auburn hair. However, Dulipe may be half-white, his father one of the white wanderers who roam these semi-civilized areas. Why should Jack be the father? It is in any case by no means certain that he could have been, the point depending, of course, on when the child was born. Remember, Jack was absolutely virgin and not in the least interested in women, either civilized or savage. It has lately become usual to credit him with the behaviour of a sex-hungry soldier, the people who are now spreading these stories apparently regarding that attitude as an inevitable characteristic of man!

The account of Aloique and the uniform case is similar to Commander Dyott's report, and can be dismissed for reasons already given.

My father distinctly stated that he was *not* going in the direction of the Rio das Mortes, for it was not unexplored and had no interest for him, yet many of the reports insist on tracing him in that direction. The suggestive name of the river seems to make it irresistible!

Senhor Morel's telephone communication did not take me unawares. My opinion at the time was that, whoever the boy Dulipe might be, it was a thoughtless act to bring him away from his home with the tribe and condemn him to the curses of civilization. But the boy had been brought out—the damage was done—and the embarrassing problem of his future welfare would be conveniently solved if I could be induced to accept him as a nephew. I foresaw the possibility of this wild boy's being put on the International 'plane and sent over to my care without so much as a by-your-leave; so with the help of friends in diplomatic circles I forestalled this risk. Meanwhile, my emphatic denials of kinship were published in the Brazilian press, and when the temporary flutter had died down I heard no more of poor Dulipe. I hope for the boy's sake he was returned to his tribe and the life he knew.[1]

About the same time it was reported that a Brazilian army officer had found a compass, and an annotated book with my father's name in it. I asked a friend of mine to try to obtain these for identification, having expected to hear some day of P.H.F.'s log-book of the last trip being found. Fortunately, my friend was able to do this, and I received the two things for inspection. The compass was a toy, such as a boy might play with, or a man wear on his watch chain; and the book contained religious matter scribbled over in pencil. What was alleged to be my father's name was nothing of the sort. My own opinion was that the book had belonged to a missionary; it had certainly nothing to do with any of the three members of the Fawcett party. I returned them with these observations; but they are still referred to as belonging to Colonel Fawcett!

From time to time there have been other expeditions, as well as isolated reports of skeletons and shrunken heads found. To mention all the attempts—genuine or merely alleged—to clear up the 'Fawcett Mystery' would occupy too much space, even if I had the records of them available, which I haven't. Suffice it to say that those not mentioned here are of little if any importance, and of some my opinion is expressed adequately in Senhor Galvão's words.

The latest report was published in the European press in April, 1951, but dates back six months before, when Senhor Orlando Vilas Boas of the Central Brazil Foundation won a 'confession' from Izarari, chief of the Kalapalos, dramatically delivered on his deathbed, to the effect that he, Izarari, had clubbed Fawcett and his two young companions to death. The three whites came with Aloique, chief of the Nafaquas, he said, and the old man's son consorted with one of his, Izarari's, wives. Then, next day, the old one demanded carriers and canoes to take them on their journey, and this request being refused on the grounds of intertribal strife, he slapped Izarari's face! The enraged chief picked up his war club and beat out the brains of the old white man. At once the two young whites attacked him, but in a moment that doughty club had laid them dead on the ground beside the other.

Izarari had a son, Yarulla, in his early twenties, called by his com-

---

[1] It was in February 1952, after the above was written, that the truth about Dulipe was published in Diario da Noite and O Jornal, two of the largest Rio de Janeiro newspapers, under the title "Twilight of the Gods". The boy is indeed an albino. His parentage is known, and there is no white blood in him. The physical defects usual to albinos made him useless to the Kuikuros and the other friendly Xingú tribes, and, unwanted and despised, he was seized upon for the purpose of a journalistic hoax.

The erstwhile 'White God of the Xingú' is living in Cuyaba, and the latest news of him states that he has taken to bad ways—is a bad lot—worthless!

panions '*Carayba*'. His complexion was lighter than that of the others—it was as though he had white blood in his veins. Ah!—the answer was obvious—he was Jack Fawcett's son![1]

Comatzi, who became chief on Izarari's death, was after much persuasion induced to disclose the grave of the murdered explorer, and bones were dug up that have now been examined. The bodies of the younger ones were thrown in the river, said Comatzi. At all events, they have not been found.

The bones were examined by a team of experts of the Royal Anthropological Institute in London, and were pronounced not to be those of my father. To whom they belonged has not been discovered, and there is a certain amount of doubt whether they are a white man's. The 'Fawcett Mystery' continues, and the reader, who has the whole background if he has read this far, can form his own opinion. Mine can be given briefly.

One possibility that could have induced the party to make for the Kalapalo territory, in the opposite direction to the intended route, is this. Let us suppose that, after leaving Dead Horse Camp, Raleigh's bad leg failed to heal—or was freshly infected by the continued attacks of insects. After a week or two the animals could go no farther for lack of food, and the party shouldered packs and went on towards the Xingú on foot. Shortly before reaching the river Raleigh went down with blood poisoning, at best a brief step from any superficial infection in tropical South America, as I know only too well. There was one slight hope of saving him, and that was by getting him out in time. To return by way of Dead Horse Camp and Bacairy Post was impossible, for Raleigh was unable to walk, and could only move supported by the others. Fortunately they were not far from the Xingú, and after great difficulty the trio reached its banks. Fortune was again kind; a party of Bacairys was found. They had several canoes, and traded one for the only equipment the party could afford to lose—the scientific instruments.

The Xingú River is joined by the Kuluene, and the Kuluene reaches farther south—and nearer Cuyaba—than any of the other affluents. To get up the Kuluene might not be possible for only two men with the burden of a sick companion, but if it could be accomplished half the distance back to civilization might be covered—and as Raleigh could not be carried, a canoe was the only way. Had they done this the journey would have brought them to the Kalapalos, at the junction of the Kuluene and Tanguro Rivers. . . .

Or it may be that Raleigh recovered after leaving Dead Horse Camp, and the three went on in the intended direction, only to find that the dreaded Morcegos were impossible to pass. After repeated attempts to

---

[1] Izarari had white blood in him, I am told. His son, Yarulla, a shy, handsome youth, is quite the pick of the Kalapalos. When I asked Snr. Vilas Boas if he believed that Yarulla was my 'nephew', the great *sertanista* replied that he knew he was not.

get through they were forced to give up. If able to procure a canoe, they might have decided to return by way of the river. . . .

Another possible explanation is that they made valuable finds at the waterfall—so valuable that the urgency of disclosing them swallowed up the immediate intention of reaching 'Z'. There could then have been cause for them to come out by way of the river and the Kalapalos. . . .

What I am searching for, you see, is an explanation of their possible presence in the Kuluene district. That they *were* there I am not yet prepared to accept. It would be far more reasonable to suppose that if Indians wiped them out, it was some savage and unfamiliar tribe such as the Morcegos, and not the half-tame Indians of the rivers, through whose villages missionaries and explorers find no difficulty in passing. Of course, if my brother was in the habit of seducing chiefs' wives, and my father of slapping chiefs' faces, there would be grave risk for them from any Indian tribe, however tame. Such tales as these, manifestly ridiculous as they are, may arise from jealousy. A man so utterly opposed to violence towards the Indians as to allow himself and his party to be shot at with poisoned arrows for a considerable time, and refuse to retaliate, is not the one deliberately to offer a mortal insult to a chief!

There is yet another possibility. They may have managed to penetrate the barrier of savage tribes and reach their objective. If that were so, and if the tradition is true that the last remnants of the ancient race had indeed protected their sanctuary by ringing themselves round with fierce savages, what chance would there be of returning—thus breaking the age-long secrecy so faithfully preserved?

Up to the time of writing these words the fate of my father and the two others is as much of a mystery as it ever was. It is possible that the riddle may never be solved; possible also that before this book is in my readers' hands it will be a mystery no longer. He knew the risks they faced better than any other civilized man, and admitted that there were tremendous odds against their returning.

"If we should not come out," I remember him saying, "I don't want rescue parties to come in looking for us. It's too risky. If with all my experience we can't make it, there's not much hope for others. That's one reason why I'm not telling exactly where we're going.

"Whether we get through, and emerge again, or leave our bones to rot in there, one thing's certain. The answer to the enigma of Ancient South America—and perhaps of the prehistoric world—may be found when those old cities are located and opened up to scientific research. That the cities exist, I know. . . ."

INDEX AND GLOSSARY